GUIDEBOOK TO

ZEN AND THE ART OF MOTORCYCLE MAINTENANCE

GUIDEBOOK TO

ZEN AND
THE ART OF
MOTORCYCLE
MAINTENANCE

RONALD L. DiSANTO, PH.D., AND
THOMAS J. STEELE, S.J., PH.D.

WILLIAM MORROW AND COMPANY, INC. NEW YORK

Quotations from *Zen and the Art of Motorcycle Maintenance* copyright © 1974 by Robert M. Pirsig. Used by kind permission of Robert M. Pirsig.

Recognizing the importance of preserving what has been written, it is the policy of William Morrow and Company, Inc., and its imprints and affiliates to have the books it publishes printed on acid-free paper, and we exert our best efforts to that end.

Library of Congress Cataloging-in-Publication Data

DiSanto, Ronald L.
    Guidebook to Zen and the art of motorcycle maintenance / Ronald L. DiSanto and Thomas J. Steele.
        p.   cm.
    Includes index.
    ISBN 0-688-08461-3
    ISBN 0-688-06069-2 (pbk.)
    1. Pirsig, Robert M. Zen and the art of motorcycle maintenance.
  I. Steele, Thomas J. II. Title.
CT275.P6483D57 1990
917.304'92—dc20   90-37374
                                                          CIP

Printed in the United States of America

First Edition

1 2 3 4 5 6 7 8 9 10

BOOK DESIGN BY JAYE ZIMET

MAPS BY ARLENE GOLDBERG

FOR CHRIS, OF COURSE

ACKNOWLEDGMENTS

Around the turn of the century, some waggish undergraduates at Oxford learned that Rudyard Kipling got a shilling a word for his writing, so they wired him a shilling and instructed him to send them one of his very best words. Kipling wired back: "Thanks." We think he was right about that being one of the best words there is, and we hope it will handle our many debts to many generous people.

We must first thank Robert M. Pirsig, who endorsed our plan to write this book, introduced us to James Landis, his editor at William Morrow and Company, generously shared personal materials with us, and helped us along with his comments, while always leaving us our freedom of interpretation. He also introduced Ron to Sylvia and John Sutherland and introduced Tom to Gennie and Bob DeWeese.

We thank Professor Richard Rodino of Holy Cross College, chair of the section on Pirsig's *ZMM* at the 1981 national convention of the Modern Language Association, who helped us assemble the bibliography and provided abundant encouragement; Professor Forrest Shearon of Eastern Kentucky University, who allowed us to use a chronology of the trip which served as the foundation of Section 1; and Professor Mary Oates O'Reilly of Rider College, who permitted our use of the questions that start Section 10.

Closer to home, we thank our Regis College students who performed so expertly during a semester-long course on *ZMM* in the fall of 1985; the Regis College Faculty Development Committee for a summer research grant that enabled us to get a good running start on the work; and the Regis College librarians, especially Richard Hansen. Ron thanks his daughters, Carolyn and Catherine, and Tom thanks his fellow Jesuits in Denver and Albuquerque.

C O N T E N T S

AUTHORS' NOTE

The introductory part of Section 3 ("A Mystical Map") and Sections 4 and 5 ("A Philosophical Backpack") were written by Ron DiSanto. While the co-authors take joint responsibility for this material, it was thought best to leave the first person singular style intact.

GUIDEBOOK TO

ZEN AND THE ART OF MOTORCYCLE MAINTENANCE

S E C T I O N 1

C H R O N O L O G Y

This chronology is almost altogether drawn from a very helpful footnote in Forrest B. Shearon's "Visual Imagery and Internal Awareness in Pirsig's *Zen and the Art of Motorcycle Maintenance*," *Kentucky Philological Association: Best Papers* (1983), pp. 53–62. We are very grateful to Professor Shearon for permitting us to revise and expand it for use in this book. Chapter and page numbers refer to Bantam's paperback edition.

DAY OF TRIP	DAY OF WEEK	CHAPTER(S) AND PAGE NOS.	PLOT ACTION (CHAUTAUQUA)
1	Monday	1–3 3–34	Leave Twin Cities; storm; sleep at the motel thirty miles east of Ellendale, North Dakota (technology versus nature/romanticism; "spectators" versus workers who care; scientific laws as "ghosts")
2	Tuesday	4–5 34–57	Sleep under July moon, Llewelyn Johns Recreation Area, Shadehill Reservoir, South Dakota (being versus seeming; Goethe poem)
3	Wednesday	6–7 57–79	Across South Dakota-North Dakota and North Dakota-Montana lines, up from heat to cool; hotel in Miles City, Mont. (classic versus romantic; analytic "knife"; subjective choosing)

DAY OF TRIP	DAY OF WEEK	CHAPTER(S) AND PAGE NOS.	PLOT ACTION (CHAUTAUQUA)
4	Thursday	8–10 83–103	Miles City, hotel in Laurel (division of cycle into components and functions; alienation; politics; inductive and deductive thinking, scientific method; Einstein on hypothesis)
5	Friday	11–12 104–128	Laurel, Red Lodge to Cooke City, Wyoming, Yellowstone Park; Gardiner, Montana, for night (lateral drift; high country; Hume, Kant; Benares Hindu University; illusion and A-bombs)
6	Saturday	13–14 128–154	Through Bozeman, DeWeeses' party (Church of Reason; politics; assembly directions and peace of mind; technology and art; Greek Sophists; Quality)
7–9	Sunday– Tuesday	15 154–164	Loaf, say good-bye to Sutherlands, visit Montana State University campus (Quality)
10	Wednesday	16–18 167–203	Backpack into mountains, narrator puts Chris down; camp out (good first phase—exploration of Quality, refusal to define it; bad second phase—dividing world)
11	Thursday	19–21 203–232	DREAM; return, stay in Bozeman hotel (more of bad second phase—subjective-objective impasse, Quality beyond either, is event; worse third phase—monism, Quality is Tao; art, religion, and science)
12	Friday	22–23 232–246	Say good-bye to DeWeeses; leave for West Coast via Butte, Missoula, Lolo Pass; sleep out in forest; DREAM (Poincaré, convenient tautologies, elegance)
13	Saturday	24–25 246–269	Grangeville, White Bird, Riggins, New Meadows, Tamarack, Cambridge; sleep in Brownlee Campground (caring and stuckness; quietness of body, mind, and value)

DAY OF TRIP	DAY OF WEEK	CHAPTER(S) AND PAGE NOS.	PLOT ACTION (CHAUTAUQUA)
14	Sunday	26 270–294	Baker, Unity, Dixie Pass, Prairie City, Dayville, Mitchell, Prineville, Bend; sleep out in dusty subdivision (gumption; *mu;* real cycle is yourself)
15	Monday	27–28 297–319	DREAM; LaPine, Crater Lake, Klamath Lake, Medford, motel in Grant's Pass (Quality [*aretê*] is all of Greek thought; University of Chicago Aristotelians, mythos-logos)
16	Tuesday	29–30 319–361	Crescent City, California, Arcata, unnamed town north of Weott (loneliness; Aristotle's writings, dialectic, philosophers versus rhetoricians, pre-Socratics; Kitto; Plato's Good is idea, not value; analogy in *Phaedrus;* Phaedrus' breakdown)
17	Wednesday	31–32 361–373	Weott, Leggett, Mendocino County coast; Ukiah, Hopland, Cloverdale, Asti, Santa Rosa, Petaluma, Novato, San Francisco Bay (reconciliation of Phaedrus and narrator, of father and son)

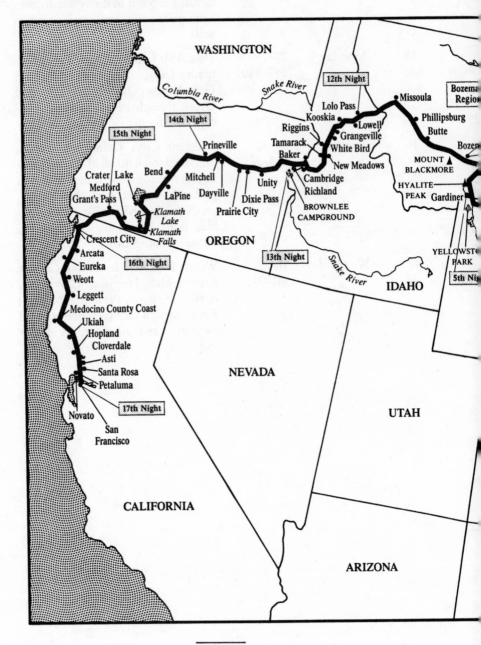

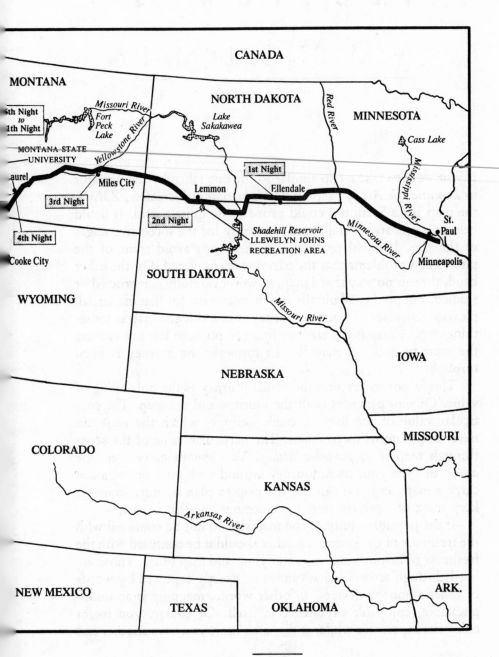

CANADA

MONTANA

NORTH DAKOTA

MINNESOTA

Missouri River

Fort
Peck
Lake

Lake
Sakakawea

Red River

Cass Lake

5th Night
to
11th Night

MONTANA STATE
UNIVERSITY

Yellowstone River

1st Night

Mississippi River

aurel

Miles City

Lemmon

Ellendale

Minnesota River

St.
Paul

3rd Night

2nd Night

Minneapolis

4th Night

Shadehill Reservoir
LLEWELYN JOHNS
RECREATION AREA

Cooke City

SOUTH DAKOTA

WYOMING

Missouri River

IOWA

NEBRASKA

MISSOURI

COLORADO

KANSAS

Arkansas River

NEW MEXICO

TEXAS

OKLAHOMA

ARK.

SECTION 3

A MYSTICAL MAP

If you were to take a trip similar to the one taken by the narrator in *Zen and the Art of Motorcycle Maintenance* (hereafter, *ZMM*), the map from Section 2 could prove to be quite useful. It could help you prepare mentally and physically for the successive stages of the trip. It could perhaps even help you avoid some of the pitfalls and problems that the narrator encountered. On the other hand, there is no way that a map, however carefully constructed or studied, can predict all pitfalls and problems or, for that matter, all pleasant surprises. An actual journey is one thing; a map is something else. A map is a metaphor that can point to but not capture the journey itself. A map is *seen through;* the journey is *lived through*.

This is not to say that the actual journey is the only thing of value. Quality pervades both the journey and the map. The particular value of the lived-through journey, which the map can never duplicate, is its *freshness*. The particular value of the seen-through map is its *portable utility*. You cannot carry someone else's, or even your own, journey around with you, but you can carry a map; and you can use the map to plan a future journey, keep track of a present one, or remember one that is past.

If the portable utility of the map should not be confused with the freshness of the journey, neither should it be confused with the freshness of mapmaking, map studying, and map using. Those are lived-through activities that cannot be exactly captured by words or other symbolic devices. In other words, mapping is an unduplicatable, enjoyable experience in itself. Of course, you might enjoy the experience while, at the same time, you have another end in view (e.g., taking a motorcycle trip). Your mapping in that case is both lived-through and seen-through.

When an activity has this dual character, it can happen that the lived-through character of the experience so dominates its seen-through character that you hardly notice the extrinsic goal that your activity facilitates. Your attention is riveted on the intrinsic goal—the mapping activity itself. The face of Quality that shows itself to you is the moment's freshness and beauty. On the other hand, it can happen that the seen-through character of the experience so dominates its lived-through character that you hardly notice the freshness and beauty and are wholly intent on the extrinsic goal. In that case, the face of Quality that shows itself to you is utility. (In a way, when you are focusing on utility, you are tuning in to the freshness and beauty of moments that will be lived later. The freshness/beauty face of Quality is never entirely absent. To use a metaphor whose pertinence will perhaps be better understood later on in this section, the ox has never gone astray.) A third possibility is that you maintain the lived-through and seen-through characters of the experience in some sort of dynamic equilibrium. You pass back and forth between a state in which you are impressed by the present moment's own worth and a state in which you are driven on by the anticipated future.

What has just been said is meant to apply not only to mapping, in the narrow sense of that term, but to all human symbolic activity. Symbolic activities such as the writing I am doing right now and the reading that you are doing in a different "now" have particular value of their own simply in their very performance. To be sure, writing is a difficult activity, but the difficulty cannot obliterate the delight to be found in the shaping of thoughts and words. Similarly, despite the element of struggle in reading, there is a delight to be found in the exploration of another person's images and ideas. Moreover, the activities of writing and reading have utility as well as intrinsic worth. My writing activity, for example, is useful in that it leads to the production of written words on paper. However much I am centered on the internal exploration of certain questions and ideas, I also have an eye toward the external product. I realize that that product can by no means replace or wholly contain the thinking process that leads to it—the external word is not the thinking process; the map is not the journey—however, the external word can extend the utility value of the thinking process by adding the dimension of portability. Since that portability has been exploited to the point where you are now reading my words, you are perhaps getting a sense of some of the things that I, the writer, am thinking about (journeys, maps, kinds of value, symbolic activity), and you may be finding this somewhat interesting. In addition, your reading may be useful in that it leads to your taking some further intellectual trips of your own. Perhaps one or more such trips will result in external words, written or spoken, which in turn will function as portable see-through devices to help others not only get a sense of your inner journey but also initiate or continue inner journeys of their own. And so on.

Without symbolic activities such as writing and reading, speaking and listening, there could be no sharing of our inner journeys. Without symbolic activities such as imagining and thinking, there could be no inner journeys in the first place. By "imagining," I mean the formation of internal pictures, whether still shots or motion pictures. By "thinking," I mean an internal process that includes such mental operations as wondering and expressing my wonder in specific questions, enjoying insights that meet those questions and expressing these insights in internal words, wondering about the validity of my insights and expressing this wonder in further, reflective questions. I cannot imagine or think of an inner journey that would not be constituted by some blend of imagining and thinking.

It may be that we are drawn into a journey by something other than the sorts of activities that make up the journey. Perhaps a nonsymbolic form of awareness pulls us into our symbolic activities. (That was, in a way, the climactic insight of the narrator, that the train of symbolic consciousness is pulled and guided by a presymbolic Quality awareness. See *ZMM*, pp. 254–255.) If that is the case, and if we assume the importance of the nonsymbolic awareness that pulls us, it only goes to confirm the importance of the symbolic activities into which we are pulled. Moreover, it is in the context of those symbolic activities that we come to understand and appreciate the importance of the nonsymbolic.

What if the nonsymbolic awareness (in Phaedrus' terms, Quality awareness) is pulling us not just *into* symbolic activities but also *through* and *beyond* them? In the spiritual traditions of both the East and the West—I am thinking not about particular religions, but about the mystical element to be found in them all—we find the claim that eventually one must let go of the activities of thought and imagination in order to enter regions of consciousness that such symbolic activity cannot reach. The journey then becomes no longer a matter of metaphysical musings and horizontal ramblings but a matter of vertical plunging (or rising) toward what T. S. Eliot referred to in the *Four Quartets* as "the still point of the turning world." We might say that the journey becomes journeyless. Suppose that those mystical traditions are right in suggesting that the completion of our journey requires the curtailing, if not the cessation, of ordinary rational consciousness. What then? Does this imply that our symbolic activities, including our metaphysical musings, have been worthless? Hardly. We *learn* about the nonsymbolic (whether presymbolic or postsymbolic) in and through symbolic activity and its product (which is also its common medium), language. *Learning* about getting beyond rational, symbolic activity requires doing the very thing that is to be gotten beyond.

Moreover, what is useful at a later point in a journey may not be useful at an earlier point, and vice versa. From a later vantage point, we might look back in memory at an earlier part of the journey and see illusion and futility. We might say, for example, how silly of us to have put so much stock in rational disputation! Yet at the time it may have been good and even necessary for us to stretch our verbal powers in that way. Perhaps our learning to appreciate the beauty of a verbal thrust or parry led to our learning to appreciate other forms of beauty. Perhaps our development of this form of rationality, the fact that we left no unfinished business in this area, is precisely what made it possible for us to reach the point where we can now recognize the illusion and let go of reliance on an exclusively verbal rationality. Perhaps we are profoundly better off *now* for having passed through *then* what *then* seemed right but *now* likes like a futile activity. Maybe there are some illusions that it is better to pass through than to skirt.

Similarly, if there is some value in the *process* of letting go (and not simply in the subsequent state), this would seem to imply that what is let go has at least a utility value. The process could not occur without it. Put simply, we can't *stop* thinking if we haven't *been* thinking; we can't fall silent if we haven't been speaking.

In sum, our inner journeys seem to require thinking, talking, and other symbolic activity, even if it is the case that all that symbolic activity is sparked by some sort of nonsymbolic intuition and even if that symbolic activity is leading us toward a place where the symbolic activity must give way to something else.

In the light of all this, let's have a look at what is going on in *ZMM*. What is going on is a motorcycle trip and a spiritual journey. In a sense, the motorcycle trip includes the spiritual journey, for the trip provides the narrator with the opportunity to review and extend Phaedrus' philosophical and psychological searchings. In a deeper sense, the spiritual journey includes the motorcycle trip, for the real cycle of the trip, as the narrator tell us, is the self (*ZMM*, p. 293).

What gets this spiritual journey going? On one level, the driving force is the narrator's intellectual desire to work out a view of reality that includes an answer to the question he poses in his very first Chautauqua, What is best? (*ZMM*, p. 7). That question animates his attempt to understand and deal with a series of related dichotomies that seem to underlie a good deal of contemporary pain and confusion, dichotomies such as that between an aesthetic way of viewing things and a rational/technical way of viewing them and that between a reliance on subjectivity and a reliance on objectivity. The question meets its answer when the narrator achieves (or perhaps better, retrieves from Phaedrus) a unifying insight into Quality. On another level, the driving force of the spiritual journey is the narrator's attempt, mostly unselfconscious, to complement a unifying metaphysical insight with an integrating self-insight and a new way of relating to others that is based on such authentic self-insight. The narrator carries out this identity/relational struggle through internal and external conversations with his friends, with his son, and with the ghost from his past that he names Phaedrus. The journey on this level is marked by flight as well as progress. The element of flight can be detected (at least hind-read) in the narrator's disparaging description of Phaedrus as an "evil spirit," in his somewhat cavalier proposal to bury this ghost, and in his weak attempts to distance himself from Phaedrus' project (see *ZMM*, pp. 57, 58, 60, 323). Despite his escapist temptations, the narrator manages to attain the needed identity/relational insight. The full implementation of that insight remains to be lived out, just as the full implications of his metaphysical insight remain to be worked out. But the narrator is well on his way, and we are assured at the end that "it's going to get better now" (*ZMM*, p. 373).

The vehicle of the narrator's spiritual journey is the spiritual motorcycle, the self. (See *ZMM*, p. 293.) But what self? Clearly, on one level, the *rational* self. The rational self is powered and moved by a desire to understand. Fired by that desire, it raises questions, presses for and attains insights, raises further reflective questions, and so on. Throughout the process, the rational self is engaged in symbolic activity. In raising and answering questions, it produces and uses concepts. Those concepts are not the journey itself, but they are necessary see-through devices without which the rational journey could not proceed. We catch the narrator on such a rational journey on almost every page of *ZMM*, as he seeks to understand the differences, tensions, and frustrations that he discovers within and among his traveling companions and the people that he meets. He expresses his understanding by borrowing from Phaedrus such concepts as the "classical mode of reality," "romantic mode of reality," "underlying form," and "immediate appearance." He uses these and other conceptual markers as take-off points for further travel on his journey through the "high country of the mind" toward a wider and deeper understanding of self and the world.

On another level, the vehicle of the narrator's journey is not the rational self with all of its symbolic products and tools but another more inclusive, more mysterious self, the existence of which is the crowning insight of the narrator's rational self. That crowning insight is that Quality is the "track" that carries all subjects and objects (*ZMM*, p. 254), and not only the track (or guide) but also the "cause," "source," and "creator" of subjects and objects (*ZMM*, pp. 215, 222, 263, 280). What this means, in the present context, is that both the narrator's rational self and the objects created by that self (as see-through devices for getting at other objects) are powered and driven by Quality. But by what self is Quality apprehended? Not by the rational self, for the rational self is one of its products. It must be apprehended by a transcendent self that is similarly prior to and more encompassing than the rational self. That mysterious, more encompassing self apprehends Quality not through rational/conceptual/symbolic processes but through a kind of "preintellectual awareness" (*ZMM*, p. 240) for which "peace of mind is a prerequisite" (*ZMM*, p. 265). In a sense, the self that apprehends Quality is not other than what it apprehends, for "at the moment of pure Quality, subject and object are identical" (*ZMM*, p. 261).

Is there a convenient label for that mysterious self that enjoys a nondualistic relationship with Quality? We could continue to call it the rational self, with the proviso that we keep in mind that we now have an enlarged conception of rationality. The narrator himself, at one point in his journey, speaks of the need to "expand the nature of rationality" (*ZMM*, p. 150). Later on in the journey, he speaks of Phaedrus as having shown a way "by which reason may be *expanded*" (*ZMM*, p. 230, italics Pirsig's). Still later, while distancing himself from Phaedrus' project, the narrator speaks of Phaedrus as having pointed to "a new spiritual *rationality*" (*ZMM*, p. 323, italics Pirsig's). However, it might be somewhat confusing, after what has been said thus far, to continue to use the language of rationality. Besides, my purpose here is not to duplicate the language of the narrator (or of Phaedrus) but to map the journey of the narrator (i.e., to provide symbolic see-through devices that are distinct from the symbolic products of the journey itself). So I prefer not to refer to the narrator's journeying self as his rational self.

A second possibility is that we call the self in question the "subliminal self." It is a term, used by Poincaré, that the narrator saw as corresponding exactly to what Phaedrus called "preintellectual awareness" (*ZMM*, p. 240). However, this term is under-suggestive, in the present context, as to the role and importance of the kind of consciousness we are talking about. So I prefer not to use that term either.

The kind of language I propose to use here is one that Phaedrus, given his decision to fight his battle from within the "Church of Reason," declined to use, namely, the language of *mysticism* (see *ZMM*, p. 207). I want to say, in brief, that the ultimate and inclusive vehicle of the spiritual journey taken by Phaedrus and described by the narrator was the *mystical* self. In saying so, however, I want to try to preclude another sort of confusion. The word "mysticism" is frequently associated, in popular usage, with occult phenomena and with people allegedly adept at reading or controlling such phenomena. What I have in mind here is not the popular usage but the way the word has been used, within the spiritual traditions of both the East and the West, to refer to the height of spiritual attainment. In this latter sense, "mysticism" is always associated with some sort of unitive consciousness, a consciousness experientially united with ultimate reality.

What is considered *ultimate reality* may be variously named in different mystical traditions. It may be called Brahman or Tao or Buddha or God or Quality. Those who use these different terms may have different connotations in mind when they use them. What matters with respect to the possibility of mysticism, however, is that, whatever the attendant connotations, the terms be understood to refer to what is ultimate.

Similarly, there may be different ways of speaking of the *union* involved in mysticism. When it is important to obliterate all notion of twoness, the word "identity" may hold sway. When it is important *not* to obliterate all notion of twoness, the word "communion" or "encounter" may be found more acceptable. (Martin Buber's I-Thou language comes to mind.) In either case, as a way of underscoring the fact that some sort of recovery has occurred (whether it be a matter of regaining what has actually been lost or of waking up from the illusion of loss), it may be appropriate to speak of *reunion*. Whatever nuance the language of union is given, if there is to be talk of mysticism, some sort of deep union must be involved.

It perhaps cannot be emphasized enough that to speak of mysticism is to speak of an *experience* of union and not merely speculations about union. The experience is so precious that one who has had a taste of it may try to maintain it indefinitely and dwell in it to the exclusion of everything else. Why mess around with mundane matters when ultimate reality is there for the having (or being)? Certainly, the idea that mystics are dropouts who live in "another world" is not unfounded. The mystical tradition itself gives rise to that idea. However, the notion does not reflect the whole or the best of the tradition. Buddhism and Christianity, for example, emphasize the importance of extending the experience of the Ultimate into everyday experience. Dropping out must be complemented by reentry. Mystical experience is the base from which one lives in fuller union with everything and everyone, doing what ordinary people do but with a radically transformed and transforming consciousness. (An example of this type of mysticism is to be found in the Zen Oxherding Pictures, which will be discussed soon.)

With the above notion of mysticism in mind, let us look at the narrator's journey as a mystical voyage. Only Phaedrus consciously and deliberately set out on a mystical quest, of course; the narrator thinks he is a mere biographer. But since the narrator goes in pursuit of Phaedrus, naïvely intending to bury him forever, he must perforce travel the path of Phaedrus' quest—with ironic results, as Katherine Hayles points out (1984; p. 72; listed in Bibliography, Section 9): "Rather than 'burying' Phaedrus, the narrator's discourse is resurrecting him." At the outset of his journey, the narrator like everyone else knows about the Ultimate, which he names with Phaedrus' term "Quality." However, the narrator's contact with the Ultimate is sporadic and incomplete. Feeling the lack of complete union, he is not at ease and goes forth unconsciously on a search. That search requires that he summon up all of his rational powers to deal with the "dis-ease" that he sees permeating society as a whole, the smaller network of relationships in which he is involved, and even himself. Quality permeates all this as well. And in a way the narrator already "knows" this. But his knowledge lacks the more complete and unitive dimension that would allow him to be at peace with himself and with everyone and everything else. And so he is led to work through and beyond rationality as ordinarily understood, with the help—ironically—of the ghost from the past whom he thinks he's trying to bury. At the end of the book, which is only a point on life's total journey, the narrator has come home to a Quality that was never really lost by reaching a vastly fuller union with his son, within himself, and with the whole world.

Is there a map that we can use to follow this mystical journey more closely? Well, in a way *ZMM* itself is such a map. The author's recounting, while it is neither Phaedrus' journey nor the narrator's, is nevertheless a means whereby we can get a sense of those journeys. However, sometimes a book is illumined by another book, the tale of one journey by the tale of another, one map by another map. Is there another, perhaps more explicitly mystical, map that can throw further light on the journey in *ZMM*? Within the Zen tradition, we find *The Oxherding Pictures*, a series of pictures, along with verse and prose commentaries, having to do with a man's search for a lost ox and the aftermath of that search. It is meant to symbolize the stages of the journey toward full enlightenment.

The series as we know it today goes back to a twelfth-century Chinese Zen master, Kuo-an Shih-yuan, better known in the West by his Japanese name, Kakuan. Prior to Kakuan, there existed other sets of pictures, having similar purposes, which ended with the image of a large, empty circle, suggesting that the end of the enlightenment journey is characterized by a state of self-transcending emptiness. For Kakuan, that was not enough. He added two more pictures, the last of which is entitled, "Entering the Marketplace with Helping Hands." He felt that the fullness of enlightenment involves its radiation amid the everyday desires and concerns of one's fellow human beings. The fact that Kakuan's ten-picture version of the Oxherding Pictures is the commonly accepted one today shows that Zen is one of those forms of mysticism, alluded to earlier, that does *not* locate the be-all and end-all of the journey in the attainment and cherishing of unitive experience. Such experience is to be radiated, not jealously guarded.

The Oxherding Pictures give us a simple story and a profound message. A man searches for an ox, finds it, catches and tames it, and rides it home. He then proceeds to forget first the ox and then himself. Finally, after "returning to the Source," he enters the marketplace with "helping hands." We might say that the man has passed through a series of reunions: reunion with the ox, reunion with himself, reunion with the Source, reunion with his fellow human beings. We might also say that the man has passed through a series of detachments: detachment from the ox, detachment from himself, detachment from reunion experience, and detachment from detachment.

I offer these pictures here as a sort of mystical map for the spiritual journey of *ZMM*. I do not mean to suggest that the reader will find exact counterparts of the ten Oxherding Pictures in Phaedrus' and the narrator's journeys, but I do believe that a study of the pictures, worthwhile all by itself, might help the reader see some things that otherwise might not be seen. Perhaps in the process some interesting comparisons will emerge.

By way of example, consider the first Oxherding Picture. We are told in the commentary attached to the picture that the ox has "never really gone astray" but that the man cannot see it because he has turned his back on his true nature. Compare that remark with the one made by the narrator at the beginning of his motorcycle trip: "I've wondered why it took us so long to catch on. We saw it and yet we didn't see it. . . . The truth knocks on the door and you say, 'Go away, I'm looking for the truth,' and so it goes away" (*ZMM*, p. 5). Also, note that at the end of the commentary on the first Oxherding Picture, we are told that the man "hears cicadas chirping in the trees." In the light of a later line (found in the commentary on the third picture) about the value of listening intently to "everyday sounds," we may take the chirping of the cicadas to signify the pervasive presence of what the man is ultimately after. Returning our attention to *ZMM*, might we say something similar about the humming of a motorcycle? If there is a profound difference between the sounds of nature and the sounds of human artifacts, the answer is a clear no. But what if "the Buddha, the Godhead, resides quite as comfortably in . . . the gears of a cycle transmission as . . . in the petals of a flower"(*ZMM*, p. 16)?

The following rendition of the Oxherding Pictures is taken from Philip Kapleau's *The Three Pillars of Zen* (Garden City, N.Y.: Anchor Books, 1980), pp. 314–323. The brush-and-ink drawings are by Amy Metier, a contemporary American artist. To the Oxherding Pictures I have appended a contemporary commentary by Lex Hixon, found in his *Coming Home* (Los Angeles: Jeremy P. Tarcher, 1989), pp. 60–67, 78–80. My comments up to this point, the traditional Oxherding Pictures, and Hixon's fine commentary all add up to maps upon maps. May I reiterate, as a final reminder, that a map is one thing and an actual journey something else. Fare forward, traveler!

1 / SEEKING THE OX / The Ox has never really gone astray, so why search for it? Having turned his back on his True-nature, the man cannot see it. Because of his defilements he has lost sight of the Ox. Suddenly he finds himself confronted by a maze of crisscrossing roads. Greed for worldly gain and dread of loss spring up like searing flames, ideas of right and wrong dart out like daggers.

> Desolate through forests and fearful in jungles,
>   he is seeking an Ox which he does not find.
> Up and down dark, nameless, wide-flowing rivers,
>   in deep mountain thickets he treads many bypaths.
> Bone-tired, heart-weary, he carries on his search
>   for this something which he yet cannot find.
> At evening he hears cicadas chirping in the trees.

2 / FINDING THE TRACKS / Through the sutras and teachings he discerns the tracks of the Ox. [He has been informed that just as] different-shaped [golden] vessels are all basically of the same gold, so each and every thing is a manifestation of the Self. But he is unable to distinguish good from evil, truth from falsity. He has not actually entered the gate, but he sees in a tentative way the tracks of the Ox.

> Innumerable footprints has he seen
>> in the forest and along the water's edge.
> Over yonder does he see the trampled grass?
> Even the deepest gorges of the topmost mountains
>> can't hide this Ox's nose which reaches right to heaven.

3 / FIRST GLIMPSE OF THE OX / If he will but listen intently to everyday sounds, he will come to realization and at that instant see the very Source. The six senses are no different from this true Source. In every activity the Source is manifestly present. It is analogous to the salt in water or the binder in paint. When the inner vision is properly focused, one comes to realize that that which is seen is identical with the true Source.

> A nightingale warbles on a twig,
>   the sun shines on undulating willows.
> There stands the Ox, where could he hide?
> That splendid head, those stately horns,
>   what artist could portray them?

4 / CATCHING THE OX / Today he encountered the Ox, which had long been cavorting in the wild fields, and actually grasped it. For so long a time has it reveled in these surroundings that breaking it of its old habits is not easy. It continues to yearn for sweet-scented grasses, it is still stubborn and unbridled. If he would tame it completely, the man must use his whip.

> He must tightly grasp the rope and not let it go,
>   for the Ox still has unhealthy tendencies.
> Now he charges up to the highlands,
>   now he loiters in a misty ravine.

5 / TAMING THE OX / With the rising of one thought another and another are born. Enlightenment brings the realization that such thoughts are not unreal since even they arise from our True-nature. It is only because delusion still remains that they are imagined to be unreal. This state of delusion does not originate in the objective world but in our own minds.

He must hold the nose-rope tight and not allow the Ox to roam,
   lest off to muddy haunts it should stray.
Properly tended, it becomes clean and gentle.
Untethered, it willingly follows its master.

6 / RIDING THE OX HOME / The struggle is over, "gain" and "loss" no longer affect him. He hums the rustic tune of the woodsman and plays the simple songs of the village children. Astride the Ox's back, he gazes serenely at the clouds above. His head does not turn [in the direction of temptations]. Try though one may to upset him, he remains undisturbed.

Riding free as air he buoyantly comes home
    through evening mists in wide straw-hat and cape.
Wherever he may go he creates a fresh breeze,
    while in his heart profound tranquility prevails.
This Ox requires not a blade of grass.

7 / OX FORGOTTEN, SELF ALONE / In the Dharma there is no two-ness. The Ox is his Primal-nature: this he has now recognized. A trap is no longer needed when a rabbit has been caught, a net becomes useless when a fish has been snared. Like gold which has been separated from dross, like the moon which has broken through the clouds, one ray of luminous Light shines eternally.

Only on the Ox was he able to come Home,
But lo, the Ox is now vanished, and alone and serene
　　sits the man.
The red sun rides high in the sky
　　as he dreams on placidly.
Yonder beneath the thatched roof
　　his idle whip and idle rope are lying.

8 / BOTH OX AND SELF FORGOTTEN / All delusive feelings have perished and ideas of holiness too have vanished. He lingers not in [the state of "I am a] Buddha," and he passes quickly on through [the stage of "And now I have purged myself of the proud feeling 'I am] not Buddha.' " Even the thousand eyes [of five hundred Buddhas and patriarchs] can discern in him no specific quality. If hundreds of birds were now to strew flowers about his room, he could not but feel ashamed of himself.[7]

Whip, rope, Ox and man alike belong to Emptiness.
So vast and infinite the azure sky
    that no concept of any sort can reach it.
Over a blazing fire a snowflake cannot survive.
When this state of mind is realized
    comes at last comprehension
    of the spirit of the ancient patriarchs.

9 / RETURNING TO THE SOURCE / From the very beginning there has not been so much as a speck of dust [to mar the intrinsic Purity]. He observes the waxing and waning of life in the world while abiding unassertively in a state of unshakable serenity. This [waxing and waning] is no phantom or illusion [but a manifestation of the Source]. Why then is there need to strive for anything? The waters are blue, the mountains are green. Alone with himself, he observes things endlessly changing.

> He has returned to the Origin, come back to the Source,
>   but his steps have been taken in vain.
> It is as though he were now blind and deaf.
> Seated in his hut, he hankers not for things outside.
> Streams meander on of themselves,
>   red flowers naturally bloom red.

10 / ENTERING THE MARKETPLACE WITH HELPING HANDS / The gate of his cottage is closed and even the wisest cannot find him. His mental panorama has finally disappeared. He goes his own way, making no attempt to follow the steps of earlier sages. Carrying a gourd, he strolls into the market; leaning on his staff, he returns home. He leads innkeepers and fishmongers in the Way of the Buddha.

Barechested, barefooted, he comes into the marketplace.
Muddied and dust-covered, how broadly he grins!
Without recourse to mystic powers,
    withered trees he swiftly brings to bloom.

TEN SEASONS OF ENLIGHTENMENT

ZEN OX-HERDING

LEX HIXON

Enlightenment is not an isolated attainment of ancient or legendary sages but a process flowering through members of every culture, a process in which our consciousness gradually becomes transparent to its own intrinsic nature. Various traditions have developed subtle languages to describe phases of this process. These dimensions of Enlightenment are not scholastic projections; they reflect the complex tissue of awareness as it gradually becomes purified or clarified by awareness of itself.

The seeker of Enlightenment must become as close an observer of consciousness as the Eskimo is of snow condition. Enlightenment is not simply an expanse of whiteness any more than snow is, but a process developing through various seasonal changes. Ten seasons of Enlightenment are evoked by the Ox-herding pictures, evolved in twelfth-century China, in which the spiritual quest is depicted as the search for an elusive Ox that roams wild in the rain forest. This Ox symbolizes the intrinsic nature of consciousness, the mystery of what we are. In Buddhist teaching, our intrinsic nature is revealed to be that we have no intrinsic nature, that is, the essence of our consciousness is void, free, or open. The dimensions of Enlightenment suggested by these ten pictures become progressively more comprehensive as this essence of consciousness, or what Zen masters call our *True Nature*, becomes clearer and clearer.

The first Ox-herding picture, or phase of Enlightenment is called Seeking the Ox. This marks the moment when we become explicitly aware of the process of Enlightenment. We now imagine the mystery of our True Nature to be an object of search. Prior to Seeking the Ox, our spiritual growth has occurred in the disguise of ordinary life, for all desires express in more or less clarified ways the longing for ultimate fulfillment, or Enlightenment. Now we have become formal spiritual seekers, a development that is indispensable for focusing our conscious energy toward True Nature. Yet this development also involves a fundamental illusion which Zen tradition exposes in an uncompromising way. We read from the traditional commentary on the Ox-herding pictures: *The Ox has really never gone astray. So why search for it?* By seeking our True Nature, we are creating an illusory duality between the one who seeks and the object that is sought. Why search for True Nature, which is already present as the consciousness by which one carries out the search? Our True Nature is never lost and therefore can never be found. We cannot discover a satisfactory answer to the puzzle *Why search?* and this not-finding-an-answer brings about the gradual cessation of search which is the flowering of Enlightenment.

The ancient commentary continues: *Having turned his back on his true nature, the man cannot see it. Because of his defilements he has lost sight of the Ox. Suddenly he finds himself confronted by a maze of crisscrossing paths.* The seeker is pictured wandering through a mountainous jungle or rain forest. The maze of paths represent the complex possibilities for thought and action in any given culture and within each individual. The seeker assumes that the Ox has taken one of these ways or byways, but no matter how sincerely he follows the various paths, he will never find the Ox of True Nature along any particular path. The Ox is eventually understood to be the entire maze of paths, the infinite rain forest as well as the seeker who wanders through it. Our True Nature is none other than the fundamental principle of Being which Zen masters also speak of as *Original Mind.* The commentary describes this illusory quest for the Original Mind, which can never be lost but from which we have turned away: *Desolate through forests and fearful in jungles he is seeking an Ox which he does not find. Up and down dark, nameless, wide-flowing rivers in deep mountain thickets he treads many bypaths.* There is exhilaration and adventure at this stage of search, yet also a growing sense of desolation and even despair. The seeker has left behind ordinary desires only to become lost in transcendental ambition. This is an impossible quest for the concept of quest itself obscures the True Nature which we seek and which is not beyond our own present seeing or hearing. The commentary on this first Ox-herding picture ends suggestively: *At evening he hears cicadas chirping in the trees.* The music of the cicadas provides a subtle clue to the seeker's True Nature. This humming sound pervades all the structures of seeking. The seeker is exploring the trackless wilderness, frustrated and weary, but the soothing song of the cicadas is omnipresent, subtly permeating all dimensions of his mind and senses.

The second Ox-herding picture, or phase of Enlightenment is called Finding the Tracks. The commentary reads: *Through the Sutras and teachings he discerns the tracks of the Ox. He has been informed that, just as differently shaped golden vessels are all basically the same gold, so each and every thing is a manifestation of the Self. He has not actually entered the gate, but he sees in a tentative way the tracks of the Ox.* The tracks are the wisdom teachings, expounded by various illumined beings, that the sound of the cicadas, and indeed all phenomena, are the same light of Original Mind, or True Nature. The seeker now becomes the finder, but as there was illusion inherent in the seeking so is there illusion in the finding. The tracks of the Ox are none other than the seeker's own tracks through his own consciousness.

Innumerable footprints he has seen in the forest and along the water's edge. Over yonder does he see the trampled grass? Signs of the Ox's presence are noticed everywhere. The forest no longer seems desolate. Yet, following these tracks will not lead anywhere because, as the commentary continues, *Even the deepest gorges or the topmost mountains cannot hide this Ox's nose, which reaches right to Heaven.* The Ox is the entire realm of Consciousness that seekers of the first stage and beginning practitioners of the second stage are exploring, leaving their own tracks everywhere. However, following these tracks is a fruitful and indispensable illusion, without which the seeker would not be drawn deeper into the actual practice of meditation on the intrinsic nature of all phenomena as Original Mind. Children often need to be presented with an incomplete picture to move them in the right direction.

The third Ox-herding picture is called First Glimpse of the Ox. The commentary expands on what was hinted by the song of cicadas: *If he will but listen intently to everyday sounds, he will come to realization and at that instant see the very Source.* The noise of city traffic is the Ox bellowing. This encounter with the Ox does not come through hearing esoteric teaching or the abstract contemplation of the sutras but through direct experience. No longer is the Ox imagined to be somewhere out in the jungle. As the commentary suggests: *The six senses are no different from this true Source.* Any of our sense perceptions or thoughts can become a glimpse of the Ox. The commentary continues: *In every activity, the Source is manifestly present. When the inner vision is properly focused, one comes to realize that which is seen as identical with the true Source.* The practitioner who has glimpsed the Ox is consciously Enlightened, for he or she is no longer seeking the Ox or finding its tracks. The Ox is known to be omnipresent, not in abstract contemplation but in direct experience. Reflects the commentary: *The nightingale warbles on a twig, the sun shines on undulating willows. There stands the Ox. Where could he hide?* The Source cannot hide, because it exists through all forms, though they differ in structure and appearance as suns, nightingales, and willows. Yet this third phase of Enlightenment provides only an inebriating glimpse, an ecstatic realization which comes and goes. Further struggle and discipline are required to expand and stabilize such flashes of insight.

The fourth Ox-herding picture is Catching the Ox. *Today he encountered the Ox, which has long been cavorting in the wild fields, and actually grasped it. For so long a time has it reveled in these surroundings that the breaking of its old habits is not easy. It continues to yearn for sweet-scented grasses: it is still stubborn and unbridled. If he would tame it completely the man must use his whip. He must tightly grasp the rope and not let it go, for the Ox still has unhealthy tendencies.* The intransigent character of the Ox experienced in this stage is expressed literally in Japanese as *wild strength*. This is the raw energy of Enlightenment for which nothing matters, the complete abandon that perceives creation and destruction as one. Such energy must be tempered and refined, a function of advanced spiritual disciplines which cannot begin until one has generated profound insight into the omnipresence of Original Mind. For, prior to such insight, spiritual disciplines are simply an expression of the illusion of seeking. We must now hold and embrace the Ox, sustain our perception of True Nature with such disciplines as total compassion, perfect nonviolence, unwavering truthfulness. These are the *whip* and *rope*. We are dealing with the wild strength of the Ox, which can prove dangerous. Distortions of genuine spirituality are possible at this stage. If discipleship and disciplined practice are prematurely abandoned, the energy of Enlightenment can dissipate into arbitrary and self-willed activity. That the Ox is *still stubborn and unbridled* and *yearns for sweet grasses* reflects the fact that primal awareness has been eternally at play in an infinite field unlimited by human conventions. The conventional surface thinking that operates our daily lives has developed as a byroad, apparently partitioned from the open field of True Nature. When this illusory partition is broken through and the wild Ox enters into conventional human awareness, the advanced practitioner's system of values and even his physical nervous system must be reconstituted so as to harmonize the energy of Enlightenment with personal and cultural being.

The fifth Ox-herding picture, Taming the Ox, indicates a more intense intimacy with True Nature. The previous phase, Catching the Ox, is to sustain and control spiritual insight under all conditions. Taming the Ox is more subtle. An effortless intimacy or friendship with the Ox is now being established. All movement of thought is to be integrated into the realization of True Nature. All phenomena are *tamed* by the childlike friendliness of the one who is ceasing to be an advanced practitioner by becoming an illumined sage. Reads the commentary: *With the rising of one thought, another and another are born. Enlightenment brings the realization that such thoughts are not unreal, since even they arise from our True Nature. It is only because delusion still remains that they are imagined as unreal.* We might suppose that Taming the Ox would begin by the elimination of all thoughts, or at least certain thoughts regarded as negative, impure, or unreal. But that is not the way of Enlightenment, which operates fundamentally by inclusion rather than by exclusion. Taming the Ox is the unlearning by the practitioner of convictions concerning discipline, purity, and discrimination that were important in earlier stages. When we follow the tracks of the Ox, which appear as the teachings of various sacred traditions, we learn to discriminate between the unreal and the real, between our inveterate human illusions and the wisdom of the sages. Now we discover all thoughts to be intrinsically the same, since they each arise from Original Mind. Only because traces of illusion remain is any thought imagined to be different from Enlightenment. Yet without this provisional spiritual illusion of discrimination between ultimate truth and relative truth, between insight and ignorance, there would have been no clarification of True Nature but only the chaos of ordinary desire.

Taming the Ox begins to dissipate this illusory discrimination between spiritual life and ordinary life, a distinction that is no longer useful. The one who is becoming a sage makes friends with the limitations of the ordinary ego rather than withdrawing into the transcendental ego of the spiritual seeker or advanced practitioner. This is the first hint of the mysterious ordinariness into which the sage eventually disappears. Describing the Ox at this stage, the commentary reads: *Properly tended, it becomes clean and gentle. Untethered it willingly follows its master.* The point of this taming is to untether the Ox, to release the primal awareness which we have focused as a particular body and mind. The Ox becomes a free companion, not a tool for plowing the field of Enlightenment. This is a graceful process, not a violent unleashing of energy. All movement becomes balanced.

The sixth Ox-herding picture, or phase of Enlightenment, is Riding the Ox Home. The advanced practitioner now becomes the illumined sage: *The struggle is over. Gain and loss no longer affect him. He hums the rustic tune of the woodsman and plays the simple songs of the village children. Astride the Ox's back, he gazes serenely at the clouds above.* In the final film of the Japanese classic, Samurai Trilogy, the spiritual warrior prepares for his ultimate duel by becoming a farmer again. Laboring hard in the fields during the day, he carves wooden Buddhas in the evenings by firelight. Eventually he wins his final Samurai encounter, transcending his role as warrior or practitioner, not with a steel but a wooden sword that he carves quickly and surely, drawing on the strength and reverence he developed in the carving of Buddhas. He creates the wooden Buddha and the wooden sword because wood grows directly from the earth. This earthiness of the sage does not mean that he or she is always rural, or rustic. The symbolism here is simplicity, naturalness, spontaneity. The sage, having untethered his own being and the being of all phenomena, begins to blend with the ordinary flow of life. He is pictured sitting comfortably on the Ox: *Riding free as air, he buoyantly comes home through evening mists in wide straw hat and cape. Wherever he may go, he creates a fresh breeze, while in his heart profound tranquility prevails.* The sage begins spontaneously to radiate Enlightenment, which is no longer simply an insight alive privately within him but a breeze of blessing felt by all who come into his presence. Yet while there is no longer any problem of discovering, catching, or taming the Ox of True Nature, this phase still involves subtle illusion. The sage is still relating to the Ox as a separate being, even though this being is now so intimate that one can ride it effortlessly, without having to pay the slightest attention to where it is going. The Ox must disappear utterly as a separate entity. The Ox must be expressed fully through our own person.

The seventh Ox-herding picture is called Ox Forgotten, Self Alone. The sage finally regards himself as the full expression of True Nature: *There is no twoness. The Ox is his Primal Nature: this he has now recognized. . . . Only on the Ox was he able to come Home. But lo! the Ox has now vanished, and alone and serene sits the man. . . . Yonder, beneath the thatched roof, his idle whip and idle rope are lying.* All spiritual practices and concepts are now idle. There is no longer any question of having to attain or to discipline. The contemplative way has become indistinguishable from daily life. Meditation, nothing more special than walking or breathing, has become the natural activity of the sage and no longer implies any sense of separation or motivation. *Only on the Ox was he able to come Home.* That lingering twoness between the practitioner and his or her True Nature was necessary all along the way until this stage of Coming Home. A new image emerges here. The Ox symbolized True Nature during the period of illusory quest, discipline, and attainment, but the image of Home no longer contains these illusions. Yet although the separate Ox has disappeared, the Enlightened sage himself still exists as a particular embodiment of True Nature. He enjoys serenity and solitude. This subtle twoness created by the separate existence of the sage himself is yet to be dissolved into the perfect singleness of Original Mind. As the roles of seeker and practitioner gradually disappeared, so also the role of sage must cease to limit illumination.

The eighth Ox-herding picture is called Both Ox and Self Forgotten. The final illusory barrier has evaporated: *All delusive feelings have perished, and ideas of holiness, too, have vanished.* The sage of the previous level has no personal sense of his own holiness but does entertain a sense of reverence for True Nature as expressed through his own conscious being. Instead of blending completely with True Nature, he remains in a contemplative mood and experiences a bliss that still retains a trace of twoness. But on the eighth level, represented by empty space, there is only awakened Enlightenment: no contemplator and no contemplation, no serenity and no disturbance. *He lingers not in Buddha and passes quickly on through not-Buddha.* Awakened Enlightenment itself cannot assert *I am Buddha,* any more than it can assert, *I am not Buddha.* Any such assertion implies the existence of someone who frames the assertion. Here there is no one, not even the sage. Both Ox and Self Forgotten is represented by the traditional Zen circle, the single brushstroke leaving the paper shortly before the point of closure. If there were not that opening, further growth could not occur and the process of Enlightenment would be frozen into empty space. This profound state of emptiness needs to open into fullness. Otherwise it would be excluding the flow of life outside itself, and another illusory sense of subtle duality would arise. The empty circle should contain a landscape. The stream of lifeforms continues to flow as trees, fish, insects. Life is not to be locked out by Enlightenment.

The ninth Ox-herding picture is called Return to the Source. Mountains and pine groves, clouds and waves are appearing from nowhere. The open space of emptiness is melting into a kind of springtime: formless awareness is growing back into forms again without losing its formless, or perfectly unitary, nature. The Enlightened being is no longer faced with the illusion of Enlightenment: *From the very beginning there has not been so much as a speck of dust to mar the intrinsic purity.* After the First Glimpse of the Ox, the practitioner senses every activity as emerging directly from the Source, yet must traverse all the subtle intervening levels of development in order actually to return to that Source. The sage's homecoming had to dissolve into the circle of emptiness before he could completely disappear and simply *be* the Source. But there is no annihilation. All manifestation is now observed by awakened Enlightenment as its own emanation: *This waxing and waning of life is no phantom or illusion but a manifestation of the Source. Why, then, is there a need to strive for anything? The waters are blue, the mountains are green.* Enlightenment simply *is* the blue lake and the green mountain. In earlier stages there has been a dramatic quality of realization, but in the ninth stage this drama fades, leaving only freshness or plainness: *The waters are blue, the mountains are green.* But where are the human beings? There remains a subtly trans-human flavor in this Return to the Source. The process of Enlightenment has come so far, through so many simplifications, that there is difficulty in recognizing and accepting the constructions of human personality and society: *It is as though he were now blind and deaf. Seated in his hut, he hankers not for things outside.* There is a subtle twoness here between the Source flowering as pine or cherry trees and its manifestation as the chronic delusion and suffering of human civilization. This very Return to the Source must deepen to include the return to mundane life.

The tenth Ox-herding picture, which obliterates oneness as well as twoness, is called Entering the Marketplace with Helping Hands. Awakened Enlightenment takes the form of a fat, jolly rustic who wanders from village to village, from mundane situation to mundane situation. His body is overflowing with life-energy.

His being is full of compassionate love. His open hands express perfect emptiness. *The gate of his cottage is closed, and even the wisest cannot find him.* He has gone beyond, gone completely beyond, not to move farther away from humanity but to return completely into the human world. He has even abandoned the Source as a citadel where Enlightenment may subtly isolate itself. *The wisest cannot find him,* because it is not he that wanders about but simply the activity of awakened Enlightenment. He does not experience any intrinsic difference between himself and the villagers, or even the village landscape: *His mental panorama has finally disappeared. He goes his own way, making no attempt to follow the steps of earlier sages.* Advanced practitioners and even sages feel intense reverence for previous sages, and thereby may regard themselves as subtly separate from those Great Ones. But the awakened Enlightenment expressed in this tenth stage is fully identical with the Enlightenment of all Buddhas, past, present, and future. Who is there to follow? The cheerful one who fully manifests Enlightenment follows no path. He carries a wine gourd, symbol of the Tantric ecstasy which transforms the wine of the delusive human world from poison into nectar. *Carrying a gourd, he strolls into the market. He leads innkeepers and fishmongers in the Way of the Buddha. Barechested, barefooted, he comes into the marketplace. Muddied and dust-covered, how broadly he grins! Without recourse to mystic powers, withered trees he swiftly brings to bloom.* By being perceived as intrinsically Buddhas, not only fishmongers and innkeepers but all human beings in the marketplace of desire are swiftly brought to bloom.

S E C T I O N 4

A PHILOSOPHICAL
BACKPACK—EASTERN
PHILOSOPHY

In his intellectual journey, which includes a retrieval of Phaedrus'
intellectual journey, the narrator covers a good bit of philosophical
territory. Sometimes he passes through a region so quickly that if
you aren't already acquainted with it, you will hardly notice it's
there; sometimes he pauses and calls explicit attention to various
features of the philosophical terrain. In either case, if you bring to
the journey some relevant philosophical information and insight—
a philosophical backpack, as it were—you stand a better chance of
noticing and appreciating both the territory and the route that the
narrator takes through it. I offer the next two sections as a philosophical backpack for the journey or as a supplement to whatever
philosophical backpack you are already carrying.

The narrator journeys back and forth between the Eastern and
Western hemispheres of thought. What catches his eye, in both
hemispheres, is whatever speaks to the three interrelated philosophical concerns that he constantly carries with him: a concern
about knowledge, a concern about reality, and a concern about
values. What is human knowledge? Is it some sort of sensuous
contact with an external, material reality? Is it some sort of subtle
creation of and encounter with mental "ghosts" (e.g., concepts
and laws) that are devoid of matter (see *ZMM*'s discussion of
science and ghosts, pp. 28–32)? Is it something objective? Subjective? Both? Neither? Next, what is reality? Is it the complete set of

extramental, material things? A collection of ghosts that have no existence apart from the mind? A process, like a moving train, whose leading edge is the source and container of all that is (see *ZMM*'s train analogy, pp. 254–258)? Is reality objective? Subjective? Both? Neither? Finally, what are values? Are they simply spontaneous, variable, inexplicable *feelings* (positive or negative), or is there *reason* to them as well as rhyme? Are they simply relative to individual or cultural tastes, or is there some common core—Value or Quality—that is the source and measure of the relative variations? How is this Value to be known? Is it real—perhaps the reality of realities—or illusory? Is it objective? Subjective? Both? Neither?

Through the Chautauquas that mark out his intellectual journey, the narrator draws you into a conversation that revolves around questions such as the above. The point of the present backpack is not to outline or summarize the Chautauquas but rather to enhance the conversation. You will find some things in this backpack that may help you understand some bits of the conversation that you might have missed. You will find some other things that may entice you to go further into the questions and extend the conversation beyond the explicit confines of *ZMM*. I have arranged the contents of the backpack under the two broad headings "Eastern Philosophy" and "Western Philosophy" simply to underscore the fact that *ZMM*, as its very title suggests, is an East-West book. The intellectual journey of *ZMM* is fueled by both Eastern and Western sources; the conversation to which you are invited is a conversation that includes both Eastern and Western traditions of thought.

As we explore the Eastern and Western compartments of our backpack, I will attempt to do three things: to highlight some of the key features of the thought tradition under inspection; to indicate where and how some of those features make their appearance along the intellectual route of the narrator; and to suggest some ways in which you might want to extend the conversation and further your own journey.

I will begin by removing from the backpack and unfolding for you a set of information packets on Eastern philosophy. The packets pertain to Eastern religion as well, for religion and philosophy are not sharply divided in Eastern thinking. Religion is the all-inclusive search for and relationship to ultimate reality, meaning, and value; philosophy is the explicitly rational component of the search. The religious search includes all sorts of devotional and meditational practices and experiences that are quite distinct from rational speculation, and it includes ideas that are born from such practices and experiences rather than from rational speculation; but it also includes rational speculation, as well as an attempt to give rational articulation and systematic order to meditative experience and the ideas born therefrom. Religion thus includes philosophy. The packets that I am about to unfold are primarily concerned with the philosophical component of Eastern Religion.

Our backpack includes a packet on Hinduism, one on Buddhism in general, one on Confucianism, one on Taoism, and one on Zen Buddhism. The first two packets deal with native traditions of India; the third and fourth, with native traditions of China; the fifth, with a tradition that began in India, reached an initial flowering in China, and attained its full flowering in Japan.

HINDUISM

Upon opening the information packet on Hinduism, you may be struck by the Hindu tradition's age. From the point of view of Western historical scholarship, Hinduism, in its primary component, goes back to the third millennium B.C. At that time, a group of tribes who called themselves "Aryans" and wandered in regions north and west of what came to be called India already possessed at least the seeds of a significant body of spiritual wisdom. Those tribes invaded India from the northwest and came upon a civilization that probably had already been flourishing since the fourth millennium B.C. That native civilization, the secondary component of the Hindu tradition, had a spiritual tradition of its own that provided fertile soil for the spiritual seeds brought in by the invading tribes. If you think of the Hindu tradition as beginning at the point when seeds and soil first met, you will say that the tradition is about four thousand years old; if you think of the tradition as beginning with its primary component, you will say that it is as much as five thousand years old.

Either way, you will be looking at the matter from an external viewpoint. If you look at the matter from a viewpoint internal to Hinduism, you will say that the tradition's age is immeasurable, for from this internal viewpoint time is seen not as a single straight line but as a series of circles or cycles within ever larger circles or cycles. The largest of those cycles, a sort of day and night of the universe, consists of a period of billions of years during which the universe gradually evolves and reaches a state of full flourishing followed by a period when it deteriorates until it disappears into a state of pure potentiality that also lasts for billions of years. When the night of pure potentiality is over, the day of evolving actuality emerges anew; and so on, endlessly. The historical Hinduism that emerged with that group of nomadic tribes in the third millennium B.C. was one manifestation, during one universe-day of the wisdom that lasts through the unending succession of universe days and nights. If you identify that everlasting wisdom—which intermittently appears to intelligent beings who make only intermittent appearances themselves—with the essence of Hinduism, you will conclude that Hinduism is not a mere 4,000 or 5,000 years old but rather as old as infinite time.

If you are inclined to take seriously the particular events of history, the atrocities and tragedies as well as the blessings and triumphs, you may find the Hindu view of time somewhat disturbing; for it seems to devalue history and the particularities of history. How can any particular event or sequence of events be taken as all that important when whole histories—indeed, whole *universes*—are bound to come and go, to emerge, evolve, decline, and disappear into pure potentiality? If such apparent devaluation of the particular disturbs you, consider yourself in the company of the young Phaedrus, who was disturbed to the point of having to leave India (see *ZMM*, pp. 126–127). More on this later.

As you peruse the packet on Hinduism, you will be struck by the tradition's incredible richness. It is full of cults, centering on a variety of gods and goddesses. At the same time, however, you'll see that the many gods and goddesses are simply faces or appearances of the One God (Brahman). You will encounter solemn rituals carried out with meticulous formality by priests; you will also encounter simple acts of devotion—such as dressing a statue of a deity and offering it flowers and food—performed with unsophisticated piety by peasants. You will hear proclaimed a variety of paths to salvation: reflection on the sacred texts of the tradition, devotion to this or that god or goddess, the performance of one's duty (as determined by one's caste and stage of life), and the practice of a kind of wordless meditation that goes beyond all reflection, devotion, and action. You will hear salvation spoken of both as a deep interpersonal communion with God and as the realization of one's identity with God. You will come across six traditionally acknowledged philosophical systems and note that in their central assertions they seem to contradict one another.

As you view and review the rich array of contrasting practices and seemingly contradictory beliefs, you may begin to wonder whether there is any core of practice and belief that is indispensable to Hinduism. Are there some things that every genuine Hindu must believe and do? Or does anything go here? But remember the Hindu view of time: If the eternal wisdom is manifested and re-manifested through an endless succession of ages and worlds, it would follow that no one set of particulars can contain or exhaust that wisdom and that, by the same token, almost any set of particulars may somehow get at it. In this connection, you might recall part of the narrator's summary of what Phaedrus learned in India about Eastern religion. Phaedrus learned that doctrinal differences among Hinduism, Buddhism, and Taoism are not nearly as important as such differences are among Judaism, Christianity, and Islam, because with Eastern religion "verbalized statements about reality are never presumed to be reality itself" (*ZMM*, p. 126). What Phaedrus learned about doctrinal differences *among* Eastern traditions holds for differences *within* the Hindu tradition, and for the same reason: Words are not to be equated, in reality or in importance, with what they signify. Words are not absolute containers but relative pointers. Similarly, the viewpoints and insights that give birth to words are not absolute but relative. This point is made within Hinduism by the word that is used to denote the philosophies that developed within the tradition. Each of those philosophies is called a *darshana,* a "way of seeing."

The relativity hinted at by both the Sanskrit word and the English phrase is more fully conveyed by an old Hindu parable: Six blind people surrounded an elephant and began to investigate it with their hands. But when asked to describe what was in front of them, each one of them produced a rather different observation, some of which even seemed to be outright contradictory ("smooth," "rough," etc.). Will you say that some of their descriptions are right and others wrong? Are all of them wrong? The answer to those questions depends on how you understand what the people are doing. If you think of them as trying to capture the total reality of the elephant in words, you will conclude that they have all failed and that their descriptions are all wrong. On the other hand, if you see them as simply pointing with words at what they "see" in front of them, each from a relative and limited standpoint, you may wonder about the linguistic aptness of this or that description but you will be unlikely to say that any of the descriptions are simply wrong. From the Hindu viewpoint, all philosophies and indeed all of the constructions of human knowledge amount to what is "seen" by blind persons from their relative standpoints.

Let us consider one of the Hindu philosophies or ways of seeing, the Vedanta. This philosophy is appropriate both because it seems to typify for Westerners who are exposed to it the intriguing "otherness" of India and also because it seems to have played a prominent role in Phaedrus' intellectual development.

Since the word *Vedanta* means "end of the Veda," I will begin by saying something about the *Veda*. I earlier spoke of a body of spiritual wisdom brought into India by ancient Aryan tribes. The ancient Aryans called that body of wisdom *Veda*, or "knowledge." They meant not just any sort of knowledge but all the knowledge that counts, salvific knowledge. That body of salvific knowledge took the form, over time, of four layers or levels of writing. Sometimes the word *Veda* is used to denote only the first, foundation level of writing; sometimes the word refers to all four levels. In either case, the four levels together constitute the Vedic tradition and are all important to the development of Hinduism. The level with which we'll concern ourselves is the fourth and final one. On it, philosophical speculation is explicit and deep; and some of the ideas and suggestions found on the first level are brought to a certain culmination. Hence, the writings on the fourth level, which are most commonly called the Upanishads, are sometimes also referred to as Vedanta, or "end of the Veda." The Vedanta school of Hindu philosophy purports to carry forward the task of philosophical speculation by paying special attention to the wisdom contained in the Upanishads.

What is the wisdom contained in the Upanishads? To answer, I must say something about the word *Upanishad*. The Sanskrit roots mean "sit down near"—Upanishadic wisdom is the sort that you might get by sitting down near your guru or spiritual master and engaging in a dialogue. It is quite distinct from the sort of wisdom that you might get by a detached pursuit of truth for truth's sake, and it is miles apart from the knowledge that you gain when your objective is a course grade or some other credential.

Moreover, the Upanishadic wisdom obtained through intense interaction with a guru is not quite the same as that attained simply by a careful reading of the Upanishads. An intellectual attempt that is not also a spiritual search can get no further than a surface hold on Upanishadic truth. Upanishadic wisdom is, in the last analysis, something that needs to be realized nonconceptually. Hence, I cannot pretend to be transmitting Upanishadic wisdom to you. What I aim to do is simply explain the concepts that might provide the intellectual bearings for a spiritual search that eventually does away with the need for intellectual bearings.

To get an idea of Upanishadic truth, you need to have some understanding of two key concepts, "Brahman" and "Atman." The word *Brahman* comes from the Sanskrit root that means "to grow." The Upanishadic thinkers used this word to refer to the source of all beings, that from which everything in the universe grows. Brahman is thus a creator of sorts, but not like our Western God, who creates out of nothing a world that is distinct from God. Brahman grows into or *becomes* the many things of the world. At the same time, Brahman is not exhausted by the world of things but remains its own reality, which is true reality. One must not reduce Brahman to the many things that Brahman somehow becomes; rather, the many are to be reduced to Brahman.

The Upanishads are filled with stories in which spiritual masters enjoin spiritual seekers to peel away the layers of the universe in order to discover the subtle essence of all. This discovery, which is to be prized beyond all else, is not attainable through ordinary ways of knowing, for ordinary, perceptual/conceptual knowledge is geared toward marking off qualities from other qualities and objects from other objects, while Brahman is neither a particular object nor a particular quality but that which underlies all objects and qualities, the unqualified ground, the Pure Object. No wonder, then, that it is spoken of as "that from which words and thought return without having attained it" (Taittiriya Upanishad, Ch. II, sect. 4, l.1). Nonetheless, although concepts cannot get a hold on Brahman, they can be used to point the way toward it. The Upanishads are full of analogies that are meant to provide a notion of Brahman (e.g., the salt that pervades the water and is in our awareness without itself being an object of direct perception). And lest seekers confuse the analogy with the reality, they are continually reminded that Brahman is *neti, neti,* "not this, not this." Analogies and negations do not attain the goal but they at least mark off a path from which seekers will eventually leap into transcendental consciousness.

Why seek Brahman? The answer to that question has to do with the Upanishadic characterization of Brahman as *sat* ("being"), *cit* ("consciousness"), and *ananda* ("bliss"). Brahman is infinite being, infinite consciousness, and infinite bliss. The knower of Brahman will gain release from the endless rounds of suffering, death, and rebirth that mark a time-bound existence. But how can this knowledge take away the knower's own limitations and misery? Wouldn't it only emphasize the disparity between it and the knower's life circumstances? The answer requires an analysis of another key concept, "Atman."

The word *Atman* means "Self." The self denoted by this word is not the surface self but the deepest self. In the Upanishads, the seeker is challenged to work down past all the nonultimate layers of the seeker's being to the essential core, the self that is most real and lasting. The seeker is to prize that self above all else and know it fully. It is not the physical self, the person seen in a mirror, the object of sensory consciousness. Nor is it the self found in dreams, roaming freely in the world of dream objects. Nor is it the self associated with deep sleep, neither a physical object among physical objects nor a dream object among dream objects, but an objectless subject that is opaque to itself. Rather, the core self is encountered, in its purity, on a level of consciousness for which the Upanishadic thinkers lacked an adequate descriptive label. It is a level of consciousness beyond the first three levels (awakeness, dream, and deep sleep) called *Turiya*, or "the Fourth," the self-luminous source and illuminator of all objects of consciousness. It is consciousness itself, the Pure Subject.

We cannot know the Pure Subject, the Atman, by simply *learning* about it. We must avoid any confrontation, any duality between subject and object. In a way, we already know it—the Atman is never really devoid of Self-knowledge. The task of the seeker is somehow to tap into that Self-knowledge. Following the lead of the pertinent philosophical tradition, you might call this tapping "transcendental knowledge" or "realization." Whatever the label, the important thing is that you remember the special character of the knowledge that is sought: a nondualistic entry into a nondualistic Self-presence.

When we have that Self-presence, we realize the climactic lesson of the Upanishads—Atman and Brahman are one. The Pure

Subject is the Pure Object. As it is put in second-person form, *tat tvam asi*, "you are that." You, the real you, the Atman, are that, the ground of all beings, Brahman. Whether you peel away the onionlike layers of the universe or the onionlike layers of yourself, you reach the same point, the point at which the fullness of reality (*sat*), the fullness of consciousness (*cit*), and the fullness of bliss (*ananda*) are present. It is a point from which, despite the seeming vagaries of your time-bound existence, you have never really departed. No wonder, then, that the knowledge of Atman (which is also the knowledge of Brahman) is to be prized: To know it is to be it, and to be it is to enjoy eternally the fullness of being.

Tat tvam asi teaching is of central importance to the Upanishads and, therefore, to the Vedanta school of philosophy. Moreover, according to the narrator of *ZMM*, Phaedrus realized that this teaching, overcoming the separation of subject and object, is important not just to Hinduism but to *all* of the Oriental religions (*ZMM*, p. 126). Quite clearly, the teaching is important to and finds a resonance in Phaedrus' philosophy of Quality. As the narrator puts it: "Phaedrus felt that at the moment of pure Quality perception, or not even perception, at the moment of pure Quality, there is no subject and there is no object. . . . At the moment of pure Quality, subject and object are identical. This is the *tat tvam asi* truth of the Upanishads" (*ZMM*, p. 261).

Meditation is typically a prerequisite for the realization of Upanishadic truth. This idea also finds a resonance in *ZMM*'s philosophy of Quality. The narrator tells us that "peace of mind" (which we may take as very much related to the practice and fruits of meditation) is a prerequisite for Quality perception. He then describes peace of mind in terms of three levels of quietness: physical quietness, mental quietness, and value quietness. Physical quietness is illustrated by "the ability of Hindu mystics to live buried alive for many days" (*ZMM*, p. 265). Mental quietness is characterized by an absence of "wandering thoughts," value quietness by an absence of "wandering desires" (*ZMM*, p. 265). All three levels of quietness have a relation to the practice of meditation in the Hindu tradition. The first level is perhaps best thought of as preparation for meditation practice, the second level as the heart of the practice itself, and the third level as its effect in daily life. In other words, before you meditate, you need to attain a state of physical relaxation; while you meditate, you need to clear your mind of thoughts, so that Atman consciousness may take over; and after you meditate, to the extent that your consciousness has been transformed, you should be able to deal serenely with the ups and downs of everyday existence.

What the narrator of *ZMM* calls "value quietness" is reminiscent of a theme found in another sacred scripture of Hinduism, the *Bhagavad Gita*. The *Gita* contains a philosophy of action that complements the philosophy of knowledge and reality contained in the Upanishads. In the *Gita*, Krishna (an incarnation of the Godhead, Brahman) tells Arjuna (a warrior who is filled with doubts as he is about to enter battle) that action in the world, action amid ambiguity and ambivalence, does not necessarily defile the doer. As long as it is performed in the right spirit, action can be a path to salvation. Action in the right spirit is *nishkama karma*, "desireless action," that is, action without any desire for rewards. It parallels the narrator's description of value quietness as a state in which one "simply performs the acts of his life without desire" (*ZMM*, p. 265).

Clearly there are points of convergence between certain strands of Hindu philosophy and the philosophy developed in *ZMM*. But there are also points of divergence that will become clearer as we explore further aspects of the Vedanta philosophy.

The elements of Upanishadic wisdom discussed here are only a part of the Vedanta philosophy. The Upanishadic texts are subject to varying interpretations. In addition, there are many questions that the texts neither explicitly raise nor directly address. The result is that the school of philosophy that seeks to carry forward Upanishadic wisdom is a house divided into three rather different-looking apartments, called nondualism, qualified nondualism, and dualism. The names correspond to the different ways of responding to the question, What is the relationship between the *many* beings that make up the world of our experience (including those particular beings that we ordinarily call ourselves) and the *one* underlying reality that the Upanishads refer to as Brahman and Atman? If you believe that the one true reality of the many is Atman/Brahman and that manyness is a mere appearance or illusion, you reside in the "nondualist" apartment of the house of Vedanta. If you believe that the core reality of the many is Atman/Brahman but that the many add to that core a distinct reality of their own, you reside in the "qualified nondualist" apartment. If you believe that the reality of the Supreme Being, Atman/Brahman, is radically distinct from the reality of the many beings to which the Supreme gives rise, you reside in the "dualist" apartment.

A concept that is central to the nondualist Vedanta philosophy is *maya*. The word *maya*, usually translated as "illusion," comes from the same Sanskrit root as *magic* and carries some of the same connotations. To say that the world is maya is to say that it is a sort of magic show. We may be enthralled by it, but we need to remember that things aren't, after all, as they appear to be; we are being tricked. To use a metaphor that is very common in the Hindu tradition, we are mistaking the rope for a snake. Our mission in life is to get beyond the illusion and grab hold of the rope, Brahman, to the point where all else, including ourselves, disappears. If the mission is accomplished, the result (which is also the cause and, indeed, the only genuine reality) will be infinite being, consciousness, and bliss.

Given the concept of maya, what might you say about the elephant in front of you if you were a nondualist Vedantin? You might say that it is rough and hairy but that its roughness and hairiness are, after all, an illusion brought about by ignorance. You might add that really there is no elephant in front of you but only an elephantine consciousness that is all in all. But suppose you are pressed a bit on this business of maya and asked about things other than elephants. It may not seem all that momentous to delete, philosophically, an elephant or two—but what about the terrible injustices, horrendous sufferings, and tragic events of world history? Are they to be philosophically deleted as well? Are they mere illusions? Was the bombing of Hiroshima an illusion?

So asked the young Phaedrus, when he was a student at Benares Hindu University, and his professor smiled and answered yes. The exchange led to Phaedrus' departure from India. (See *ZMM*, pp. 126–127.) The departure is readily understood as a young man's conscientious response to an unconscionable point of view; but what about the professor's response? Is that the authentic and inevitable conclusion of the philosophical tradition (nondualist Vedanta) that the professor was expounding?

Perhaps the professor had his reasons for smiling and answering as he did; but I think it important to point out that he might have responded differently without doing injustice to the tradition. He might have said, for example, that there are levels of truth and reality. A higher-level truth might delete a lower-level truth *on the higher level* without deleting the lower-level truth *on its own level;*

a higher-level reality might cause a lower-level reality to vanish *on the higher level* without rendering the lower-level reality illusory *on its own level*. Thus, we who live on the lower level, the level of empirical consciousness, must regard as real and take very seriously events like Hiroshima, even though we believe that such events disappear on the highest level. We are where we are, and we shouldn't pretend to be where we aren't. When we say that the things of our world are mayic, illusory, we are speaking of what is true from the standpoint of the highest level. (Paradoxically, when we reach that standpoint, "we" won't be around and there will be no "standpoints.")

The same point is carried by an old story about Shankara, the great eighth-century Vedanta philosopher. Shankara was being challenged with regard to his teaching that the world is maya. "What would you do," the challenger asked, "if you were being chased by a wild elephant?" "I would run," Shankara replied. "Why would you run?" the challenger continued. "After all, by your own account, the elephant is merely an illusion." "I would run," Shankara retorted, "because *I* am part of the same illusion."

If Phaedrus' professor had responded along such lines, Phaedrus might have felt less compelled to leave India. In any case, he did not leave India without a good bit of Hindu philosophy. Even the notion of maya, in spite of its theoretical and practical difficulties, seems to have found a place in his thinking. After all, to say that the subject-object duality needs to be transcended is also to say that that duality is in some sense an illusion. Moreover, Phaedrus apparently reached a point in his development when the commonplaces of our culture took on the character of an illusion to be overcome, a dream from which to wake. At that point, Phaedrus apparently had a trans-mayic experience of sorts. We might wonder whether that experience is best understood as an insanity experience, as an enlightenment experience, or as both. In any case, the narrator's description of the experience carries overtones of the Vedantic philosophy that we have been considering: "He [Phaedrus] crosses a lonesome valley, out of the mythos, and emerges as if from a dream, seeing that his whole consciousness, the mythos, has been a dream and no one's dream but his own, a dream he must now sustain of his own efforts. Then even 'he' disappears and only the dream of himself remains with himself in it" (*ZMM*, p. 358).

Much more could be said about this experience and its tie-ins with Hindu philosophy and Hindu spirituality; but right now it is best to bring our perusal of Hinduism to a close and put the packet on Hinduism to one side. It's time to have a look at Buddhism.

BUDDHISM

As you begin to unfold the packet on Buddhism, you might be struck by the fact that that tradition, unlike Hinduism, can be traced to a definite person whose historical time and place can be marked off with reasonable assurance and accuracy. Later on, when you have unfolded the packet at greater length, you may have occasion to note that from a viewpoint internal to Buddhism, things are not so simple. For now, however, you are not wrong to think that Buddhism began with a man, Siddhartha Gautama, who was born in northeastern India in 560 B.C.

A second thing that you may notice is that Buddhism seems to be both an offshoot of and a reaction to Hinduism. Siddhartha was born into the Kshatriya caste, the political-military caste of Hindu society. He was undoubtedly raised in an environment permeated by Hindu rituals and beliefs. We can only speculate about whether and to what extent the Hinduism of the time was alive spiritually or smacked of dead ritualism; but we do know that at a certain point Siddhartha did not find the tradition spiritually sustaining. He felt compelled to leave his family, reject the forms of Hinduism that were available to him, and launch out on a spiritual quest of his own. The net result of his quest was not simply a new branch of Hinduism but a new and rival tradition. Hinduism, it may be noted, eventually dealt with that new tradition in the same way it would always deal with rivals—it "overcame" it by absorbing it— Gautama the Buddha became a part of the Hindu pantheon. (From Phaedrus' perspective, that sort of conquering by absorption was similar to the ancient Greeks'—the Sophists' Virtue, *aretê*, was stripped of its character as Value or Quality and enthroned as the leading Idea—the Idea of Good—in Plato's pantheon of Ideas. See *ZMM*'s discussion of Plato and the Sophists, especially pp. 342–343.)

As you read the traditional account of Siddhartha Gautama's life, you may come to the conclusion that while it contains a core of historical fact, it is richly and unabashedly embellished with fable and fantasy. I don't think it is a mistake to look at the account in that way, as long as we don't jump to the further conclusion that all the truth worth seeking in the account is to be found only in the "facts" purified of all fable and fantasy. If we understand that the account is meant to open the reader to *spiritual* truth in addition to historical truth, we may find it worthwhile to attend as much to the embellishments as to the core.

When Siddhartha was born, so the traditional account goes, his father was told by seers that the child was destined to become either a man with vast political power or a man with vast spiritual power. The prediction put Siddhartha's father at a fork in the road. Should he choose for his son the path toward worldly rule or the path toward spiritual leadership? His choice would affect his son's life; but though it would place the son on a definite road, it would not preclude the son from reaching his own crossroads. The son's eventual decision would alter both the momentum and the meaning of the father's choice. Decisions made at such crossroads have implications both for what is to be and what has been. They alter the *conditions* of future experiences (for others as well as for the chooser); and they alter the *meaning* of past experiences (for others as well as for the chooser). In this light, you might want to look at the father-son relationship in *ZMM*. The father's crossroads decisions, both before and during the motorcycle trip, definitely shape Chris's experience of the trip; but Chris's decisions, especially the later ones, have an even more powerful, transformative effect on his father's understanding of what happened before the trip.

Siddhartha's father chose for his son the well-traveled road of worldly power and success. He tried to keep his son on that road by surrounding him with palatial pleasures and comforts. Siddhartha was exposed only to the pleasant side of life. It seemed for a while that the father's plan was working and that Siddhartha's choices were mirroring and confirming his father's choice. For example, Siddhartha chose a beautiful woman, Yasodhara, to be his wife and won her in a contest of arms. As it turned out, however, Siddhartha's arriving at his own crossroads would change everything.

When Siddhartha was in his mid-twenties he had a series of experiences usually referred to as the Four Sights. As the story goes, despite his father's efforts to keep Siddhartha's out-of-palace trips free from all ugliness, one day the young man came upon an old person. Since old age was outside the realm of Siddhartha's prior experience, Siddhartha asked his trusted traveling companion, Channa, to explain what was befalling the old person and to say whether the occurrence was unique or common. Channa briefly explained the nature of old age and told Siddhartha that the condition was the common lot of human beings. That response led Siddhartha to do some heavy thinking back at the palace. On a second occasion, Siddhartha came upon a sick person. Since sickness was also outside the realm of Siddhartha's prior experience, he asked Channa about the nature and regularity of that occurrence. Channa explained the nature of sickness and told Siddhartha that the condition was the common lot of human beings. This led to more heavy thinking back at the palace. On a third excursion, Siddhartha saw a corpse being carried in a funeral procession. He repeated his question. Channa repeated his answer. More heavy thinking back at the palace. On a fourth occasion, Siddhartha came upon a monk, simply dressed, with a begging bowl in his hand and a serene look on his face. It was another novel experience.

This time Siddhartha's thinking led to resolute action. He arose in the middle of the night, bid a silent good-bye to his sleeping wife and sleeping child—by now, Yasodhara had given birth to a son, Rahula (a name that, significantly, means "bond" or "impediment")—and made for the palace gates. The gates, which the father kept tightly barred at night, miraculously opened for Siddhartha, allowing him to leave the grounds and begin his world-transforming religious quest.

If you approach the story of Siddhartha with a hunger for "facts," you will probably still be hungry after hearing it. You will glean from the story that Siddhartha was married, that he had a son, and that he left home when he was about twenty-five; but you are unlikely to find the story of the Four Sights credible. How could a young man in his mid-twenties, a married father, have no knowledge of old age, sickness, and death? Impossible! You know it, I know it, every intelligent and mature person knows it, and, surely, the original storyteller knew it too. However, it's quite possible for the original storyteller and every intelligent and mature hearer to find food for thought where credible "facts" are missing. Consider the difference between *knowing factually* that people grow old, get sick, and die and *knowing existentially* that you and persons you cherish are subject to old age, sickness, and death. In the case of factual knowing, your knowledge might well be integrated, in an abstract manner, with all sorts of other factual knowledge, such as knowledge about rocks and trees and bees. In the case of existential knowing, that sort of abstract integration would be beside the point. What you have gotten hold of is a new awareness that calls for a new way of appropriating what you already know and a new way of living your life! The knowledge—the gut experience—has gotten hold of you. It has placed you at a crossroads and there is no turning back to life as hitherto lived.

One of the paths at your crossroads may lead back to your own version of Siddhartha's palace, but that does not mean that the path leads back to your old life. You have a new awareness of the transitory nature of life, and that new awareness is bound to color everything. Perhaps you will try to kill that awareness by giving yourself to palatial comforts and pleasures with a vengeance. What in your innocence was the zest of life will now be a deadening drug; and you can count on having to increase the dosage and adjust the form of the drug so that it maintains its deadening effect.

Perhaps the prospect of a deadened life seems less appealing than death itself. In that case, you may feel yourself somewhat drawn by a second path at your crossroads, a seemingly short one, the path to suicide. If life is so absurdly painful, why prolong the agony when it can be ended quickly? But if you take the dead end, you cut yourself off from the possibility of finding a deeper meaning that removes the absurdity and the pain. What if such a meaning is somewhere to be found? Do you really want to end it all without having tried hard to find it? Besides, if you are in Siddhartha's shoes, you have probably been brought up with the idea that death doesn't really end it all. After you die, you are reincarnated again and again. The seemingly short, dead-end path is neither short nor a dead end. It dips down and around and eventually takes you back to the same crossroads.

If you can't go home and you can't escape, what can you do? You can take the third path at your crossroads, the path of a personal, spiritual search for life's meaning. Perhaps the memory of the monk with the serene look on his face will suggest to you that a spiritual search might be worthwhile. If you take that path, you will leave behind not only your father's palace but also your father's *answers*—with no guarantee that you will find believable, livable answers of your own. Besides, in leaving behind all that, you are not simply leaving behind ego-centered pleasures, comforts, and securities; you are also, seemingly, shirking your social *responsibilities*. What about your spouse and your child and the other people who count on you? On the other hand, how responsible is it to base your life on yesterday's certitudes when today you have had an experience that calls them into question? Isn't the heart of responsibility your readiness to *respond* to the situation in which you find yourself? What if that situation includes a powerful doubt—a doubt provoked by a soul-shaking, Four Sights experience—about the meaning of your life as you are living it? Are you being responsible when you ignore this doubt or when you face it squarely? When you continue to tell yourself that the old answers still hold you or when you admit that they don't? When you grit your teeth and go on fulfilling the responsibilities that go along with the old answers or when you saddle your horse, leave behind what has previously defined (and confined) you, and move out in search of new meaning and new life? Is it not possible that you might conscientiously reach the conclusion sometime that you need to let go of plural responsibilities in order to recover the one great responsibility?

In any case, Siddhartha's way of dealing with his shocking new awareness of some rather old facts was to begin a search for a new understanding of life's meaning. You might imagine that, as he set out on his search, he felt both the exhilaration that generally accompanies a fresh start and a certain fear regarding the unknown, unpredictable future into which he was heading. Would he find what he was looking for or would his search end in darkness, just as it started in darkness? Given that his father had the habit of keeping the palace gates securely locked at night, would Siddhartha's search be blocked at the very outset? As the story goes, Siddhartha's search was neither destined to end in darkness nor blocked by locked gates at the outset. The gates opened miraculously of themselves—an event whose symbolic aptness should not be overlooked. When you have been thrown into confusion and you have been struggling both to get clear and to get by, you can reach a point at which you are so drained that, despite a maximum of willpower (or perhaps *because* of a maximum of willpower), you are going nowhere. You are down to your last ounce of energy and just about ready to say that the whole struggle has been worthless when the miracle happens. Somehow a door opens for you. And you feel uplifted and ready to continue the struggle, even though the confusion has not entirely disappeared. In this context, you might want to consider the plight of Chris in *ZMM:* Dissatisfied with his father's certitudes but too confused himself to throw much light on the problem in the relationship, he was unable to move things toward a solution until somehow a door opened, a door that separated him and his father.

The gates opened. Siddhartha had the break he needed. He took the break, passed through the opening, and set out on his spiritual journey. He could not turn back. The mythos within which he had lived was now broken. Broken mythos, broken life. What had broken the mythos was his existential realization that life was riddled with old age, sickness, and death. Life thus riddled was itself a riddle. Siddhartha had to solve the riddle if he was to maintain the hope of overcoming life's brokenness. Could he solve the riddle?

The traditional account tells us that Siddhartha spent a number of years and explored a variety of paths in search of a solution before he finally reached a breakthrough, which occurred in the aftermath of another internal crisis. We can only guess about what brought on the crisis, since, in the story, no mention is made of it. All we know is, Siddhartha came upon a tree on the bank of a river. As he approached the tree, a woman came up to him and offered him a bowl of rice. Perhaps the woman had an inkling of the special role her action might play in the unfolding spiritual drama, or perhaps she had no inkling at all and was just doing what many people at that time would do when they encountered someone who looked like a beggar. Whatever, her simple action helped Siddhartha move toward the climax of his spiritual journey. (You might want to consider some parallel instances in spiritual literature where a woman's simple action impels a journeyer toward a higher stage. For example, in the New Testament [John, ch. 2], it is at the instigation of his mother, Mary, that Jesus works the first of his miracles, turning water into wine at Cana. Closer to our main concern here, it is Sarah's innocent remark, "I hope you are teaching Quality to your students" [see ZMM, p. 160], that impels Phaedrus forward on his spiritual journey.) Accepting the bowl of rice from the woman, Siddhartha moved toward the tree. Somehow, the conjunction of the rice, the tree, the river, and whatever had been churning in his mind led him to feel that he was at another crossroads. Would he continue on as he had been journeying or would he, right here and now, with this rice as his food, this tree as his shelter, and this river as his focal point, bring the journey to a climax one way or another? He chose the latter, resolving to eat his rice and to take no further nourishment until, sitting and thinking beneath the tree, he reached either transforming insight or death, whichever came first. As it turned out, he won through to transforming insight and became *Buddha*—"Awakened One," or "Enlightened One." The tree under which he accomplished this momentous feat came to be called the *bodhi* tree, i.e., the "enlightenment tree." The river did not receive a like title, but rivers in general are symbolically associated, in Buddhist lore, with enlightenment as well as with what precedes and follows enlightenment experience. The bowl of rice was later commemorated by Siddhartha, as he lay on his deathbed, as one of the two most significant meals in his life, the other being the recently consumed meal (probably poisonous mushrooms) that brought on the sickness that led to his final departure.

Of what did Siddhartha's enlightenment experience consist? Words cannot capture the experience; they can only point. If you would like to know what it was like, from the inside rather than from an external point of view, you will have to find your own version of a sustaining bowl of rice, a shelter-giving tree, and a focus-providing river. And if you do that, there will be no guarantees as to the outcome. Recall that Phaedrus, after walking the streets with "his mind spinning" (*ZMM*, p. 356), finally settled into his apartment bedroom (his bodhi tree?) and stared for "three days and three nights" (*ZMM*, p. 358) at the bedroom wall (his river?). The outcome was that Quality finally made itself clear to him and put his soul at rest (*ZMM*, p. 359); the outcome was also that he was declared insane. What went wrong here?

Supposing that you are enough of a risk-taker not to be turned back by a lack of guarantees, you still might not want to bother with a bowl, a tree, and a river unless you have some indication that the enlightenment experience is worth seeking. Can something be said about enlightenment, from an external point of view, that might help someone decide whether it's worthwhile to try to get inside? To put the question in terms familiar to readers of *ZMM*, is there some "classical" formulation of enlightenment—some breakdown of the category *enlightenment* into component categories—that might provide, if not a *substitute* for the "ecstatic" feel of the experience, at least an *analogue* to that feel? Can we get some understanding of motorcycle riding even though we have not yet ventured to ride one?

Before facing such questions about the nature of Siddhartha's enlightenment, we might do well to pause for a moment and pay some special attention to this word "enlightenment." While the word is central to the whole Buddhist tradition and also to the origin and development of the modern era in the West, there is a marked difference in the Eastern and Western connotations of the word. In the Buddhist tradition, the word is used to refer to the transforming experience by virtue of which Siddhartha came to be called "Buddha." Buddhists seek to live the sort of life that tallies with such experience and thereby attain a similar experience. In the Buddhist tradition, you cannot, in the last analysis, divorce the word "enlightenment" from its reference to a certain kind of *experience*. In the West, the word is frequently associated with a particular historical period (roughly, the seventeenth and eighteenth centuries) and, more generally, with an ideal that came into prominence during that period, namely the ideal of putting the whole of human life under the rule of *reason*, which means, first, that you don't take something as a truth to be believed or as a principle to be put into practice simply on the word of an authority, however powerful or exalted the authority might be or seem to be. Rather, you must believe what you believe and live as you live on the basis of reasons that are judged to be sufficient in and of themselves. Trust reason and not authority. That does not preclude your relying, from time to time, on the opinion of experts— after all, you don't have enough time and energy to carry out a rational investigation of everything. However, your reliance would be very "unenlightened" if it were rooted not in the premise that the expert had reached a certain conclusion "scientifically" but in the premise that the expert had some special, nonrational access to an esoteric body of truths.

Putting life under the rule of reason also assumes that you don't base your beliefs and practices on untutored and untested personal experience. Although your experience may carry with it a certain momentum of its own, you must not unthinkingly give in to that momentum. After all, your experience may prove to be illusory or, if not illusory, subject to a different and more rational interpretation than the one you might spontaneously give to it. Try your experience at the bar of reason, test it in the laboratory of logical method.

How? First, prepare your experience for court proceedings by submitting it to a process of rational articulation. (If you try to take unarticulated experience to court, you won't even get the judge to look at it.) Put your experience into words. However, not just any words will do. What you want is a set of words that translates the experience into one or more propositions or claims about how things are (or are not), about what really is (or is not) the case. As much as possible, you need to free your claims of the feel and the energy that were attached to the original experience. Admittedly, that feel and energy may have been what made the original experience impressive and momentous, and that fact may tempt you to try to use language that somehow creates a duplicate experience; but you should resist the temptation. This is not a time to wax poetic. You are not preparing to enter the theater of the happily lyrical; you are preparing to enter the court of the would-be rationally enlightened. You want your life, with all of its beliefs and practices, to be "enlightened," illumined and guided by rationally ascertained truths and free from slavish dependence on non-rational feelings and impulses; so you must be willing to strip your experience of its feel and energy in order to isolate and put to the test the claims that the experience suggests.

At this point, an objector might say that the process of rational articulation has the effect of discarding experience and replacing it with something quite different, a set of claims. If that is so, how can it be said that *experience* is to be tried in the court of reason? Isn't it rather the case that what is to be tried is a poor substitute for experience, one that *reason* has had a hand in producing? The objection is well taken. It is clear that what is to be taken into court is not experience in its own proper state, and it may well be said that something is lost in the process; but as Phaedrus saw, recalling Thoreau, "You never gain something but that you lose something" (*ZMM*, p. 341). Phaedrus' insight came in the context of his wrestlings with Greek thought and concerned the loss that comes with the movement toward scientific understanding. It is the very sort of loss that our present objector is lamenting. If you are a seeker of rationally enlightened life, you may share in the lament, but you need to keep in mind that there is something to be gained—indeed, a whole new world. You are about to exchange the old world of immediacy, a world characterized by powerful feelings and urges and by a language laden with such feelings and urges, for a new, more mediated and more rationally controlled world with a language of its own. Because you think that new world is worth entering, you must be willing to submit your experience to the transmutation process that allows you to enter the new world's courtroom.

After transforming your experience into propositions or claims, you are ready to enter the court of rational discourse. In that court, you will find a number of rooms well stocked with other instances of rationally articulated experience as well as conclusions drawn from such instances; indeed, you will find claims upon claims upon claims. If you investigate closely, you will find that the rooms are not all alike. Some rooms (in the winners' section of the court) contain claims that are well supported by other claims that are, in turn, well supported by other claims, and so on. Other rooms (in the losers' section of the court) contain claims that are contradicted by other claims, which latter claims are well supported by other claims that are, in turn, well supported by other claims, and so on. Still other rooms (in the jury-still-out section of the court) contain claims that are neither thoroughly supported by other claims nor thoroughly refuted by them.

In which sort of room will your own claims end up? You won't know until they have undergone their trial. And even after the trial, you can't count on your claims staying in the same room forever. They could pass from the winners' section through the jury-still-out section to the losers' section and back again several times. (In the court of reason, there is no counterpart to the legal presumption of innocence; nor is there a limit to the number of appeals that might be made.)

How does the trial proceed? A full response to that question would be out of place here. Suffice it to say that, while there have been and continue to be differences among the advocates of enlightenment about how the court of reason should proceed, it is generally agreed that the proceedings should have a *public* rather than a private character and should honor appeals to *logic* rather than to intuition.

To say that the trial should have a public character is to say that the meaning of all the claims involved in the trial should not be accessible only to a privileged one or few who have some special gift or experience. If, for example, you bring to the court of reason the claim, "Yatquil is dubahd," and you say that only those few who have your own special gift could possibly have an inkling of what you mean by the claim, it will likely be thrown out of court, for there is no way that a trial centering on it could have a public character.

To say that the trial should honor logic rather than intuition is to say that the court is interested in finding out how well the claims in question link up with other already accepted claims and also that the court is not interested in hearing about how intensely the claimant "sees" the truth of the claim. If, for example, you attempt to back up your assertion that capital punishment is a deterrent with the exclamation, "It's so clear!" you will not score any points with the judge.

And what does enlightenment have to do with all of this? Are you enlightened if all or most of your claims end up in the winner's section? Are you unenlightened if all or most of your claims end up in the losers' section? The answer to both questions is no. What makes you enlightened is not the disposition of your claims but rather your own disposition regarding what goes on in the court. If you are ready to stand by the present and future verdicts of the court and to adjust your own beliefs and practices to those verdicts, then and only then are you truly enlightened. Of course, it's to be expected that your allegiance to reason and its methods will pay off in an increase in the number of true claims and a decrease in the number of false claims that you carry around with you. But again, what makes you enlightened is not the tally sheet as such but rather your commitment to the truth *as disclosed by reason*. Because of that commitment, you are willing to give up the security that might come with putting your life in the hands of some benevolent, external authority, just as you are willing to give up the excitement that might come with following your own unreasoned feelings and impulses. You are willing to give up those things because you are convinced that life under the rule of reason is really a liberation of sorts, indeed the best sort of freedom available to human beings. Welcome to the world of the rationally enlightened!

Suppose that you have entered the world of the enlightened in the Western sense of the word "enlightenment." Are you in the company of Siddhartha? Hardly. Siddhartha had a powerful, illuminating experience that resulted in his viewing and living life in a profoundly different and more satisfying way. He had solved the perturbing riddle of old age, sickness, and death. You can be Westernly enlightened without ever having had a powerful, illuminating experience and without ever having solved any of life's major riddles. Indeed, it may be due to your enlightened state that you think the jury of reason is still out, and likely to stay out, on those riddles.

Well, if there is no necessary connection between the Western and the Buddhist versions of enlightenment, are the two at least compatible? Can you be enlightened in both ways? Perhaps. But you should not fail to notice that there is an almost inevitable tension between a life centering on one version and a life centering on the other. If you are living comfortably in the world of the Westernly enlightened, you are probably suspicious of any fuss that is made over so-called enlightenment experience, however powerful the experience might be. People on drugs can have all sorts of intense experiences without thereby being one whit closer to the truth about reality. The only important aspect of the experience is the truth of the claims that emerge from it. And that truth can only be ascertained by the careful, painstaking process of examining arguments and counterarguments. Are there solid arguments for the claims associated with "enlightenment experience"? If so, the experience is either unnecessary or, at best, quite subsidiary. If not, the experience is worthless.

On the other hand, if you are on a Buddhist enlightenment trip, you are probably bemused by the fuss made over living under the "rule of reason." What good does it do to heap arguments upon arguments and little truths upon little truths if the whole structure does not get you one whit closer to an answer to the questions of life's meaning? If those big questions seem impervious to rational methods, why cling to the methods? Is it rational to be so rational? Perhaps the Westernly enlightened can be likened to people who lock themselves in a house and then say that the outside, if there is an outside, is beyond their ken. (You might recall here Phaedrus' eventual disenchantment with the philosophizing of Kant—that great philosopher of the Western Enlightenment period. Through his Oriental experience, Phaedrus had gained a "feeling of escape from a prison of intellect," whereas Kant's writing was "just more of the prison again"—*ZMM*, p. 120.)

This tension can exist not only *between* individuals but also *within* an individual. Consider, for example, the tension that brought about a temporary split between the narrator and Phaedrus in *ZMM*. Phaedrus seems to have been grasped by something akin to a Buddhist enlightenment experience. At the very least, we can say that whatever got hold of him was not simply a conclusion of a rational argument or even of a whole series of rational arguments. He had a powerful illuminating experience! To be sure, all sorts of reasoning preceded that experience—Phaedrus was clearly a highly reflective individual, used to following out chains of reasoning to the nth place. But his enlightenment experience was a far cry from just another rational link in a rational chain. It was not simply a well-supported proposition that he could add to his stockpile of well-supported propositions. In fact, it was not a proposition at all. In describing that experience, the narrator tells us that "the sudden accumulated mass of awareness began to grow and grow into an avalanche of thought and awareness out of control" (*ZMM*, p. 228). On the other hand, the narrator seems to want to downplay its importance. After describing the experience, he tells us that Phaedrus' discovery "at some mountaintop of personal experience," while "spectacular," is "very unimportant" (*ZMM*, p. 229). The narrator then proceeds to spell out rationally and in workmanlike fashion some of the practical implications of Phaedrus' discovery. What is important to him is not personal experience, not the illumination that might be internal to such experience, not the momentum that might be unleashed by illuminating experience, but rather the calm, controlled, rational, Aristotelian appraisal of experience. However much he might seem to salute Phaedrus' discoveries and call for a new, expanded version of rationality, you can detect in his *modus operandi* the workings of a devotee of Western enlightenment who would, if he could, totally control and domesticate the residue of Phaedrus' experience by the imposition of rather familiar rational methods. That MO is basically the MO of the Chautauquas, which were originally intended to "improve the mind and bring culture and enlightenment to the ears and thoughts of the hearer" (*ZMM*, p. 7). (You may safely assume that the "enlightenment" in question is the Western sort.) In his Chautauquas, the narrator takes up issues that are related to and sometimes directly derived from "fragments" (see *ZMM*, pp. 60, 169) of Phaedrus' experience and thought. The narrator deals with them by making all sorts of conceptual distinctions and producing all sorts of rational arguments and, above all, urging the maintenance of a rational perspective that avoids dangerous extremes—like the extreme (evinced by Phaedrus) of pushing rationality to the limit and then taking a mystical plunge. In short, the narrator's (Western) enlightened way of dealing with Phaedrus involves a careful avoidance of Phaedrus' Buddhist or near-Buddhist enlightenment. To be sure, the narrator provides a summary of the last phase, the "third mystical wave of crystallization," of Phaedrus' enlightenment trip, but the narrator does it in the context of giving the "specter" of Phaedrus "his walking papers" (*ZMM*, pp. 221 ff.).

What is the purpose of pointing out this tension between the narrator's and Phaedrus' approaches to enlightenment? Is it to raise the question whether the narrator or Phaedrus (or both, or neither) is "right"? Not really—though you are free, of course, to raise such a question. The point is rather to illustrate tension within a single individual. An assumption underlying the illustration is that the narrator and Phaedrus are somehow a single individual as well as a duality. We could enter some pretty deep waters trying to sort out the ways in which "oneness" or "twoness" more appropriately signifies the reality. It think it is best to avoid those waters at this point—though you are free, of course, to enter them. If you do decide to enter them and even if you don't, you might want to consider such questions as these: Just what did happen between the narrator and Phaedrus at the end of the book? Is it best to call what happened a reunion? A new integration? The dropping of an illusion? A resurrection? Whatever happened at the end, did it happen because of or in spite of the narrator's rational methods and efforts? Finally, can one individual be enlightened in both ways?

The tension that we've been talking about can exist not only between and within individuals but also between groups, even between whole cultures. Indeed, that tension is at the heart of the split—to paint the picture in broad brushstrokes—between the Eastern and Western hemispheres of philosophy. Perhaps the split is not unbridgeable. Perhaps the tension is not irresolvable. Phaedrus, for one, came to believe that the tension might be resolved. His hopes centered on the philosophy of Quality that he was developing. When he wrote to the chairman of the Committee on Analysis of Ideas and Methods at the University of Chicago, he suggested that his thesis on Quality might be "a major breakthrough between Eastern and Western Philosophy, between religious mysticism and scientific positivism" (ZMM, p. 311). Does Phaedrus' philosophy provide the seeds of a resolution to the tension between two versions of enlightenment? Could someone who endorses that philosophy have a foot in both hemispheres? What do you think?

I think it is time to return to our question about the nature of Siddhartha's enlightenment. Perhaps our side trip into the fields of Western enlightenment will help us gain some perspective, if only by way of contrast, on what went on beneath the bodhi tree. What was Siddhartha doing underneath that tree, and what happened to him in the doing? Whatever he was doing, whatever he was undergoing, we can be sure that his enlightenment did not come down to a rational proposition, or a set of rational propositions, or a string of sets of rational propositions. Nor did his enlightenment come down to the rational process whereby such propositions are grounded, the process that we talked about earlier as "acceptance at the bar of reason." Neither rational processes nor rational products nor both together add up to the enlightenment that we're talking about. His enlightenment was simply not rational, not a product of reason.

To say that Siddhartha's enlightenment was not a product of reason is simply to say that the enlightenment experience itself cannot be reduced to the business (or some part of the business) of forming and linking premises and conclusions within a chain of reasoning. It is not to say that his enlightenment was not preceded by rational processes and rational propositions, by thinking of the sort that the Westernly enlightened would applaud. Nor is it to say that his enlightenment was not followed by rational thinking. His postenlightenment teaching—which he carried on for some forty-five years—contains numerous examples of a rational mind at work, a mind drawing conceptual distinctions, analyzing claims, producing and refuting arguments. The rationally discriminating, sand-sorting Buddha of which the narrator speaks, "the Buddha that exists *within* analytic thought, and *gives that analytic thought its direction*" (*ZMM*, p. 70, italics Pirsig's) is certainly not belied by Siddhartha's postenlightenment activity.

Siddhartha's enlightenment experience, while not *rational*, might well be thought of as *intellectual*, at least if you associate the intellectual with insight into or an understanding of things. In and through his enlightenment experience, Siddhartha understood life more fully than he had ever understood it before. It would be a mistake to think of the experience as some sort of "raw feel," like a powerful itch that we might ascribe to a creature that we take to be totally lacking in intellectual consciousness. Whatever else the experience was, it was illuminating and visionary—it threw light on things and involved a new seeing.

In the Westernly enlightened scheme of things such insight is never enough. Insights need to be verified or falsified through a process of reasoning, hypotheses need to be checked by rationally controlled experiments. The intellectual is subordinate to the rational. In the normal run of things, insights amount to intelligent guesses that require further checking out before they can be safely and wisely followed. If you fail to do so, you run the risk of chasing mental will-o'-the-wisps. However, Siddhartha and his followers would want to claim that what is true in the normal run of things is not true in the case of enlightenment experience. Enlightenment experience is not a *part* of the scheme of things. It is the *source* of the scheme of things. In this case, the rational is subordinate to the intellectual.

If you don't check out enlightenment experience at the bar of reason, where do you check it out? In brief, you don't. The experience is *self-validating*. When Siddhartha went out to teach, he did not carry with him a hypothesis that he wanted to submit to further scrutiny. He didn't say to his followers, "I have an idea here that I'd like to get your help on in sorting out. Maybe you could help me see if there are some further questions that I ought to raise or some further pieces of evidence that I ought to consider." Rather, he summoned all the powers of imagination and reason at his disposal to help his hearers move toward where he was, toward the point where the need for questions and evidence falls off. He wasn't out to validate his trip; he was out to bring people along.

What else can be said about this nonrational, intellectual, self-validating enlightenment experience? Perhaps two more things are worth mentioning here. The first is that the experience is said to be blissful. If Siddhartha hadn't found it so, his enlightenment would not have provided him with an answer to the problem of old age, sickness, and death; his enlightenment would have been simply an intellectual addition to the pain of life, a part of the problem rather than a solution, as in the case of a diseased person whose understanding of the disease carries with it a loss of all hope of recovery. As it was, Siddhartha found a solution and did not refrain from referring to it as "bliss." The second thing to be said is that when Siddhartha was questioned about his experience and about the philosophy that he expounded in the light of that experience, he sometimes responded with what is called in the Buddhist tradition a "noble silence." Words can point, but they can also mislead. Sometimes it's best to keep quiet. Enough said about enlightenment experience.

What about Siddhartha's philosophy? Before I say something about it, I want to state clearly that Siddhartha's philosophical exposition should not be confused with his enlightenment. The exposition followed the enlightenment. The exposition was not something Siddhartha needed to fill in the gaps in his own attainment, but rather something he freely offered to others as a sort of guide. It was up to the others whether they would take the exposition in that direction. That is still the case. You can take Siddhartha's philosophy as a sort of intellectual map pointing you in the direction of enlightenment. If you do so, you must realize that the map is neither the destination nor the journey. Moreover, at a certain point in the journey, you may find that the map itself is no longer useful. You may need to put it aside in favor of another, less intellectual, more "mystical" map. And at a certain further point, you may need to be entirely mapless. On the other hand, you may choose to use Siddhartha's philosophy (or later Buddhist developments) in the world of the Westernly enlightened, in which case you will want to test its claims at the bar of reason.

If you choose to do the latter, you should be aware of Siddhartha's disposition toward that sort of thing. He himself was an eminently practical thinker, for whom the test of ideas was their capacity to solve life's problems and cure life's ills. If the final cure is the enlightened life and the enlightened life is life rooted in enlightenment experience, the best ideas are those that help one to move toward enlightenment experience. Those ideas may or may not be presently favored by the court of reason; and they may or may not be very far along in the series of tests by which the court settles its claims. If you decide to wait for a final verdict—which is only relatively final, since appeal procedures may follow—before you use those ideas, you may die before you can. That is a very impractical way of relating to ideas. To use Siddhartha's own metaphor, it is like the case of a person wounded by a poison arrow, who disallows the removal of the arrow and the commencement of treatment until certain questions are answered: Who shot the arrow? What was the shooter's profession? What sort of wood is the arrow made of? From what species of bird came the arrow's feathers? And so on.

The heart of Siddhartha's philosophy can be found in the first sermon that he preached after his enlightenment experience. In it, Siddhartha taught the doctrine of the Four Noble Truths. If you understand that doctrine, you understand the basics of Buddhist philosophy. If you are philosophically inclined, you might want to delve into other teachings of Siddhartha that develop or complement that doctrine and into the speculations of the numerous schools of Buddhist philosophy that emerged over the centuries. We don't have time to do much of that here, since there are other packets to peruse. But, if you're interested in removing the arrow, the Four Noble Truths will be enough to help you get started (and, as a bonus, you might even get an idea about the source of the arrow).

The first truth is that life is suffering. The Pali word *dukkha*, which is generally translated as "suffering," carries a connotation of something being out of joint. Life, as ordinarily lived, bears the character of painful out-of-jointness. How so? The question can be answered in at least two ways. One is to list the various pains that human beings are bound to encounter, in Hamlet's words, "the thousand natural shocks that flesh is heir to." Siddhartha's list included, as you might well guess, the things that shocked him into his journey toward enlightenment: old age, sickness, and death. Another way is to point out what it is about life that makes the stream of painful experiences seem so inevitable: life's impermanence or transience (*anitya*). Things may be going well now, but nothing nice lasts forever. Life flows. And, given this flow, sooner or later, you will come up against things that you find repulsive, and you will be separated from things that you find attractive. In the midst of this painful flow, is there anything substantial to which you can cling? Siddhartha's answer is: Nothing. Nothing outside of you. Nothing inside of you. Nothing. The Hindus, you might recall, proclaimed the doctrine of the Atman, the blissful, eternal Self that is your ultimate reality, your final home. Siddhartha proclaimed the contrasting doctrine of *anatta*, according to which there is no substantial self and, for that matter, no permanent substance at all.

The second truth is that the cause of suffering is desire (*tanha*). The sort of desire referred to here is ego-centered desire, as opposed to what might be called "transcendental" desire. Ego-centered desire focuses your attention on your individual self. Transcendental desire focuses your attention and your efforts on what may take you beyond your individual self and even call your individual selfhood into question. You might say that Siddhartha's search for the solution to life's riddle was an example of the workings of transcendental desire. Clearly, he did not have that sort of desire in mind when he said that desire is the cause of suffering. But even transcendental desire can be counterproductive, if it is expressed in an ego-centered way. There is an old Zen story about this. A disciple asked a Zen master how long it would take to gain enlightenment. The master responded, "Seven years." The disciple asked, "How long will it take if I try very, very hard?" The master responded, "Fourteen years."

Life is transient and offers nothing solid to cling to, but that fact in itself, according to Siddhartha's teaching, is not the cause of our suffering. We suffer because we want it otherwise. We want there to be permanent things that we, as enduring individual selves, can count on and enjoy ceaselessly. And because reality does not match our wanting, because we are really not permanent, separate selves but fluctuating processes that reflect and participate in larger, more inclusive processes, our wanting sets us up for disappointment. And we suffer. The cause of our suffering is our desire, but we might just as well say—and Siddhartha did say it, many times—that the cause of our suffering is our ignorance. We are under the illusion that permanence and substance are to be found within and without, and we are under the further illusion that apart from such permanence and substance no joy is to be found. Under the spell of this double illusion, we cling to what we take to be our separate selves. Our ignorant illusions breed our egocentric desires. And those desires, in turn, keep the illusions going. And we suffer.

Is this a pessimistic philosophy of life? It would be if it stopped there, but it doesn't. The third noble truth is that an end to suffering (and more positively the attainment of deep joy) is a genuine possibility, because suffering, like everything else that occurs in the flow of life, is a *conditional* reality. It comes into being as a result of certain conditions, it changes when those conditions change, and it ceases altogether when the conditions cease. Ignorant desire and desire-filled ignorance are the conditions that make for human suffering. Eliminate those conditions and you eliminate the suffering. And you *can* eliminate the conditions. That is hardly a pessimistic outlook on life!

How can you eliminate the conditions? How can you eliminate the "illusion" of separate selfhood, when every morning you look in the mirror and seem to have the "illusion" confirmed? How can you eliminate desire, when desire seems to be such an integral part of what "makes you tick" as a human being? (As Saint Augustine, in the fourth century, put it, "What are we, if not wills?") And even if it were possible to eliminate desire from your life, wouldn't the net result be a kind of living death?

If you want theoretical answers to such questions, you can find them in the Buddhist tradition, but you won't find them in Siddhartha's doctrine of the Four Noble Truths. After proclaiming the possibility of the cessation of suffering, Siddhartha did not offer a theoretical justification for his emancipation proclamation. Rather, he offered, in the fourth Noble Truth, a practical program, usually referred to as the Eightfold Path. That path consists of right thought, right aspiration, right speech, right action, right livelihood, right effort, right mindfulness, and right meditation. When you think of the Eightfold Path, it is perhaps better to imagine a revolving eight-spoked wheel rather than a staircase. When you climb a staircase, typically you go up one step at a time, leaving behind each earlier step. The parts of the Eightfold Path, on the other hand, are not steps that you pass beyond, once and for all. Like eight spokes on a wheel, they keep on coming around. Again and again and again, they touch the ground of your daily life. And like spokes on a wheel, they radiate from a central point. The reason to take the Eightfold Path is not to get somewhere else, vertically or horizontally, but rather to find your center, a center wherein ignorance, desire, and suffering vanish. Although each part of the path is qualified, in standard English translation, by the word "right," it would be a mistake to think of that qualification in terms of a rigid "ought." In fact, it might be a good idea to substitute for the word "right" a word that is central to *ZMM*, "quality." What you need is quality thought, thought that does not ignore the transiency in life, thought that does not ignore the role played by desire in human suffering, thought that does not ignore the possibility of a whole new way of approaching life. Right or quality thought, in other words, is thought permeated by the ideas contained in the first three Noble Truths. But such thought, by itself, won't get you where you need to go, unless you aim to put it into practice. So you also need quality aiming, quality aspiration. Such aspiration, in turn, will be fruitless unless it is complemented by the way you conduct your daily life. You need to see to it that your everyday speech, your everyday actions, and your everyday work reflect and reinforce your new thinking and aspiring rather than old, egocentric patterns. In other words, you need quality speech, quality action, and quality livelihood. And since none of this is likely to "pay off" immediately, you need to stay with the program and make quality effort.

But what is the point of all this effort? The point is to wake up to a new consciousness, a new center. The final two steps of the Eightfold Path amount to a sort of wake-up program. The first part of the program, the seventh step of the path, is quality mindfulness. If you are going to wake up, you would do well to begin by noticing all that is going on in the field of your awareness. Perhaps you will notice that your mind behaves like a drunken monkey, rambling from one object to another, so that when you are doing something, you are not really doing that thing, since your mind is in a thousand places. What if you could get control of the monkey? What if you could learn to focus and amplify your awareness so that you could be fully engaged in what you are doing? When walking or fixing or cooking or eating, you would be totally walking or fixing or cooking or eating. Perhaps you would find the flow of life's activities more enjoyable, because you would *be there*. In any case, from the Buddhist perspective, by such heightened, focused, and controlled awareness—quality mindfulness—you would be preparing your consciousness for the new dawn.

Controlled and engaged attention is not enough, though. If egocentric desire is to vanish, control and engagement must be complemented by letting go and detachment. How do you learn to let go? How do you learn to become detached? The whole Eightfold Path is designed to teach you that, but quality meditation—the second part of the wake-up program—is especially designed to do so. When you meditate, you find a quiet place, you sit still, you focus your attention on your breathing, on a recurrent sound, or on some object, and *you wait*. You are not in control here. Nothing can be forced. The fruit will ripen when it's ready. In the meantime, you pass back and forth between your everyday maintenance activities (like walking, fixing, cooking, and eating) and your meditation practice. There is no telling how long you will have to wait, but eventually you will begin to notice a difference in your life. And then one day you may see a *big* difference. Welcome to the world of the enlightened.

Since the Eightfold Path is more a wheel than a staircase, the path doesn't end once you've reached the fruits of the eighth step. The wheel keeps turning. The peace and enlightenment that lie at the center of the wheel keep on influencing and shining through all the points of the turning wheel, making the "earlier" steps of the path even more "right," more quality-filled. (You can hear an echo of this idea, including an echo of traditional Buddhist language, in one of the narrator's discussions about the relation between peace of mind and working on a motorcycle: "Peace of mind produces right values, right values produce right thoughts. Right thoughts produce right actions and right actions produce work which will be a material reflection for others to see of the serenity at the center of it all"—*ZMM*, p. 267.)

The basics of Buddhist philosophy, in sum, are these: Life, as it is ordinarily lived, is shot through with suffering; the root cause of such suffering is ignorant desire; the cause of suffering and suffering itself can be eliminated; and there is an Eightfold Path to get you there. If you take this philosophy seriously, following in the footsteps of the Buddha, you will be dedicating yourself to the pursuit of two important Buddhist virtues: compassion and wisdom. You will exhibit compassion because you realize how easy it is to be caught up in the illusions and desires that keep the cycle of suffering going; recall that the Buddha spent some forty-five years, after his enlightenment experience, teaching others. You will seek wisdom because you realize that you can only gain release from this cycle by wising up to your illusory desires and opening yourself up to enlightenment.

Before I wrap up this packet on Buddhism, I want to speak briefly to a question that may be on your mind. Siddhartha, alias the Buddha, was a historical human being who lived and died some twenty-five hundred years ago. If the Buddha is dead and gone, you may wonder, how can the Buddha reside "in the circuits of a digital computer or the gears of a cycle transmission" or, for that matter, "in the petals of a flower" (*ZMM*, p. 16)? The answer turns on a conceptual development within Buddhism. Over the centuries, the thought developed that, while Siddhartha was gone, somehow the Buddha was still with us, for Siddhartha was not all there was to Buddha. Perhaps, in part, that thought developed in a devotional context. Imagine that you are grateful for the liberating teachings that the Buddha has left you and that you express your gratitude in words and acts of reverence for the Buddha. Might not your reverent action contribute to a belief that somehow the Buddha still lives? Perhaps, too, the thought developed in a more speculative context. If we can all gain enlightenment, might there not be some principle, residing in us all, that makes enlightenment possible? If so, might not that principle be the real Buddha, the Buddha that never dies? In any case, the developing thought eventually crystallized into the concept of the "trikaya," or the "three bodies" of Buddha. The first body, the "body of transformation" (*nirmanakaya*), is that of one who shows the way to enlightenment while living on earth. Siddhartha was an example of the first body. The second body, the "body of bliss" (*sambhogakaya*), is that of numerous Buddhas residing in other places in the universe, notably places more "pure" and more conducive of enlightenment than earth. Amida Buddha, the Buddha that millions of Japanese invoke in faith and devotion, is an example of the second body. The third body, the "truth body" (*dharmakaya*), is the cosmic principle of enlightenment. This is the Buddha who plays a significant role in Zen, the Buddha that Zen practitioners find in themselves, in a flower, and even in a dung heap. If there is a Buddha to be found in the gears of a cycle transmission, it is the truth-body Buddha.

When we began to peruse the packet on Buddhism, you may recall, we noted that Buddhism, unlike Hinduism, can trace its origin to a definite historical time. However, from the perspective of the three-body concept, things are not so simple. Buddhas populated the universe and existed on planet earth long before Siddhartha showed up, and the principle of Buddhahood has been around forever. Regarding that principle and its tie-ins with *ZMM*'s Quality, we will have more to say later, when we turn to the packet on Zen. Right now, however, let's turn our attention to Confucianism.

CONFUCIANISM

As you remove the packet on Confucianism, you may wonder why this packet is here, in this backpack. In *ZMM*, there are direct references to Hinduism, Buddhism, and Taoism, but none to Confucianism. So what is the point of exploring Confucianism? How can such an exploration provide any pertinent background to the book?

Despite the absence of direct references, the spirit of Confucius can be detected in *ZMM*, especially in some of the narrator's Chautauquas. In fact, I think a case might be made that the narrator tends to play the Confucian to Phaedrus' Zen Buddhist. Perhaps, after perusing this packet, you will find some merit in this contention, and you may even wish to put your hand to building the case. At any rate, perhaps this brief exploration of Confucianism will help you put into better focus what the narrator is up to.

As you look through this packet, you may be struck by the contrast between the Confucian coloration of life and that depicted in the packets on Hinduism and Buddhism. Perhaps they are best seen as reflections of contrasting tendencies between the Indian mind and the Chinese mind. If your mind is of the Indian bent, you feel a strong transcendental pull. You want to move beyond ordinary consciousness, which you see as deluded and pain-producing, toward a kind of consciousness in which all is a blissful unity, in which the many in their manyness are to be dealt with compassionately but not taken too seriously. Given this transcendental tendency, you feel the need to go within yourself, to meditate, to open yourself up to mystical experience. Even if life's problems are felt in the context of interpersonal relations or social institutions, you locate the root of those problems within, and you also look for the ultimate solution within.

If your mind is of the Chinese bent, by contrast, you are drawn not to transcend ordinary, everyday consciousness but rather to make such consciousness more effective, more practical. You perceive interpersonal and social problems as calling for interpersonal and social solutions, and you do not expect to come upon such solutions by closing the door, sitting down, and meditating. Rather, you feel the need to investigate and understand the many in their manyness, in the hope that thereby you will develop the capacity to perceive and meet the demands of distinct situations as they emerge. You are pulled not by the mystical but by the ethical and the political. (You might want to compare this broad and admittedly oversimplified characterization of the Indian and Chinese minds with what the narrator says about Plato and Aristotle: "Plato is the essential Buddha-seeker who appears again and again in each generation, moving onward and upward toward the 'one.' Aristotle is the eternal motorcycle mechanic who prefers the 'many.' " See *ZMM*, p. 331.)

Does that mean that the Indian mind is concerned with the spiritual, whereas the Chinese mind is not? I think not. Rather, I think it would be best to view the matter in terms of two different approaches to the spiritual. For the Indian, the spiritual is something that you seek to *focus* on. To do so, you must engage in special practices (devotional and meditational) that are removed from the activities of everyday life. Because you consider the spiritual to be immensely more important than anything else, you do not allow everyday problems and concerns, individual or social, to distract you from your spiritual efforts. For the Chinese, the spiritual is not something that you make focal. It is in the *background*. In the foreground are the concrete realities of worldly life. Your task as a human being is to deal harmoniously with those realities. That does not mean that the spiritual is unimportant. Foreground can neither be perceived nor appreciated apart from the background. But your task remains to focus on the foreground. In the performance of that task, the spirituality that is proper to you as a human being will emerge and may even enter your consciousness in a more prominent way. As Confucius put it autobiographically, "I study things on the lower level but my understanding penetrates the higher level" (*Analects*, XIV, 37). Had Confucius attempted to study the higher level directly, could he have succeeded? The Indian seems to say yes. The Chinese seems to say no. The narrator of *ZMM*, seeming to favor the Chinese, says, "Quality is what you see out of the corner of your eye" (*ZMM*, p. 308).

If you were born in a land characterized by the Indian type of spirituality and it were somehow augured that you were destined for greatness, your parents might well wonder which form of greatness, worldly or spiritual, would be yours. A foregone conclusion would be that you could not have it both ways. In such a context, your parents, like Siddhartha's father, might be confronted with a crossroads choice. On the other hand, if you were born in a land characterized by the Chinese type of spirituality, the augury of greatness would not demand an either-or choice between the worldly and the spiritual. You could and should have it both ways. In such a context, the question would not be *whether* you should be raised for worldly greatness but *how*, it being assumed that genuine worldly greatness and genuine spiritual greatness go together. In broader terms, since you cannot achieve genuine worldly greatness without contributing to society, the question would be, What makes for the well-being of society? That was the question that Confucius dealt with. It was a question that confronted him and others of his era with a certain intensity, since at the time the Chou Dynasty was breaking down. Conflict and chaos were winning out over community and cosmos. Eventually the conflict would reach such proportions that a lengthy period (403–221 B.C.) would merit the historical label Period of the Warring States. But even in the time of Confucius (551–479 B.C.), the lack of social cohesion presented a challenge to the intellectually, socially, and spiritually engaged.

What makes for social well-being? (You might notice at the outset a similarity between the Confucian project—to address the question of well-being in a context of social disintegration—and that of the narrator of *ZMM*. The narrator's initial Chautauqua question, "What is best?"—*ZMM*, p. 7—would not have been out of place in the Confucian setting.) Before we consider the response of Confucius, let us have a quick look at several alternative responses that were developed in China around or shortly after the time of Confucius: the Legalist response, the Mohist response, and the Taoist response. The Legalist says that you bring about social well-being by producing and promulgating and enforcing a detailed set of laws with teeth in them. Reward good (legal) behavior and punish severely bad (illegal) behavior. The net result will be law and order, which is all the social well-being that anyone can realistically expect to achieve. The Mohist (following Mo-ti, who lived in the fifth century B.C.) says that you bring about social well-being by preaching and practicing an all-embracing, nondiscriminating love. You cannot eliminate social conflicts and disorders unless you eliminate factions, and you cannot eliminate factions unless you replace restrictive, discriminating love—the sort of love that makes you care intensely about some people while you are apathetic or even positively hateful toward other people—with a love that seeks equally the good of everyone. The Taoist says that you bring about social well-being by abandoning the pretensions of civilization and returning to a simpler and more natural way of life. The best mode of governance is nongovernance; if the government is best that governs least, that government is perfect that does not govern at all.

What does Confucius say? Before I venture a response, let me say a word about who Confucius was. In a word, he was a teacher, China's "Number One Teacher," to use the common honorific title that history has given him. Like Plato in the Greek world, Confucius had aspirations toward political office not because he craved power but because he believed quite strongly that society would benefit if his teachings were put into practice. Also like

Plato, he did not get very far with his political ambitions. He held a middling political position for a short period of time but never attained the sort of position that would have allowed him to implement his sociopolitical ideals directly. Hence, he was confined to a more indirect method, the method of the itinerant teacher. Like the narrator of ZMM, Confucius taught as he traveled, and again like the narrator of ZMM, his teachings had to do with maintenance—not simply with the maintenance of the social machinery but also with the maintenance of the underpinnings of that machinery, and above all with the proper maintenance of the self. (As the narrator puts it: "The real cycle you're working on is a cycle called yourself"—ZMM, p. 293.) Of course, it should be understood, in the case of Confucius as well as in the case of ZMM, that maintenance doesn't just mean keeping things as they are. When things are out of order their being fixed is an important part of their being maintained. Confucius' call for proper personal, social, and political maintenance was also a call for reform. He was both a teacher and a social reformer.

What does this teacher/reformer say in response to the question, What makes for social well-being? Speaking against the Legalist, he says that laws with teeth in them are not enough: "Lead the people with governmental measures and regulate them by law and punishment, and they will avoid wrongdoing but will have no sense of honor or shame. Lead them with virtue and regulate them by the rules of propriety, and they will have a sense of shame and, moreover, set themselves right" (Analects, II, 3). In other words, outward conformity, which is all the Legalist worries about, is an inadequate index of social well-being. It is important that people act from within (setting themselves right) and that their actions stem from quality inner dispositions (like honor and shame). To bring that about, leaders should be concerned with developing moral force (the word te, here translated as "virtue," carries the connotation of moral power or force) rather than physical force. Of course, the power of moral example, while it might ignite in people a desire to act rightly, won't tell people how to act rightly. Where does the how come from? In Confucius' view, it comes not from the promulgation and enforcement of laws but from education in li (here translated as "propriety").

The concept li has wide and deep significance for Confucius and Confucianism. Included in that broad concept are proper modes of behavior (you might say "quality actions") that people in the Western world are apt to put under several distinct categories: morality, etiquette, ritual, *savoir-faire*. If you have gotten hold of *li*, you know and are prompted to do the right thing, which could be treating a person as a person rather than as a thing (a moral imperative) or dining with proper utensils (a matter of etiquette) or bowing in the right way (a rule of ritual) or letting your cycle cool at the right time (a bit of *savoir-faire*). Does getting hold of *li* mean, then, that you have memorized a lengthy set of social rules and that you are ready to follow those rules slavishly, without adaptation or flexibility? This is one way, a rather crusty way, of understanding the process; but it is a way that puts you perilously close to the Legalist way of meeting the social problem, and it does not seem to be the way of Confucius. Confucius seems rather to have had in mind the development of a civilized mind-set that, among other things, would help you know when and how to bend the rules as well as when to follow them strictly. After all, the point of *li* is not *li* itself but the harmony it creates (see *Analects*, I, 12). Sometimes you can establish or reestablish harmony by a slight swerve from the "right way" of doing things. (Recall, for example, the episode of the slipping handlebars in *ZMM*, pp. 46– 47. The narrator suggested that John's slipping handlebars might be fixed with a shim made out of a beer can. To John, the thought of fixing his new BMW with a piece of beer can seemed crude, inappropriate, a departure from *li*. But who was more in touch with the *li* of motorcycle maintenance, John or the narrator? Whom would Confucius have sided with?)

The Confucian way differs from the Legalist way by stressing *li* rather than law, education rather than enforcement, example rather than punishment. In at least one way, however, the two ways are similar. Both put stress on providing some details. General prescriptions are not enough. If you provide people only with a few vague laws, says the Legalist, you can't really expect Law to accomplish its task. You have to give people lots of laws that cover lots of situations and tell them exactly what they should, may, or may not do. In addition, you have to give people detailed information about the punishments that will come their way if they dare to break the laws. You can expect to see Law do its thing and society benefit only if you provide such details. The Confucian, similarly, says that if you provide people with only a few very general ideas about how things are done well, you can't really expect education to accomplish its task. You have to give people lots of concrete examples of how the ancients did things and, accordingly, how things should be done now. (Confucius referred to himself as a *transmitter* of the wisdom of the ancients rather than an originator—see *Analects*, VII, 1. It is generally acknowledged that, despite his modest self-appraisal, he modified and innovated while transmitting. In any case, he frequently couched his moral and social advice in terms of the moral example, *te*, and propriety, *li*, of the ancients.) Different social situations (e.g., a time of mourning versus a time of ordinary carrying on), different social relations (e.g., the relation of husband and wife versus the relation of parent and child), and different social positions (e.g., that of the old versus that of the young) all call for different ways of behaving. Unless you help people catch on to the differences, you can't expect them to develop a civilized mind-set, for civilization requires an appreciation of difference as well as commonality. Hence, if you provide a variety of concrete examples and at least some detailed prescriptions, you can expect to see education do its thing and society benefit.

Perhaps this aspect of the Confucian way will remind you of a certain aspect of the narrator's method as a Chautauqua teacher. The narrator doesn't attempt to teach motorcycle maintenance (which, we must constantly remember, is also self-maintenance) by offering a few general rules or prescriptions. While he does offer advice on a general level—e.g., "You should remember that it's peace of mind you're after and not just a fixed machine" (*ZMM*, p. 284)—he doesn't simply leave things on that level. He breaks down general prescriptions into more specific prescriptions. He illustrates specific prescriptions by concrete examples. He follows up examples with further suggestions. In sum, he pulls you into details.

Why does he do this? Perhaps in part his teaching style is simply a reflection of his own orientation. By his own admission, he is more the Aristotelian motorcycle mechanic who is at home with the "many" than the Platonic Buddha-seeker who is after the "one," more a person who prefers to "find the Buddha in the quality of the facts" around himself than one who seeks to find the Buddha directly (*ZMM*, pp. 331—332). (Maybe you can hear, in the narrator's self-appraisal, an echo of Confucius' "I study things on the lower level but my understanding penetrates the higher level"—*Analects*, XIV, 37.) On the other hand, the narrator's teaching style seems to be not only a reflection of his orientation but also a requirement of what he is teaching. He is not teaching "peace of mind" but "motorcycle maintenance." You want peace of mind, as he reminds you, but you want it *in addition to* and not *instead of* a fixed machine. If you want both peace of mind and a well-running cycle (or self), and not one at the expense of the other, there is no way that you can avoid attention to detail. You need to tune into the *li* of maintenance. You need to attend to the diversity of parts and the diversity of problems that pertain to proper (i.e., peace-filled and effective) maintenance. That is what the narrator tries to get you to do. I think Confucius would approve.

For a good example of what we've been talking about, have a look at the Chautauqua on gumption (*ZMM,* pp. 272–293). The narrator begins by connecting the word "gumption" with the word "enthusiasm," which literally means being "filled with God." From the narrator's viewpoint, to be filled with God is to be filled with Quality. When you have gumption, you and your work are filled with Quality. How do you maintain that gumption, that relationship with Quality? How do you lose it? Those are the questions that the narrator proceeds to address. I think it is important to notice what the narrator does *not* do in meeting those questions. He does not go into an excursus about the direct search for Quality. He does not invite you to follow him on a mystical trip. If you want to go on a mystical trip and seek a direct encounter with Quality (in the hope, perhaps, that such an encounter will provide you with an inexhaustible supply of gumption), you'll have to look elsewhere for guidance. Perhaps you can follow Gautama Siddhartha to some tree by a river and there make your special, concentrated effort to encounter Quality. Or perhaps you can follow Phaedrus into a small room, close the door, sit on the floor, and gaze at the wall. But don't expect the narrator or Confucius to come along with you. Mystical trips are for others. The narrator and Confucius are content to let Quality—of which the Confucian analogue will be considered later (see p. 98)—emerge in the context of their performing well and helping others to perform well the tasks of everyday life. (Of course, you might contend that theirs is simply another, more subtle version of a mystical trip—the trip you're taking is almost always bigger than you think it is). How then does the narrator deal with the question of gumption maintenance? He launches into a well-ordered, descriptive account of the variety of "gumption traps" that you might encounter in the context of your maintenance activity. You can see the analytic knife, the primary tool of Western enlightenment, at work, dividing the traps into external setbacks and internal hang-ups and dividing setbacks and hangups, respectively, into various types. But you can see more than the analytic knife at work, for the account is prescriptive as well—not in a heavy-handed way (the way of the Legalist) but in a gentler way, that advises, warns, encourages, and coaxes (the way of the Confucian). There also seems to be another tool working with the analytic knife (although it seems rather far removed from motorcycle maintenance): a hoe, a Confucian hoe. The hoe is a good tool for someone who is not given to mystical flight, but who wants to stay down-to-earth and make things grow. With a hoe you break and turn the earth, both weeding and cultivating. That's what Confucius was trying to do through the pithy remarks and responses that characterize his teaching as we know it, and that's what the narrator tries to do through the more rambling style of his Chautauquas.

Where does the cultivation start? Where do you put the hoe first? And once the cultivation has started, how does it proceed? In response to those questions, two comparable texts come to mind, one from the Confucian tradition and one from *ZMM*. The Confucian text is *The Great Learning*, a short work whose author and date are uncertain but which had achieved a certain prominence by the time of the Han Dynasty (205 B.C.–A.D. 220). It is one of the so-called Four Books of the Confucian tradition. The other three of the Four Books are the *Analects* (a collection of Confucius' sayings), the *Mencius* (a collection of the teachings of Confucius' most influential follower, Mencius, who lived in the fourth century B.C.), and the *Doctrine of the Mean* (a work that came into prominence around the same time as *The Great Learning*). The Four Books were singled out by the neo-Confucianists of the eleventh and twelfth centuries A.D. as constituting the heart of Confucian thought. They became, and remain, a sort of bible of the Confucian tradition and the basis of Confucian education. If you want to get into Confucian thought more deeply than is possible through this packet, you will do well to study the Four Books.

Listen to what *The Great Learning* has to say about the cultivation process: "When things are investigated, knowledge is extended; when knowledge is extended, the will becomes sincere; when the will is sincere, the mind is rectified; when the mind is rectified, the personal life is cultivated; when the personal life is cultivated, the family will be regulated; when the family is regulated, the state will be in order; and when the state is in order, there will be peace throughout the world" (from the translation of Wing-tsit Chan in his *Source Book in Chinese Philosophy*).

From the point of view of *The Great Learning*, the process of cultivation is clearly an inside-to-outside sort of thing. You first put the hoe to work inside yourself and cultivate your personal life. Then, and only then, are you ready to put the hoe to work outside yourself and cultivate the family, then the state, and finally the world. The ultimate goal is worldwide peace and harmony, but you can't start there. Nor can you effectively start at the level of state politics or even family relationships. If you want to do something good for society (and all good Confucians want to do something good for society), you've got to start with yourself, *inside* yourself.

As to exactly where inside yourself you start, there has been considerable discussion within the Confucian tradition about the meaning of "investigation of things" (in Chinese, *ko-wu*). Does it mean that, with senses and intellect fully engaged, you try to understand the natures, the inner workings, of the things and processes that you find around you? If that is what it means, then it's clear that the process of personal cultivation should not be an isolating phenomenon. You don't begin to cultivate yourself by withdrawing from everything else, but rather by *attentive engagement* with the world. By the same token, you don't put the hoe to work inside yourself by making yourself the *focus* of your hoeing but rather by your effort to use and stretch your mental powers. On the other hand, could the phrase *ko-wu* be interpreted in a more mystical manner, so that the beginning of the process of personal cultivation would consist of your withdrawing from the objects around you, entering a room, closing a door, and looking into your own mind for unitive knowledge? Could you "investigate things" by directly hoeing your own mind? I don't think this latter interpretation would have found its way into the Confucian tradition apart from the Buddhist influence; the first interpretation seems more in keeping with the original thrust of Confucianism. But the fact remains that both interpretations are a part of the Confucian tradition. (The polarity of the "eternal motorcycle mechanic" and the "essential Buddha-seeker"—*ZMM*, p. 331—keeps cropping up.)

For present purposes, we needn't explore further these two

rival interpretations. (You may wish to do so on your own, of course. Such an exploration could be a form of hoeing in its own right and prove to be quite fruitful. Anytime you can get the mechanic and the Buddha-seeker to interact at a quality level, some interesting things are bound to happen. That certainly was the case in *ZMM*. If you do decide on a further exploration, just look for material that deals with "neo-Confucianism," keeping a special eye out for discussions of the philosophies of Chu-Hsi, on the one hand, and Wang Yang-Ming, on the other.) Right now I just want to repeat the point that *The Great Learning* finds the root of social flourishing in personal cultivation. If you want to reform the world, you first have to reform yourself.

You have listened to what *The Great Learning* has to say about the process of cultivation. Now listen to what the narrator of *ZMM* has to say: "Peace of mind produces right values, right values produce right thoughts. Right thoughts produce right actions and right actions produce work which will be a material reflection for others to see of the serenity at the center of it all" (*ZMM*, p. 267). Earlier, when we were considering the Buddhist Eightfold Path, we had occasion to notice a Buddhist resonance in this passage (see above, p. 83) But it has a Confucian resonance as well. The starting point of effective work in the world is inside of you, in right thoughts, in right values, and—most deeply—in peace of mind. There is at least a loose correlation between the narrator's chain of internal development (peace of mind linking with right values, right values linking with right thoughts) and the chain found in *The Great Learning* (extended knowledge linking with sincere will, sincere will linking with rectified mind). It might be an interesting exercise to try to determine just how loose or tight the correlation is. My concern here, however, is simply to point out that the narrator is on a Confucian wavelength when he calls attention to the internal, personal basis of social reform and well-being. As the narrator continues with this theme, you can hear an echo of *The Great Learning* getting louder and more distinct:

> I think that if we are going to reform the world, and make it a better place to live in, the way to do it is not with talk about relationships of a political nature . . . or with programs full of things for other people to do. I think that kind of approach starts at the end and presumes the end is the beginning. Programs of a political nature are important *end products* of social quality that can be effective only if

the underlying structure of social values is right. The social values are right only if the individual values are right. The place to improve the world is first in one's own heart and head and hands, and then work outward from there. [*ZMM*, p. 267, italics Pirsig's]

Now it is time to pause and note where we've been and where we're going. We set out to examine the Confucian response to the question of the best way to attain and maintain social well-being (especially in a time of social disintegration). We decided to try to clarify the Confucian response by comparing and contrasting it with alternative responses: the Legalist, the Mohist, and the Taoist. So far, we've compared it with the Legalist response, and, in the process of doing so, we've had occasion to note some similarities between the Confucian approach and that of the narrator of *ZMM*. Now we're ready to compare Confucianism with Mohism.

The Mohist, you might recall, says that social factions and conflicts are rooted in a lack of the right kind of love. The right kind of love is all-embracing, nondiscriminating love. If people practice that kind of love, society will flourish and everyone will be happy. It's important to notice, if you want to understand Mohism correctly, that the Mohist objective is social flourishing and universal happiness. All-embracing love is seen as a means to that objective and not as an end in itself. A Mohist, by self-definition, is a utilitarian and not a moral zealot. A moral zealot says, "Do x simply and solely because x is the moral thing to do, regardless of consequences, even if the net result is misery for yourself and others." A utilitarian, on the other hand, says, "Do x because of the alternatives available, x is the best way to achieve socially desirable results." From the Mohist utilitarian perspective, the practice of all-embracing, nondiscriminating love is the best way, and indeed the only way, to overcome social disintegration and achieve social well-being.

What does the Confucian say to this? Well, for one thing, the Confucian might well borrow a statement that you recently heard the narrator make: "I think that kind of approach starts at the end and presumes the end is the beginning" (*ZMM*, p. 267). Perhaps worldwide love is a crucial element in the world transformation that you ultimately want, but you can't start with it. You have to start with love at less comprehensive levels. To return to the chain of causation proclaimed in *The Great Learning*, if you want to love on a worldwide level, you first have to learn to love your own state; if you want to love your own state, you first have to love your own family; if you want to love your own family, you first have to love yourself. Self-love, not the universal love of the Mohist, is the Confucian starting point.

To get clear about this, you need to take note of a couple of things. First, note that Confucian self-love is not some sort of narcissistic self-absorption. To love yourself in a Confucian way is not to gaze at yourself in a mirror but to cultivate yourself, to get that hoe working around your mind and heart. You get the hoe working by dealing conscientiously with the people and things in your environment. Thus, self-love is understood to be practical and nonindividualistic. Second, note that Confucian self-love is not a whole unto itself but part of a whole, a part that requires its complement. The whole in question is a virtue or quality that is central to the thought of Confucius, *jen*. The word *jen* has been variously translated; "humaneness" "human-heartedness," "humanity," "goodness." The ideograph underlying the word symbolizes a human being and twoness. Hence, following the ideograph, you might translate the word as "human-to-humanness." You might also translate the word as "love," provided you understand the word in its comprehensive, Confucian sense. In any case, to be a person of *jen* is to be both conscientiously self-loving and compassionately other-loving. (Confucius alludes to this combination of self-love and other-love as the "one thread" that runs through his teachings—*Analects*, IV, 15.) Self-love, as a part of *jen*, calls for its complement, other-love. Other-love, in turn, takes self-love as its guide. As Confucius put it, in words that provide a "negative" complement to the Golden Rule: "Do not do to others what you do not want them to do to you" (*Analects*, XV, 23). More positively: "A man of humanity, wishing to establish his own character, also establishes the character of others, and wishing to be prominent himself, also helps others to be prominent" (*Analects*, VI, 28).

If the Confucian way involves the expansion of self-love into other-love, is there not, after all, a great deal of similarity between the Confucian way and the Mohist way? You can safely say that there is *some* similarity. Both call people to transcend selfish love and move toward a more universal love. The similarity seems to stop here, however. We have already noted a difference with respect to *timing*. From the Confucian point of view, the Mohist unrealistically calls for this love all at once, when it can develop only over a long period of time and in the proper sequence. In addition to the difference in timing, there is a difference regarding the *kind and degree* of the love that is sought. The Mohist ideal is to love everyone equally—in the same way and in the same amount. From the Confucian point of view, this egalitarian ideal is unnatural and impossible. For example, you can't expect people to love strangers as much as they love the members of their own family. A difference in degree is inevitable and appropriate. After all, love is a matter of practical effort and not just a matter of sentiment. Since you don't have an infinite amount of practical energy to spend, the natural place to spend the bulk of what you do have—the natural place to develop and express your kindness—is within your own family, with your own kin. (Recall the narrator's remark about his reticence to send Chris to psychiatrists: "They can't have real *kind*ness toward him, they're not his *kin*"—*ZMM*, p. 55, italics Pirsig's.) Just as differences in the degree of love are inevitable and appropriate, so also are differences in kind. The kind of love you have for your child is, quite naturally, different from the kind of love you have for your spouse, and both of those are different from the kind of love you have for a parent. The indiscriminate love of a Mohist flies in the face of such natural differences.

Another way of getting at the difference between Confucian love and Mohist love is to note the connection between love and propriety (*jen* and *li*) in Confucian thought. For the Confucian, love finds its appropriate expression, its content, in and through the mores, the *li*, of civilized society. If you want to be a loving person, a person of humanity, you have to act in culturally appropriate ways that bespeak your humanity. As Confucius succinctly put it: "To master oneself and return to propriety is humanity" (*Analects*, XII, 1). On the other hand, the *li*, the ways of propriety, find their characteristic animating influence, their true inner *form*, in *jen*, in humane love. In other words, "appropriate" ways of acting aren't truly appropriate if they don't come from a humane heart. As Confucius put it: "If a man is not humane, what has he to do with *li*?" (*Analects*, III, 3). In sum, Confucian love is tied up with the structures of civilization and with the distinctions that are pertinent to those structures. It is *civilized* love, a love that knows distinctions. Such love does not respond to the Mohist call.

We have seen how the Confucian way of promoting social well-being differs from the way of the Legalist and the way of the Mohist. How does it differ from the way of the Taoist? A brief answer will suffice for now, since we have yet to peruse the packet on Taoism. A Taoist claims, you might recall, that you improve society by returning to a simpler and more natural way of life. I'm sure that, from what has already been said, you have a pretty good idea of how the Confucian would respond to this. For the Confucian, humanity and civilization are intimately connected. You develop your humanity (*jen*) by tuning into and making a part of yourself the whole of civilized mores (*li*). Hence, to decivilize is to dehumanize. A Confucian feels that the Taoist program for social improvement, if successful, throws out the baby with the bathwater. The tub is clean, but there is no one in it; the "improved" society is devoid of human (i.e., *jen*-filled) beings.

The last thing I'd like to look at before we move on to the packet on Taoism is a Confucian concept that is an analogue to *ZMM*'s Quality, the concept of the "Mandate of Heaven" (*Ming T'ien*). This concept was around before the time of Confucius, but Confucius gave the concept new life and a central role in his philosophy. The Mandate of Heaven was for Confucius a transcendent reality that required human attention, not as an object of focal awareness but as that which puts the objects and tasks of everyday life into proper focus. (Do you see the analogy with Quality?) Before we unpack the concept further, a bit of background is in order.

Long before the time of Confucius, the Chinese came to believe in a spirit world that included various deities as well as ancestral spirits. The chief spirit was Shang-ti, the Lord on High, who was probably thought of as the primal ancestor. During the time of the Chou Dynasty (1111–249 B.C.), the Chinese revered Shang-ti as the supreme being. During that same period, however, the supreme being came to be referred to by another name, Heaven (T'ien). While Heaven was thought of as the abode of the spirits (and, thus, of Shang-ti), it also came to be thought of as a moral power or agency above human beings, an agency whose will called for human attention and acceptance. (It isn't difficult to see the connection between these two senses of "Heaven": If Heaven is the abode of ancestral spirits, and if those ancestral spirits are truly wise, then the directives that issue from that abode must carry moral weight.) Before Confucius, the will of this moral agency was primarily referred to in connection with rulers. A ruler who maintained a tie with the Mandate of Heaven deserved to remain a ruler; a ruler who lost the Mandate of Heaven did not. Herein lay a justification for revolution, one that the original rulers of the Chou Dynasty used with regard to their overthrow of the previous ruling house, the Shang. The Chou rulers claimed that the Shang had lost the Mandate of Heaven.

What does Confucius do with this concept of the "Mandate of Heaven"? He broadens its relevance and emphasizes its importance. The Mandate doesn't just have relevance at special times to what *rulers* do. It has continual relevance to what *anyone* does or doesn't do. The Mandate functions as a sort of measuring stick of the quality of human living. If you maintain a connection with it, your actions are good; they have quality. If you lose your connection with it, your actions are bad; they lack quality. To be a superior person (a *chun-tzu*), a person characterized by quality action, you need to know and respect the Mandate of Heaven (see *Analects*, XVI, 8, and XX, 3). How do you come to know it? Not by some sort of direct insight; it is not an object that you can directly focus upon. Rather, you come to know the Mandate (the "higher level") by conscientiously attending to what is in front of you (the "lower level"). It's a bit paradoxical. To be a quality person, you've got to know the Mandate; but your knowledge of the Mandate is something that emerges in the context of your acting as a quality person. If you want to resolve this paradox rather than leave it intact, you may well find yourself speculating along the lines of *ZMM*'s philosophy of Quality: A preintellectual awareness (Knowledge A) of the Mandate allows you to perform the quality actions that in turn make possible a fuller insight into and conceptualization of the moral order enjoined by the Mandate (Knowledge B). Knowledge A precedes the designation of subjects and objects, whereas Knowledge B is right in the thick of such designation. This sort of a distinction might help us make sense of an autobiographical statement of Confucius: "At thirty my character had been formed. At forty I had no more perplexities. At fifty I knew the Mandate of Heaven" (*Analects*, II, 4). Did Confucius have no knowledge of the Mandate prior to the age of fifty? If so, how is it that his character was formed and perplexities were gone? Might it not be the case that, prior to the age of fifty,

Confucius had a preconceptual, nonfocal awareness of the Mandate and that such "knowledge" enabled him to develop his character and get rid of perplexities? Might not the knowledge referred to in Confucius' statement be knowledge of the conceptual sort, knowledge that is a condition of philosophizing but by no means a condition of quality living? Or, to speculate more boldly, might the knowledge referred to be the sort that Phaedrus was eventually open to, a sort of mystical plunge into a postconceptual illumination?

Perhaps enough has been said to indicate some possibilities of mutual illumination between Confucianism and *ZMM*. It's time to move on.

TAOISM

In our exploration of the packet on Taoism, we are going to focus our attention on one kind of Taoism, a kind that is usually referred to as "philosophical" Taoism. There are several kinds of Taoism, which all claim descent from the teachings of the founder of Taoism, Lao-tzu. But the commonality stops rather abruptly there. Under the umbrella of "nonphilosophical" Taoism, you will find, among other things, a church that includes priests who perform various rituals for fees—rituals designed to expiate sins or draw favors from the spirit world. If you observe one of those rituals and then retire to your room to read Lao-tzu's book, the *Tao Te Ching*, you will no doubt wonder how anyone could have ever found any inspiration for such rituals in the book. If you do some further exploring under the umbrella, you will discover a variety of historical movements (e.g., the Chinese alchemy movement and the hygiene movement) that seem aimed at the attainment of a long life or, at the limit, a kind of physical immortality. Again you will be hard-pressed to find an endorsement for such movements in Lao-tzu's book. Perhaps you will be willing to say that, for Lao-tzu, a long life is the likely by-product of following the way of life that he proposes, but you might note a big difference between seeing something as a by-product and making that something a main objective. Lao-tzu's main objective is to live a *natural* life, not to live a *long* one, especially when the pursuit of a long life involves unnatural efforts and practices. In sum, you will find some fascinating things under the umbrella of nonphilosophical Taoism, but those things put you on a different wavelength from that of Lao-tzu's book. Which wavelength do you want to be on? For present purposes, stay on Lao-tzu's. That's where you'll catch some vibrations that resonate to what is going on in *ZMM*.

The *Tao Te Ching* (which means literally "The Classic of the Way and Its Power") comprises eighty-one "chapters" that are actually eighty-one short poems. The whole book amounts to only about five thousand words, a very small book indeed. The spirit of Taoism is the spirit that gives rise to sayings like "Small is beautiful," and "Less is more." You can read the *Tao Te Ching* in less than an hour; but you can spend a lifetime reading it. Less is more.

The question of the origin of this book has become a matter of unending scholarly investigation and debate. Was it written by Lao-tzu in the sixth century B.C., as tradition attests, or was it written much later? Was it written at one time by one author or over a period of time by several authors? If you want to bother with questions like those, by all means have at them sometime; but here and now I suggest that you just listen to the traditional story of how the *Tao Te Ching* came into being and let the story work on you. There is something very Taoist about letting stories work on you. From a Taoist perspective, you are every bit as productive when you are receptive as when you are assertively active. If it's good for you to go after information and insight, it's also good to let information and insight come after you.

As the story goes, Lao-tzu, an older contemporary of Confucius, worked as a librarian at the royal archives. One day, he decided to quit his job, leave town, and ride a water buffalo into the western sunset. Maybe he was tired of his work. Maybe he was tired of the world of books. Maybe he was tired of the ways of civilization. Maybe all three. Whatever moved him, he made his way toward the western gate of the town, and at the gate, something fortuitous happened. (Fortuitous things frequently happen at gates—for they present opportunities as well as obstacles. Recall the miraculous gate-opening that allowed Siddhartha to continue his self- and world-transforming quest. Recall, too, the equally miraculous glass-door-gate opening that occurred at the end of *ZMM*—an opening that allowed the narrator both to rediscover who he was and to be reunited with his son.) What happened was quite simple but, when you think about it, quite strange. The gatekeeper asked Lao-tzu to write down his wisdom and leave it behind for posterity. What gives here? Are gatekeepers in the habit of extracting wisdom from travelers before the travelers are allowed to continue their journey? Had this librarian, a recluse, gained a reputation that extended to the city gates? Did this gatekeeper see something special in Lao-tzu that prompted the request? Whatever prompted the request, Lao-tzu went along with it and produced the eighty-one poems that make up the *Tao Te Ching*. Having thus supplied food for the journey of millions, Lao-tzu was free to continue his own journey.

In the *Tao Te Ching*, you can find food for the journey of everyday living, food for metaphysical journeys, and food for mystical journeys. The versatility of this food is rooted in the versatility of the Tao. The Tao (or Way) has a Te (or Power) that can reach you at many different levels. On the level of everyday life, the Tao is the way of good living, a way that empowers you to live more naturally and more fully while, paradoxically, you are doing less. On the level of the metaphysical, the Tao is the way that things came into being and that which powers their continuation in being—a way that, paradoxically, is more nothing than something. (The word "metaphysical" is being used here with reference to that branch of philosophy—"metaphysics"—that is concerned with knowing what reality is, fundamentally, and why it is. The word is not being used in the popular sense that associates the "metaphysical" with occult powers and strange phenomena.) On the level of the mystical, the Tao is the way of unitive knowledge, a way that empowers you to let go of your individual self and be one with the energy behind the universe.

So let's have a closer look at the three levels of the Tao, beginning with the everyday level. That is the level with which most of the *Tao Te Ching*'s passages are concerned. The book, reflecting the general tendency of the Chinese mind (see above, pp. 85—86), is focused on the realities of everyday living rather than on the Transcendent. Given that focus, it has much to say in response to the narrator's initial Chautauqua question, "What is best?" (*ZMM*, p. 7), and in response to the Confucian question, "What makes for the well-being of society?" (see above, p. 86). How does the *Tao Te Ching* respond to those questions? In brief, what is best is what is natural, and what makes for the well-being of society is natural living.

You may well ask, "What does it mean to live naturally?" The Taoist answer is that you live naturally when you affirm and accept the harmony of *yin* and *yang* within yourself and outside yourself. To understand this, you need to get clear about the Chinese terms *yin* and *yang*. They refer to two dynamic principles whose interaction accounts for all that exists and occurs in the universe. The dynamic character of those principles should be underscored: Yin and yang are not static; they are elemental processes. And since they are at the heart of each and every thing and event in the universe, it is best, from a Taoist perspective, to think of *everything*—whether it be a "thing" or an "event"—as a process of yinning and yanging. What we call things are simply slower processes than what we call events. The yin-yang process is going on everywhere—in the mountain as well as in the hurricane.

Yin is the yielding, receptive, "female" force, and yang is the firm, assertive, "male" force. Yin is a kind of negative energy, while yang is a kind of positive energy. (Don't think of "negative" and "positive" here as "bad" and "good"; think rather of the complementary forces that make up electricity.) Perhaps a few examples will help you get clear both about the specific characteristics of yin and yang and about their pervasiveness.

As you read this page, you are taking in printed signs through your eyes—that's yin. However, your seeing the words isn't just a matter of taking in; it's also a matter of going after. You focus your eyes—that's yang. As you read, thoughts come, and you let them be there—that's yin. However, your thinking isn't just a matter of letting thoughts play on your mind. You also go after thoughts. You bring to your reading specific questions and concerns that shape the thoughts that will come to you—that's yang. Perhaps, at a certain point, you tire of concentrating (a yangish activity) and you give in to a bit of daydreaming (a yinnish activity). But you are startled from your reverie when you remember (yin) that you have an appointment. You look at your watch and quickly plot (yang) the series of moves that will get you where you need to be. As you purposefully stride (yang) across the floor, the floor accepts your purpose and your footsteps (thus playing yin to your yang). You walk outside and find that you are in the rain (thus playing yin to the sky's yang). Then you suddenly remember (yin) that it's Tuesday and your appointment is Wednesday. You breathe in deeply (yin), exhale forcefully (yang) and decide (yang) to take an aimless stroll in the rain (the epitome of yinnish behavior).

Perhaps from these examples you will get the idea that if you look hard enough (yang), you can find (yin) the forces of yin and yang at work (yang) or at play (yin) in just about anything. You will also see, quite rightly, that there is a necessary complementarity to yin and yang, so that someone or something is always playing yin to someone or something else's yang. If you look even further into the matter of yin-yang dynamics, you may discover that it's part of the natural order of things, part of the Tao of the universe, that the yin-yang process continually tends toward a kind of equilibrium or harmony. Nature seeks a balancing of yin and yang. That doesn't mean that if nature has its way you will always and everywhere find exactly equal amounts of yin and yang. Different degrees and kinds of yin and yang are appropriate for different moments and places in the cosmic process. There is balance when both yinning and yanging are going on in appropriate ways and appropriate degrees at appropriate times in appropriate places.

Does nature have its way? Does the Tao win out? Does harmony prevail? Yes, yes, yes. But also not necessarily, not necessarily, not necessarily. Eventually yes, but at any specific moment not necessarily. Eventually, the Tao will see to it that a proper balance of yin and yang is restored, but at any specific moment things can be more or less out of kilter. The hurricane hits the land and unleashes a torrent of destructive power. If you happen to be watching, you are not likely to cry out, "What wondrous balance! What glorious harmony!" What you see is imbalance, disharmony. There is far too much yanging going on! But excessive yanging can't go on forever. Eventually the hurricane's power is spent. Calm returns. And in the yin of calm, the myriad forces of nature move toward recuperation and renewal. Harmony is restored. As Lao-tzu put it: "Return is the movement of the Tao" (*Tao Te Ching*, 40; Mitchell translation). But why, you may ask, do things move too far in one direction in the first place? Why is there not a balance that would make reverse flow unnecessary? Where is the *te* of the Tao? Is it powerless? The answers to those questions turn on the nature of the Tao's power, which is not totalitarian, but subtle and unimposing. As Lao-tzu put it, starkly and paradoxically: "The Tao never does anyting, yet through it all things are done" (*Tao Te Ching*, 37). That doesn't mean that the Tao is totally inert. Energy flows continually from it, in the currents of yin and yang and in the tendency to keep those currents in harmony. But the Tao doesn't impose its energy on things in such a way as to take from them their own part in the cosmic drama. The universe is not simply the playing out of the internal script of the Tao. The universe is Tao and more. What more? Well, there is such a thing as chance in the universe, and there is also such a thing as human choice. The hurricane's excessive accumulation and expression of yang energy is an example of chance. The Tao does not eliminate the excesses of chance; it only mitigates their effects by swinging things back in the other direction. The case of human choice is similar. Human beings can ignore the need for balance and choose to be excessively yangish or yinnish. The Tao won't prevent the excess but it will eventually bring about a reversal. Have you ever allowed yourself to wallow in sadness to the point where you found yourself bursting into rage? Have you ever worked so long and hard and stubbornly that you eventually collapsed, physically and emotionally? The Tao does not impose itself, but it eventually has its way.

Perhaps now the basic Taoist prescription for the good life is clearer. Be natural. Don't fight the flow of the Tao's energy. Go with the flow. If a little more yang is called for, be a little more yangish. If a little more yin is called for, be a little more yinnish. But don't go to excesses. Keep some yin at the heart of your yang and some yang at the heart of your yin. If you refuse to be natural in that way, if you ignore or fight against the Tao's flow, it will eventually catch up with you, and a turning back will take place. In the meantime, though, you can count on a lot of unnecessary suffering.

If the Taoist prescription went only this far, you might see a lot of compatibility between the Taoist approach and the Confucian approach to social well-being. After all, the Confucian also aims at harmony, and the Confucian would have no trouble subscribing to the call to avoid excesses. Similarly, you might feel that a Taoist and the narrator of ZMM seem to agree. The narrator, too, is after harmony. Beginning with his very first Chautauqua, he is concerned with the tension and disharmony between what he calls a technological, square, classical approach to modern life and an antitechnological, groovy, romantic approach. You don't have to stretch the categories very far to see that the narrator is talking about a clash between excessive yang and excessive yin.

However, the Taoist goes much further than simply calling for harmony. The Taoist has some specific things to tell you about how to get there. If you read the *Tao Te Ching*, you will be struck by the number of passages and the variety of images that suggest a yinnish approach to life. It's as if Lao-tzu is telling you: "See harmony, but don't expect to get there unless you give a special place to the yin in your life. The yang will pretty much hold its own, even if you don't give it special attention. Neglect the yin, however, and the yang will take over, disharmony will prevail, and the natural way of living will be lost." Why this emphasis on the yin? I don't know for sure what Lao-tzu had in mind, but maybe he felt that he was writing the *Tao Te Ching* for a developed civilization, which by its very nature emphasized the yang over the yin. Perhaps he felt that it was necessary, in the name of harmony, to counter that emphasis and call attention to the need for yin.

How is it that developed civilizations have a sort of built-in tendency to emphasize the yang over the yin? Just think of the many ways in which they shape and structure the activities of everyday life. From dawn to dusk and from dusk to dawn, you can see the yang energy of culture at work, prescribing the way to do things. The way you dress, the way you eat, the way you relate to people, the way you work, the way you fill your free time—it's all more or less prescribed for you. Through all those prescriptions, culture asserts its power over your life. In addition to prescribing the way you fill your time, culture surrounds you with products that continually reinforce its hold over you. You find very little of nature in the raw. Rather, nature is shaped to satisfy the desires and imperatives that civilized life both creates and feeds on. You find forms and objects of art that influence your tastes to conform to cultural norms. You find commodities that help you perform everyday maintenance—body maintenance, vehicle maintenance, shelter maintenance, etc.—more pleasantly, more easily, or more efficiently. Along with the commodities comes the subtle or not-so-subtle message that the particular activities supported by those particular commodities are an absolutely necessary part of a human life. (Do you really have a clue as to what life is about if you don't wear a headset and jogging shorts when you jog?) While hardly noticing it, you are led to identify human living as such with this or that particular form of civilized living. If you try to ignore cultural prescriptions and products and resist culture's domination, you may soon feel that you're a misfit, in which case you may eventually feel compelled to take a culturally prescribed "cure." Alternatively, you may feel compelled to "drop out." If you take that route, there's a good chance that you will try to do so in culturally prescribed ways—with an appropriate T-shirt and bumper sticker. The yang power of culture can be practically insuperable. A Confucian might say yes to the overarching yang power of civilization and see in civilization's prescriptions the *li* (rules of propriety) in and through which people discover, express, and develop their humanity. A Taoist, on the other hand, would say no to this power and see in it an excess that prevents both natural living and social well-being. It prevents natural living because the loud voice of civilization all but stifles the call of nature, and it prevents social well-being because the hustle and bustle called for increases tension and makes conflict more likely.

What would the narrator of *ZMM* say? I think he would say both yes and no, but mostly yes. He is concerned not with the yang power of developed civilizations in general but with the yang power of twentieth-century Western technological culture. The narrator sees in that culture—despite problems such as mass warfare, pollution, and a "mechanized existence" for many—a tremendous improvement over the "agony of bare existence" that characterized primitive civilizations. In his estimation, the movement from the primitive to the modern can only properly be described as "upward progress" (see *ZMM*, p. 112). On the other hand, he does find an evil in modern technology's tendency "to isolate people into lonely attitudes of objectivity." His solution, however, calls not for a reversion to a more primitive life-style but for a turning toward Quality in the midst of the tasks of the technological culture (see *ZMM*, p. 322; see also p. 261).

Perhaps you are wondering why Lao-tzu would emphasize yin values in response to the yang power of civilization. After all, you might ask, if we are in fact the victims of cultural domination, isn't the net effect that we are inert, passive, excessively yinnish? Don't we need to muster more yang rather than more yin? Don't we need to assert ourselves, fight against the social control that comes with a developed civilization, and regain control over our own lives? Shouldn't we counter social yang with personal yang? If, instead, we follow Lao-tzu's suggestion and celebrate yin values, cultivating them further within ourselves, won't the problem simply get worse?

How would Lao-tzu respond to such a line of questioning? I think, if he were here today, he would say something like: "I sympathize with your concern. We need a lessening, not an increase, of civilization's impositions on our lives. But the way to get there is not by fighting yang with yang. Do you really think that you can successfully counter social yang with personal yang? Aside from the rare case of a 'successful' revolution—which is really no more than a shift to a new regime, a new power with a new set of cultural impositions—the more common case is that personal yang gets coopted by social yang. Your effort to be an individual gets translated into books, clubs, cocktail chatter, and new areas of professional expertise. The net result is a new social game and a stronger, because more subtle, form of cultural domination. And even if you could somehow assert yourself, what good would that do? Given all the yang energy that you would have to muster, do you think that you would be at peace with yourself? Do you think that you would be thereby contributing to the harmony of society? No, the way to solve the problem is not to counter yang with yang. There is a two-fold solution. On the social level, what is needed is a deyanging of society, a decivilizing of civilization. Once that happens, people won't feel a need to fight against cultural domination, because they will feel more space in their lives. On the personal level, what is needed is greater yin in response to nature, greater receptivity to the flow of the Tao. The two parts of the solution are meant to support each other. When civilization is no longer at fever pitch, you are freer to respond to the call of nature. When you are interested in responding to the call of nature, you are freer to reject the trappings of a developed civilization."

On the basis of this imaginary response, you might well suspect that Lao-tzu would be quite sympathetic with the Johns and Sylvias of contemporary culture. John and Sylvia of *ZMM*, you recall, felt a tremendous antipathy toward the "it all" of our highly technological culture and wanted desperately to get away from it, even though they felt there was no escape (*ZMM*, pp. 14–15). From Lao-tzu's perspective, such feelings are a quite understandable response to an overly yangish society. A similar set of feelings (coupled with an insight into other possibilities) drove Lao-tzu to the western gate and perhaps had something to do with his leaving behind his wisdom in the form of the *Tao Te Ching*.

The narrator of *ZMM*, on the other hand, while not out of sympathy with John's and Sylvia's feelings about technology, thinks that "their flight from and hatred of technology is self-defeating" (*ZMM*, p. 16). What does he mean by that? How is an antitechnological attitude self-defeating? Well, just consider the way John relates to his motorcycle. In his effort to flee from technology, he makes little effort to understand just how the cycle functions, and he does little to develop the art of cycle maintenance. So what happens when things go wrong, when the cycle malfunctions? John curses the machine and perhaps goes into a bar—if one is available—for a beer. Temporary relief, but no solution. The cycle remains unfixed (unless, of course, someone of the narrator's ilk plays the savior), and John's bad feelings about technology remain and continue to grow. The more the feelings grow, the less inclined John is to develop and apply the art of maintenance. Without the needed maintenance, the cycle's problems are likely to mount. With the mounting problems come more curses, more beer, and more unproductive bad feelings. It all adds up to a vicious cycle (pardon the pun). That is what the narrator probably means when he says that the antitechnological attitude is self-defeating.

What would Lao-tzu say in response to the narrator? I think he would be willing to grant that the antitechnological attitude is self-defeating as long as it is taken in the direction that John takes it. But is that the only way to go with the attitude? Maybe, instead of cursing the cycle, John should get rid of it. Maybe the cycle, whatever benefits it brings, is part of an overly yangish society that simply has to be deyanged. It would be interesting to get the narrator and Lao-tzu into a conversation about that. So let's do it.

LAO-TZU: John's feelings about the technological society come from the not yet muted voice of nature within him. He should listen to that voice, leave his cycle behind, and seek a less yangish society, one that is simpler and closer to nature.

NARRATOR: You can't turn back the clock. Nor should you want to. Better to deal with the problems that come with progress than with those that come with a struggle for bare survival.

LAO-TZU: You don't have to go back to the point of struggle for survival. You just have to simplify to the point where there is more space and a greater possibility of getting into the flow of the Tao.

NARRATOR: How will you know when you've reached the right point? How will you know when to stop? And, once you've stopped, how can you keep the momentum of progress from returning?

LAO-TZU: There is no formula that you can consult for the knowledge of when to stop. The wise know when to stop. The nonwise don't. If you want a picture of what the simple, nonyangish society might look like, listen to this poem that I wrote many years ago:

If a country is governed wisely,
its inhabitants will be content.
They enjoy the labor of their hands
and don't waste time inventing
labor-saving machines.
Since they dearly love their homes,
they aren't interested in travel.
There may be a few wagons and boats,
but these don't go anywhere.
There may be an arsenal of weapons,
but nobody ever uses them.
People enjoy their food,
take pleasure in being with their families,
spend weekends working in their gardens,
delight in the doings of the neighborhood.
And even though the next country is so close
that people can hear its roosters crowing and its dogs
    barking,
they are content to die of old age
without ever having gone to see it.
                                   [*Tao Te Ching*, 80]

NARRATOR: Your picture might have strong appeal to a few, but it will have very little appeal to most people. Having gotten used to the conveniences, comforts, pleasures, and possibilities that technological progress creates, they can't imagine returning to such a confined existence. For them, the choice is to find peace *within* the technological society or else be resigned to anxiety and frustration.

LAO-TZU: How can you find peace within such a high-strung society?

NARRATOR: You find it not by avoiding the things that make twentieth-century life enjoyable but by caring about what you are doing when you are dealing with those things [see *ZMM*, p. 25].

LAO-TZU: But if the things that you are dealing with make

such high demands on you, drain you of your energy, yang you to pieces, why care about dealing with them? Why not instead return to the simple life and care about sunshine and fresh air and good, plain food?

NARRATOR: Whether you are caring about sunshine or cycles, if you are really caring, you are not being drained and dissipated, because caring involves being in relation to Quality—"care and Quality are internal and external aspects of the same thing" [*ZMM*, p. 247]—and when you are in relation to Quality you are full of gumption [*ZMM*, p. 272]. Quality energizes you.

LAO-TZU: I will grant you that a caring attitude is important for the harmony that you and I both seek. From your Chautauquas, I gather that you are fully aware that caring has both a yang dimension and a yin dimension. In its yang dimension, it involves taking active steps to make things right and to keep things right. The motorcycle won't take care of itself. In its yin dimension, caring involves being open and receptive to the pull of what you call Quality and I call Tao. Genuine caring must have both dimensions. If you're not receptive, tuned in, your work is likely to be sloppy, full of mistakes. If you only tune in and don't put your hand to the task, you make a good contemplative but an unsatisfactory worker. In neither case can you be in harmony with your technological environment.

NARRATOR: It sounds like you understand what I'm saying. Where do we differ?

LAO-TZU: I understand on the abstract level; on the concrete level, I see a huge problem. You have said to me that my simple society is only for the few. I say to you that genuine caring and peace of mind in the midst of the technological society is for the few. Few can be *in* the hubbub without being *of* the hubbub. Most are overwhelmed. In the blare, the complexity, the glare of an overly yangish society, their caring is reduced to coping. They are out of touch with the Tao, out of touch with themselves.

What is needed? "Blunt your sharpness, untie your knots, soften your glare, settle your dust" [*Tao Te Ching*, 56]. In a word, simplify society so that the Tao and its power—or, if you like, Quality and caring—can be fully felt.

You can take this conversation further if you like. For our purposes here, enough has been said to indicate the importance that Lao-tzu attaches to the simplification of society. Simplicity is one of several yin values that the *Tao Te Ching* calls attention to and celebrates through a variety of images. Let's have a look at some of those images and the values that they suggest.

One image is the "spirit of the valley" (*Tao Te Ching*, 6). The valley, which is yin to the mountain's yang, suggests a kind of productive receptivity. It receives a sound and produces an echo. It receives water from rain and melting snow and produces grasses and flowers. To have the spirit of the valley is to appreciate and show forth the power of receptivity. (It is interesting that the narrator says "Zen is the 'spirit of the valley,' not the mountaintop"—*ZMM*, p. 220. The phrase "spirit of the valley" is actually Taoist. Moreover, the narrator himself notes elsewhere that the Buddha can be found at the top of a mountain—*ZMM*, p. 16. Perhaps the slight confusion should be downplayed, given that Zen may be aptly described as what happens to Buddhism when Buddhism meets Taoism. Perhaps, too, the slight confusion is psychologically apt in the context in which it occurs. The narrator utters the statement in the context of trying to escape a reunion with the ghost of Phaedrus at the top of a mountain.)

Another image is that of the infant. (See *Tao Te Ching*, 10, 20, 28, 55, 76, and see Steele, below, p. 282.) The infant, who is yin to the adult's yang, represents suppleness as opposed to rigidity. As Lao-tzu notes, we enter life supple and exit life rigid. If we want to be on the side of life, we need to recover the infant's suppleness. (*ZMM*'s beer-can shim episode—pp. 46–47—comes to mind again. If you're too "adult"—too formed, too—there's no way you'll be able to see the shim in the can. You need a baby's fresh eyes to see the shim and a baby's suppleness to respond to what you see.)

A related value, the value of the indefinite, is conveyed by the image of the "uncarved block" (see *Tao Te Ching*, 15, 19, 28, 32, 37, 57). An uncarved block of wood, like a baby, is simple, unformed. It has not been made into a definite object that serves a definite function. It has not been given a definite shape that might appeal to someone's eye for the beautiful. Because it lacks a definite function and a definite beauty, you might be tempted to think that in its present state it lacks value. "Carve it into something useful or beautiful," you might say. Lao-tzu, on the other hand, suggests that you give the matter a second look. When the block of wood is carved, it gains something, but it also loses something. By the very fact that it becomes one definite thing, it loses its original potential for being any number of things. A valuable actuality is gained, but an even more valuable reservoir of potentiality is lost.

What if the block of wood could always be returned to its original, uncarved state? Then you could have both the value of the definite things that are carved and the value of the indefinite potential that exists when the block is uncarved. But is that possible? Can it be both ways? With a block of wood, no, but with yourself, yes. You can retain the uncarved block within you and return to it over and over again. How so? Think of a definite talent that you might develop or a definite social role that you might play or a definite profession that you might enter. Now imagine two different ways of relating to that talent, role, or profession. The first is the desire-filled way. You want it badly, you cling to it, you totally identify with it. You carve yourself out to match it. If *it* is lost, *you* are lost. The second is the desireless way. You do what needs doing, but you do not totally identify with any particular talent, role, or profession. You keep a part of yourself—the most important part—within yourself. You retain the uncarved block. In circumstances that tempt the desire-filled, the irrevocably carved, to jump off of high buildings, you are ready, as always, to go with the flow of the Tao. You are ready to develop a new talent, play a new role, or enter a new profession (or perhaps avoid professions, since professions tend to promote high definition or total carving).

Perhaps the favorite image of Taoists, one suggesting a number of yin values, is that of water. If you want to be a good Taoist, be like water and seek the low places. To do so is to favor survival. You can't get knocked down if you're already low to the ground. Moreover, there can be greatness in the low places. "All streams flow to the sea because it is lower than they are. Humility gives it its power" (*Tao Te Ching*, 66). If you want to be a good Taoist, be like water, "which nourishes all things without trying to" (*Tao*

Te Ching, 8). If you want to be a good Taoist, be like water—there is "nothing . . . as soft and yielding" and, at the same time, nothing better "for dissolving the hard and inflexible" (*Tao Te Ching*, 78).

If you take these images and values seriously, you will open yourself up to the power of the Tao in everyday life. Supposing that you do so, how will you feel about the art of motorcycle maintenance? Will you avoid motorcycles and their maintenance altogether? Perhaps that is the "purer" route, but it isn't necessarily the only route. If you are committed to a world that includes cycles and computers, perhaps you will find in Taoist images and values some further tips for avoiding gumption traps and gumption loss.

Now let's look at the Tao's power on another level, the metaphysical level. If you are journeying on that level, your concern is not simply to deal harmoniously with the realities of everyday life but rather to understand reality itself at the deepest level. If you are journeying on that level, with that sort of concern, you have a fellow traveler in Phaedrus.

Phaedrus eventually asked the metaphysical question and reached the answer that Quality is at the heart of reality. His metaphysical musing intensified when he began to wonder whether Quality is something subjective or objective. His answer, in many ways the crowning philosophical insight of *ZMM*, was that Quality is neither subjective nor objective, but rather the *cause*, the *creator*, of subjects and objects (see *ZMM*, p. 215). It was at this point that Phaedrus began to surmise that his own understanding of ultimate reality converged with that of the *Tao Te Ching*. Perhaps Tao and Quality were one and the same, the indefinable source and substance of all things. With that thought in mind, he picked up the *Tao Te Ching*, a book that he had read many times before, and read it again with new eyes. Happily, he discovered that he could aptly substitute "Quality" for "Tao" throughout the text. He had reached the mind of Lao-tzu and, by the same stroke, found his own philosophy vindicated. (See *ZMM*, pp. 226–228.)

There is no point in listing here all the points of convergence that Phaedrus saw between Taoist metaphysics and his own (see *ZMM*, p. 227, and *Tao Te Ching*, 1, 4, 6, 14). Rather, I'd like to consider a parallel that is not explicitly made in *ZMM*. The parallel concerns the dynamics of creation—more specifically, the fact that the created world comes into being through the interaction of a polarity, a complementary twosome.

In the Taoist scheme of things, the Tao, the unnameable One, gives rise to the myriad nameable things by way of the Two, yin and yang. The Tao is neither yin nor yang but is the ground of both and permeates both. Yin and yang produce by their interaction all that can be named and defined. In Phaedrus' parallel scheme, as I understand it, Quality, the unnameable One, gives rise to the myriad nameable things by way of the Two, subject and object. Quality is neither subject nor object but is the ground of both and permeates both. Subject energy and object energy produce by their interaction all that can be named and defined.

If this is a genuine parallel, there must be a similarity between the yin-yang polarity and the subject-object polarity. Is there? I believe so. When subjects and objects interact, something asserts and something receives; something acts and something undergoes; something works and something is worked upon. All of which amounts to yanging and yinning. But which is which? Is subject-energy yang and object-energy yin or vice versa?

What makes that question especially fascinating is that you can divide the whole of Western philosophy down the middle in terms of your answer. If you say that the subject is yin and the object yang, your answer echoes the keynote of Western philosophy from the time of the first ancient Greek philosophers (sixth century B.C.) up to the time of the first "modern" philosophers (seventeenth century A.D.). If you say that the subject is yang and the object yin, your answer echoes the keynote of Western philosophy from the beginning of the modern era up to the present. The ancient tendency was to think of knowing primarily as a kind of receptivity, an openness to reality. To be a knower was to allow yourself to be acted upon by what is. For the most part, the active, shaping role of the knower was unnoticed. And where an active role was recognized, as in the case of Aristotle's "agent intellect," the role was limited to some sort of a nonshaping, preparatory phase in the process of knowing. Aristotle viewed the "agent intellect," the active part of the knower, as a sort of light-thrower. The "agent intellect" did not shape the object or impose categories upon it. It simply provided the light within which the object might be received by the "passive intellect." There, in the "passive intellect," in the receptive part of the knower's consciousness, is where knowledge as such occurred. And knowledge as such was objective for the very good reason that the knower's consciousness was determined by the object. The to-be-known object yanged, and the knowing subject yinned. (I am speaking here of the *keynote* of ancient and medieval Western philosophy and don't want to suggest this was the only view. Phaedrus, for one, tuned in to the alternative philosophy of the ancient Sophists and found in its "man is the measure" theme an echo of his own philosophy, which gave a much greater role to the human subject—see *ZMM*, pp. 337–345, especially p. 338.)

With the beginning of the modern era the keynote changed. Immanuel Kant noted that when you know something you don't know it simply by *taking in* sensory data. Rather, you know it by *imposing* certain mental categories upon the data. Your knowing is something active and shaping, not something passive and shaped. To use the narrator's example (*ZMM*, pp. 117–119), when you have knowledge of a motorcycle, you don't simply rely on sensory data. If you relied only on sensory data, then given variations in light and in other conditions, you would think of the cycle as a series of fluctuations of color, temperature, shape, texture, and so on. But you don't think of the cycle in that way, as simply a series of fluctuations. You think of it as a *constant thing* that somehow undergoes and underlies various sensory changes. Where is the sensory datum that corresponds to "constant thing"? It is not to be found, for "constant thing"—Kant would say "substance"—is not a sensory datum but a category in your mind that you inevitably impose upon data to escape getting lost in the whirl of sensations.

Kant claimed that his insight into the shaping activity of the human mind amounted to a sort of Copernican revolution. He was right. From his day on, the *object* would be considered less and less the fixed star, the primary determinant of knowledge; more and more that role would fall to the *subject*. The subjective character of human knowledge and the yangish character of the human subject would become ever more prominent in Western thinking. Kant thought the categories of the human mind were common to all human beings. Later thinkers would point out that human knowledge also involves the imposition of categories that are relative to particular cultures and to individual histories. The object of knowledge would thus be seen as multiple layers of categories produced by multiple layers of human, subjective activity.

The subjectivizing of human knowledge and the yangizing of

human subjectivity intensified when the question arose, Why do human beings impose categories upon things in the process of knowing them? Nietzsche's answer, which has resonated throughout the twentieth century, was that human beings are not really interested in knowing things but in making them amenable to their own desires and needs. Underlying and permeating the human desire to know is a "will to power," a drive toward self-expansion and self-assertion. With *knowing* thus reduced to *willing*, it became easier and easier to talk about human beings, in their knowing activity, as not just *shaping* but even *creating* their world. Phaedrus, for example, said that we "create the world in which we live. All of it. Every last bit of it" (*ZMM*, p. 225). (In Phaedrus' view, that creation occurs under the stimulus of Quality. Does this addition—the stimulus of Quality—make a difference with regard to the subjective/objective character of our world? Phaedrus certainly thought so. It's an interesting and important question.)

Whether the ancients or the moderns are right about the nature of knowledge, it should be clear that there is an analogy between the yin-yang polarity and the subject-object polarity. Perhaps you might be interested in developing that analogy. And perhaps you might wonder why Phaedrus didn't.

One answer is simply that his mind took a different turn. Having gotten turned on by the parallel between Taoist metaphysics and his own, he soon found himself swept away. Metaphysical musing gave way to a mystical plunge. In the narrator's language, the metaphysical wave of crystallization gave way to a mystical wave of crystallization from which Phaedrus "never recovered" (*ZMM*, p. 221).

One difference between the metaphysical and the mystical, a difference noted by Phaedrus (*ZMM*, p. 226), turns on the possibility of definition. If you can define the ultimate, you are treating it as a metaphysical entity; if you cannot define it, you are treating it as a mystical entity. Another difference, which Phaedrus did not so much note as *embody*, concerns the relation between the knower and the known. When you know something metaphysically, you maintain a certain distance from it; you can talk about it. When you know something mystically, the distance vanishes and you can't talk about the known because you've entered it and *are* it. Perhaps Lao-tzu had mystical knowledge in mind when he said, "Those who know don't talk. Those who talk don't know" (*Tao Te Ching*, 56).

Phaedrus could talk when he was comparing Lao-tzu's metaphysical speculations with his own, but at a certain point Tao talk and Quality talk gave way to a thunderous silence. The narrator uses the image of an avalanche to describe what happened. "Before he could stop it, the sudden accumulated mass of awareness began to grow and grow into an avalanche of thought and awareness out of control; with each additional growth of the downward tearing mass loosening hundreds of times its volume, and then that mass uprooting hundreds of times its volume more, and then hundreds of times that; on and on, wider and broader; until there was nothing left to stand" (ZMM, p. 228).

Those who know don't talk. But we've got some further talking to do—about Zen.

ZEN BUDDHISM

As you look through the packet on Zen Buddhism, it may occur to you that Zen is a weave of two contrasting strands: the boring and the zany. The boring strand—I am using the word *boring* to designate an impression from the outside rather than an experience from the inside—involves monks spending endless hours seated in meditation. If you were to ask those monks what they are doing, they might well respond with an expression that is more or less a trademark of a certain brand of Zen: "Just sitting." What could be more boring than that? The narrator of ZMM, referring explicitly to that "boring" Zen practice, tells us that "Zen has something to say about boredom"; but like a good Zen master, he doesn't tell us what that something is. Instead he puts the question to us—or better, puts us to the question (ZMM, p. 286; see the note to p. 266 in Section 11): "In the center of all this boredom is the very thing Zen Buddhism seeks to teach. What is it? What is it at the very center of boredom that you're not seeing?" Very early in his narrative, the narrator hinted at this Zen connection between boredom and vision when he voiced his hopes for Sylvia: "I thought maybe in this endless grass and wind she would see a thing that sometimes comes when monotony and boredom are accepted. It's here, but I have no names for it" (ZMM, p. 18). Did Sylvia see it? There is at least a hint, a bit later in the narrative, that she saw something that would draw the approving nod of a Zen master:

"Sylvia has tears in her eyes from the wind, and she stretches out her arms and says, 'It's so beautiful. It's so empty' " (*ZMM*, p. 42). If Zen has something to say about boredom, it has a great deal to say about emptiness. Recall, for example, the eighth Oxherding Picture, the great empty circle, in Section 3.

You can find the zany strand of Zen, among other places, in the interchanges between Zen masters and their students. What goes on in those interchanges? Sometimes a master takes a stick and whacks the student across the back, and the student responds by "getting *satori*," i.e., by having an enlightenment experience. At other times the master puts to the student a puzzling question or offers a puzzling response to the student's question. The student then takes that puzzle, or *koan*, and wrestles with it, works with it, plays with it, becomes it, until satori dawns whereupon the student goes back to the master to have the enlightenment experience "confirmed." (Watch out for another whack across the back!) The koan that the student receives from the master might be a question that has a playful, nonsensical air about it (e.g., "What is the sound of one hand clapping?") or it might be a response that sounds, more or less, like a deliberate non sequitur (e.g., "What was the meaning of the twenty-eighth Zen patriarch's coming to China?" "The cypress tree in the garden."). Zany whacks, zany words. What is the point of all this zaniness? Is it all just an exercise in creativity?

If you look at Zen activity this way, you should probably get rid of that little word "just." And you should realize that this creativity aims toward a new way of seeing. That is what Zen, both its boring and zany strands, is all about: new seeing, fresh seeing, direct seeing. "When I first began to study Zen," an old Zen saying goes, "mountains were just mountains, streams were just streams. After I had studied Zen for a while, mountains were no longer mountains, streams were no longer streams. But when I really understood Zen, the mountains were again just mountains, and the streams were just streams." All the boring Zen sitting and all the zany Zen whacks and words are meant to help the Zen practitioner recapture the "beginner's mind" and see afresh the mountains and streams.

Why do you need Zen or any other special practice to see things directly and freshly? Aren't you already doing that? Wasn't the speaker just quoted doing that at the outset of Zen study? Why study or practice something just to get back to where you were before you started? Those are good questions. The last even has the ring of a koan about it. However, the assumption behind them— an assumption that needs to be challenged—is that your present seeing is immediate, nonmediated. You assume that you are seeing "just mountains," when in fact you are seeing mountains as filtered by a variety of mental paraphernalia. The paraphernalia—including moods, expectations, imperatives, and a host of verbal categories that function as containers and confiners—can weigh you down and distort what you see. The narrator of *ZMM* refers to such depressing and distorting mental paraphernalia as "internal gumption traps," more specifically "value traps" and "truth traps" (*ZMM*, pp. 279–290). Interestingly, he includes "boredom" among such traps: "Boredom means you're off the Quality track, you're not seeing things freshly, you've lost your 'beginner's mind' and your motorcycle is in great danger" (*ZMM*, p. 285). Why does the narrator see boredom as a trap, given his claim—noted above, p. 118.— that at the heart of boredom lies the thing that Zen seeks to teach? There's no mistake here. Boredom can be both an obstacle and an opportunity. How you experience it—and consequently how you deal with it—may depend on where you are in your journey. You may or may not be ready to sit and see boredom through to its depths, to the point where it opens up on fresh seeing.

Given the variety and the subtle workings of the mental paraphernalia that can block your vision, you may well need special study, special techniques, and above all else special guidance to liberate yourself and reopen the channels of fresh seeing. The guide, the Zen master, has an important role to play. A good guide can help you both see and get beyond whatever keeps you from enlightenment experience. Perhaps what holds you back is a dualistic mind-set, an either-or point of view. The Zen master can provide an appropriate koan for dislodging that mind-set. Maybe the Zen master Joshu had this in mind when he produced, in the ninth century, his now famous koan in response to the question: "Does the dog have the Buddha-nature?" As *ZMM*'s narrator interprets it, Joshu's response, "*Mu*"—literally "No thing"—was meant and is meant to challenge a dualistic mind-set and its narrowness of vision by calling the either-or type question into question. If you're locked into either-or, yes-or-no thinking, you may need an appropriate *"Mu"* to shock you out of it, to open up and expand your awareness (see *ZMM,* pp. 289–290).

Perhaps what keeps you from direct seeing is one or more false assumptions about the seer or the to-be-seen. The Zen master can give you a koan or an exercise that leads to the shattering of those assumptions. By way of analogy, recall the *ZMM* episode in which Phaedrus the teacher, alias Phaedrus the Zen master, coaxed a five-thousand-word essay out of an otherwise wordless student by asking her to focus on the upper left-hand brick of the opera house in Bozeman. The student falsely assumed that she had nothing to say, because she assumed that she could see nothing new. Perhaps she also assumed that much insight could only come from much material, that much could not come from little. By giving her a one-brick focus, a sort of visual koan, Phaedrus helped her to let go of her assumptions and open her eyes. In the narrator's words: "She was strangely unaware that she could look and see freshly for herself, as she wrote, without primary regard for what had been said before. The narrowing down to one brick destroyed the blockage because it was so obvious she *had* to do some original and direct seeing" (*ZMM,* p. 171).

Whether it be Joshu's *"Mu"* or Phaedrus' brick, a Zen tool is just that—a tool. It has no special magic outside of its being properly used. And proper use depends upon the combined effort of master and student. It's up to the Zen master to determine the what, when, and how of the tools to be used. Sometimes what's needed is a whack, sometimes direct advice, sometimes a zany word, sometimes a shout, sometimes silence. It's up to the student to follow the master's skillful lead with diligence, persistence, and flexibility. When the interaction is Quality-filled, when the student yins to the master's yang and yangs to the master's yin, there can occur that "special transmission" that has been Zen's hallmark from its very beginning. And as a result, the mountains and streams are seen afresh.

Special interaction, special transmission, fresh and direct seeing—that would be one way of summing up the Zen tradition. How did the tradition get started? The story goes that Siddhartha Gautama, alias the Buddha, decided to use a prop, a Zen tool, for one of his sermons. Having gone up on a hillside to preach, he silently held up a flower. Everyone in the crowd below awaited his words. Everyone, that is, except one person, Kashyapa. Kashyapa smiled. He had caught on to something. A special transmission had occurred, and somehow Gautama became aware of it. He walked down to the smiling Kashyapa, handed him the flower, and conferred upon him the honor, the power, and the task of being the first Zen patriarch. The Flower Sermon, as it came to be called, said loudly and clearly that enlightenment experience doesn't depend upon words and concepts for its flowering.

Of course, words would often be used in the Zen tradition both to talk about enlightenment and to make the point that enlightenment doesn't depend on words, but that doesn't nullify the point of Gautama's Flower Sermon. You can use words as a net to try to capture a nonverbal reality, in which case it may be difficult to let go of the net without losing the reality; or, in Zen fashion, you can use words as pointers that vanish as soon as the pointed-to begins to be seen. A pertinent Zen image is the finger pointing to the moon. If you want to point to the moon, you've got to put your finger up there in the field of vision; but if you don't want your finger to become the object of attention, you've also got to take your finger down at the appropriate time. What is the appropriate time? How long do you leave the finger up there? How long do you dangle the words? How can you ensure that the finger will not be confused with the moon, that clever words will not be confused with enlightenment? There is no formulaic answer to those questions. Different situations call for different timing and different words. It all comes down to an art, the art of the Zen master. Koans as we know them from the outside—koans as they might be contained and even "explained" in books—are but the frozen by-products of this art form. Koans in their living reality, as they emerge through the master's art within the master-student interaction, are the pointing fingers that give way to the moon.

If you want to talk about Zen's origins, you've got to mention Kashyapa, but there is little to say about him apart from recounting the Flower Sermon. If you want to learn about Zen's flowering, you've got to move ahead several centuries, to the sixth century A.D. (some say the fifth century), the time of Bodhidharma. Bodhidharma was the twenty-eighth patriarch in the line that goes back to Kashyapa. Since he was the person who brought the Zen tradition to China, he was also the first patriarch of Chinese Zen (Ch'an). In Zen lore, Bodhidharma is famous for three things: a four-line summary of Zen, a strange interview with Emperor Wu (Zen's zany strand again), and a nine-year sojourn in a cave (Zen's boring strand again). Let's have a look at each of the above in turn.

Bodhidharma's description of Zen goes:

> A special transmission outside of scriptures.
> No dependence on words or letters.
> Direct pointing to the soul of the human.
> Seeing into one's nature and becoming Buddha.

The first two lines repeat things that have already been noted about Zen. In the Zen tradition, we expect to find enlightenment transmitted through nonordinary ways of teaching, like holding up a flower or suddenly whacking someone on the back or using language in a way that stands language on its head. That doesn't mean that there are no scriptures in the Zen tradition. Like every other school of Buddhism, Zen makes use of scriptures and even has its favorite ones (such as the *Lankavatara Scripture,* which is said to have been brought by Bodhidharma to China, and, especially, the *Platform Scripture,* which is said to have its root in sermons preached by Hui-neng, the sixth patriarch in the Chinese tradition). However, Zen explicitly makes the point that enlightenment can occur apart from the use of scriptures. What's more, Zen teaches that if you *depend* upon scriptures or, more generally, upon verbal language, you are making a mistake. By such dependence, you are confining your awareness to *rational* ways of apprehending reality; you are riveting your attention to your head center. If you want to attain enlightenment, you've got to be open to other ways of seeing and to another center of consciousness. (Phaedrus' pursuit and thrashing of the ghost of rationality—*ZMM,* pp. 71, 88—and the narrator's call for an expansion of the nature of rationality—*ZMM,* p. 150—are variations on this Zen theme of getting beyond words and letters, getting beyond conventional logic, getting beyond the head center and moving toward a new center.)

Bodhidharma's third line, "Direct pointing to the soul of the human," indicates that the Zen finger always points not just *away* from you, toward the moon, but also *at* you, toward your inner being. Zen activity seeks to illumine the seer as well as the seen, the subject as well as the object. Had the tradition remained in the land of its birth, transcendentally oriented India, Zen's inward pointing might have been confined to closed-eyed meditation practices and to texts and words that facilitated and promoted such introspective practices. As it is, given the move northeastward toward less introspective cultures, that inward pointing takes on many forms, including some that seem to focus attention externally: blows and shouts, puzzles concerned with external things (like the cypress tree in the garden), and practical advice that seems to be concerned with no more than everyday maintenance (for example, the advice contained in this koan story: A student went to a Zen master and asked about enlightenment. The master then asked, "Have you had your breakfast?" The student answered, "Yes." The Zen master retorted, "Then go wash your bowl."). It is important to note that all of this apparently outward-pointing activity is also, from the viewpoint of Zen, inward-pointing activity. If the pointing is Quality-filled, if it hits the mark, it will not only give you new eyes for seeing the mountains or washing your bowl or fixing your cycle, it will also allow you to see yourself afresh. The division between the external and the internal is not absolute. The Zen finger can point to both at the same time; otherwise it is not the Zen finger. And by the same token you can be working on both at the same time; otherwise it's not Zen work you're doing. As the narrator of *ZMM* puts it: "The real cycle you're working on is a cycle called yourself. The machine that appears to be 'out there' and the person that appears to be 'in here' are not two separate things. They grow toward Quality or fall away from Quality together" (*ZMM*, p. 293).

Bodhidharma's line, "Seeing into one's nature and becoming Buddha," tells what occurs if the pointing activity is successful. You will understand what you are and become enlightened. At the heart of you is the Buddha-nature, the *dharmakaya* or truth body of the Buddha that we talked about earlier (see above, p. 84). To see this is to become it; but in a way you don't "become" it, because it's not a matter of taking on something new. Rather, you are allowing what has always been there to shine through. At the moment of enlightenment experience, the Buddha-nature (in *ZMM*'s terms, Quality) shines through everything. You can see it in yourself; you can see it in mountain peaks and flower petals; and, as *ZMM*'s narrator has it, you can see it "in the circuits of a digital computer or the gears of a cycle transmission" (*ZMM*, p. 16).

The idea of an all-pervading Buddha-nature is an important one within the Zen tradition. If you emphasize it, as Zen does, you are likely to deemphasize the historical Buddha. Siddhartha Gautama may have shown the way, but as a historical individual he is long gone, whereas that which gave his words and deeds their quality, the Buddha-nature, is right here and right now. If you focus attention or veneration upon the historical figure, you may fail to see the reality that is within you and around you. (That is the point of the Zen saying, "If you see the Buddha on the road, kill him.")

If Bodhidharma's four-line summation of Zen suggests to you a speaker who doesn't waste words, your opinion will be confirmed when you tune in to Bodhidharma's interview with Emperor Wu. When Bodhidharma arrived in China, the emperor was already a devout Buddhist. (Buddhism existed in China for centuries before its Zen form found its way there.) Bodhidharma's arrival was an occasion for the emperor both to learn more about Buddhism and also (perhaps especially) to try to impress a celebrated Buddhist monk. So the emperor invited Bodhidharma to his court, told him about all of his accomplishments on behalf of Buddhism (such as building Buddhist temples and having Buddhist scriptures copied), and asked him how much merit he had accrued thereby. (The concept of merit or good karma, it should be noted, was an established part of the Buddhist tradition at that time. Merit was not to be confused with the ultimate goal of enlightenment, but it was thought of as a sort of stepping-stone. By accumulating merit you could reach the point where, in the present life or a future one, you were ready to move on to enlightenment.) Bodhidharma responded, "No merit at all." What did he mean by that? Was he challenging the Buddhist tradition on this point and suggesting that the concept of merit was a faulty one? Was he suggesting that merit rested not on external accomplishments but on the right internal attitude and that the emperor lacked that attitude? Was he playing the role of Zen master, selecting words that might shock the emperor out of complacency and into readiness for enlightenment? Whatever Bodhidharma meant, the emperor, doubtlessly taken aback, shifted the conversation and asked Bodhidharma to tell him what was the most important teaching of Buddhism. Bodhidharma responded simply, "Vast emptiness." Was he referring to the ancient Buddhist doctrine that nothing is substantial or permanent, that all is a constant flow? Was he somehow suggesting to the emperor that, in contrast to what Buddhism is all about, the emperor was ego-filled, lacking the openness and receptiveness ("beginner's mind") that both lead to and reflect enlightenment? Apparently rankled by Bodhidharma's response, the emperor asked, "Who are you who answers me in this way?" Bodhidharma responded, "I don't know." Again, what did he mean? Was he suggesting that enlightenment brings with it loss of individual identity? (If so, is that loss the common denominator of enlightenment and insanity? Phaedrus had a vision of Quality even as "he" disappeared—ZMM, pp. 358–359. Did he, perhaps, become enlightened and insane at the same time?) Was Bodhidharma's response somehow calling into question the ego behind the question? Whatever Bodhidharma meant, his "I don't know" would echo down through the centuries as a koan in the Zen tradition. Bodhidharma then left the emperor's presence and took up residence in a cave for nine years.

Why a nine-year sojourn in a cave? Wasn't that a strange way to introduce the Zen tradition to the Chinese? Perhaps he was making the point that what Zen has to offer is not to be gotten cheaply. If so, that point was corroborated by what happened at the end of the nine-year period. The story goes that after nine years, a would-be disciple, Hui-k'o, came to Bodhidharma's cave to receive instruction. Bodhidharma refused. Hui-k'o waited outside the cave through all kinds of weather. Eventually, to show his earnestness, he cut off his arm and presented it to Bodhidharma. Only then did Bodhidharma break away from his solitude and take on Hui-k'o as a student. What Zen has to offer is not to be gotten cheaply. (Perhaps that is one of the unintended side lessons of ZMM.)

What did Bodhidharma do in the cave? He simply sat and stared at a wall. He was a wall-gazer for nine years! It might not seem to be such a great activity to those who are in a hurry to get things done, but for those who are acquainted with Bodhidharma's story, it symbolizes both the earnestness of Zen activity and the simplicity of Zen attainment.

With that story and that symbolism in mind, you might want to consider the prominent roles of a couple of walls in ZMM. First, there is the Korean wall. The narrator alludes to a memory fragment from Phaedrus' days in Korea. The fragment contains "a picture of a wall, seen from a prow of a ship, shining radiantly, like a gate of heaven, across a misty harbor" (ZMM, pp. 106–107). The narrator tells us that that fragment "seems to symbolize something very important, a turning point" (ZMM, p. 107). What does it symbolize? We are given a hint when we are told that Phaedrus was reading on that ship a book by F.S.C. Northrop, *The Meeting of East and West*, that calls for greater attention to the " 'undifferentiated aesthetic continuum' from which the theoretic arises" (*ZMM*, p. 108). Did the wall perhaps symbolize the "undifferentiated aesthetic continuum," the preconceptual element in human knowing? We are given a clearer answer later on, when the narrator relates Phaedrus' philosophy of Quality: "Once you begin to hear the sound of that Quality, see that Korean wall, that nonintellectual reality in its pure form, you want to forget all that word stuff, which you finally begin to see is always somewhere else" (*ZMM*, p. 222). The Korean wall is thus a symbol of Quality or, in Zen terms, the Buddha-nature. Seeing the wall is, in *ZMM* as in Zen, a symbol of enlightenment.

The second significant wall is in the bedless bedroom of a Chicago apartment. Phaedrus sits cross-legged and stares at that wall "for three days and three nights" (*ZMM*, p. 358). (You catch a hint of Bodhidharma here, even though it's not a nine-year gaze.) Eventually, the narrator tells us, Phaedrus' consciousness comes apart and he moves out of the "mythos" and even "disappears" (*ZMM*, p. 358). (You catch mostly a reference to insanity here.) But significantly, in this very state, "Quality . . . makes itself clear to him and his soul is at rest" (*ZMM*, p. 359). (The hint of Bodhidharma returns.)

After the time of Bodhidharma, perhaps the most important figure in the Chinese Zen tradition is the sixth patriarch, Hui-neng, who lived in the seventh century. According to the traditional story, Hui-neng was an illiterate rice pounder at the monastery run by the fifth patriarch, Hung-jen. (Hui-neng's illiteracy is important in the story; it's another way of making the Zen point that enlightenment does not depend on "words or letters.") Hung-jen decided to conduct a poetry contest to determine his successor. Whoever showed the best understanding of Zen in a poem would be the next patriarch. The head monk at the monastery, Shen-hsiu, produced a poem that all the other monks, except one, thought was unbeatable. The one exception was Hui-neng, who produced a poem of his own in response to that of Shen-hsiu. Shen-hsiu's poem went like this:

> The body is the tree of Perfect Wisdom.
> The Mind is the stand of a bright mirror.
> At all times diligently wipe it.
> Do not allow it to become dusty. [Chan translation]

Hui-neng's poem went like this:

Fundamentally Perfect Wisdom has no tree.
Nor has the bright mirror any stand.
Buddha-nature is forever clear and pure.
Where is there any dust? [Chan translation]

Hui-neng's poem won the contest, and Hui-neng became the sixth patriarch.

Why did it win? How did it show a greater understanding of Zen? Without attempting a thorough explanation, I'd like to suggest a possible answer. When you read Shen-hsiu's poem, you might get the image of a monk sitting, back straight like a tree, and spending endless hours in meditation, attempting to purify the mind. But when you read Hui-neng's poem, this image vanishes. Enlightenment doesn't depend upon straight-backed meditation any more than Siddhartha's enlightenment depended on the tree beneath which he sat. Nor does enlightenment depend upon your mind, since the "bright mirror" has no "stand." Nor is diligent wiping essential, since the Buddha-nature is already clear. Rather, enlightenment or Buddha-nature is a self-supporting, self-illuminating reality that is always present and can be experienced at any time. (This doctrine resembles Phaedrus' philosophy of Quality. Quality is neither subjective nor objective but prior to subjects and objects, mind and matter. It does not depend upon subjects and objects; they depend upon it. It is the self-supporting reality at the heart of all that exists. See ZMM, pp. 215, 221–223.)

Hui-neng's victory was not total. Shen-hsiu apparently had enough of a following that a controversy developed which eventually led to a split within Zen. The followers of Shen-hsiu became associated with the "Northern" school, the school of "Gradual Enlightenment," while the followers of Hui-neng became associated with the "Southern" school, the school of "Sudden Enlightenment." The Gradual Enlightenment School put an emphasis upon the repeated practice of seated meditation (zazen), Bodhidharma's specialty, and taught that enlightenment occurs little by little over a long period of time. The Sudden Enlightenment School put an emphasis upon a variety of newly developing techniques, such as the koan, and taught that enlightenment experience occurs in an instant and can come at any time, e.g., in the midst of all sorts of everyday activities, such as chopping wood, drawing water, cleaning a bowl, and—we might add—shimming handlebars.

The Sudden Enlightenment School didn't deny the fact that enlightenment might be preceded by a lengthy period of preparation; nor did it belittle the importance of such preparation. It *did* take issue with the idea that formal meditation practice is the only pertinent preparation for enlightenment. If the Buddha-nature is within everyone, laypersons as well as monks, illiterate rice pounders as well as refined scholars, the process that precedes its self-manifestation can be going on in a variety of life contexts. It can be going on in people whose lives consist mainly of everyday maintenance activities just as it can in people whose lives revolve around long hours of daily zazen.

Some of the heirs of the Sudden Enlightenment School went so far as to deny the preparatory value of zazen. They likened the attempt to reach enlightenment through zazen to trying to produce a mirror by rubbing a brick. This does not necessarily mean that you have to throw out zazen. Maybe what you have to throw out is the idea that zazen is a *means* to the attainment of enlightenment. Maybe you should think of it as an expression of Buddha-nature, as a form of Buddha-nature-in-action. Maybe you should think about it as an exercise in "beginner's mind": just keeping yourself open, with no goal in mind. Maybe you shouldn't think about zazen at all and just do it.

Zen took root in Japan in the twelfth and thirteenth centuries and there reached its full flowering. The tendencies and practices of the Gradual Enlightenment and Sudden Enlightenment schools were carried forward within the two most important schools of the Japanese tradition, the Soto School, which emphasized zazen, and the Rinzai School, which emphasized the koan. Numerous art forms developed under the influence of Zen and were suffused with its spirit. A list would include the tea ceremony, haiku poetry, Nō drama, flower arranging, ink brush painting, rock gardening, swordsmanship, and archery, to name just a few.

Why did Zen have such wide influence? Several factors may have been involved, but one that should be singled out is the Zen idea, expressed especially within the Rinzai tradition, that the Buddha-nature can show itself at any time and place, that enlightenment experience, *satori,* can occur in any context. If you accept that idea, you will think of enlightenment not as the special prerogative of straight-backed meditating monks, but as an event that may occur as you are doing the most mundane things—like preparing food or washing clothes or fixing a motorcycle. And if it occurs, you might have a new appreciation for the activity within which it occurs, since you are looking at it with fresh eyes. You might find yourself repeating an old Zen saying, "How wonderful! I carry wood! I draw water!" or, in the spirit of *ZMM,* "How wonderful! I shim a handlebar! I extract a screw!" In addition to new appreciation, you might experience a new level of performance, since you are fully engaged in what you are doing. What can distract you if you find the Buddha (or Quality) there? The narrator of *ZMM* makes this point when he compares "just sitting" in the Zen tradition to "just fixing" in motorcycle maintenance. In either case, what matters is that you be fully identified with what you are doing, for that implies "caring," the inverse side of Quality (*ZMM,* pp. 266–267). New appreciation, new level of performance—it all adds up to art. Your activity, however ordinary, has become art. If you were going to write a book about your activity, you might well entitle it *Zen and the Art of* ———.

If the experience of enlightenment amid everyday activity can turn everyday activity into art, how does that bear upon the specific art forms influenced by Zen? Were those art forms originally everyday activities? Some were. Tea drinking went on before the tea ceremony was developed. (Tea drinking, it might be noted, became a part of Japanese culture largely under the influence of Zen monks, who advocated tea's value for alertness in meditation as well as for general health.) Swords and bows were used before the pertinent Zen art forms were developed. On the other hand, some of the art forms were not developments of everyday activities but only came into existence as art forms, e.g., haiku poetry and ink brush painting. These art forms were frequently used to express the simplicity and the beauty to be found in everyday experiences and everyday objects, but you wouldn't say that the art forms themselves were everyday activities.

Whether the art forms were originally everyday activities or not, you can still ask why Zen became an important factor in their development. Why did the practitioners of Zen turn to such art forms? The answer revolves, at least in part, around the Zen idea of a "special transmission," the idea that enlightenment experience can be *transmitted* from mind to mind apart from the ordinary mode of teaching, which uses words to *explain* something. The Zen mode uses words and nonwords to *point* to an experience. Zen masters, who made use of a variety of materials and instruments to do the pointing, apparently saw in the various art forms Zen fingers, alternative media through which to effect a "special transmission," so they sought to suffuse those art forms with the teachings and spirit of Zen. You can find in the art forms symbols of the Zen idea that all reality is one. (For example, in Zen archery the archer and the target are one.) You can find symbols of the Zen idea of emptiness—the wonderful, nonsubstantial, ever-changing openness at the heart of things. (For example, in ink brush painting, empty space receives great attention.) You can find symbols of the Zen idea that *samsara*, the continuous cycle of transience and suffering, and *nirvana*, the cessation of that cycle, are one. (For example, haiku poetry expresses life's transience and somehow conveys the beauty of that transience.)

Two narratives recounting this combination of art and Zen resulted from a German couple's experiences in Japan between the two world wars. Eugen Herrigel, a philosophy teacher interested in mysticism, learned Zen by studying archery with a Zen master, and his wife Gustie learned Zen by studying flower arranging. Their books, *Zen in the Art of Archery* and *Zen in the Art of Flower Arrangement*, provided the inspiration for Robert Pirsig's memorable title.

Is this then the point of Zen's commingling with the arts, to convey Zen teachings? Yes and no. The teachings are worth conveying, but as teachings, as rationally discussible propositions about the way things are, they are not what Zen activity *ultimately* seeks to transmit. They can perhaps function as intermediate stages, but they are not what the Zen finger finally points to, which is enlightenment experience, an experience that gives you a new way of seeing what is in front of you and around you and within you. If through participation in the arts you have been led to such an experience, you will appreciate the Zen ideas that are embodied in the arts, but you will also be aware of the gap between the experience and the ideas. You won't mistake the finger for the moon.

The specialized arts, then, no less than everyday maintenance activities, can be a vehicle for the transmission of enlightenment experience. Once you've had such experience are you at the end of the Zen road? No. For one thing, your enlightenment can be deepened by more Zen practice and more instances of enlightenment experience. For another, enlightenment is not a personal treasure that calls for jealous guarding, but a gift that needs to be gladly shared. Recall the depiction of the Zen journey that is contained in the Oxherding Pictures (Section 3). After you've caught and tamed the ox and ridden it home, you forget the ox and yourself as well. This state is represented, in the eighth picture, by the great empty circle. At this point you are resting in the realization of the total oneness that comes with enlightenment. You don't stay there, however. The tenth picture, "Entering the Marketplace with Helping Hands," suggests that you make a point of reentering the everyday world and letting your enlightenment shine among others.

The narrator of *ZMM* makes a point of calling for the marketplace Zen that the tenth Oxherding Picture depicts; and he does it in the context of downplaying Phaedrus' personal achievement. He claims that the discovery of a Quality/Buddha connection "at some mountaintop of personal experience" is unimportant if not made relevant "to all the valleys of this world, and all the dull, dreary jobs and monotonous years that await all of us in them" (*ZMM*, pp. 229–230). How is the discovery to be made relevant? The narrator tells us, a little later on, that the process begins when a person's awareness of Quality starts to flow into Quality decisions. Those Quality decisions have a positive effect not only on the person and whatever job the person is doing but also on other people, "because the Quality tends to fan out like waves." Someone else sees the Quality job and "feels a little better because of it, and is likely to pass that feeling on to others, and in that way the Quality tends to keep on going" (*ZMM*, p. 323).

I think the narrator does well to call for radiation of enlightenment, but what about his downplaying Phaedrus' attainment? Is that perhaps a bit hasty? Would there be anything to radiate without enlightenment? Does enlightenment occur without a personal struggle? Zen tradition proclaims the ubiquity of the Buddha-nature and thereby attests to the possibility of enlightenment occurring anywhere, anytime; but at the same time, in its practices and its life stories, it attests to the importance of personal earnestness and exertion. So why doesn't the narrator give Phaedrus his due? Why doesn't he praise Phaedrus' effort and attainment? Does it come down to a defense mechanism of the narrator? At that point in his journey, was he wary of what might happen to him if he did not keep a proper distance from Phaedrus? Does it come down to the fact that Phaedrus did not simply become enlightened but actually became insane, thereby shutting himself off from the marketplace Zen that the narrator wished to celebrate? Should Phaedrus, could Phaedrus, have gone a different route? Or was the route fine and the only problem a lack of proper guidance when he reached the point of wall-gazing? Might things have ended up differently if a Zen master had been there with Phaedrus, in that bedless bedroom, when Phaedrus crossed that "lonesome valley" (*ZMM*, p. 358)?

I put this last question to the author of *ZMM*. Perhaps before you set aside the Zen packet and the Eastern portion of the backpack you would like to hear his answer. He began, on a general level, by talking about the connection between enlightenment and insanity. He didn't think all insanity was a form of enlightenment or all enlightenment was a form of insanity, but he did think there was an overlap. He made reference to a description of enlightenment in a Zen monastery, contained in Philip Kapleau's *Three Pillars of Zen*, according to which the enlightened "sits transfixed, unable to move, as if encased in a block of ice." Pirsig then pointed out that an unprepared psychiatrist coming upon such a scene "would immediately make a diagnosis of catatonia and hospitalize the person found in this state," whereas the Zen master "tries to end the state by snapping his fingers or giving a sharp command that will ease the student out of his unpatterned reality and back into the conventional form of patterned social behavior of the monastery. It is considered a dangerous time." At that point in the conversation, I pressed Pirsig a bit about what a Zen master would have done in his own case, the case described in *ZMM*. Pirsig responded, "It's impossible to say what a Zen master would or would not do under a given set of circumstances, but I think I would have been a lot happier if one had been around."

SECTION 5

A PHILOSOPHICAL
BACKPACK—WESTERN
PHILOSOPHY

As you remove and peruse the Western portion of your philosophical backpack, perhaps the first thing you will notice is the analytic knife, the standard instrument of classic Western reason (discussed and exemplified in *ZMM*, pp. 63–67 and 223). Altering the image from packets of information, we might say that the Western part of the backpack is made up of compartments (Reality, Knowledge, and Value) and that the compartments are in turn divided into such categories as idealism and realism, which are split into subdivisions, such as naïve realism and critical realism. Before you examine the contents of these compartments, you should be aware of a couple of things.

First, dividing philosophy into compartments is rather an arbitrary task. Nothing in the nature of humanity requires that it be done at all, and nothing in the nature of philosophy or in the nature of talk about philosophy requires that it be done in exactly *this* way. In a different context and for different purposes, philosophy might be divided differently or left undivided. Here it has been divided into the basic triad of Reality, Knowledge, and Value simply because that fits in well with the philosophical concerns of *ZMM*. My hope is to provide a handle on Western philosophy that is also a handle on the philosophies of Phaedrus and the narrator.

Second, our three compartments are not three separate, unrelated, airtight bins of thought. Questioning in one of the compartments flows into questioning in the other two; an answer in one of the compartments has repercussions in the other two. For example, you might ask whether reality is necessarily mind-dependent, i.e., whether whatever exists can only exist insofar as it is present to some form of consciousness (a question in the Reality compartment), and you might go on to ask how an alleged reality that existed outside the field of awareness of any and every mind could be known (a question in the Knowledge compartment). If your answer to the Reality question is the idealist answer that everything real is real in and for some mind or other, that answer will have repercussions in the Value compartment. You won't be able—at least not logically—to think of things as having value in themselves, apart from the activity of a valuing mind.

In other words, philosophical thinking flows freely wherever the desire to understand and the questions generated by that desire take it. It does not come prepackaged, compartmentalized. Only *after* this thinking has left behind its products—a proposition or set of propositions that asserts and argues for a particular view—can the compartmentalization occur. A compartmentalizer, who may or may not also be the original thinker, can then take these thought products, compare them with others, and say that they pertain to this or that compartment and that they represent this or that category within the compartment. The compartmentalizer might work with compartments already available or craft some afresh; the person with the knife can slice reality one way or another—or not slice it at all. But neither the carving nor the compartmentalizing should be confused with the original thinking that is the heart and soul of philosophy.

You might look at this section, with its compartments and contents, as a sort of intellectual menu. A menu can list and describe various food offerings in ways that are both informative and tantalizing, but the menu itself is not the meal, and the menu cannot guarantee that the food will be tasty, digestible, and nourishing. That depends upon the match between, on the one hand, the food and cooking and, on the other, your palate and digestive system. The following menu of philosophical positions is bound to leave you feeling empty if you don't taste and chew some of the intellectual food that's offered, but even the best of philosophical cooks can't guarantee a match for your intellectual palate.

To change the metaphor, you might look at this section as a sort of intellectual map (see the introductory part of Section 3). A map has the advantage of portable utility, but it offers no substitute for the freshness of an actual intellectual journey. It can describe various places and tell you how to get to them, perhaps offering more than one route, but it can't take the place of your choosing a destination or a route, taking the trip, and arriving someplace. Nor can a map predict the satisfaction or dissatisfaction that you will feel during the trip or upon arrival. Similarly, this section describes various philosophical positions and some of the reasoning that has led thinkers to those positions, but it cannot take the place of your deciding to follow (and perhaps extend) or dismiss a particular line of reasoning, nor can it predict what might happen if you sample an unfamiliar way of thinking.

When intellectual mapping activity and its products are confused with or substituted for actual intellectual journeying, something very important is lost. Flesh and blood people like Phaedrus who try both to penetrate the mystery of life and make sense of their own lives—philosophers in the original sense, "lovers of wisdom"—are replaced by professional philosophers, specialists in abstract thinking who by their proficiency have earned a badge that can be worn or removed as the occasion demands. ("What do you want to be when you grow up?" "I want to be a philosopher." "I think I know a place where you can get that badge.") And just as a way of thinking is divorced from a way of living, so the resultant thought products—in the form of writings—are divorced from both the living and the thinking, and those who develop the skill of inspecting, naming, and classifying those thought products also usurp the name "philosophers," thus effecting a further degradation of the name. ("What do philosophers do?" "They investigate and classify the philosophical residue of other philosophers." "I think you've just given a 'circular definition.'" "Good point. I think you'd make a good philosopher.")

I think it's important here, before the mapmaking and the map reading begin, to draw attention to the difference between philosophy as a way of life, a life centering on the search for wisdom, and philosophy as badge-earning activity, activity that demonstrates either the ability for high-powered abstraction or the ability to analyze and categorize the philosophical residue of others. The point is not that one is bad and the other good—Quality can show itself in both. The point is that, if both are to flourish, philosophy as badge-earning activity should not be allowed to masquerade as philosophy pure and simple. Calling attention to the distinction between a map and a journey is one small effort in the direction of preventing the masquerade. Mapping activity can stimulate an intellectual journey and point to a philosophical way of life, but it is not in itself either one, and it can just as easily—perhaps more easily—point to and participate in philosophy as badge-earning activity.

I do not mean to suggest that mapping activity is worthless. That would be to trivialize in advance what I am about to do. ("Poisoning the well"—in this case, my own—is what a "good philosopher" might call it.) I just want to warn against a costly confusion—and perhaps also protect myself against the invective of Phaedrus. Phaedrus, you will recall, had angry words for those professional academicians who followed in the footsteps of Aristotle the Mapmaker, not the harder-to-find Aristotle the Journeyer. These professionals have reduced teaching and learning to naming and classifying and have thereby "smugly and callously killed the creative spirit of their students" (*ZMM*, p. 325). Such teachers might have been less prone to murder had they been more alive to the distinction between a map and a journey. Perhaps my emphasizing the distinction will call off the wrath of Phaedrus. Perhaps it will also modulate the voice of another ghost that you might hear in what follows, "the ghost of Aristotle speaking down through the centuries—the desiccating lifeless voice of dualistic reason" (*ZMM*, p. 326).

If you do experience a little desiccation from the carving, labeling, and compartmentalizing that follows, perhaps you will find relief in the flowing waters of the dialogue that appears as the final portion of this philosophical backpack. While the intellectual technique of naming and classifying, in philosophy and elsewhere, goes back to Aristotle, the dialogue as a mode of philosophical discourse goes back to Aristotle's teacher, Plato. I think it's quite fitting that this backpack conclude with the mode of discourse favored by "the essential Buddha-seeker" rather than with the mode favored by "the eternal motorcycle mechanic" (see *ZMM*, p. 331)—after all, *ZMM* concludes with the return of Phaedrus to the driver's seat.

REALITY

When you ask broad questions about reality, you have entered the area of philosophy known as metaphysics. The word itself was coined by Aristotle's followers sometime after Aristotle's death, when it was used as the title for a particular set of Aristotle's treatises. Why it was called *Metaphysics* is open to question. One speculation is that the title originally referred to the location of the work within the collection of one of Aristotle's followers (Adronicus of Rhodes). Since this set of Aristotle's treatises was located on the shelf "after" (*meta* in Greek) a work that dealt with "nature" (*physica* in Greek), the set was called *Metaphysica*. Another speculation is that Aristotle's followers coined the word as a way of saying that the treatises, because of their greater abstractness, should be studied only *after* the treatises dealing with nature. A third speculation is that the title was meant to indicate that the treatises went intellectually "beyond"—*meta* means "beyond" as well as "after"—the work on nature. Whatever the motivation behind the title, the book that was gathered together under the title raised questions that cut wide and deep. It asked about the fundamental principles, the causes and constituents, not simply of this or that sector of things, but of all things, of whatever is, of *being* as a whole. Ever since the time that Aristotle's wide-ranging book was given its title, metaphysics has been the area of philosophy in which the broadest questions about reality are asked. As was stated earlier, the work "metaphysics" has also come to be associated with the occult, with strange, seemingly inexplicable phenomena that go beyond what is ordinarily considered natural. When the word "metaphysics" is used in *ZMM* it is used in the Aristotelian, not the occult, sense.

Here are some examples of metaphysical questions: What is the nature of reality? Is all reality of one basic kind? What is it? If there is more than one kind, how many kinds are there and what are they? If mind or consciousness is a basic principle, how basic is it? Can there be any reality that is not contained in a mind? Is there one source or more than one source for all the things that are? If there is one source, does that source have an existence that is independent of all the things that come from it, or has it somehow entered into all the things that come from it, or is it somehow both independent of (transcendent) and present within (immanent) the things that come from it? If there is more than one source, what is the relation between or among them? Are they on the same level, or is there a hierarchy? Are they antagonistic or cooperative? Whatever the source or sources, are they subject to change in any way or are they absolutely immutable? Is change real or illusory? Is permanence real or illusory? Are the many things of our experience really many or are they really one? Are they both one and many? Why is there anything at all rather than nothing?

As you can see, these are not the questions that you typically take along with you to spark a conversation at the hair salon. Why in the world would anyone ever ask them? One answer is that people ask them because they *can,* just as they climb the mountain because it is there. Another answer is that sometimes a crisis that removes a taken-for-granted sense of security brings on a metaphysical search for a new basis of security. If, for example, you are used to thinking of the gods as the immortal sources of everything else and you begin to lose faith in the existence of the gods, you may begin to search for some other permanent reality or realities that explain what is. According to the narrator's reading (*ZMM*, p. 336), this is how metaphysical speculation got started in ancient Greece.

REAL OR IDEAL?

Is reality "real" or "ideal"? That may seem like a strange question to ask, but it is not so strange if you know what the terms "realism" and "idealism" came to mean in the history of Western philosophy. At the outset, you should note that the philosophical use of those terms is quite different from that found in everyday conversation. In everday conversation, we might say that a person who tends to be a bit cynical about the purity of human motivation or who at least is very practical and down-to-earth is a "realist," whereas a person who tends to believe the best about people or who, in any case, strives to reach and maintain the highest standards is an "idealist." This is not the distinction that Western philosophical mappers have had in mind.

To become clear about the philosophical distinction, you first have to understand what is meant by "mind." A mind is a center of consciousness or awareness. As you read this section, various things may enter your awareness: the texture and coloration of the printed page, meanings of words and phrases and statements, questions about what I'm driving at and what difference that might make, and so on. Those things are "in" your mind—mental contents. If you reflect upon the awareness that somehow holds them, you are reflecting upon your mind. Notice that in doing so, you are not sensing or thinking about the physical object that we call the brain (unless perhaps this stuff is giving you a headache). Whether or not the mind is totally dependent upon the brain is a further question. Whatever the answer to that question, the fact remains that you can be aware of your awareness without being aware of the physical object that neurophysiologists study. It's that awareness of awareness that you should "keep in mind"—don't worry about what your brain is doing—as we talk about the distinction between philosophical realists and philosophical idealists.

Basically, a philosophical "realist" is a person who believes that a thing can be real without being either itself a mind or contained in a mind. Reality is not, as such, mind-dependent. Whatever is to be said about the prevalence or importance of mind in the universe, it is one thing to be real and another to be mental. A philosophical "idealist," on the other hand, says that a thing is real only insofar as it is a mind or contained therein. Reality, as such, is mind-dependent. A nonmental reality is a contradiction in terms. A realist looks at a motorcycle and says that it could really exist— or at least its real existence is conceivable—even if somehow all minds, all awareness, in the universe ceased to be. An idealist says that the motorcycle is mental stuff, through and through. Take away mind and you take away the cycle. In a mindless universe, a universe without awareness, there would be no visual consciousness. In such a universe, what would a motorcycle look like?

You can divide up philosophical realism in various ways. For example, you can divide it up according to how realists support their realism. If you divide it this way, your carving activity may yield "naïve realism," "critical realism," and "pragmatic realism." A "naïve realist" supports realism by saying that little or no support is called for. Of course things can be real without being present in a mind. It's a matter of common sense, like the sun rising and setting! The naïve realist says, Do you want to know how I refute the idealist position? I refute it by kicking this stone! (Samuel Johnson is reported to have refuted Bishop Berkeley's idealism in just this way.) The vast majority of human beings on planet earth are probably naïve realists, whether or not they have ever paid explicit attention to philosophical questions or debates.

(Of course, if you ask me how I know this, I might say something silly, like "It's a matter of common sense!") By the way, the word "naïve," as it's used here, is not a pejorative term. It is simply the mapper's way of noting the fact that realism can be and is embraced on more or less spontaneous grounds.

A "critical realist," on the other hand, takes the claims and arguments of idealists more seriously and believes that it's not enough to embrace realism spontaneously. It has to be carefully argued, not just proclaimed; and the case for realism has to be made in the face of the case for idealism. The critical realist is "critical" not in the sense of being "negative" but in the sense of being "careful and reflective."

The case for idealism might run something like this: When you are aware of something, what you are aware of is *in your mind.* You cannot be aware of what is *outside your mind.* If you say that you are aware of something outside your mind, for example a motorcycle, you are making the contradictory claim that you are aware of a motorcycle that is not in your awareness. If you are a determined realist, you might say, of course, that the mental motorcycle is caused by an extramental one, and you might add that you know the extramental motorcycle through the medium of the mental one. But how do you support such claims? Anything you could refer to by way of support, any evidence you could offer— for instance the exhaust fumes—would also be in your mind; otherwise you couldn't refer to it. So you still haven't bridged the gap between your mind and the alleged extramental thing. Sooner or later you will have to join the company of idealists and admit that it's all in the mind.

Before offering a counterargument, the critical realist might point out that such a line of thinking flirts with "solipsism," the view that "I myself alone" exist, as a mind, since everything else is only an entity in my awareness. The idealist might respond that the logic of idealism allows for the existence of more than one mind. Many of the things in my mind may be there through the influence of other minds, including the mind of my realist opponent. That makes more sense than saying that the things in my mind are somehow caused by things of an entirely different nature, extramental things. What could those mysterious extramental things be like? Any positive conception I could have of them would be in terms of some form of consciousness (visual consciousness, aural consciousness, tactile consciousness, intellectual consciousness, etc.). Even my *conception* of the extramental is bounded by the mental. As to what the alleged extramental might be *in itself*, I haven't a clue. When I talk about other minds, on the other hand, at least I know what I'm talking about. Moreover, the idealist might continue, minds don't have to be on the same level. There can be a Big Mind, a Universal Mind, a Creative Mind, that causes and maintains everything that exists. Thanks to that Mind, everything that enters your mind doesn't begin to exist only when it enters your mind. It's already in the Universal Mind. And thanks to that Mind, the book that you're reading won't vanish out of existence when you leave the room!

As to the counterargument of the critical realist, to draw it out, let us use our analytic knife to carve out of critical realism a subcategory, "transcendental realism." Transcendental realists owe a lot of their inspiration to Immanuel Kant (1724–1804), who was actually a transcendental idealist, not a transcendental realist. As a transcendental idealist, Kant rooted his version of idealism in the attention he paid to the *internal or necessary conditions* of possible experiential knowledge. He said that if you paid attention to those internal prerequisites, you would see that you can never really know things as they are in themselves, but only as they are shaped by your mind. The internal conditions that Kant had in mind included your sense of space and your sense of time and a number of species-wide categories, such as "substance," that you carry around with you (see *ZMM*, pp. 116–119 and p. 116, above). Since the time of Kant, the word "transcendental" has been associated in philosophy with a kind of thinking that seeks to support a position by calling attention to the internal conditions of knowing. Transcendental realists say that when you pay close attention to the conditions inherent in the process of knowing, you end up in the realist camp rather than the idealist camp.

A transcendental realist might argue as follows: When you have a desire to know something, you are consciously aiming toward what is—not toward a copy of what is or a mere substitute for what is or a mere mental content, but toward *what is*. Thus in your very desire to know, there is already an anticipatory awareness, a general notion of what reality is. It is toward the to-be-known toward which your desire to know is directed. Will you reach the target? That will depend upon your own resources and what you are trying to know. In some instances you will be successful through a combination of experience, understanding, and judgment. To the data of experience you will bring questions that somehow indicate what you want to know. The tension of questioning will every so often yield to the eureka experience of insight. You've reached an understanding of how things might be, of a possible unity or relationship that you previously didn't know. However, not satisfied with an understanding of how things *might* be, you will press on. You will bring to your understanding reflective questions that seek to determine what conditions must be fulfilled if you are to know that your understanding is correct. If you are successful in determining the conditions, you will push on to see if you can determine whether or not the conditions are fulfilled. If you are successful in that, you will be ready to make judgments. You will have reached the to-be-known toward which you were aiming. You will be able to say something about what is, about reality. You don't have to confine your talk to mental contents, in spite of what the idealist says. You will have aimed further than that and gotten there. (You can find an extended version of this sort of argument in the work of the twentieth-century Canadian thinker Bernard Lonergan [1904–1984], especially in his master work, *Insight.*)

You might notice that the sort of argument that comes out of transcendental realism illustrates what was said earlier about the interrelatedness of the compartments of philosophy. Transcendental realists make use of epistemological considerations—claims reached within the compartment of Knowledge—to back up a metaphysical position—a position within the compartment of Reality. When they are doing that, of course, they are not thinking of themselves as passing from the Reality compartment to the Knowledge compartment and back again (unless they are trying to map their journey while they are taking it). They are simply going with the flow of their own questioning. There might have been a time when it was quite easy for seekers of wisdom to confine their attention to questions about reality without finding themselves raising questions about knowledge. That day is gone. At least, it's gone for thinkers who have passed through the trails carved out by the philosophers who ushered in the modern era, philosophers like Descartes and Hume and, especially, Kant. Once you've traversed those trails, you're bound to find Reality considerations and Knowledge considerations flowing into each other. The map is not the journey, but the journey is influenced by the maps you've seen.

The naïve realist says realism is simply a matter of common

sense. The critical realist says that the case for realism can and should be carefully argued, notably by using Knowledge considerations. The pragmatic realist says that the realist position is proved by asking the practical question, What difference does it make? If thinking of your life and the world in realist terms ("Reality is more than mental contents") is *more fruitful* than thinking of your life and the world in idealist terms ("It's all in the mind"), then realism makes a positive difference and you've got good grounds for adopting it. From a pragmatic viewpoint, the ultimate test of the truth of any position is whether or not that position *works*. Realism works.

How might a pragmatic realist argue that the realist perspective works better and is more fruitful than the idealist perspective? The argument might go something like this: When you're operating within a realist perspective, you don't expect reality to appear and act in ways that conform to all of your present thoughts about it—reality is more than mental contents. Your mental contents can be missing something. You can be *mistaken!* So you constantly try to bring your thoughts into line with a reality that is more than your thoughts, thus opening yourself up to progress in knowing. Similarly, as a realist you don't expect reality to conform to your wishes and desires—reality is not simply a projection of the mind. Reality *impinges* on you! So you constantly try to adjust your desires and your actions to the demands of a reality that overrides the constructions of wishful thinking, thus opening yourself up to progress in harmonious living. Belief in external reality leads to progress in knowing and living. Realism works.

But does idealism also work? asks the pragmatic realist. If you're operating within an idealist perspective and believe that everything is an event in the mind, is there anything that can call into queston the contents of your mind? Anything that can make you think that you may have been mistaken? Is there anything that can act as the standard for improving your understanding of things? Anything that can keep you from wishful thinking? Or that can spur you on to more harmonious, well-adjusted living? External reality might have done all of those things, but you've banished external reality. Perhaps, in spite of your idealist position, you act *as if* there were an external reality that urged you on to correct your thinking and adjust your living. But if that is the case, why not simply admit that realism works and is therefore true?

An idealist is not rendered speechless by such a realist challenge. The conversation never ends. An idealist can claim that what drives you toward greater perfection in knowing and living is not some extramental reality, but other minds, and above all the Big Mind. The Big Mind lures you on toward the perfection of its own mental universe. Thanks to the pull of the Big Mind, you are not satisfied with whatever is in your consciousness at a given time. You seek a fuller Truth and a greater Good, a Truth and a Good that owe their existence to the Big Mind. To this idealist counter, the pragmatic realist might respond that while such thinking might provide a certain comfort and even a certain motivation, you don't need it to function well in everyday life, whereas you do need the notion of extramental reality. If you see a car coming toward you, you'd better view it as an extramental reality and make an appropriate extramental move, and you had better not waste time thinking about what the Big Mind may be trying to impart to your little mind!

This last pragmatic realist move leads us to note a further point about pragmatic realism. It is not just a way of establishing the general realist outlook. It is also a way of working out the details within that outlook, a way of figuring out what counts as real. If you're thinking of something and want to know whether it's real, ask what difference the alleged reality makes in the world. If it doesn't make the slightest difference, if the world and your life in the world would be exactly the same even if the alleged reality were absent, that's a sign that you're not thinking of anything real at all. On the other hand, if in supposing the alleged reality's absence you see that the world would be quite different, perhaps even dysfunctional, that's a sign that you're thinking of something quite real.

Phaedrus performed a thought experiment along these lines when he was thinking of how to respond to people who questioned the existence of undefined Quality. He tried to imagine a world without Quality and found that in significant ways such a world would function abnormally. That to him was proof enough that Quality exists, whether or not it's defined. (See *ZMM*, pp. 193–194.) Interestingly, the narrator locates Phaedrus' response within "a philosophic school that called itself *realism*" (*ZMM*, p. 193, italics Pirsig's). The narrator must have had some version of pragmatic realism in mind.

So far we've divided realism according to the criteria by which it's established: spontaneously, theoretically, or pragmatically. We can also divide it according to the sorts of things that realists allow in their world. One swift move of the knife and you have the categories "materialism" and "antimaterialism." A materialist thinks of the real world as populated by material things and nothing else. An antimaterialist denies that material things are the whole story of reality. Note that the antimaterialist needn't deny the existence of matter. An antimaterialist who is also an idealist would, of course, but an antimaterialist who is also a realist simply wants to make room for nonmaterial realities. The problem isn't matter. The problem is the materialist restriction.

To help us better understand the category of materialism, it might be useful to subdivide it into "deliberate materialism" and "nondeliberate materialism." If you're a nondeliberate materialist, you think of reality in material terms, but you don't say things like, "All reality is material" or "Those who believe in immaterial realities are wrong." You don't say such things because the distinction between the material and the nonmaterial hasn't occurred to you, at least not with any clarity. Your thinking is simply confined to categories that those who do make the distinction would call material. A number of the pre-Socratic, cosmological thinkers of ancient Greece seem to be categorizable as nondeliberate materialists. Those thinkers were trying to get at the one constant reality underlying and somehow permeating the many, changing things that make up the world, and when they thought they reached it, they called it water or air or fire (see *ZMM*, p. 336). You might call their thinking materialist, but they certainly weren't arguing explicitly and deliberately for materialism as opposed to antimaterialism. (Phaedrus makes a similar but perhaps more radical point about those thinkers, when he says that at that point in time "there was no such thing as mind and matter," since the dichotomy of mind and matter hadn't been invented yet— *ZMM*, p. 337.)

An example of deliberate materialism is modern "scientific materialism," according to which things only have real existence insofar as they have matter and energy; otherwise they exist only in the mind. (Despite the suggestion given by the label, if Phaedrus is right, such a view is "commoner among lay followers of science than among scientists themselves"—*ZMM*, pp. 209–210.) If you want to adopt this view critically rather than naïvely, you will have to take into account the antimaterialist challenge to scientific materialism.

One version of that challenge is to be found in *ZMM*. In a way, the whole philosophy of Quality is a challenge to scientific materialism. More specifically, the narrator and Phaedrus make explicit remarks about the incoherence of scientific materialism. The narrator does so in the context of a ghost-story-telling session, in which he points out that scientific laws, from the scientific materialist viewpoint, are unscientific and unreal because they lack matter and energy—just like ghosts. After expanding on such ideas at some length (*ZMM*, pp. 28–32), the narrator confesses that he has "stolen" them from Phaedrus (*ZMM*, p. 33). As the narrator later recounts, Phaedrus reached a similar insight when he was thinking through his defense of Quality. Scientific materialism threatened to impale Quality on the "subjective horn" by saying that if Quality is not scientifically knowable, i.e., composed of matter and energy, it is therefore unreal and unimportant. Phaedrus saw that scientific concepts and laws themselves would be impaled and reduced, too. (See *ZMM*, pp. 209–211.) If you want to defend scientific materialism, then, you will have to say something about the status of scientific laws and concepts. More generally, you will have to say something about the status of mind. As the narrator puts it: "The problem, the contradiction the scientists are stuck with, is that of *mind*. Mind has no matter or energy but they can't escape its predominance over everything they do" (*ZMM*, p. 31, italics Pirsig's).

If you're a scientific materialist, you'll have to respond to this challenge, it seems, along one of two lines. The first is to the effect that concepts and minds (including the minds of scientists) are scientifically unreal but nonetheless important. If you say that, however, you seem to take away the point of the distinction between the real and the unreal. If the unreal can be as important as the real or even more important, perhaps the search for knowledge of reality ought to give way to a search for knowledge of the important. (In a way, Phaedrus' philosophical journey moved in the direction of such a shift. As an aspect of Quality, Importance is at the top of the metaphysical hierarchy, and intellectual reality, including scientific knowledge, is subordinate to it. However, Phaedrus did not hesitate to equate Quality with Reality, since he was not held back by scientific materialism.)

The second line of response is to the effect that concepts and minds do, after all, have a kind of matter or energy to them and are therefore real. Notice here that you can't get away with a facile identification of mind with brain. It's clear that you can be aware of your mind and what's going on in it, your awareness and its contents, without being aware of your brain, its cells, and its functions. Similarly, someone could conceivably study the brain of a living person without knowing what is going on in that person's mind. There is *some* distinction between mind and brain. The matter and energy of the brain are scientifically detectable, but that is not the case with the alleged matter and energy in awareness and ideas. So if you're a scientific materialist, how will you back up your claim? Perhaps you will say that while mind and brain are distinct, mind is *reducible* to brain. Then the question becomes, What do you mean by "reducible"? If you mean that the matter and energy in the brain somehow permeate awareness and ideas, you are back to your unsupported claim. If you mean that mind, though not itself a form of matter, is totally *dependent* upon the brain and its functioning, it sounds like you are ready to admit that material reality isn't the only kind there is. (And, by the way, you won't establish the mind's total dependence simply by pointing out correlations between mental activity and brain activity. A number of logical fallacies—such as "causal oversimplification," "neglect of common cause," and "cause-effect confusion"—are easily committed along this line of reasoning.)

Among the antimaterialists, none is more important in the history of Western thought than Plato (427–347 B.C.). There is something to the view of Whitehead, cited approvingly by Phaedrus, that the rest of Western philosophy is nothing but "footnotes to Plato" (*ZMM*, p. 302), although we can't take this to mean that later thinkers did not take significant and varying journeys of their own. Later thinkers—at least the ones who left behind maps of their journeys—felt compelled to make use of the map left by Plato, if not as a means for getting their bearings on the journey itself, at least as an important reference point for when they got around to describing where they had traveled and where they had arrived. Plato's map became and remains the standard reference point. Phaedrus developed and formulated his philosophy of Quality, for example, with reference to Plato's similar but significantly different philosophy of the Good.

In Plato's view, material reality is a second-class, subordinate type of reality. The first-class type is a "Form" (also called an "Essence" or an "Idea"). If you want to understand what a Form is, first think of some beautiful object or person; then note that that object or person, however beautiful, is not Beauty Itself, not the absolute summit of beauty, not the ultimate standard by which all beautiful things and persons are measured. Tomorrow you might encounter something or someone more beautiful, and the day after you might encounter something or someone more beautiful yet. (For example, at the beginning of *Romeo and Juliet*, Romeo thought he was in love with a beautiful woman, but he soon discovered, when Juliet entered his life, that he hadn't known what love or beauty was.) If your ultimate standard of beauty were some particular object or person, you wouldn't be able to recognize surpassing beauty. The particular object or person would be the unsurpassable measure. Such recognition is not impossible, however, because, more or less faintly or sharply, you retain a notion of Beauty Itself—the "Form" Beauty. (If you are in love, you might be tempted to equate the standard with some particular person. In that case, maybe you ought to vary the example and think about the difference between a particular instance of justice and Justice Itself or between a particular instance of happiness and Happiness Itself—either that or accept the Platonist analysis that the person with whom you are in love is for you an exceptionally strong "reminder" of Beauty Itself.)

Forms lie behind and are the measure of every particular thing or event in the world. They are the measure not only of what we designate by abstract nouns like "justice" and "beauty" but also of what we designate by concrete nouns like "tree" and "horse." At the same time, in Plato's view, there is a marked contrast between the world of Forms and the world of particulars. Forms are non-material, whereas particulars are material. (The exception is the particular human intellect, which thus bridges the two worlds.) Forms are permanent and changeless; particulars are changing. (Your ideas about Forms can change, but not the Forms themselves—hence, it's probably wise to avoid the label "Ideas.") Forms are indestructible; particulars are destructible. (Again, the exception is the human mind.) Forms are knowable intellectually—notably through the "dialectic," a process that moves toward the highest understanding of reality through the interaction of questions and answers or positions and counterpositions; particulars are knowable through the senses. Forms are perfect and most truly real; particulars imperfect and less real—they have a relationship to Forms that is analogous to that between shadows and the things that cast them. (*ZMM*'s explicit discussion of Plato's forms is found on pp. 330, 342–343.)

Aristotle (384–322 B.C.) accepted the reality of the nonmaterial entities that Plato called Forms. However, being more the "motorcycle mechanic" than the "Buddha-seeker" (*ZMM*, p. 331), he couldn't accept his teacher's devaluation of particular things; so he made a crucial move. He located the Forms *within* concrete, particular things. Now instead of two separate worlds, one of Forms and one of particulars, there was one world, a world of particular things.

Particular things, in Aristotle's view, have a certain permanence about them (a permanence that Plato finds only in the world of Forms), even while they are subject to change: A tree changes colors without ceasing to be a tree; a horse grows in size without ceasing to be a horse. And what is the root of this permanence or constant identity? It is the thing's *internal form,* or intelligible structure, a sort of "master pattern" that the intellect can detect when it penetrates beyond the thing's changing sensory qualities. Every particular thing in the universe has such a form, or structure, or pattern (or built-in "program," to use a computer analogy) and thus maintains a basic identity throughout its variations. On the other hand, particular things do change because of their "matter." Reality is thus made up of particular things that are each composed of form and matter. Those particular things are called "substances" (from the Greek, by way of a Latin translation that literally means "that which stands beneath"), because, owing to the internal presence of form, they have a constant identity that "stands beneath" the various changes that the senses detect.

Phaedrus claimed that with Aristotle's doctrine of particular substances, and not before then, the "modern scientific understanding of reality was born"—*ZMM*, p. 343. What did he mean by that? He probably meant something like this: The shift from a world of Forms to a world of *substances that contain forms* meant that you looked *within* things, not beyond them, for their explanation, and it meant that the sensory world was seen not as a distraction but as a gateway to the understanding of reality. This model paved the way for the empirical method of modern science, a method in which the full engagement and cooperation of senses and intellect is crucial.

Both Plato and Aristotle were "realists" in the sense that we have been using that term. Both accepted the reality (in Plato's case, the secondary reality) of material things; neither said that "being real" and "being mental" were synonymous. Plato and

Aristotle were also "realists" in another sense, a sense that opposes realism to nominalism. A nominalist says that universal terms like "beauty" or "justice" or "horseness" or "humanness" are just names that we use to group together and talk about a number of particular things—and that those terms don't refer to anything real. Particular beautiful things really exist, but beauty as such does not really exist. Particular human beings really exist, but humanness as such does not exist. As opposed to a nominalist, a realist says that universal terms do refer to real entities. Plato says the terms refer to Forms that exist apart from particulars. Aristotle says the terms refer to forms that are real components within real existing things.

Thus, Plato and Aristotle are realists in two philosophical senses; materialists are realists in the first sense discussed, but not in the second; idealists are realists in the second sense but not in the first.

Are you thoroughly confused now? If not, how would you categorize the views of Phaedrus and the narrator?

ONE OR MANY?

Is reality one or many? If you say that it's basically one, you are a "monist." If you say that it's basically more than one, you are a "pluralist." If as a pluralist you say that reality is basically twofold, you are a "dualist." (Among pluralistic models, dualism alone has acquired a distinct numerical label, because the representatives of dualism have been many in number and strong in influence. Hence, Phaedrus found it somewhat awkward that he had reached a metaphysical position that seemed to invovle *three* basic realities—*ZMM*, p. 214.)

When you ask about reality's oneness or manyness, you might be wondering whether there is one or more than one *source* of all that is. If you answer that there is one and only one source, you are a monist of sorts. Jews, Christians, and Muslims—believing as they do in God the Creator—are all monists in this sense. But this type of monism—a "monism-of-source"—is a rather weak type of monism, since there can be one Source and at the same time a radical difference between that Source and everything else. ("Monism" is used in this weak sense in *ZMM* on p. 214.)

To arrive at a stronger type of monism, ask whether reality is one in *kind* as well as in source. Is there one and only one basic kind of thing that is both the source and the substance of all that exists? Some of the early Greek cosmological thinkers (see *ZMM*, pp. 336–337) answered yes and hence were monists in a stronger sense. Thales of Miletus (sixth century B.C.), for example, said the One was water; Anaximenes (sixth century B.C.) said it was air. They both were saying that the many things of our experience are simply expressions of the One—different forms of water or air— and not, at bottom, anything different. Notice how much stronger—more One-ful—is their kind of monism than a monism-of-source: A Jew or Christian or Muslim, while granting that everything depends on the One God, isn't likely to grant that God's creatures are, at bottom, nothing different from God. A monism-of-kind is further exemplified by both thoroughgoing materialists and thoroughgoing idealists. The materialist says that everything is simply a variation on the theme of matter/energy; the idealist says that everything is simply a variation on the theme of mind. Both say that all is one in kind.

This stronger sense of "monism" is exemplified in *ZMM* on p. 226. Phaedrus came to see that he had shifted from his original position—a position involving three distinct entities: Quality, mind, and matter—toward an "absolute monism," with Quality being the "source and substance of everything." He thus found himself in the company of the great German philosopher, Georg W. Hegel (1770–1831). Although Phaedrus didn't explicitly note it, he also was in the company of another famous monist, Baruch (Benedict) Spinoza (1632–1677). Spinoza's monism is perhaps worth noting here, because Phaedrus' opponent at the University of Chicago, the chairman of the Committee on Analysis of Ideas and Study of Methods, was a Spinozist (*ZMM*, p. 309)—a touch of irony.

If you accept both a monism-of-kind and a monism-of-source, you still haven't reached the limit of monism. You can ask whether reality is one in *number*. Is there really one and only one thing? Is the common view that there are many distinct and separate things mistaken? Is our experience of manyness somehow illusory? A "monist-of-number" will say yes to all of those questions. There is not simply one source that gives rise to everything else; nor is there simply one kind of reality that is shared by the originating One and everything else. Rather, there is simply no "everything else"; there is only the One. The many in their manyness are an illusion. They don't really exist in plurality. They are either false mental projections (a sort of cosmic dream or cosmic trick) or else real parts of the One (like the parts of your body), but in neither case do they have a separate reality of their own. All is One; One is all.

Enough said about monism. What about pluralism? For present backpack purposes, it will be enough to note a few things about *dualism*. Like monism, metaphysical dualism can be carved into several forms. For example, as with monism, we can split *source* from *kind* and thereby carve out two distinct dualisms. However, in contrast with monism, a dualism-of-source is "stronger" than a dualism-of-kind. If you believe in a dualism-of-source, you believe that there are two radically different principles or agents that give rise to all that exists; and most probably you also think that the world is a battlefield wherein those two agents and their offspring are in a constant struggle for supremacy. Reality is a struggle of Good against Evil, Light against Darkness, Spirit against Matter. (An example of this sort of dualism is Zoroastrianism, a religious and philosophical tradition that began in ancient Persia. Manichaeism, an offshoot of Zoroastrianism, attempted a synthesis between this sort of dualism and Christianity.)

Which of the two principles will win out? Perhaps you cherish a strong hope as to the outcome—but if you know for certain, then you're not the sort of dualist we're talking about. If you know for certain, it must be because you know that one of the two allegedly ultimate principles is really in charge, in which case only one of the two principles is truly ultimate (and history is just a stage for playing out a prewritten drama).

If you believe in a dualism-of-kind, you hold that there are two eternally distinct kinds of reality. You might hold that the two distinct realities are to be thought of as *separate things*. (For example, along with Plato you might think of Forms and particulars as separate things, or along with René Descartes [1596–1650] you might think of minds and bodies as separate—or at least separable—things.) On the other hand, you might think of the two distinct realities not as separate things but as two *distinct components* within a single thing. (For example, along with Aristotle you might think of form and matter as the coconstituents of a thing, or along with Taoist philosophy—see pp. 103–104—you might think of yin and yang as complementary forces running through every single thing or event.)

In either case, a dualism-of-kind doesn't necessarily imply a battle between the two kinds. Although you find a hint of such a battle in Plato's philosophy, inasmuch as the world of sensory particulars is said to distract you from the task of knowing the Forms, there is talk of the two working together. Sensory knowledge of a particular can be the occasion of your "recollecting" a Form, and in turn the knowledge of a Form (e.g., Justice) can provide the standard for adjusting and improving particulars (e.g., a concrete political situation). When you turn to Aristotle's modification of Plato's philosophy, the hint of a battle is gone, the suggestion of cooperation strengthened. Matter looks to form for structure and purpose; form looks to matter for a context in which to realize structure and purpose. Similarly, in Taoist philosophy, yang and yin are more like dancing partners than opposing boxers; they are meant to produce balance and harmony rather than mutual elimination.

If you like, you can split dualism-of-kind into *egalitarian* and *hierarchical* dualism. In the former case, your two kinds or principles are considered equal—or at least no explicit judgment is made as to the superiority of one over the other. In the latter case, one of the two kinds is considered superior. Plato's dualism of Forms and particulars is an example of hierarchical dualism. Another example is spirit-matter dualism in the context of a monotheistic religion. In that context, spirit is typically regarded as a higher form of reality than matter, since God is thought of as spiritual; on the other hand, matter is not to be thought of as worthless or as the enemy of spirit, since God is thought of as Creator of all, of matter as well as spirit. The hierarchical dualism in such a context remains a dualism-of-kind, not an antagonistic dualism-of-source. (Hence, the Manichaean attempt to blend a dualism-of-source with Christianity could have succeeded only at the expense of Christian monotheism.)

A clear example of egalitarian dualism is not easy to find in Western thought. Aristotle's dualism of form and matter is perhaps less blatantly hierarchical than Plato's dualism, since form and matter are explicitly thought of as complementary; but form is still considered the higher principle. Twentieth-century thinkers such as Martin Heidegger (1889–1976) and Jacques Derrida (1930–) hold that Western dualisms are so many variations on the theme of *presence* and *absence* and that, no matter what the variation, preeminence is always given to the principle representing presence.

Thus form (in contrast to matter) gives something definition and thereby calls it out of the background into the foreground, making it more present; mind (in contrast to body) makes something present in awareness. Are such thinkers right? Are there no exceptions? Maybe there are, but none come to mind.

If you want a clear example of egalitarian dualism, you perhaps need to turn to the East, to the yin-yang philosophy that is found within Taoism. Yin, the "female" principle (space, receptivity, openness—"absence"), and yang, the "male" principle (solidity, assertion, focus—"presence") are thought of as equally important as well as complementary. This equality is perhaps due to the fact that the Tao, the One that gives rise to the two, is not thought of as exclusively yin or exclusively yang but as both or, better, neither—or, perhaps better still, beyond "both" and "neither," since linguistic distinctions come only with the arising of duality. In this connection, you might want to consider the relation between Taoist thought and Phaedrus' philosophy of Quality (see *ZMM*, pp. 226–228 and above, pp. 114–115). Just as Tao is neither yin nor yang, so Quality goes "between the horns" (*ZMM*, p. 213), between subject and object, mind and matter. Just as Tao, if heeded, continually brings about a harmonious interaction of yin and yang, so Quality, if heeded, continually brings about a harmonious interaction of subjectivity and objectivity. An egalitarian duality rooted in Quality or Tao is seen as the antidote to antagonistic or hierarchical dualisms.

A final note before leaving "the one and the many." *ZMM* can easily be read as an antidualist book. In his Chautauqua discussions about "what is best" (*ZMM*, p. 7), the narrator tries to overcome various dualisms that seem to make for unharmonious contemporary living, such as the dualism of a classic, scientific, protechnological mentality and a romantic, aesthetic, antitechnological mentality. The narrator's attempt can be viewed as an extension of Phaedrus' climactic antidualist insight into Quality. A further and final bout with dualism, and the overcoming of "the biggest duality of all" (*ZMM*, p. 363), occurs when the narrator faces and somehow resolves, by one stroke, both the *intrapersonal* conflict betweet Phaedrus and himself and the *interpersonal* conflict between Chris and himself. As you tune in to this antidualist theme in *ZMM*, it may be helplful to keep in mind that dualism is not all of one stripe and that, accordingly, *ZMM*'s call for a nondualistic way of thinking and living is not necessarily a rejection of all dualities. In this connection, it may be useful to note in advance that dualism, as well as being a position in the Reality compartment—a metaphysical position—is also a position within the Knowledge and Value compartments—an epistemological and axiological position. You may well find that the antidualist theme of *ZMM* is played more loudly and more clearly in those compartments.

CHANGING OR CHANGELESS?

Before you leave the Reality compartment, consider one more metaphysical question: Is reality changing or changeless? Clearly, what is in your *experience* is changing; and that holds both for your experience of the external and your experience of the internal. The book that is in front of you wasn't always in front of you and won't always be in front of you. It came to be there and will cease to be there: That is external change. The thoughts running through your mind right now weren't always there and won't always be there: That is internal change. If you equate reality with your experience, you will say that reality is changing, and perhaps you will wonder how anyone could ever think otherwise.

To begin to think otherwise you have to do one of two things (or both): find an unchanging dimension of experience or stop equating experience with reality. Some of the cosmological thinkers of the ancient Greek world (see *ZMM*, pp. 336–337) apparently took the latter route. They began to draw a distinction between the way things appear in experience and the way they really are, between surface *appearance* and underlying *reality*. On the surface, you might find many different changing and interacting things (such as minerals, plants, and animals), but beneath this world of variety and change lies a single, constant reality (such as water or air).

Why draw such a distinction? Why suppose a constant reality in addition to changing appearances? Perhaps what those early thinkers had in mind was something like this: If you equate reality simply with the changing and changeable things of experience, you might as well equate reality with chaos—but that is unthinkable. The world is a cosmos, an ordered and beautiful whole, not chaos, a disorderly and ugly flux. And you can't have a cosmos without an element of stability, without a constant that complements change.

One early Greek thinker, Heraclitus (540–475 B.C.), seemed to defy this rational need for the stable and constant. In equating reality with fire and in saying things like "All things flow" and "You can't step into the same river twice," he seemed to be saying that all is flux, that there is no such thing as an abiding substance. However, Heraclitus also claimed that there was a *logos*, a rational scheme, according to which the never-ending fluctuations occur. So it seems that Heraclitus too, despite his well-known emphasis on change, or "becoming," supposed something that made for stability.

The celebration of the stable and changeless reached its zenith in the philosophy of Parmenides (sixth–fifth century B.C.). He didn't just add another voice to the chorus that called for a stable complement to the changing aspect of reality; he banished the changing aspect altogether and equated reality with the changeless. How could anyone seriously hold such a view? Isn't change an obvious fact? It's an obvious appearance, Parmenides might say, but not an obvious reality. The truth about reality is reached through reasoning, not through the senses. (If we were presently browsing through the Knowledge compartment rather than the Reality compartment, we would say that Parmenides was a "rationalist" rather than an "empiricist.")

How does reasoning lead to the view that reality is changeless? Here is one way of reconstructing Parmenides' reasoning: What is not, Nonbeing, cannot *be*, because if it were, it would not be *Non*being. Hence, Nonbeing is impossible. But if Nonbeing is impossible, Being, what is, is necessary. (We can't say that there can't be *Nothing* without saying that there has to be *Something*.) Now, since Being is necessary, Being always is. (We can't say *both* that Something simply has to exist *and* that that Something might at some time not exist.) But if Being always is, it can neither come into existence nor pass out of existence. (We can't say that Something always is without also saying that this Something neither starts nor stops.) To say that Being neither comes into existence nor passes out of existence is to say that Being is changeless and, by the same token, that change is unreal. (When we say that Something really changes, we are saying that at least a part of this Something ceases to be or begins to be.)

In yielding to what he took to be the demands of reason, Parmenides made claims that flew in the face of common sense and thus invited ridicule. Even so, he did not lack supporters. His most famous supporter, Zeno of Elea (495–430 B.C.), countered the ridicule with a series of paradoxes designed to show that change is illusory (see *ZMM*, p. 337) or at least that the idea of change involves logical difficulties. If you would like a sense of what those paradoxes were like, consider what is involved in your putting down this book. If you want to put the book down, you first have to move it *halfway* from where it is now to where you want to put it. You can't move it all the way without moving it through the halfway mark. But to get the book all the way to the halfway mark, you first have to get it halfway to the halfway mark because, again, you can't move it all the way without first moving it half of the way. Similarly, you can't get the book all the way to this quarter mark without first getting it halfway to the quarter mark. And so on indefinitely. Think about it. There are an infinite number of halfway points to traverse. If it takes a unit of time, however infinitesimal, to traverse each point, it will take an infinite number of units of time—hence, infinite time—to traverse them all. Thus, you can never put this book down—even if you don't find it gripping. Changing its location is a metaphysical impossibility. (Parmenidean laughter!)

The Parmenidean claim that change is illusory and totally unreal did not become a mainstay of Western thought. However, thanks to Plato, the changeless that Parmenides equated with reality pure and simple did come to be thought of as the *most real* part of reality. As *ZMM*'s narrator rightly notes, Plato worked out a synthesis that "tried to resolve differences between the Heraclitans and the followers of Parmenides" (*ZMM*, p. 343), a synthesis of the philosophy of the changing and the philosophy of the changeless. What is important to note here is that in that synthesis the changing and the changeless do not fare equally well. The changeless comes out clearly on top. Eternal Forms are deemed the truest reality, the most real, the really real; the changing particulars are deemed a second-class reality, less real than the Forms. Whatever reality those changing entities have, they have because they somehow *participate* in, share in the being of, the Forms. Take away that *participation* and you take away their reality.

Plato sounded a theme loudly and clearly: What is most real is what is most constant. You can hear that theme played in countless variations throughout the centuries of philosophy that came after Plato. For example, you can hear it in Aristotle's claim that reality is composed of particular *substances*, entities that retain a constant self-identity even while they pass through various adventures of superficial change, and you can hear it in the many different substance-philosophies that have arisen since the time of Aristotle (such as Descartes's dualistic philosophy, according to which there are two kinds of substance, "thinking things" and "extended things," and Spinoza's monistic philosophy, according to which there is one and only one substance, God or Nature). All substance philosophies share two beliefs: first, that a constant, self-identical entity somehow underlies whatever change occurs, and, second, that this self-identical entity is the primary reality and any changes are secondary—what is most real is what is most constant.

You don't have to study philosophy to be tuned in to this theme. It's such a catchy melody that you are probably tuned in to it in a number of everyday contexts. To notice it, just ask yourself what you take to be the most real instance of something or the core reality of something. Isn't it always something that lasts? What do you take to be the most real instance of, say, love? If you have ever used the phrase "true love," haven't you used it to refer to a kind of love that isn't shaken by hardship, a love that lasts? What do you take to be the core reality of a particular society? Isn't it some characteristic or set of characteristics that keeps on turning up, century after century, amid the appearance of variation? What do you take to be the core reality of yourself? What is the real you? Whether or not you reach a satisfying answer to this question, when you ask it aren't you looking for a constant, whether it be something manifest or hidden? Whether it be a matter of nature or nurture, the old Platonic theme continues to be heard—what is most real is what is most constant.

Of course, the countertheme—that change is more basic and more real than constancy—has also been sounded and heard throughout the centuries. The followers of Heraclitus have not been completely silenced, even though the influence of Plato's synthesis has muted their contribution to the symphony of Western thought. Moreover, in the twentieth century, the Heraclitan countertheme has increased in volume—thanks to the contributions of both scientists and philosophers.

The main scientific contributors have been the physicists. From the standpoint of twentieth-century physics, reality is basically a field of energy of which the elementary particles are condensations. Moreover, those elementary particles—for example, electrons—are only simplistically thought of as "particles"; complementarily, they are to be thought of as "waves," as vibrating events. Material reality is a field of vibrations, dynamic through and through. The book you are holding, despite its apparent stability, is awhirl with activity. (Despite Zeno's paradoxes, it's a wonder that the book doesn't fly out of your hands!) From the standpoint of contemporary physics, the Parmenideans were right to claim a distinction between appearance and reality but wrong in their claim about where the illusion lies. What is illusory is constancy, not change.

The main philosophical contributors to the Heraclitan countertheme have been Alfred North Whitehead (1861–1947) and his followers, who are generally called "process thinkers." From the standpoint of process philosophy, the basic and most real realities are neither Platonic Forms nor Aristotelian substances but infinitesimal events on the micro level (termed "actual entities" or "actual occasions"). Such events, which might be thought of as drops of experience, link up to form the macro objects of our experience (things like trees and birds and bees). Despite our tendency to think of those objects as *substances,* as self-contained things (a tendency perhaps rooted in the grammatical structures of certain languages), they are not really substances. Rather, they are societies of *processes* interacting within ever larger societies of processes. Reality is process and nothing but process.

How does *ZMM*'s metaphysics fit in here? What is this philosophy's answer to the question whether reality is basically the constant or the changing, substance or process? Clearly, from the standpoint of Phaedrus and the narrator, what is most basic and most real is Quality. What then is Quality? Is Quality a substance or a process (or neither)? You might see an initial resemblance between Phaedrus' "Quality" and Plato's "Good." The narrator himself says that he would have thought the two identical were it not for certain notes that Phaedrus left behind (*ZMM*, p. 332). However, a key difference between the two is that while Plato's Good is a fixed Form, Phaedrus' Quality is "not a *thing*" but "an event," a causal event that produces subjects and objects (*ZMM*, p. 215, italics Pirsig's). Score one for process. Moreover, according to the narrator's train analogy (*ZMM*, pp. 254–255), Romantic Quality is not any "part" of the train—neither the engine, nor the boxcars, nor any of the train's contents—but rather the cutting edge of the *moving* train, of experience itself. Score two for process. On the other hand, Phaedrus responded to the question

"Why does everybody see Quality differently?" by noting that people carry around with them different sets of analogues based on different sets of experiences: "People differ about Quality, not because Quality is different, but because people are different in terms of experience" (*ZMM*, p. 224). This response suggests that Quality has a sort of fixed identity. (If Phaedrus were focusing on the process character of Quality, he might have simply said that Quality *is* different at every moment.) Score one for substance. Moreover, to return to the train analogy, while Romantic Quality is identified with the train's leading edge, Quality itself is identified with the "track" (*ZMM*, p. 254). Now the track is clearly meant to guide the train's motion (score another for process), but the track itself is something already there, a fixed entity (score one for substance).

Both the train analogy and the scorecard suggest that *ZMM* offers the beginnings of a new metaphysical synthesis, one with an emphasis opposed to that of Plato. Perhaps you will find in this inchoate synthesis a train of thought worth developing. If so, you might find fuel for the task by doing some reading in the area of process philosophy. In particular, you might find it thought-provoking to draw out some comparisons and contrasts between what *ZMM* says about Quality and what certain process thinkers (notably Charles Hartshorne and Alfred North Whitehead) say about God.

KNOWLEDGE

It is time to turn our attention from the Reality compartment to the Knowledge compartment, the compartment of philosophy that has traditionally been called epistemology (from the Greek word *episteme*, meaning "knowledge"—hence, "study of knowledge"). In doing so, we will temporarily put metaphysics in the background; but don't be surprised if you find your focus shifting back and forth between Reality and Knowledge. When you are exploring the "high country of the mind" (*ZMM*, p. 111), the highest peaks and widest panorama of human intellectual aspiration and achievement, it's quite natural to find your eyes jumping between a metaphysical gaze and an epistemological gaze. You may even reach a point where the two gazes seem to blend into one.

Here are some typical epistemological questions: What does knowledge involve? What are you doing when you are knowing? Is human knowing primarily a matter of sense experience? of some sort of intellectual intuition or insight? of rational activities or rational categories? of some sort of conscious or subconscious choice? Is human knowing a structured set of activities rather than a single activity? Whatever activities are involved in knowledge, what guarantees the proper performance of those activities? How is such performance recognized? Supposing proper performance of the right activities, what is reached thereby? Does human knowledge reach or fall short of reality? Does human knowledge *disclose* or *create* reality? What are the limits of human knowledge? Are the limits of human knowledge the same as the limits of reality?

For present backpack purposes, you can confine your attention to two major questions: What are you doing when you are knowing? and What are you reaching when you are doing it? When you ask the first question, you are wondering not about the content of knowledge but about the activity of knowing. You are wondering whether there is a particular activity or set of activities whose presence guarantees the presence of knowledge or whose absence indicates the absence of knowledge. When you ask the second question, you are wondering about the status of the content you reach through the activity. You are wondering, for example, whether what you reach is reality in the fullest sense, some less than fully genuine version of reality, or not reality at all.

EXPERIENCE, REASON, OR SOMETHING ELSE?

What are you doing when you are knowing? If you say that what you are primarily doing is experiencing, you can be labeled an "empiricist." If you say that what you are primarily doing is using reason in one way or another, you can be labeled a "rationalist." If you say that what you are primarily doing is willing or choosing or selecting, consciously or subconsciously, you can be labeled a "voluntarist." If you say that you are primarily feeling, you are an "emotivist." If you say that you are primarily intuiting, you are an "intuitionist." The list could go on.

You can take the analytic knife and carve up empiricism into "broad empiricism" and "narrow empiricism." If you are a "broad empiricist," you insist with every other empiricist that knowledge be grounded in experience, but you do not insist that the pertinent experience be the sort of data that are delivered by the five senses. You do not equate "experience" with "awareness of sensory objects." Perhaps you will say—with John Locke (1632–1704)—that experience includes not only sensory data but also awareness of conscious activities, such as the activities of sensing, imagining, and understanding. For example, as you read this, you are not only experiencing black marks against a white background (a sensory datum); you are also experiencing your act of *seeing* those marks. Your act of seeing is not a sensory datum alongside the sensory datum of the black-on-white marks, but it is a datum of experience and a potential building block of knowledge. On the other hand, if you are a "narrow empiricist," you tend to think of experience only in terms of sensory data. Your basic contention is that we gather knowledge—at least *factual* knowledge—by gathering and working with the reports of our senses. Hence, if presented with a factual claim, as a narrow empiricist you are quick to ask about the sensory data that are available to support the claim. If no indication of pertinent sensory data is forthcoming, as a narrow empiricist you are quick to dismiss the claim.

If you're an empiricist, you don't deny that reason has a role to play in knowledge. You simply see that role as secondary. You are likely to point out, again with Locke, that when we enter the world, our minds are like blank tablets. As we fill those tablets with more and more sensory data, we begin to make various comparisons and contrasts and to notice spatial or temporal conjunctions among data. On the basis of those comparisons, contrasts, and conjunctions, we form various concepts and principles that we can use in connection with further sensory data to increase our factual knowledge. From an empiricist perspective, it is important to note that our concepts and principles (which are generally associated with "reason") would not be in our minds at all were it not for the stimulus of sense experience. Sense experience is the heart and soul of knowledge.

If you are a thoroughgoing narrow empiricist like David Hume (1711–1776), you may go so far as to say that factual knowledge in the strictest sense is only that which is verified within sense experience. In that case, you will regard various rational concepts and principles that are *not* verified within sense experience as *not* yielding genuine knowledge (however much they might be practically useful). Take, for example, the concept of "substance," that of a constant, self-identical entity that underlies the various changes and fluctuations that the senses detect. Since in your sense experience you find no such constant entity but only a series of fluctuating impressions, you have to say—from a radical empiricist perspective—that no substances are *known* to exist.

At this point you might be tempted to say that while empiricism, at least in its narrowest form, may be a nice place to visit, you can't live there. You have to live as if there were substances, stable entities. You have to live as if the motorcycle you're riding is a constant thing and not just a series of impressions. So you might opt for a less radical version of empiricism, or you might opt for one or another epistemological opponent of empiricism. (One such opponent would be the version of rationalism provided by Kant, a version according to which the substantiality of the motorcycle is guaranteed by a rational category, "substance," without which no knowledge of motorcycles or anything else could possibly occur—see *ZMM*, pp. 114–119.)

If you are an empiricist, you don't necessarily deny that reason can deliver truths of its own, truths that are known through rational calculation or a rational manipulation of symbols rather than through attention to experiential data; but you are quick to point out that such "truths of reason" (also called "a priori truths" or "necessary truths") are not factual and, hence, bring us no news about the world. For example, mathematical truths—such as the truth that the angles of a triangle add up to 180 degrees—are truths of reason. They tell us about the relations among certain symbols but they don't tell us if those symbols have any referent in the "real" world, much less where the referent can be found. Knowing the just-stated truth about triangles, we don't know for a fact that triangular objects exist or where we might find one. For all we know, there might not be a single triangular object in the whole universe—and yet it would still be rationally evident that "a triangle's angles add up to 180 degrees."

The most important kind of truth, from an empiricist perspective, is factual truth, empirical truth. Truths of reason are sterile unless and until they find application in the world of facts, a world that is known primarily through experience. Besides, the empiricist argues, even the truths of reason depend upon the formation of concepts and symbols. We can't rationally "see" that certain concepts necessarily go together (such as "triangle" and "180 degrees") if we don't have the concepts to begin with. And where do we get the concepts, if not from various conjunctions, comparisons, and contrasts that present themselves in sense experience?

A rationalist disagrees with the empiricist on several counts. A rationalist, broadly defined, is anyone who claims that the central and most important contribution to human knowledge comes from a human being's "higher faculties," from reason rather than from sense experience. More specifically, the rationalist claims, against the empiricist, that *concepts*—which are crucial to *all* human knowledge, both factual and a priori—are not simply copies or combinations or extensions of sense experience. Concepts are "things of reason."

In what way are concepts "things of reason"? The answer depends upon your version of rationalism. If you are a Platonic rationalist, you will say that your concepts are the result of your "recollection" of the Forms. Sensory experience might occasion the recollection, but the recollection itself is not a remembrance of a sensory experience but a remembrance of an intellectual vision that occurred when your mind was not trapped in a body and immersed in a world of sensory particulars. The once-upon-a-time vision of Forms remains imbedded in your consciousness, and the task of human knowledge is to raise those imbedded Forms from dimness to clarity, a task accomplished not by sense experience but by the dialectic, a process in which answers to questions are challenged by further questions and positions are pitted against counterpositions.

If you are a Kantian rationalist, you will say that the concepts involved in knowledge—at least the major ones—are "categories" of the mind, structures or molds through which you mentally lay hold of sensory objects. You don't derive these concepts *from* sensory data. Rather, you bring them *to* sensory data in order to "make sense" of the data. (Think here of the a priori category of "substance" without which we couldn't make sense of the varying patterns of sense data that we experience on the motorcycle— *ZMM*, pp. 117–119.) Paradoxically, without such rational— nonempirical—categories, empirical knowledge would not occur, for empirical *knowledge* involves making sense of data and not just collecting them.

Both Platonic rationalists and Kantian rationalists may be said to subscribe to some version of "innate ideas," insofar as both say that we do not simply derive concepts from sense experience and that at least certain concepts are part of our natural heritage as human beings. When the battle in Western philosophy between the empiricists and the rationalists was at its height in the seventeenth and eighteenth centuries, the rallying cries of the two camps were "blank tablet" and "innate ideas." Rationalism tends to go hand in hand with a belief in innate ideas, just as empiricism tends to go with the belief that the mind begins like a *tabula rasa*, or blank tablet.

As you might suspect, there are epistemological positions that seem to fall between "rationalism" and "empiricism." Kant's position might be regarded as an attempt at a middle way, insofar as Kant holds that human knowledge involves a *synthesis* of rational categories and sensory experience. However, Kant's position is much more clearly rationalist than empiricist, since he does not accept the blank-tablet notion and he does accept a version of innate ideas. Perhaps a genuine example of a middle position is that of Aristotle. Aristotle holds that we develop human knowledge by studying the concrete, particular things that can be observed with our senses. He does not depreciate the sensory world or the role played by our senses. If you think of Aristotle in *contrast* to Plato, you may well think of him as an out-and-out empiricist. On the other hand, Aristotle holds that when you study particular things, the key moment—as far as growth in knowledge is concerned—is when you grasp a thing's internal form. The form of a thing is not a piece of sensory data but an intelligible dimension of the thing. You grasp it not by some particular activity of one or more senses but by an act of understanding, an intellectual act, an insight. Hence, if you think of Aristotle in terms of what he has in *common* with Plato—an acceptance of form as a nonsensory reality—you will not regard Aristotle as an empiricist. You won't say that he is a rationalist, either, since he clearly emphasizes experience rather than some alleged a priori element in knowledge. Perhaps you will call him an "intellectualist," since he locates the heart of knowledge in an intellectual (nonsensory) act.

An epistemological "voluntarist" locates the heart of knowledge neither in the senses nor in reason but in the will, in the human capacity to tend toward or intend something and to express that intention through choices. What is it that you are willing or intending when you are in the process of coming to know something? Different versions of "voluntarism" will involve different answers to that question. Ironically, the one unacceptable answer from a voluntarist perspective—an answer that puts you outside the voluntarist camp rather than within it—is "truth." If you say that the will to truth is a key element in the pursuit and attainment of knowledge, you've not said anything that an empiricist or a rationalist or an intellectualist has to deny. Empiricists, rationalists, and intellectualists can all say that the human knower is gripped by the will to truth and hence motivated to direct attention to sensory observations or to the rational manipulation of symbols or to the intellectual penetration of data. The voluntarist goes beyond this—or beneath it—and claims that a will to something else is the primary element, the chief motivator and guide, in the attainment of "knowledge."

A classic voluntarist epistemology is that of Friedrich Nietzsche (1844–1900). Nietzsche held that the "will to power" is at the heart of knowledge. In seeking and attaining knowledge, the knower is seeking and attaining ways of looking at things and talking about things that increase the knower's capacities of self-expansion, full functioning, and practical control. (By "power" Nietzsche meant primarily such capacities rather than the domination by one individual or group of another individual or group—though, of course, the drive to increase such capacities can frequently express itself in a drive toward domination.) As a knower, you might claim that your pursuit of knowledge is a detached pursuit of truth for truth's sake, but in fact, Nietzsche would say, your motivation is less pure than you think it is. The will to power both motivates your search and guides your selection of "facts" and interpretations along the way. If you object that you are conscious of a will to truth but not conscious of a will to power, Nietzsche can respond (as, more generally, any voluntarist tends to respond) that the primary motive for knowing needn't be something of which you are fully conscious—the will can work subtly and in subconscious ways. If you further object that some people claim to know things that make them feel humble, even despicable, rather than proud and powerful, Nietzsche can respond that even that sort of knowledge can mask a secret will to power. Perhaps these humble knowers believe that their acceptance of a humbling self-picture or world picture will eventually bring them a reward and a position of prominence. Perhaps, too, they secretly bear resentment toward the world's "winners" and they take self-aggrandizing glee—secretly or not so secretly—in the belief that such winners will eventually be brought low. (Nietzsche did in fact interpret Christianity along these lines.)

A voluntarist says, in sum, that you "see" and "know" what you *want* to. Why do you want to see and know whatever it is that you do see and know? Maybe you are driven, as Nietzsche says, by a will to power. Maybe you are driven by some other will: a will to security or a will to pleasure or a will to beauty or a will to Quality. You can imagine any number of different voluntarist epistemologies centering on different possible objectives of the will. What they all have in common is the belief that a will to something other than "pure" truth is the primary factor within human knowing.

In pointing out the central role of will within knowledge, a voluntarist isn't necessarily making a cynical or damning observation. A voluntarist isn't necessarily saying, "You *can* and *ought* to be engaged in a pure, disinterested, detached pursuit of truth, but instead, driven by a will to something else, you follow a path of self-interest and self-deception." Rather, a voluntarist might be saying, "You *can't* be driven simply by a pure will to truth" or "You *shouldn't* be driven simply by a pure will to truth" or both.

Why *can't* you be driven by a pure will to truth? A voluntarist might say that the search for truth is always grounded in a variety of human concerns and purposes. Take away those concerns and purposes and you take away the search. Moreover, once the search is started, if you insist on being guided by nothing other than a pure will to truth, the search may never reach closure. As long as you keep on thinking—and as a pure truth-seeker you will want to keep on thinking—new candidates for the sought-for truth will continue to present themselves. If you banish every concern except a concern for truth, what will keep you from expanding the field of candidates indefinitely? What will enable you to narrow the field? If in fact you do narrow the field, if you do make judgments, isn't it because more than a pure desire for truth is operating within you?

At this point, you might consider how Phaedrus' laboratory experience contributed to his break with mainstream rational thought and launched him on his philosophical journey "in pursuit of the ghost of rationality itself" (*ZMM*, p. 97). He discovered in the lab that hypotheses tended to increase rather than decrease as they were being tested. He thus came to see that scientific method, instead of moving us *toward* a settling of truth claims, moves us *away* "from single absolute truths to multiple, indeterminate, relative ones" and thereby contributes to rather than eliminates "social chaos" (*ZMM*, p. 101). What was the problem with scientific method? Phaedrus would later see, though he didn't quite put it this way, that in the pursuit of knowledge, scientific or nonscientific, a will to Quality is needed to complement and guide the will to truth. A detached will-to-truth, devoid of Quality awareness, is incapable of getting where it wants to go (unless with Nietzsche you suppose that such a will is really a disguised form of a death wish—in which case, the will to truth may well get its wish).

The narrator eventually discovered that Phaedrus' line of thought about science converged with the line of thought of an eminent scientist, mathematician, and philosopher, Jules Henri Poincaré (1854–1912) (see *ZMM*, pp. 232–242). Poincaré came to see that the scientific crisis of his era, a crisis regarding the foundations of the sciences, was rooted in a crisis regarding mathematical truth. The discovery of new geometries to rival that of Euclid raised a question about the nature of mathematical truth. Poincaré came to the conclusion that mathematical truth was neither *a priori*, a fixed part of human consciousness, nor *empirical*, subject to continual revision on the basis of experience, but *conventional*, a matter of definitions agreed upon to suit human convenience. Poincaré extended this idea of "conventionalism" to the facts and hypotheses of science. The question then became, How are the key facts and hypotheses selected? Poincaré's answer was that the subliminal self, on the basis of a felt *harmony* or order, preselects what comes to consciousness. Thus Poincaré, like Phaedrus, saw that when reason pursues knowledge, it requires an element of will other than simply a will to truth: It requires an orientation toward a harmony comparable to Phaedrus' Quality so it can select information on the basis of that orientation. Poincaré's "conventionalism" is another example of a voluntarist epistemology.

In addition to saying that you *can't* carry out the pursuit of truth simply on the basis of a detached and disinterested will-to-truth, a voluntarist might be saying that you *shouldn't* attempt to do so. The attempt is misguided and inhuman. The search for knowledge should be carried out within the context of human values, and knowledge itself should be seen as appropriately, as well as necessarily, value-laden. This insistence is a central and recurrent theme of *ZMM*. The "genetic defect" at the heart of Western rationality, a defect that produces a "structure of reason" that is "emotionally hollow, esthetically meaningless and spiritually empty" (*ZMM*, p. 102) resides in the divorce of reason from value. That divorce, initiated in the ancient Greek world (on Phaedrus' reading) by the likes of Plato and Aristotle (see *ZMM*, pp. 342–345) and finalized in the modern scientific era, must be overcome. "The dictum that Science and its offspring, technology, are 'value free,' that is, 'quality free,' has got to go" (*ZMM*, p. 231). What is needed is an "expansion of reason" (*ZMM*, p. 150) in which the will's orientation to Quality is given a central place—a replacement of a narrowly rationalistic or empiricistic theory of knowledge with a more voluntaristic one.

An American philosopher who called for something similar was William James (1842–1910). In James's voluntaristic philosophy, Pragmatism, truth is thought of as belief that works, belief that leads to fruitful and satisfying consequences. If you want to know whether a particular belief or hypothesis that you are entertaining is true, be attentive to the consequences of the belief. If the consequences—in attitudes, in actions, and in the products of attitudes and actions—are good, if they are somehow satisfying, then you can say that the proposed belief is true; and if the consequences are not satisfying, you can say that the proposed belief is false. If later you find that a fruitful belief has become a fruitless or destructive one or, vice versa, a fruitless or destructive belief has become a fruitful one, you can say that the truth has changed. The idea that truth changes needn't be a source of intellectual embarrassment. Truth isn't to be thought of as some sort of eternal quality that certain beliefs have and others don't; it is to be thought of as something that *happens* (or fails to happen) to a belief as the consequences of the belief get played out. Truth is a *process*.

If you look closely from James's perspective, you will see a will (other than the will to truth) at work within human knowing, a will to good. The will to truth is subordinate to the will to good. Truth is a species of good, the good in the area of belief, that which it is good to believe. Hence, you should not think of the pursuit of truth as a detached, value-free exercise but as an intellectual effort directed and permeated by value concerns. You can perhaps imagine Phaedrus reading James and exclaiming, "Yes! Score one for the Sophists—the Platonic victory is not complete!" In Phaedrus' view, Plato's attempt to form a synthesis of truth (the special concern of the early cosmological thinkers) and good (the special concern of the Sophists) resulted in an "encapsulation" of good under truth. The Good became a Form, a dialectically attainable object of thought. Granted, it was the *highest* Form—but it was still a Form, a fixed, unchangeable Idea rather than what the Sophists made it out to be, ever-changing reality itself (see *ZMM*, pp. 342–343). From Phaedrus' viewpoint, James's epistemology might be understood as a reversal of Plato's synthesis and a return to the Sophists' perspective.

Before we move on from the first epistemological question (What are you doing when you are knowing?), I'd like to call your attention to two more positions that seem to have special relevance to *ZMM*'s epistemology, "emotivism" and "intuitionism." In general, an emotivist is anyone who stresses the role of human feelings in any or all areas of human endeavor. For present purposes, it is important to take out the analytic knife and slice emotivism into "noncognitive emotivism" and "cognitive emotivism." A noncognitive emotivist contrasts feeling with knowing—where feeling has a central role to play, where knowledge, if present at all, is banished to the periphery. A cognitive emotivist, on the other hand, sees feeling as a potential medium of knowledge, at least in certain areas.

These two contrasting emotivist positions are both exemplified in twentieth-century ethical thought. Ethical thought (which will be looked at more closely in the Value compartment) seeks to understand the meaning and the grounds of beliefs or judgments about the rightness or wrongness, goodness or badness of human actions. When we apply terms like "right" or "wrong" or "good" or "bad" to human actions, what do we mean by such terms? If we say, for example, that killing an innocent human being is morally wrong or that sharing with the needy is morally good, what do we mean by such statements? How do we know that our statements are correct? A noncognitive emotivist—for example, the British philosopher A. J. Ayer (1910–   )—might say that such statements simply express our feelings or attitudes toward certain actions, without expressing any knowledge about the actions. Hence, it would be just as improper to say that our statements are true or false as it would be to say that a crowd's cheers for its baseball team are truths or falsehoods. In effect, we are simply saying, "Boo, killing! Hurray, sharing!" On the other hand, a cognitive emotivist—for example, the German philosopher Max Scheler (1874–1928)—might say that your claims about killing and sharing are grounded in objective values that are knowable through human feeling rather than through sensing or reasoning. Your claims express both feeling and the value reality that feeling discloses.

(Scheler coined a new word—"value-ception" in English—to express this disclosure through feeling.) Feelings are not just blind forces; they are windows to knowledge.

If you are an intuitionist, you hold that you can know certain things by an act of direct, nonsensory "seeing," or intuition. (The word "intuition" itself is derived from a Latin word, *intueri*, that means literally "to look at" or "to gaze within.") You don't necessarily deny the reality or importance of knowledge gained through sense experience or reasoning or some combination of sensing and reasoning, and you don't necessarily deny that some things known intuitively might also be known through empirical-rational means. You do, however, deny that all knowledge is reducible to empirical and rational activity; and most probably you hold that some very important things are only knowable through intuition. For example, you might hold that value is only knowable by intuition. You don't experience it with your senses, nor do you infer it by a rational argument. You know it intuitively or not at all. You might say, with Henry Sidgwick (1838–1900), that you intuit the *oughtness* that is attached to doing or not doing certain things, like not killing the innocent; or you might say, with G. E. Moore (1873–1958), that you intuit the *goodness* of certain actions, like sharing with the needy. In either case, you will be claiming that your nonsensory intuitive act directly apprehends its proper object in much the same way that an act of seeing directly apprehends color.

At this point, you may, quite rightly, detect a family resemblance between intuitionism and the version of cognitive emotivism we have just discussed. Both claim a type of direct knowing that is not reducible to observation or inference. Both would be comfortable with the dictum of Blaise Pascal (1623–1662) that "the heart has its reasons that Reason doesn't know at all." The distinction between the two positions seems to turn on the "felt" (or "intuited") propriety of using the language of feeling or a language that connotes a kind of intuitive seeing. You could, of course, say that you *both* feel and intuit value.

Two things that intuitionists frequently say about intuition are worth singling out here, because they have special relevance to *ZMM*'s epistemological insights. One is that intuition is a sort of "inside" knowledge, a knowledge had by a sort of sympathetic entry into the thing known rather than by an external examination;

a kind of knowledge by identity rather than by confrontation. This is the idea of intuition that you can find in the writings of Henri Bergson (1859–1941), who described intuition with phrases like "intellectual sympathy." It is also the idea of intuition that young Phaedrus encountered in the writings of Albert Einstein, who said that the universal laws of the cosmos could only be reached by "intuition, resting on sympathetic understanding of experience" (quoted in *ZMM*, p. 99). That idea would be carried forward in the narrator's reflections (undoubtedly inspired by, if not inherited from, Phaedrus) about the relation of Quality to *caring* (*ZMM*, pp. 25, 247). Just as for Einstein the intuition of cosmic laws is rooted in a sympathetic understanding of experience, so for the narrator the intuition of Quality is rooted in caring about what one is seeing and doing. But for the narrator the flow goes both ways. Caring—which, you might care to note, involves both willing and feeling—is reciprocally related to Quality. The more you care in your knowing and doing, the more you see (or intuit) Quality. The more you intuit Quality, the more you care. "A person who sees Quality and feels it as he works is a person who cares. A person who cares about what he sees and does is a person who's bound to have some characteristics of Quality" (*ZMM*, p. 247).

The second frequently made and presently pertinent statement is that intuition is *holistic*. When you intuit, you see wholes in their wholeness. In contrast, when you are engaged in an *analytic* mode of thought, you seek to know things by breaking them down into parts and subparts (or, in the narrator's terms, concepts and subconcepts—*ZMM*, p. 86). The rational, analytic mode of thinking, exemplified in *ZMM*'s breakdown of a motorcycle (pp. 63–67), belongs to the "classic" mentality, whereas the holistic, intuitive mode belongs to the "romantic" mentality. In terms of *ZMM*'s landscape analogy (pp. 69–70), rational analysis is what you are doing when you are sorting the handful of sand into various piles on the basis of various criteria; intuition is what you are exercising when you grasp the entire handful of sand as a whole. As the analogy suggests, one and the same object can furnish the material for both rational analysis and intuition. While intuition might have its own proper objects (e.g., as some intuitionists suggest, value), it might also share objects with other modes of thought. You can analyze the motorcycle in terms of its parts and functions; additionally or alternatively, you can intuitively grasp the cycle as the "right thing" for you, a vehicle that suits your style. In the latter case, your intuition is still a nonsensory act of knowing, even though the motorcycle is a sensory object—the cycle doesn't carry a visible label that says "right thing."

What are you doing when you are knowing? You have been considering various answers to that question, answers centering on distinct cognitional activities and issuing in distinct epistemological positions. Suppose that you take away the "ism" from those distinct positions and consider the distinct activities that have just been called to your attention. What do you see? Perhaps you see the empiricist's *sense experience,* the intellectualist's *understanding* of the forms of things, the rationalist's *reasoning* with categories in logical patterns, the voluntarist's *willing* of what is considered valuable, the cognitive emotivist's *feeling* of values, and the intuitionist's *intuition* of unanalyzed (though not necessarily unanalyzable) meanings and values.

Now look a little more closely. Do you perhaps see those six activities conveniently arranging themselves into two distinct epistemological trinities? Do you see emerging a "classic" epistemological trinity of *sense experience, understanding,* and *reasoning*? Can you imagine an implementation of scientific method that does not involve all three of those activities? Do you also see emerging a "romantic" epistemological trinity of *feeling, intuition,* and *will*? Can you imagine a "groovy" approach to life from which any of those is absent? It is perhaps not difficult to see the classic trinity as a *structure,* a set in which each element plays its proper role. It is quite a bit more difficult to see the romantic trinity as a structure—and maybe that's fitting.

You don't find a fully developed epistemology in *ZMM,* but you do find epistemological ideas that seem to be awaiting and even crying out for development—for example, the idea that there is a preconscious moment in knowing, a moment of Quality awareness or Quality intuition, which ought to be taken very seriously (*ZMM,* pp. 221–222). This is not the place to attempt a full development of the sort of epistemology that *ZMM* implies. It is, however, the place to note that an epistemology true to the spirit of *ZMM* would be an *inclusive* epistemology, one that overcomes the "noncoalescence between reason and feeling" that makes technology come across as ugly (*ZMM,* p. 149), one that bridges the classic-romantic split by somehow interweaving the classic and romantic epistemological trinities.

The first epistemological question, the question that we have been asking, focuses on the *activity* of knowing. The second epistemological question focuses on the *content* that is reached through that activity. This second question can be put in several ways: What is the status of the content of knowing? What are you knowing when you are doing what knowing requires? What do you reach when you genuinely know something?

When you know, does your knowing attain an object that is somehow independent of the mind with which you come to know it? If your answer is yes, you can be called an epistemological realist. If your answer is no, you can be called an epistemological idealist. As an epistemological idealist, you hold that what you know is always an object *within* your mind rather than an object *beyond* your mind, a mental reality rather than an extramental reality.

Earlier, in the Reality compartment, you had a look at *metaphysical* realism and idealism. Now you are having a look at *epistemological* realism and idealism. Interestingly or frustratingly (depending on how your mind works), the metaphysical and epistemological positions can be found in various combinations. You can be both a metaphysical realist and an epistemological realist. In that case, you hold that there is a reality that exists outside of mind or independently of consciousness (metaphysical realism), and you also hold that through your knowing activity you can actually reach such reality (epistemological realism). The motorcycle is a nonmental thing, and you can know it as it is. A second possibility is that you are a metaphysical realist and an epistemological idealist. In that case, you hold that there is an extramental reality (metaphysical realism) but that your knowledge takes you no further than a mental version of it, a version shaped by the structures and activities of your knowing mind (epistemological idealism). This was, more or less, the position of Immanuel Kant, who held that there was an extramental reality, a "thing-in-itself," a "noumenon," but that human knowledge is confined to the "thing-for-us," the "phenomenon"—an object of knowledge that has been shaped by the mind. The motorcycle is a nonmental thing, but you can only know a mind-shaped image of it. A third possibility is that you are a metaphysical idealist and an epistemological idealist. In that case, you hold that all reality is mental and that your knowledge is confined to your mind's version of it. The motorcycle is always a mental thing, a projection of some consciousness or other, and you know it in the version that suits the consciousness that is yours. The fourth and final possibility is that you are a metaphysical idealist and an epistemological realist. In that case, you hold that reality is essentially mind-dependent, but the Mind on which it depends is not the human mind, and the human mind, in its knowing activity, can go beyond itself and reach the products of that Mind. The motorcycle *ultimately* derives its existence from the knowing activity of the Big Mind, but you can know it as it is with your little mind—which is also ultimately a product of the Big Mind. Certain "objective idealists" who followed Kant as well as certain "transcendental realists" (see above, p. 142) seem to hold something like this fourth position. (You're probably even more confused now. But be patient. . . .)

While these distinctions are rattling around in your mind, you might find it worthwhile to inspect yet another distinction, the distinction between subjectivity and objectivity. It merits attention here because the distinction frequently arises in talk about knowledge (as well as in talk about reality), notably in lively discussions and debates among true believers in the just delineated four metaphysical-epistemological positions. More specifically, the terms merit attention because they figure prominently in *ZMM*'s philosophical talk. Phaedrus reached the climax of his metaphysical thinking in the context of facing a dilemma regarding the subjectivity or objectivity of Quality. His response to that dilemma provided the narrator with the basic tools for carrying out the philosophical task of *ZMM*, the overcoming of a certain kind of subject-object dualism and its spillover into other dualisms. If we want to understand *ZMM*'s philosophical thrust, sooner or later we have to pay some attention to the meaning of subject-object talk.

Basically, a subject is a knowing mind or a center of consciousness and an object is that which the mind knows or that which is present to consciousness. The terms "subject" and "object" are correlative: A subject is called a "subject" insofar as it is aware of an object; an object is called an "object" insofar as it stands, or at least *can* stand, in a certain relation to a subject. Take away all subjects and you take away all objects. Take away all objects and you take away all subjects. (Certain schools of Hindu thought would seemingly disagree with this and say that it is possible to

1 7 6

reach a certain state of transcendental awareness in which all objects are absent and only the Pure Subject, Atman, remains. However, the present point about the correlativity of subject and object is a point about the basic meanings of words rather than about the ultimate nature of reality. If the Hindus are right about Atman, then Atman is a "Subject" only in a sense that goes beyond the basic meaning of "subject." Of course if you're in that state, you don't give a hoot about such terminological distinctions; you don't talk about it as a subject state—you don't talk about it at all.)

To see how subject-object talk becomes controversial, consider a readily available context—the context furnished by this book you are reading. As you read, you are aware of something. Given the distinction that has just been made, you can say that you are a subject and that what you are aware of as you read is an object. So far, there is not likely to be any disagreement among the proponents of various metaphysical and epistemological positions. Suppose you are asked what the object is. How do you answer? Suppose you answer, "Written words," and are asked, in turn, whether those words are simply visual entities, objects of sight, or also something else. You answer that the words are signs of meanings and that you are aware of those meanings through your mind. The object of your reading activity is meaning as well as visible words. (The throng of philosophical eavesdroppers is getting a bit restless—but there is no voiced disagreement yet.) Now you are asked, point-blank, whether you are reaching anything "real" when you read. (The eavesdroppers are at the edge of their seats.) You answer that the meanings themselves are not anything real, since they are merely mental, but that through those meanings you are coming to know certain realities, and that those realities are the ultimate objects that you are contacting through your reading. (Now the disagreements begin. By your response, you please the metaphysical and epistemological realists as well as the rationalists. But you alienate the metaphysical idealists, who are miffed about your exclusion of the mental from the real, the epistemological idealists, who are nonplussed about your supposition that mental contents reveal extramental realities, and the empiricists, who are baffled about your claim to know reality through a grasp of meanings rather than through sensory perceptions.)

Notice that, in this hypothetical scenario, the word "object" itself arouses no controversy. No one finds fault with the bare claim that there are objects in your awareness. The controversy begins when you start to say certain things about the nature and status of those objects. Similarly, no one finds fault with the bare claim that you are a conscious subject. Controversy only arises when you begin to describe your activity as a reading subject.

Suppose, to vary the scenario slightly, you say that, when you read, you create meanings rather than discover them and that really there is no meaning in the text until you create it. If you say that, you please the voluntarist but disturb the rationalist. Perhaps the rationalist is disturbed to the point of berating you for being so subjective. Now notice what has happened. Subject-object talk has taken a strange semantic turn. It is perfectly okay to be a "subject"; but it's bad to be "subjective." Take a more or less neutral word and add a seemingly neutral suffix, and what do you get? A negatively charged word. How does that happen? Why is it an accusation to call someone subjective whereas it is simply descriptive to say that someone is a subject? Why is it bad for people to treat people like objects but good for people to be objective? How is it that "subject" and "object" are complementary, each calling for the other, whereas "subjectivity" and "objectivity" are commonly thought of as opposed, so that where one increases the other decreases?

The short and generic answer to all of these questions is that the history of language is complex and not revealed in dictionary listings of words and their derivatives. The longer and more specific answers would no doubt show how various thoughts about reality, knowledge, and value got packed into certain words at certain times through the influence of the dominant voices (individual or collective) of those times.

Of course, there can be different dominant voices at different times, and so words can carry layers of meanings. If we were to examine the words "subjective" and "objective" closely, we would probably find such layers of meaning, some more prominent than others; and each layer would contain a belief about reality, a belief about knowledge, and a value judgment all rolled into one and packed tightly into the word.

Consider, for example, the pejorative use of the word "subjective." When we use that word in a pejorative manner, we are not saying that it's bad for a subject to be a subject, a center of consciousness. We are not saying that a subject should become a more or less inert and opaque object or that the subject should become less a subject by deadening awareness. Rather, we are obliquely criticizing the *kind* of conscious activity that the subject is engaged in. Certain kinds of activity are called for since they lead to the right kind of relation to the object, and certain other kinds of activity ought not be performed since they lead to the wrong kind of relation. When the wrong kind of activity is present or the right kind of activity is absent, the word "subjective" is used pejoratively. What kind of activity is wrong? What kind of activity is right? The answers depend on what kind of epistemological and metaphysical beliefs are associated with the word.

You can use the word "subjective" pejoratively in more than one way. One way is to say that a certain statement is "subjective" and to mean by that that the statement is "unrealistic" and "nonempirical." Suppose that you are an empiricist (and also a naïve realist) and you don't find any empirical support for the statement in extramental reality. You might then infer that the statement is based on the wrong sorts of cognitional activities (e.g., on alleged intuitions), and accordingly you might wish to criticize the statement. You find that the word "subjective" already conveniently packages your criticism (because of one of the layers of meaning contained in it—a layer in which nonempirical consciousness is deemed inappropriate), so you express your criticism, at least initially, by means of that convenient label. Eventually, you may find yourself in a debate about knowledge and reality, but for now the label will do.

A second way to use the word "subjective" pejoratively is to accuse someone (e.g., an opponent in a disagreement) of being subjective and mean that he or she is being arbitrary or unreasonable or capricious. In such a case, you are advocating a rationalist approach to the settling of an issue. There is a correct way to think about things or do things in this situation, and reason—the use of appropriate concepts in logical patterns of thinking—will show the way. You want your opponent to listen to the voice of sweet reason, not the voice of his or her preferences or feelings or inklings; and perhaps also you want to avoid spending the time and the energy that sensitivity to feelings requires. You find packed into the word "subjective" a negative attitude toward nonrationalist, perhaps romantic, modes of consciousness, so you pull out this word and label your opponent with it. In this case, your use of the label may be counterproductive, since it is likely to incite more of the romantic modes of consciousness that you are calling into question by your use of the word "subjective."

As these two examples indicate, both empiricists and rationalists can use the word "subjective" in a negative way. In each case, subjectivity, which is "bad," is implicitly opposed to a kind of objectivity, which is "good"; but in the two cases, distinct—though not necessarily opposed—notions of subjectivity and objectivity are involved. In the empiricist view, you reach the true object of your knowing activity and are thus "objective" when your statements are grounded in sensory experience, but when your statements are not grounded in sensory experience, unfortunately, you are "subjective." In the rationalist view, you reach the true object of your knowing activity and are thus "objective" when your statements are grounded in rational activity, but when your statements are not grounded in rational activity, unfortunately, you are "subjective."

To make this distinction in another way, the empiricist is typically committed to a *correspondence theory* of truth, whereas the rationalist is typically committed to a *coherence theory* of truth. According to the correspondence view, truth consists of a match between what is in the mind and what is in reality. When what you're thinking matches up with or corresponds to external reality, then what you're thinking is the truth. How do you know that your beliefs correspond to reality? You know it through sensory experience. (At least that's the way an empiricist would put it.) According to the coherence theory, truth consists primarily of the sticking-together-ness, or coherence, of the various elements that enter into a given belief and of the various beliefs that enter into a point of view. When the contents of your mind cohere with and do not contradict one another, then you are in possession of truth. How do you know that your mental contents are coherent? You ascertain it through rational methods, such as analyzing, categorizing, and drawing inferences. Whether you think of truth in terms of correspondence or in terms of coherence, when you call someone's talk subjective you are implicitly saying that it falls short of the pertinent criteria for truth.

Can the terms "subjective" and "subjectivity" be used in a positive (not just neutral) way, and "objective" and "objectivity" in a negative way? They can. It has been done—notably by the great Danish philosopher Søren Kierkegaard (1813–1855). Pitting his own type of thinking (which has come to be called "existentialist") against that of the rationalists of his day, such as Hegel, Kierkegaard called for "passionate subjectivity" as opposed to lifeless objectivity. His was the kind of thinking that *ZMM*'s narrator would like to see somehow *included within* Western rationality. You can, if you like, follow Kierkegaard's lead and speak positively of subjectivity and negatively of objectivity. Notice, however, that it is one thing to speak positively of subjectivity and another to impart to the word "subjectivity" a positive charge, so that the word itself is readily available for positive use in a variety of contexts. This latter task may take some time. Notice, too, that in following Kierkegaard's semantic lead, you are seeking a reversal of positive and negative charges but not really a change of meaning. Subjectivity is still associated with the "romantic trinity" that we talked about earlier, and objectivity is still associated with the "classic trinity." (This is a strange semantic fact. Aren't classic activities—such as reasoning—activities of a human subject? Are there no objects in romantic consciousness?) Finally, notice that a reversal of charges only continues the opposition of "subjectivity" and "objectivity." There is a change of regime but not a genuine revolution. A genuine semantic revolution would convert a hierarchical dualism of opposed forces into an egalitarian duality of complementary aspects.

Now that you've taken notice of subject-object talk in a broad way, you are perhaps prepared to tune in more closely to the subject-object talk in *ZMM*. As a point of departure, consider the apparent dilemma that Phaedrus faces when his colleagues put to him a question concerning the Quality that he has been touting. They ask him whether Quality is objective, residing in observable objects, or subjective, residing only in the mind of the observer. Phaedrus sees that if he says that Quality is objective, either he will have to explain why Quality is not scientifically detectable or he will have to show how it *is* detectable. On the other hand, if he says that it is subjective, Quality will be dismissed as "a fancy name for whatever you like" (*ZMM*, p. 205). This initial posing of the dilemma illustrates some of the things that have just been noted. First, objectivity is presented as the "good guy" and subjectivity as the "bad guy." Phaedrus saves the day for Quality if he succeeds in associating it with objectivity (good company) and *dis*associating it from subjectivity (bad company). Second, objectivity is associated with the empirical activity of scientific detection and hence with the classic epistemological trinity, whereas subjectivity is associated with "whatever you like" and hence with the feeling and willing of the romantic trinity. Third, objectivity and subjectivity are thought of as opposed and mutually exclusive possibilities. Quality has to be one or the other. It can't be both. Which is it?

How does Phaedrus meet the dilemma? First, he avoids the "objective horn" of the dilemma. He realizes that if he claims to see in objects something that science does not detect, he is going to come out "a nut or a fool or both" (*ZMM*, p. 207). Notice how this reaction is a concession to scientific pretensions of having a monopoly on the definition of "objectivity" (which involves an identification of the objective with the empirical) or, at least, to popular acceptance of such pretensions. Next, Phaedrus turns his attention to the "subjective horn" and grapples with the claim that Quality, if subjective, is "just what you like" (*ZMM*, p. 208). He sees that what rankles him in that phrase is the word "just," which functions as a put-down. If you get rid of the put-down word, you are left with what seems to be "an innocuous truism" (*ZMM*, p. 209). Of course, Quality is what you like. Why shouldn't it be? As Phaedrus probes the matter, he sees that authoritarians might be against this view of Quality, since from their perspective you should obey authority rather than go after what you like. Then he sees that the real challenge to this subjective view of Quality comes from "scientific materialism and classic formalism" (*ZMM*, p. 209), and so he considers each in turn.

Scientific materialism says that if Quality is subjective rather than objective, "what you like" rather than something knowable scientifically as composed of matter and energy, Quality is unreal and unimportant. Note that this involves a put-down of subjectivity in general as well as Quality in particular. Phaedrus sees that this position is naïve in that it makes scientific concepts and laws themselves unreal and unimportant, since scientific concepts lack matter and energy and cannot possibly exist apart from "subjective considerations" (*ZMM*, p. 211). The narrator makes that point with stronger language, very early on in *ZMM*, in the context of a "ghost story": The laws of science are "ghosts" and a "human invention," and "the world has no existence whatsoever outside the human imagination" (*ZMM*, p. 31). (Phaedrus, after he has worked through the subjectivity-objectivity dilemma, will use equally strong idealist language when he says that we "create the world in which we live. All of it. Every last bit of it"—*ZMM*, p. 225.) Phaedrus' rebuttal of scientific materialism clearly involves large doses of idealism. Realizing that, Phaedrus backs off from such a line of response, because idealism, though logical, just won't make it in a freshman composition course—it's "too far-fetched" (*ZMM*, p. 211). Is Phaedrus, at this point, backing off from idealism or is he backing off from *professing* idealism?

Classic formalism says that if Quality is subjective, is just what you like, then Quality is just a matter of "romantic surface appeal" (*ZMM*, p. 211) rather than something susceptible to classic "overall understanding" (*ZMM*, p. 212). The implication is that if you are in your right mind and a teacher to boot, you want understanding to take precedence over emotions, so you should give up all this subjective stuff and come back to the objective, classic pronouncements about Quality that you can find in textbooks. Phaedrus just doesn't buy this. It would require a cowardly retreat from where his thinking has arrived.

In the end, Phaedrus has an insight that allows him to split the horns of the dilemma: Quality is neither objective nor subjective but a third entity, an entity that is the parent of both subjects and objects, of mind and matter. Two questions come to mind with regard to Phaedrus' crowning insight: How does that insight overcome the dilemma? What bearing does Phaedrus' insight have on the overcoming of subject-object dualism? Let's consider each of those questions briefly before we move on to the Value compartment.

How does Phaedrus' insight overcome the dilemma? At first glance, the answer seems simple: If Quality is *neither* objective nor subjective, the problems associated with either of those labels are avoided. However, when you ask *in what sense* Quality is proclaimed to be neither objective nor subjective, things get more complicated. According to Phaedrus, Quality is neither objective nor subjective in the sense that it is neither "a part of matter" nor "a part of mind" (*ZMM*, p. 213). To say that Quality is neither mind nor matter is to make a claim about reality, a *metaphysical* claim—and an important one at that. However, it seems that Phaedrus' opponents are posing a dilemma that is at least partly, and perhaps mainly, an *epistemological* dilemma. They want to know how Phaedrus *knows* the Quality that he talks about. Does he know it objectively, through the classic methods that science has perfected? If so, they seem to be saying, let him show us the pertinent method or instrument that we too may use it and see. On the other hand, if he knows it subjectively, through romantic modes of consciousness, then his "knowledge" doesn't amount to much more than poetry—it can please, but it can't prove. (Notice how complex and potentially confusing subject-object talk can be.

The derivatives "subjective" and "objective" can be taken both as metaphysical terms, referring to kinds of reality, and as epistemological terms, referring to ways of knowing.) You might imagine Phaedrus' opponents, on this epistemological reading of the dilemma, continuing to jab at Phaedrus with the subjective horn even after Phaedrus' enthronement of Quality as the third member of the metaphysical trinity. "Granted that Quality is to be thought of as neither mind nor matter," they might say to Phaedrus, "how do you *know* that this alleged nonmental, nonmaterial reality is actually a reality and not just a creation of *your* mind?" Phaedrus can respond to that question in several ways. He can challenge the narrow view of knowledge that seems to underlie the dilemma. Objections to subjective talk may show themselves objectionable when they are subjected to objective scrutiny. He can develop and present a more adequate and inclusive view of knowledge. He can make some specific comments—he eventually does so—on how Quality is known. The point to be made here is simply that a full and Westernly rational (nonmystical) resolution of Phaedrus' subjectivity-objectivity dilemma seems to require epistemological reflections as well as metaphysical insight. (Complementarily, the narrator eventually sees that Poincaré's epistemological reflections about the preselection of facts would be well served by the addition of Phaedrus's metaphysics—*ZMM*, pp. 241–242.)

How does Phaedrus' insight bear on the overcoming of subject-object dualism? His insight is that Quality is the parent of subjects and objects. We need to unpack that insight a bit before we can draw out its implications. Quality is an event—an event "known" (but not through subject-object knowing) in a preintellectual moment of awareness. At that Quality moment, both subject awareness and object awareness (hence, both subjects and objects) are made possible. How so? Under the stimulus of Quality, the human subject creates the world of objects and through object awareness creates itself as subject (see *ZMM*, pp. 215, 221–222, 225).

In what sense do we "create" the world? More than one interpretation of Phaedrus' view is possible. If we interpret his view in a loosely Kantian manner, we will say that the world we know and are active in is a world shaped by our modes of consciousness and by various cognitional activities. The world we live in is a humanly shaped world, not a world of "raw stuff." We are creative shapers. The ultimate source and creator is Quality. Hence, when

Phaedrus discovers the Sophists, he takes to the Sophist dictum that "man is the measure of all things," since that formulation regards human beings as creative participants rather than as the ultimate source (see *ZMM*, p. 338).

To see how Phaedrus's philosophy of Quality (as well as the narrator's elaborations of it) contends with subject-object dualism, we have to become clear about the dualism in question. What sort of subject-object dualism is the problem? The problem is not the bare duality of subject and object. *ZMM* does not seek to do away with subjects or objects or even the distinction between them. The problem seems to center on the *relation* of subject and object. How do you, as a human subject, relate to the world of objects, to the things you know and the things you do, and how do you see that relation? Do you take the side of the objects and relate to the world in an "objective" manner? Do you take the side of the subject and relate to the world in a "subjective" manner? Do you see your way of relating as a matter of exclusive choice, such that you can relate in one way or the other but not in both, except perhaps at different times? Are you forced to choose between the poet in yourself and the scientist?

The forced choice between the mentality of the poet and the mentality of the scientist is rooted in a *distancing* between subject and object, a distancing that is at the heart of the subject-object dualism that *ZMM* seeks to overcome. The object is "out there"; the subject is "in here." We seem forced to choose between living in accord with what is "out there" and living in accord with what is "in here." If we choose the former, we confine our consciousness to detached modes that are apt for revealing what is out there. We don't let our subjectivity—thought of here in terms of the romantic trinity of willing, feeling, and intuiting—get in the way. If on the other hand we choose subjectivity, we can let ourselves go and be affectively engaged in what we do, give expression to our feelings, hopes, and desires, and if we like create an imaginary world. But don't confuse this imaginary world with the *real* world. The real world is the world of scientific *discovery*, not the world of poetic *creation*. In this choice between the scientist and the poet, social acceptance of our choice may depend upon who is "winning" at a particular stage of culture, the scientists or the poets. In the last few centuries, in Western culture, the scientists and their followers have tended to be the winners.

The alleged distance between subject and object begins to vanish when we start to look at the world the way Phaedrus looks at it. Subject and object are intimately related, since both spring from the Quality event and since both "grow toward Quality or fall away from Quality together" (*ZMM*, p. 293). Moreover, since the subject "creates" the object, there is no need to think of creation as the exclusive prerogative of the poet. The scientist creates also, whether or not it is recognized. And there is no cause for shame here. Being creative is bad science only when we mistakenly think of subjects and objects as distanced to begin with. Whether or not science is good science does not hinge on whether or not we keep poetic creativity at bay. It hinges on whether or not we tune in to Quality and we engage in the creating-discovering tasks of science. Similarly, good poetry (and good art in general) hinges on our tuning in to Quality. We are either poet-scientists or scientist-poets, depending on our focus. We do well what we do, and we are not arbitrary and capricious (see *ZMM*, p. 241) when through caring (*ZMM*, pp. 25, 247–248, 267) and peace of mind (*ZMM*, pp. 146, 264–267) we allow Quality to stimulate and guide the fusion of subjectivity and objectivity into creative discoveries and illuminating creations.

VALUE

The last compartment in our backpack to consider is the compartment of Value. We can keep our visit to that compartment relatively brief, not because Value is less important (Value, by its very definition, is *all* that is important) but because a number of things have already been said about Value and about Value talk in the other compartments, as well as in other parts of our backpack.

Talk about Quality is talk about Value. The name for the general branch of philosophy that is concerned with Quality or Value is "axiology" (the study of that which is worthy—*axios* in Greek). Axiology is commonly divided into ethics and aesthetics. The kind of worth that ethics focuses upon is the goodness or badness that can be found in human activity. The kind of worth that aesthetics focuses upon is the beauty or ugliness that is to be found in nature or art. Let's have a look at ethics and aesthetics in turn.

Ethics is concerned with knowing what human actions have what worth and why. What human actions are "good" or "right"? What human actions are "bad" or "wrong"? What makes human actions "good" or "right" rather than "bad" or "wrong?" As the use of quotation marks might indicate, there are different ways of understanding the key terms that are used in ethics. On its most fundamental level, ethics is concerned with sorting out the meaning of those terms. On less fundamental levels, ethics is concerned with saying something about this or that specific area of human activity or about this or that particular action.

To begin, let's make a distinction between "journey ethics" and "map ethics," between the kind of ethical thinking that might arise and be carried out within the context of your own life's journey and the kind of ethical thinking that goes on when you take up the formal study of the "maps" left behind by various ethical thinkers. In the first case, your focus is on your own actions, your own living. You begin to raise questions about what's good and bad in the way you are living and about what changes you might make. You don't just want to think or talk about what's good or right; you want it to be there, in your life. In the second case, "map ethics," the focus is on *talk* about good or bad actions and about the meaning of the terms involved in such talk. Your immediate goal is to become clear about such talk. You can, of course, pass from journey ethics to map ethics: Life's quandaries can drive you to seek light in the writings of others. You also can pass from map ethics to journey ethics: A particularly stimulating book or teacher might drive you to convert academic questions into real questions and begin an actual search instead of just faking one (see ZMM, p. 184). It is also possible, however, that you engage in journey ethics or map ethics by itself. When you isolate map ethics, you have a good example of the Platonic, formal "encapsulation" of Quality that Phaedrus was worried about (ZMM, p. 342). Good becomes simply an object of thought.

You can divide both journey ethics and map ethics into *deontological* and *teleological* forms of thinking. If your thinking is deontological (from the Greek *deon*, meaning "the obligatory"), your concern is with the *rules* (or principles or duties) that you should follow. You believe that if you know and apply the right rules, your actions will be morally good, and if you don't, they will be morally bad. The consequences of an action are irrelevant to the action's moral worth. If an action makes you and everyone else miserable but it follows the rules, it still is a morally good action. If an action makes you and everyone else happy but fails to follow the rules, it still is a bad action. If, on the other hand, your thinking is teleological (from the Greek *telos*, meaning "end" or "goal") your concern is with the *goals* or consequences toward which your actions tend. You believe that actions that tend to promote the realization of the right goals are good and actions that tend to promote the realization of bad goals are bad. Rules, at best, are guidelines that indicate what sorts of actions are likely to bring about good or bad consequences. If you follow a rule for the sake of following a rule while knowing that in so doing you will bring about bad consequences, you act wrongly. If you deviate from a rule because you see that in so doing you will bring about good, you act rightly. (Phaedrus says that Quality is the goal of method— *ZMM*, p. 305. Does that put him in the teleological camp?)

Depending on where the rules come from, a deontological approach can be authority-based or reason-based. We can accept some particular authority (familial, legal, religious, etc.) as the source of the rules of right living, or we can attempt to work out the rules rationally. The classic example of rational deontological ethics is the ethical system of Immanuel Kant. Kant held that all the rules of ethics could be reduced to a sort of master rule. He provided several different formulations of that rule, which he called the categorical imperative. What those formulations seem to have in common is that they all call for a respect for rationality itself, the source of all rules. Most of Kant's formulations amount to different versions of what has come to be called the principle of universalizability. According to that principle, whenever you are wondering about the rightness of any action that you are thinking of taking, you should ask yourself whether you can reasonably will that everyone in a similar situation, not just you, be allowed to perform the type of action in question. If you cannot rationally will it, then you should consider the action contrary to reason and, therefore, contrary to duty. You shouldn't do it. Suppose, for example, you are thinking of making a false promise in order to get out of some difficulty. Can you rationally universalize that kind of behavior? Can you rationally will anyone to feel free to make false promises to alleviate difficult situations? If there were general permission for such behavior, it is likely that you would become a victim of another's false promise and find your trust betrayed. But more to the point of Kant's logical argument, all promises would eventually become so meaningless that no one could ever rely on another's promise. The action, universalized, defeats itself. False promises make false promises impossible. You can't rationally will what is self-contradictory. Contradictions are the no-no of reason. It is not right to mess with Father Reason; so the action you're contemplating is wrong.

For a teleological ethicist, the main question is, What is the proper goal of human activity? Two examples of teleological ethics come to mind: utilitarian ethics and Aristotelian ethics. If you are a utilitarian following in the footsteps of the English philosophers Jeremy Bentham (1748–1832) and John Stuart Mill (1806–1873), your goal is to maximize pleasure or happiness and minimize pain or unhappiness *among the people affected* by your actions. Hence, when more than one course of action or nonaction is open to you, as a good utilitarian, you ask for each course of action how many people will benefit or be hurt and how much. You include yourself in this calculation, but you don't give yourself special preference. The utilitarian approach seems hard to fault until you notice that producing the greatest happiness or the least unhappiness for the majority of people can conceivably be connected with fostering or tolerating inhumane treatment of a minority—something that a deontologist should be quick to point out and condemn.

For Aristotle and Aristotelians, the goal of human activity is happiness, just as it is for certain utilitarians. However, in contrast to utilitarians, Aristotelians conceive of happiness "objectively" (there's that word again) and "naturalistically." Happiness is an objective condition that might or might not correlate with subjective satisfaction. Happiness consists of the completion or fulfillment of your human nature. By nature, you have certain tendencies and capacities that define you as a human being. Your task as a human being, your built-in, or "natural," goal, is to actuate and develop your natural tendencies and capacities rather than leave them dormant or, worse, do things that thwart their expression and development. (Notice that for Aristotle what is "natural" in us doesn't automatically come to fruition. If you don't cultivate your nature, you can easily develop and become accustomed to an "unnatural" way of living. Mencius, a Confucian thinker in ancient China, said something similar.) To the extent that you succeed in bringing your nature to completion and living out of that perfected nature, you are happy. Along with this objective state of happiness comes a certain feeling of satisfaction—from Aristotle's viewpoint, the best satisfaction available to human beings. But feelings of satisfaction, as such, should not be the ultimate goal of your striving. You can feel a sort of satisfaction while living in unnatural and unhealthy ways. You can live antisocially and inhumanely and still enjoy a kind of satisfaction. From an Aristotelian viewpoint, that sort of "happiness" is likely to be short-lived, but even while it lasts it is not the happiness that Aristotelians see as the goal of human life.

At this point you might be tempted to think that for utilitarians the goal (or good) is social, whereas for Aristotelians the goal is individual. Utilitarians talk about benefiting as many as possible. Aristotelians talk about fulfilling your own nature. However, in the Aristotelian view, human nature is intrinsically social: Aristotelians hold that we are naturally oriented toward developing our powers *within* society and *for* society. If you have no desire to cooperate with others and benefit others, something in your human nature is not being tended. Developing yourself goes hand in hand with making a social contribution. Hence for Aristotelians as well as for utilitarians, the good is social.

With these teleological approaches in mind, consider again the question about the morality of making false promises. What would a utilitarian say? A utilitarian would probably say, "It depends." The accumulated wisdom of the human race indicates that such behavior tends to generate more harm than good for all concerned, so you should probably start with the idea that making a false promise is a bad thing to do. On the other hand, if you have good reason to think that, in the particular circumstances, the net good that will come of your making a false promise—net good for all concerned, not just for you—will be greater than the net good that will come of your avoiding such a promise, then you have good reason to consider the making of a false promise morally good in this instance. (A utilitarian who would respond in this way is generally called an act utilitarian, as opposed to a rule utilitarian—a distinction that you needn't bother with here.)

What would an Aristotelian say? An Aristotelian would probably point out that we are by nature oriented toward using speech to promote a number of social ends, such as sharing knowledge, facilitating cooperation, and fostering mutual trust. The use of speech that is under consideration (making a false promise) does not fit in with our natural orientation and, in fact, works against it. It is an action that moves us away from the human good rather than toward it. It is a bad thing to do.

Now let's get out the analytic knife and split ethical thinking one more time, this time into "action-centered" thinking and "virtue-centered" thinking. Your thinking is action-centered when you focus on particular actions or on specific kinds of actions and ask whether those actions are ethically good or bad, and based on what criteria. Needless to say, the specific kinds of actions that you can ask about are numerous, and if your focus is on particular actions rather than on kinds (for example, all the actions that come into question on your life's journey, or all the actions that come up for consideration in map ethics—e.g., in a case-study approach), the number of foci is limitless. For practical reasons, you won't attempt the impossible task of inquiring about every conceivable action. You'll confine your attention to as many examples as you need to get a grasp on how different ethical systems apply their principles. Perhaps in the process you'll find yourself modifying the principles of a given system (for example, you might try to find a way to safeguard minority interests within a basically utilitarian approach); perhaps you'll find yourself shifting your own allegiance from one ethical approach to another (for example, you might decide that minority interests cannot logically be safeguarded within a utilitarian approach and that, accordingly, the utilitarian approach should be jettisoned). In any case, the thrust of your ethical thinking will be to throw ethical light on various actions and to find a guide for the decisions that determine your actions.

In a virtue-centered approach, the focus is not on the actions themselves but on the *habits* that underlie actions. If you are virtue-centered, you believe that in the actual living of a good life, cultivating good habits is more important than simply learning the decision-making technique that might be associated with action-centered ethics. So your inquiry is focused on the sources, the nature, and the purposes of habit. What kinds of habits are good habits or virtues? What kinds of habits are bad habits or vices? Are virtues meant to facilitate a sort of automatic following of rules (hence, useful in a deontological framework)? Are virtues meant to serve the attainment of life's goal (hence, useful in a teleological framework)?

Aristotle provides the classic example of virtue-centered ethics within a teleological framework. In Aristotle's view, as noted above, the goal of life is happiness, understood as an objective condition involving the full development and actuation of human nature. How do you develop and actuate your nature? By developing virtues and living out of them. Virtues are stable dispositions that facilitate your living in accord with your nature in a regular, spontaneous, and enjoyable way. If you don't develop virtue, you might live in accord with your nature part of the time, but there is nothing in you to ensure constancy in that. Moreover, without virtue, you might find that even when you act in a way that accords with human nature, you experience it as "going against the grain," since the "grain" might consist of a set of bad habits that amounts to a sort of antinature within you. Consider, for example, what life is like when you have and when you don't have the virtue that the ancient Greeks called temperance. If you have the virtue of temperance, you are disposed to consume food and drink moderately, in ways and in amounts that are healthy and that harmonize with the other activities that a full human life involves. When you have the virtue, you *enjoy* being moderate, and you don't take pleasure in eating too much or drinking too much. Moderation comes easy for you and frees you up for other things in life. On the other hand, when you don't have temperance, you might eat and drink moderately part of the time, and the rest of the time you wish you had. Moreover, if you have developed a habit of overconsumption, moderation is neither easy nor enjoyable. But the satisfactions that attend your overconsumption are short-lived and bring in their wake a host of health problems and a general stunting of your range of activity. Hence, an Aristotelian might argue, you should include virtue in your ethical thinking and not leave home without it.

What virtues are there? Aristotle divides virtues into "intellectual" and "moral." Intellectual virtues are those habits of mind that facilitate our movement toward the good of the mind, or truth. Moral virtues are those habits of feeling and willing that facilitate our movement toward the good in practical, social living. There are as many different moral virtues as there are specific arenas of life or specific "parts" of consciousness that are well served by the development of habits. (For example, the virtue of courage is pertinent to those times and places when you have to deal with the dangerous and the difficult and/or control your fear.)

What those habits have in common, according to Aristotle, is a disposition toward the mean (the golden mean, as it was later called). The mean is a degree or a kind of feeling, willing, or doing that avoids both excess and defect. It is not a fixed quantity or something that can be figured out with a mathematical formula. It can vary from situation to situation. If you have prudence (a sort of master virtue) in a specific area of human activity, you will *see* the mean, and if you have whatever other virtue is called for, you will *live* it. If you have neither, you're in trouble. (There are times in dealing with the dangerous and difficult when courage calls for standing firm and times when courage calls for walking away. If you have courage, you'll know what the mean is and hit it. If you don't have courage, ask a prudent person for advice. If you can't find a prudent person, run.)

If you want to go further into Aristotle's list of virtues, you can do so by reading his *Nicomachean Ethics*. Alternatively, or additionally, you can devise your own list by asking yourself what sorts of virtues seem to be especially called for in the contemporary world. You may well end up with a list quite different from that of Aristotle, since the societies served by the virtues differ markedly. If the narrator of *ZMM* were devising such a list, we would probably find the virtues of "caring" and "peace of mind" high on it.

Before we move on from our brief perusal of ethics to an even briefer perusal of aesthetics, you might find this a good time to reconsider Phaedrus' rage against Aristotle. Phaedrus sees in Aristotle's thinking a tremendous demotion of Quality. That demotion first is noted in Aristotle's approach to rhetoric (which is the context in which, on Phaedrus' reading, Quality makes an appearance and is celebrated by the Sophists). As Phaedrus sees it, by making rhetoric a branch of Practical Science, Aristotle isolates it "from any concern with Truth or Good or Beauty, except as devices to throw into an argument" (*ZMM*, p. 329). You might note here that for Aristotle *ethics* is a branch of Practical Science, and ethics is quite clearly concerned with *good*. Why does Phaedrus say that Aristotle's Practical Science is unconcerned with Good? If you want to give Phaedrus the benefit of the doubt, you can say that in Practical Science, Aristotle may be concerned with the human good as an objective of human striving, but he is not concerned with Good as a kind of primary metaphysical reality, in the way that Phaedrus' Quality is. Otherwise, you can say with the narrator that, in dealing with Aristotle, Phaedrus is "unfair" because he has "an axe to grind" (*ZMM*, p. 328). That unfairness appears again when Phaedrus notes that Aristotle deals with the Good in "a relatively minor branch of knowledge called ethics" (*ZMM*, p. 344). Is ethics really a minor branch of knowledge for Aristotle? It is in the context of ethics that Aristotle discusses the place of both practical and theoretical knowledge in human life. In that context (in favor of Phaedrus' interpretation), Aristotle pays high tribute to theoretical knowledge and sees it as intrinsically higher than practical knowledge. On the other hand (against Phaedrus' interpretation), Aristotle sees a life focused on theoretical knowledge as divine rather than human. The *human* good requires action and attention to practical knowledge.

At least in part, and perhaps in large part, Phaedrus' reaction against Aristotle is an aesthetic one. From Phaedrus' viewpoint, Aristotle takes *aretê*, all-around excellence (*ZMM*, p. 341), something to be known intuitively and appreciated holistically, and chops it up into a bunch of rationally divisible virtues—and the net result is ugly.

AESTHETICS

If one face of Value is moral goodness, another face of Value is beauty, the traditional concern of aesthetics (derived from a Greek word for "sensory perception"). As the word "aesthetics" suggests, beauty emerges on the sensory level. Does it stay there? If you think it does, you will agree with the saying, "Beauty is only skin deep," since the senses of themselves seem to get no further than surfaces. You might also agree with the saying, "Beauty is in the eye of the beholder," if you think that beauty's emergence on the sensory level is due to the fact that it properly exists *in* sensory experience and nowhere else.

Does beauty stay on the sensory level? Both our experience and our language suggest that it doesn't. Doesn't that which you call beautiful evoke feelings that are more than sensations or perceptions? Isn't there a sense in which things grasped intellectually can have a kind of beauty—what *ZMM*'s narrator would call "classic" beauty—that is associated with order and clarity? Can a mathematical equation be beautiful? Poincaré would certainly say so, and he's certainly not alone. And what about spiritual beauty? Aren't there ideals that draw us by their beauty? Aren't there people whom we call beautiful not because of the way they attract us on the sensory level but because of the way they live? Doesn't that indicate that we "see" (nonsensorily) a beauty beneath the surface? It seems that beauty, as we experience it, can have many modes and exist on many levels. To express this in terms of language, we can say that "beauty" is an analogical term: It can be used in different ways in different contexts. Perhaps it is fair to say that if "beauty" is an analogical term, the primary analogue is beauty on the sensory level, beauty as the kind of thing we experience when we take in a particularly marvelous Rocky Mountain sunset and say "Wow!"

We can press this business of analogy a bit further and ask how it works. Is there some element that is present in a prominent or striking way on the level of the primary analogue (the level of sensory beauty) and which is also present in a different way or to a different degree on other levels of beauty? Is there some common element that makes all kinds of beautiful things beautiful? If there is not a common element, is there at least a "family resemblance"? (The notion of a "family resemblance," as it is used in linguistic philosophy, is itself the result of an analogy. Just as we can see a resemblance among members of the same family even though there is not a single feature that all members have in common, so we can see a family resemblance among the distinct uses of certain words, even though there is not a single feature that all the uses have in common.) Is there a common element or a family resemblance among such disparately beautiful things as an ocean sunset, a sterling performance of Beethoven's Ninth Symphony, a cherished piece of writing, a motorcycle ride in the country? (I'm going to leave that question hanging—for now . . .)

Is beauty only in the eye of the beholder? Here comes the subject-object question again, popping up its ugly head, right here in the context of talk about the beautiful. It is clear that the *experience* of beauty is in the subject of the experience, in the "eye of the beholder." However, it seems equally clear that when we experience beauty, we experience *something* as beautiful and we say that that something *is* beautiful. What do we mean by this? We don't mean that we have made a metaphysical discovery about a type of reality. Nor are we calling attention to certain cognitional activities through which an entity called beauty might be rationally known. We are not making a metaphysical statement and we are not making an epistemological statement. We are making an aesthetic statement. In that kind of statement, we are equally calling attention to the object that is the focus of our experience and to the way we are experiencing the object. Both our statement and our experience are objective in some sense—in the sense that is appropriate to the context. What other kind of objectivity is called for? Is "scientific objectivity" called for? Are we supposed to make sure that some scientifically detectable property called beauty is present in Michelangelo's "David" before we dare say that the statue is beautiful (otherwise confining our statements to remarks about our subjective state)? Does science (or, more generally, the classic mode of consciousness) have a corner on the market of objectivity? (There is the classic-romantic split again.)

Aesthetics isn't just beauty talk; it's also art talk. You can see how talk about beauty might spill over into talk about art, since beauty is found in art as well as in nature. You should note, however, that talk about art within aesthetics isn't necessarily talk about the beauty of art. In fact, you can find aesthetic theories that quite intentionally leave out any discussion of beauty and understand the nature and purpose of art in such a way that talk about beauty is irrelevant.

Before you focus on the aesthetics of art, you should perhaps take note of several meanings of the word "art." In a very broad sense, "art" is contrasted with "nature" and refers to human activity and its products as opposed to that which is given in the world apart from such activity. The boundaries of art, in this sense, are the boundaries of the human-made. The word "artificial" takes off from this sense of "art." We call something artificial, in a pejorative sense, when we see in it too much of the deliberateness that is associated with human productive activity and not enough of the spontaneity that is associated with nature's way of acting.

In a second sense, still very broad, art is contrasted with science and refers to a kind of skill knowledge—savvy—that is developed through experience and practical activity as opposed to a kind of knowledge that is heavily theoretical. (Aristotle used the word *techne*—whence we get the word "technology"—to refer to art in this sense and contrasted it with *episteme*, or theoretical knowledge.) Art in this second sense of the word may also be contrasted with the state of mind of one who is inexperienced or unskillful in a given area of human activity. If you barely know how to boil water, for example, or you can only cook by following recipes doggedly, you don't yet have the "art" of cooking. If you don't know how to shim your handlebars, you're not far along in the art of motorcycle maintenance.

In a third sense, the word "art" refers to a certain set of specialized activities and their products that have historically been grouped together under the category "fine arts," activities such as painting, sculpting, dancing, and making music. This is the sense of art with which aesthetics is primarily concerned; but it is quite possible for other senses of "art" to find their way into an aesthetic theory and cause confusion for the unwary.

Talk about art can focus on the activity or experience of the artist, on the artistic product or artwork (which sometimes coincides with the artistic activity, as in dance and other "performing arts"), or on the aesthetic experience of the person who is experiencing the artwork. Whatever the focus, aesthetic theories tend to be concerned with two main questions: What is art? and What makes art *good* art?

I'm going to take out the analytic knife one more time before putting it away for good (at least as far as this backpack goes). When I first used that knife, at the beginning of the Western portion of this backpack, I noted that there was an arbitrary character about this activity (see above, p. 134). In saying this, I was echoing a point made by the narrator in ZMM (p. 66). Now, given some other things that have been said in this packet, I want to echo another point. The arbitrary character of the knife's movement means that there is a creative element in analytic thought (see ZMM, p. 70), but that creativity doesn't destroy all objectivity. Creativity is the enemy of objectivity only in the sort of dualistic framework in which you have to choose between a subjectivity that consists of arbitrariness and caprice and an objectivity that consists solely of the "hard data" that are detectable through scientific instruments. In the nondualistic framework that ZMM's philosophy points to, creativity and objectivity fuse in the light of Quality awareness (see ZMM, p. 241).

What is art? To answer that question is to say something about art's function or functions. What is good art? To answer that question is to say something about what function or functions art *ought* to have and how such functions might be carried out in an excellent manner. When I think about some of the answers to those questions that have been offered in the history of Western philosophy, it seems to me that you can divide all views according to four main ways of seeing art: art as expressing, art as pleasing, art as moving, and art as revealing.

If you see art as *expressing*, you think of the artist as, by definition, a person with something, most likely a lot, to express. You see the artist as driven by powerful notions and feelings. You see art as a satisfying projection of those notions and feelings into some art form or other. According to this view of art, how the art is taken by some receiver is irrelevant. In fact, it is unnecessary that there be a receiver. Art doesn't have to please; it doesn't have to communicate; it just has to express. Art can, of course, serve other functions as well, but its heart and soul is its expressiveness. The greater the expressiveness, the greater the art. This, clearly, is an artist-centered view of art.

At least to some extent, Nietzsche exemplifies this approach to art. He sees art as an expression of the will to power. In *The Will to Power*, he talks about the great artist as one who achieves the "grand style," a style that is unconcerned with pleasing.

If you see art as *pleasing*, you are quite likely to tie art in with the creation of various forms of the beautiful, since the beautiful (whether on the level of perceptions, feelings, or thoughts) is pleasing. However, according to this view of art, the presence of beauty as such is not essential. What matters is that the artwork be capable of stimulating some form of pleasure. The more and the better the pleasure, the better the art. This, clearly, is a receiver-centered view of art.

Aristotle points out in his *Poetics* a kind of pleasure not directly associated with presentations of the beautiful, a pleasure that is associated with a tragic play. The tragic suffering that is viewed in a tragic play elicits in the audience a "catharsis," or purgation, of certain emotions. That catharsis is or at least leads to a pleasurable feeling.

If you see art as *moving*, you believe that art is meant to goad or inspire you to some sort of action: perhaps to live more nobly, perhaps to defend a certain way of life, perhaps to start a revolution. According to this view, art's primary function is not to be found in the artwork's production, presentation, or immediate reception. It is to be found in the *lives* of the receivers. To the extent that art moves the receivers' hearts and minds in such a way as to make a difference in their lives, it is good art. If art fails to move its receivers in any way that goes beyond the place of its reception, it has failed as art. (Notice that if you say you were deeply moved by a certain artwork—say, a movie—you might mean the sort of thing associated with this view of art, but you also might simply be referring to a sort of pleasurable catharsis: You've had a good cry and you're glad for it.)

In Plato's view, art is meant to serve society by promoting moral living and responsible citizenship. When it fails to do so (for example by presenting, in attractive ways, false images of the good life), it is bad art and ought to be banned. For that reason, in the *Republic,* Plato banishes certain artists from his utopia. Art should move people properly or be gone.

Finally, if you see art as *revealing,* you believe that art is meant to disclose something about reality. It is a special window to truth. Perhaps you see art as a necessary complement to dialectically reachable propositional truth (the sort of truth that Phaedrus sees as smothering Quality). Perhaps you go further than that and see art as a kind of truth that is higher than propositional truth. (Did Phaedrus go that far?) Perhaps, to come down a few pegs, you see art as disclosing the truth about the artist, revealing the artist's soul. In any case, according to this view, the more enlightening art is, the better art it is.

In the view of Leo Tolstoy (1828–1910) art is meant to communicate the feelings of the artist. It is a limited form of revelation, but a revelation nonetheless. Among those who see art's revelatory value as going beyond this are Hegel, who talks about art as a sort of representation of the true world of ideal thought, and Heidegger, who sees in art a mode of the presence of truth.

I hope you have found in the foregoing survey of the compartments of Reality, Knowledge, and Value in Western philosophy a helpful, illuminating context in which to do some further thinking about some of the numerous philosophical ideas in *ZMM.* At this point, you might find it a helpful exercise to engage Phaedrus or the narrator in a dialogue with some of the thinkers who showed up in the three compartments. Nothing prevents you from doing that in your imagination, so have at it if you like. As a stimulus in that direction, you might want to tune in to the following.

A SHORT DIALOGUE

PHAEDRUS: I suppose you are wondering why I have asked you all to join me here at this famous table with the crack down the middle. Well, there's been a lot of talk among you about what's real and what's true and what's good. While the talk has been going on—and, to some extent, as a result of the talk—the material conditions of life have been vastly improved. The full benefit of this material progress has not yet been extended to all, and maybe something has to be done about this . . . but that's not what I want to talk with you about. The fact is that among those who have experienced the full benefit, there is a growing malaise, a kind of spiritual emptiness. It's this malaise that I've summoned you here to discuss. (By the way, in case you are wondering *how* I got you here, it was through this XL4 Vibration Reconstituter—you see, I'm quite at home in the technological world.) Anyway, this malaise seems to be—

SOPHIST: Before you go into that further, I want to say that I am glad you brought me here. I've read accounts of your journey, and I appreciate the kind, insightful, and well-chosen words you had for me. I had begun to lose all hope of vindication and suspected that the pernicious depiction of me perpetrated by this fellow on my right would go unchallenged for eternity.

PLATO: If the truth is pernicious, so be it. The truth is that you were simply concerned with teaching people how to persuade others (not to mention how to win lawsuits). And you did it for *pay*. My good friend and teacher, Socrates, was interested in higher things.

SOPHIST: Higher things? You're not going to bring up the Forms again, are you? Do you really think you benefited people by your endless discussions about these alleged essences? As Phaedrus here rightly saw and courageously said, we Sophists

	were concerned with inculcating all-around excellence in everyday life, not with some silly pursuit of—
PHAEDRUS:	Gentlemen, please! I appreciate the intensity of your interaction. I'm an intense person myself. (In fact that intensity caused me some trouble— a gap in my journey.) I want to get back to the question of the malaise. I was hoping that together we might hammer out a solution.
NIETZSCHE:	I'm glad that you used that word "hammer." I believe in "philosophy with a hammer." Add the hammer to your philosophical toolbox, Phaedrus. Put it next to the "knife." Use it to break up decadent forms of thinking and then *create* the kind of thinking that is needed. Create the valuations that will destroy the malaise.
PLATO:	What's this about *creating* thinking? Creating or making is something you do with regard to particular things on the basis of the Forms that are reached through thinking, but it's not something that applies to thinking. You don't make the thinking. Thinking is a matter of following, following the lead of *Reason,* the highest part of the soul.
NIETZSCHE:	The kind of reason you are talking about died with God. The thinking that serves life is—
ARISTOTLE:	Actually, Plato, there is a kind of thinking that is associated with making. This is a distinction you failed to make clearly. Practical thinking is rooted in doing and making and serves doing and making. It is, of course, not to be confused with theoretical thinking, which is concerned with the essential causes of things.
HUME:	Essential causes? What can you know about essential causes? You observe events happening in a certain sequence and you associate them with each other. That's all your knowledge of "causes" comes down to—an association that you have gotten in the bad habit of making. All you really know are your sensory impressions. . . .

	By the way, is anyone interested in a game of backgammon?
KANT:	David, will you ever learn? Of course one knows causes, because the human mind can't help but know things *through* the category of cause. It's a structure of the mind, a necessary predisposition to apprehend an object—by which I mean, of course, only a "phenomenal" object and not the "thing-in-itself." In fact, when you say that one is "in the habit of making an association," you illustrate this predisposition, because you say, in effect, that habit *causes* one to make this association.
SOPHIST:	Nice move, Immanuel. I like your mental agility. Now if you could only get rid of your ponderous style . . . I know someone who can help, and the fee is rather small.
PLATO:	There you go again. Always reducing things to the level of the "bronze" type of people.
SOPHIST:	I'm just trying to bring the discussion back down to earth. I seem to be surrounded by people who are given to endless and fruitless speculations. It reminds me of the pointless meanderings of the cosmologists of my era. That's what drove me to take up the Sophist position and focus on the human and the practical.
ARISTOTLE:	Your effort to make the discussion practical has some merit. However, I think it's important to make a distinction between ends and means here. The goal that Phaedrus has given us is a practical one, to solve the problem of the malaise. The means to that goal includes an analysis of the problem. That involves our distinguishing among different types and aspects of the malaise. Once we've done that, we can seek to understand the distinct causes of each type and aspect of malaise. Then we can—
SOPHIST:	That's very tidy, Aristotle; but before you get any tidier, I think we should let Phaedrus speak. What is this malaise, Phaedrus?

PHAEDRUS:	The malaise seems to center on a kind of dualism. We can't seem to get the affective and the cognitive together.
HUME:	I've gotten wind of some of your reflections about this. Don't you claim that the solution lies in something called Quality?
PHAEDRUS:	Yes. And I don't back off from that claim. I was hoping that the group of you might help me develop some of my ideas.
HUME:	I might be willing to do that, but I have a problem with this Quality that you claim to know. Is Quality a matter of fact? If so, show me the pertinent sense data.
WILLIAM JAMES:	Your view of knowing is too narrow, David. I share your appreciation for the empirical. As you might know, I even tried to find an empirical answer to the question of life after death. However, sense experience is not enough. The search for truth needs the guidance of value concerns.
HUME:	Value concerns? What does value have to do with fact? Come on, Phaedrus. Is Quality a matter of fact or isn't it?
PHAEDRUS:	You sound like my English department colleagues! How can Quality be a fact? Quality is what allows facts to emerge. Quality is prior to facts!
PLATO:	Then it's like the Forms, especially the Form "Good."
PHAEDRUS:	As I understand what you've said about this, Plato, a Form is a fixed object of thought. The Quality I'm talking about isn't like that. It has a dynamic character about it. And, what's more, it's not a form of truth. Truth is a form of it!
PLATO:	If Quality is dynamic and not something fixed, how can you even think it? Won't it change at the very moment that you go to lay hold of it in thought? How can thought even exist without the stable and fixed?
HERACLITUS	(singing): Oh, you can't step into the same stream twice, and you can't lay hold of the same thought twice, and you—

PHAEDRUS: You don't lay hold of Quality as an object of thought. You lay hold of objects of thought on the basis of Quality awareness. And you're not just "laying hold" of them. In a way, you're creating them, because you're making choices about them on the basis of Quality. Thinking is creative.

NIETZSCHE: Create boldly, then, and destroy too. Hammer the malaise to pieces.

At this moment, Chickenman enters with a slide across the floor. The conversation is interrupted by mirth, but it may be resumed later.

S E C T I O N 6

SELECTIONS FROM THE ORIGINAL MANUSCRIPT

"One hears of an eight-hundred-thousand-word draft," wrote George Steiner in his enthusiastic review, "and feels perversely deprived of it by the mere sanity and worldliness of the publisher" (*The New Yorker* [April 15, 1974], p. 147). All the drafts put together may have reached that gargantuan size, but the actual manuscript accepted by the 122nd editor to read it, James Landis at William Morrow and Company, was only about 10 or 15 percent larger than the final, published version of *ZMM*. Steiner was correct, however, in supposing that there would be a few portions of it that are especially worthy of publication; and through Robert M. Pirsig's cooperation, we are able to offer some of them here now, as well as a few excerpts from some of Pirsig's letters regarding the book.

✳

The first is a brief passage that was written to go between the twelfth and thirteenth lines on page 62 in the 1979 Bantam edition, a little more than halfway through Chapter 6. These paragraphs would have augmented the classical-romantic dichotomy.

The endless battle of the sexes is a classic-romantic battle. The stereotype of the husband in this battle is that of an eternal dullard more interested in his car and the stock market than in his own wife because these things have underlying intellectual form. The stereotype of the wife in this battle is that of eternal frivolousness. She wants everything "nice" without any real understanding of what has to be done to *have* it "nice." Because niceness is a romantic feeling rather than some intellectual concept.

Phaedrus thought the endless love-hate social agony between black and white Americans has roots in this classic-romantic duality.[1] The black family is not derived from European cultures and traditionally it is the husband who has been romantic and the wife who is classic, although, as a result of white influence, this pattern has been changing. The classical contempt for romantic frivolity, untrustworthiness, and pleasure-seeking sensuality explained much genuine and honestly derived white hostility toward blacks, he thought. That Negro men have simultaneously regarded white men as dull, awkward, and ugly is less well known, for in the romantic mode one does not make a point of spelling everything out.

Others have speculated already that the hip social phenomenon of the 1960s was caused by new understanding of black attitudes by whites and adoption of them. What was discovered was a discipline of feeling, of spirit, of soul, in the traditional black man's romantic way of looking at things, which is quite as complex and difficult as the white man's classical discipline of formal reason. And the discovery, moreover, that there was no meshing of these worlds. You go all one way or you go all the other. As I said yesterday, these modes are different visions of reality that have all things in common as objects but nothing in common themselves.

John's alienation from technology seems primarily a romantic alienation growing out of this situation.

This next segment was designed to begin at the third line on page 71 of the Bantam text. It would have augmented the discussions of definition and hierarchy.

The naturalness of this hierarchic structuring of our thought and also its weakness appears in the game "Twenty Questions," which Chris and his brother have sometimes played in the back of the car on long trips. In this game Chris will think of something and his brother will try to find out what it is by asking up to twenty questions to which answers can only be yes or no. It's a well-known game.

If his brother guesses randomly he can only examine twenty

---

[1] This echoes Eldridge Cleaver, *Soul on Ice* (New York: Delta Books, 1968), pp. 153–210 (Part IV); another appeal to black experience also occurs in *ZMM*, pp. 195–196.

grains of sand. But if he uses the analytic knife properly, splitting the pile neatly in half, learning the yes-or-no answer to which half the grain is in, and then splitting the half to learn which quarter it is in and so on, he can examine up to two-to-the-twentieth-power grains of sand. I don't know offhand how many grains of sand that is, but it's in the astronomical regions.

To know where to make the cuts a questioner must have in his mind a preconceived hierarchy of things. The thoroughness and precision with which this hierarchy is established is what gives him skill.

In theory, "Twenty Questions" is a neat game, but in practice it always degenerates into a lot of quarreling because of poor definition of the piles. A good definition not only isolates a pile from every other pile, it also locates its position in a known hierarchy of things. But a good definition is not always easy to come by, it is more a work of art on the part of the observer than a natural part of the thing observed,[1] and that is what spoils the game. The quarrels are not just caused by the bad temper of the players, Phaedrus thought. They are caused by the inadequacy of hierarchic thought to represent nature itself, which results in disagreement among the players as to what the definitions are.

For example if the questioner asks, "Is it a liquid?" and you say, "yes," and the thing you are thinking of is *glass*, then scientifically you are correct because glass is a liquid. But when the game is over and the questioner has failed to discover what you have been thinking of he will be plenty angry. That answer would throw anyone off, no matter how skilled he was.

Phaedrus thought the fault in this case was not with science, which has very specific criteria for defining liquids and solids, nor is the fault with glass, which is just glass, regardless of what quarrels arise over it. He thought the fault lay in an unproved assumption of the game, and sometimes of science too, that the hierarchies found in nature are a *part* of nature. It seemed to him that nature does not *care* whether glass is a solid or liquid. This is just a superimposition upon nature by people. Hierarchies are not nature, he said, they are a kind of *rhetoric* about nature, a statement whose significance will become more apparent later on.[2]

It seems natural enough to think of a tree as truly organized rather than just rhetorically organized into branches and sub-branches, and to think that this organization is a part of the tree rather than what you say about the tree. The same would be true of rivers and of sub-

[1] This statement has both a Sophist and a Kantian ring to it. Categories spring from the human "measurer of all things," the knowing mind, rather than from the thing known. See Section 4. p. 116.
[2] Here, with the reference to rhetoric, the Sophist ring gets louder.

stance in its macro-hierarchy of galaxy-star-planet-moon and micro-hierarchy of crystal-molecule-atom-particle. But close observation shows that if these hierarchies *are* a part of nature, nature is astonishingly indifferent to them, going its own way whether they are there or not. A branch of the banyan tree touches the ground, takes root and the tree has a new trunk—a total violation of its hierarchy. Rivers change their course so as to alter the hierarchy of their branches. Outer electrons in a copper wire pay virtually no attention to which molecule they are supposed to belong to. And in astronomy the prevailing rule is "Anything not prohibited will happen." In an infinite universe any finite possibility becomes a sure thing.

One thing not prohibited in astronomy is that the prohibitions themselves will be found incorrect. When this is combined with the previous statement it logically reduces to "Anything will happen." The hierarchy and the system of questions which generate it are a part of the sand of consciousness and of the landscape from which it is derived, but they do not govern it, they merely describe it in one of many ways.[3] How that way of description can be integrated without change into a kind of understanding which goes beyond analysis and does not depend upon it is the subject of this Chautauqua and its strange way of looking at familiar things.

The first section of this material would have begun at the second to last line on page 125, and the second section would have appeared between the twelfth and eleventh to last lines on page 126. It would have added to the treatment of Hinduism by suggesting some of its more interesting paradoxes.

All his letters show is an acquisition of an enormous confusion of contradictions and incongruities and divergences and exceptions to any rule he formulated about the things he observed. He seemed to formulate those at the rate of several a day with a feeling of profound discovery each time. But he laments that the strength of these discoveries is destroyed each time by the immediate appearance of exceptions so numerous that the rule might as well have never been formulated in the first place. He gives as an example the rule that the Hindus regard the appearances of the world as illusory but finds an exception in the market place where one can observe bargaining go on harder and longer than anywhere. People don't bargain hard

[3] "Do not govern . . . merely describe" is reminiscent of the prescribe-proscribe-describe argument on the occasion of the publication of *Webster's Third Unabridged* in 1966.

about illusions. Except that often this bargaining seemed to have an unworldly quality about it, as though the participants didn't really care, but were bargaining ritualistically. On the basis of this rule, its exception, and its counter-exception, he asked, what can you say about the subject of Hindu unworldliness?

Some other interesting generalizations which he made but which fell apart just as quickly are:

Hinduism is very ritualistic. Some of the most spiritually advanced people he met seemed to follow no ritual at all.

Hinduism is passive and non-violent. In the Bhagavad Gita warfare is encouraged as part of one's duty. Certain castes have no other purpose in this world than to fight.

Hinduism teaches the oneness of all things. The Sankhya-Yoga system of philosophy is dualistic. The Nyaya-Vaisheshika is pluralistic. These are orthodox Hindu philosophies.[1]

On and on it went, through generality after generality, until he was ready to drop the whole process of generalizing—except that this produced the nagging feeling that there *are* general truths about Hinduism, just beyond, that he was about to grasp but never did. His problem, I think, was that the Indian tradition requires acceptance of it on its own terms. You don't sum it up correctly in terms of another way of looking at things. Because of his scientific background Phaedrus threw up his hands at the inadequacy of the proofs, tests, and logical consistencies within Indian thought without realizing that these demands for proofs were, within an Indian way of looking at things, a lesser form of knowledge trying to contain a greater one. This lesser form of knowledge was to be *transcended* for an understanding of the real base of Indian philosophy. Phaedrus did not see this, and so went spinning round and round, doing Westernized generalizations on a subject that is not well rendered by Westernized generalizations.[2]

Phaedrus, in India, never began true meditation because he hadn't

---

[1] The Sankhya and the Yoga were originally distinct philosophical systems that eventually formed a rather intimate alliance. The same can be said about Nyaya and Vaisheshika. Hence, these four philosophies are commonly referred to as two: "Sankhya-Yoga" and "Nyaya-Vaisheshika." In the first alliance, Sankhya mostly provides the theoretical framework while Yoga provides a practical program. The objective of Sankhya-Yoga is to overcome the dualism of spirit and nature and restore spirit to its lost original condition. In the second alliance, Vaisheshika presents a world view that emphasizes the diversity in the universe, while Nyaya provides the logical underpinnings of this world view. These four philosophies are orthodox not in any narrow Western sense of orthodoxy but in the sense that they are among the six traditionally recognized "darshanas" or ways of seeing.

[2] To unpack a bit the narrator's analysis of Phaedrus' plight, accepting Hinduism "on its own terms" would involve a recognition of the relativity of truth on the lower level of apprehension (as in the story of the six blind persons and the elephant) plus a recognition that reaching the higher level isn't simply a matter of dialectically reachable propositions. See Section 4, pp. 54–55, 60–61.

resolved lower-order questions of truth and falsehood which are preparatory to mediation.[3] Since the ancient formulations of Indian philosophy were made many changes have taken place in the world for which Indian formulations of thought, arising from a non-technological, agricultural life, are inadequate.

Before he sent it off to the many publishing houses, Pirsig shared the manuscript with various actual persons who appear in the narrative. After he had sent it to Gennie and Robert DeWeese but before he had gotten their feedback, he had received the reactions of his son Chris and his Twin Cities friends John and Sylvia, and his follow-up letter of December 29, 1972, to the DeWeeses reads in part:

Sylvia was kind of thrown by the way I switched everything around, and Chris was *really* shook, so I guess you probably have some of the same feelings. I explained to them that the story isn't really about them, that they are like a Greek chorus there to "Oh" and "Ah" and give a semblance of reality to a tale that seems always to ride at the very edge of incredibility and needs all the help it can get. In the first draft she and John were much more three-dimensional, but it became apparent that the center of the book must be the Chautauqua, and she and John cannot be allowed to upstage it or the person telling it. For reasons shown at the end of the story, the narrator's perception of people around him is very weak and distorted, and so this two-dimensional portrayal of Sylvia and John and yourselves becomes justified.

Her observation and yours that "it isn't really me" is correct and made me kind of unhappy when I first heard it because it was so true, and at one time out of pique and whimsy I was going to have the ghost Phaedrus appear to the narrator and say "It's a nice description but it isn't really me," and the narrator would answer back, "Yeah, well this isn't really *me* either." I don't know who all these paper people really are, just parts of a dream that appeared over the years and seemed to have some quality.

In a similar vein, Hawthorne's "Preface" to *The House of Seven Gables* says that a romance, "while it sins unpardonably so

---

[3] It should perhaps be noted that postponing the practice of meditation until some "lower-order questions of truth" are resolved is not something specifically enjoined by Hinduism. Phaedrus' linear mentality, not the mentality of Hinduism, is being reflected here.

far as it may swerve aside from the truth of the human heart—has fairly a right to present that truth under circumstances, to a great extent, of the author's choosing." In this twentieth-century romance of the journey inward, the "human heart" in question is that of the implied author, the reunited Phaedrus-narrator (see N. Katherine Hayles, *The Cosmic Web* [Ithaca: Cornell University Press, 1984], p. 82).

Pirsig's remark in his letter about the two-dimensionality of the characters occurs in the book itself in this form:

> If I were a novelist rather than a Chautauqua orator I'd try to "develop the characters" of John and Sylvia and Chris with action-packed scenes that would also reveal "inner meanings" of Zen and maybe Art and maybe even Motorcycle Maintenance. That would be quite a novel, but for some reason I don't feel quite up to it. They're friends, not characters [*ZMM*, pp. 120–121].

The largest section we have chosen to reprint is an entire chapter which, had it not been cut, would have appeared after page 164 in the Bantam edition, at the end of Part II of the book. It is particularly noteworthy for showing the relationship between the narrator and his son Chris in a more positive light, for telling more of the "truth of the human heart" about the narrator, and especially for suggesting why Chris remained loyal to him, despite the narrator's very real problems and his own, until the story's happy ending.

There are many ways of defining something, and the whole business of coming up with a definition is an art in itself. A good artist at this often starts out with an *ostensive* definition because that's both the easiest to produce and the easiest to understand. Ostensive definitions define by showing.[1]

I want now to *show* what quality is in terms of something specific and concrete. English composition isn't specific and concrete—not, at least, when it's talked about as an object. You can ball around endlessly on what is and what isn't quality in English composition and never arrive anywhere—and this certainly has been done. Vic-

---

[1] An ostensive definition is a particular example in which a general principle appears to inductive reasoning with maximum elegance and clarity. As the narrator notes, the discovery and selection of a really good ostensive definition requires great art, not merely scientific knowledge. Tautological definitions, which are the foundation of deductive reasoning, are a different matter (see *ZMM*, p. 192, and our note to p. 192 in Section 11).

torians during the last century did much talking of this sort and the result was so oppressive almost no one has brought up the subject since. To a large extent the whole social revolt of the 1920's was against Victorian "quality." But that snob-derived quality[2] wasn't what Phaedrus was talking about. So to bypass that whole scene I want to talk about Quality in an area where Phaedrus would have agreed Quality is a dominant force, but where no snob would dream of finding it—Quality in the art of motorcycle maintenance.

Chris and I are now walking from the college toward Main Street again and while we do this I want to just list, randomly, some things about motorcycle maintenance that have Quality and some things that do not. This isn't a difficult exercise but it's an important one for the Chautauqua and kind of fun too. Since it's both important and kind of fun it has a quality of its own.[3]

A clean machine with a smooth, hard pickup, moving down a country road on a seventy-five-degree day, sunlit, with someone you care for[4]—that's at the high end of the scale. At the other end is a dirty, misfiring, worn-out engine that suddenly has a loud knock as you move down a slippery city street in a rainstorm. Quality is the difference between the two experiences. It's nothing more complicated than that. It only becomes complicated when you try to analyze what it is.

Quality in motorcycle maintenance changes the performance of the second machine into that of the first one. If it doesn't do that there's no Quality. But within that overall Quality, in the progression from bad to good, there are an infinite variety of shades and variations that become more meaningful as you get into it.

If the machine makes deep knocking noises that can't be cured by any adjustment you know of, you must take out the whole engine and disassemble it to find out what the cause is. Contemplation of that job normally produces depression, a very low-quality feeling, which in severe cases prevents any work on the machine at all.

But no depression can last indefinitely unless you fight it or try to get around it. Then it just hangs on. But if you resign yourself to it, it runs its course and goes away of its own accord, and you stop

[2] This remark recalls the reference to the "Eastern ass" in Montana (*ZMM*, p. 162).

[3] The narrator and Chris are not on the bike and are not wearing helmets but are simply walking side by side down a quiet, tree-lined, residential street. Conversation "with someone you care for" should be an easy and pleasurable task. Listing is not a Quality activity in comparison with conversation. On mapping as a Quality activity, see Section 3 of this book.

What the narrator needs is an ostensive definition of Quality not in words but by manifesting a Quality relationship with Chris.

[4] Caring is a Quality attitude; the interpersonal dimension suggested here is not characteristic of many of the narrator's social relationships (see *ZMM*, pp. 24–25, 38, 146, 247, 253).

thinking about how bad the machine *is* compared to what it *was* and start to think about how good it *will be* compared to what it *is*. Then a wave of high-Quality feeling appears, and if you're skillful you can ride it like a surfer all the way to successful completion of the job.[5]

An early part of this wave is a natural curiosity to see what's wrong. The height of the wave is when you do find out what's wrong and how to repair it. The late part of the wave is a suspense that develops when you wonder if it will work when the machine's back together. This keeps you careful during reassembly. On the final test ride you listen skeptically for any signs of trouble. Then, as you are forced, minute after minute, to come to the conclusion that the machine's running perfectly, a really great Quality feeling comes over you that pays you back for all the earlier gloom. When you've gone through that moment with a machine, you really own it for the first time, in a new kind of way. What the smooth sound of the engine really tells you is that it's responded to your care.

I talked a lot about caring on the first day of this Chautauqua, and said this lack of care causes a lot of the technological hopelessness around us. I think it's important now to tie care to Quality by pointing out that care and Quality are internal and external aspects of the same thing.[6] A person who sees Quality and feels it as he works is a person who cares. A person who cares about what he sees and does is a person who's bound to have some characteristics of Quality.

Thus, if the problem of technological hopelessness is caused by absence of care, both by technologists and antitechnologists; and if care and Quality are external and internal aspects of the same thing, then it follows logically that what really causes technological hopelessness is absence of the perception of Quality in technology by both technologists and antitechnologists. Phaedrus' mad pursuit of the rational, analytic, and therefore *technological* meaning of the word "Quality" was really a pursuit of the answer to the whole problem of technological hopelessness. So it seems to me, anyway.

This is still vague because I'm only defending Quality ostensively, by example, and haven't formally stated what Quality and caring are in relation to the rest of the world—or at least to the hierarchic representation of it taught in universities. But that will come.

---

[5] This wave is not one of the waves of crystallization that later trouble Phaedrus and carry him toward his psychological trouble.

[6] The commitment of the person in attention and volition forms the experiential and subjective pole, and the worthy perceived object forms the objective pole of the unique unified entity that is existential Quality.

Before it does, you should stop this Chautauqua and try to formulate for yourself an exact technical definition of your own of what you mean by "Quality." Try it. That's the only way one can understand the magnitude of the problem involved. It's not a minor uphill intellectual effort. It's Mount Everest.[7] If you doubt this, or feel it's an exaggeration, really try it. Try to define Quality. See for yourself.

A big yellow and blue sign identifies the machinist's place again. We go in back, and he has our part ready. A dollar-fifty is all he wants. He gives a little repressed smile and slips the axle into the chain adjuster link to show us. He's made it a running fit,[8] about one-thousandth of an inch clearance on each side. That's what he's smiling about.

"I didn't have a metric reamer," he says, "so I just honed it out with some old brake-cylinder stones."

"Perfect," I say.

He represses the smile even harder and hands it to me to try. Like a bottle of wine. There's Quality in what he's just done and he knows it and it means something to him. To both of us. On the way out I twist the axle in the new holes, feeling how it slides freely but without any looseness at all. I give it to Chris, and let him slide it, so he knows what a good running fit feels like.

"We don't need that good a fit," I tell him. "But he did it anyway."

"Why?" Chris asks.

"Because he didn't like to do sloppy work."

We walk along and I wonder if Chris understands the importance of that. He can't. He's way too young. And you can't learn it just by hearing it.

At the filling station the machine is waiting for us and the attendant-owner gives us a surly look out of the corner of his eye. I ignore the look, pull out the tire irons, and lay them and the other tools on the ground where I can get them. This is no different from changing a bicycle tire, once you've got the wheel off, except that it's bigger.

I squat, unscrew the valve stem to let the air out, then lay the wheel on some rags to protect the hub. I stand up again, and with my heel push down on the tire to separate the rubber from the rim.

[7] Any mountain can serve as the symbol of the ultimate problem; compare Mount Kailas, which Phaedrus unsuccessfully tried to climb (*ZMM*, p. 189), and the mountains the narrator and Chris are soon to climb nearly to the top during their hiking and camping trip.

[8] A "running fit"—when the rear axle fits through and turns easily inside the chain adjuster link—is an ostensive definition in words of Quality in the art of motorcycle maintenance; so is the narrator's manner of changing the tire. The problem with the chain adjuster link occurred on pp. 58–59 of *ZMM* again and is mentioned again on p. 155.

I kneel down again, pick up an iron, and slip it between one edge of the tire and the rim, then push down on it to lever the tire edge over the rim, then tell Chris to hold the iron in place to keep the tire edge from slipping back under the rim. About six inches farther down the rim I insert the second tire iron and do the same thing.

Then I shove a box wrench in the gap next to the first iron, remove the first iron and insert it beyond the second, then leap frog the second beyond the first, and the first beyond the second, until the tire edge pops up around the whole rim. I stand up to stretch and see Surly is watching us. When the stretch is over I go back to it.

I pull out the tube and set it on the cycle seat. With the irons I bring the other edge of the tire over the rim the same way as the first edge until the tire is completely off the wheel. I ask Surly if he wants the old tire. He shakes his head.

I spit on my fingers, rub them on a bar of soap, and put the soapy spit on one rim of the new tire. I lever the first edge of the new tire on, then stand up and look for a mark on the tire that tells me where to locate it for the best wheel balancing. The weight of the valve throws the wheel balance off a bit and the best tires are weighted to counterbalance this, but this one apparently isn't, because there's no mark.

I insert the tube, put in the valve stem, fill it with air, and then remove the valve stem to let all the air out again. This takes out any accidental folds in the tube. The big thing you have to worry about on this job is pinches and folds in the tube or damage from sharp tool edges or spoke ends. The rubber in the inner tube has to be very soft to stay flexible and it's more than discouraging to put a tire on and discover that because of sharp edges it leaks worse than it did before. Chris did a bicycle tire once when I wasn't around and when he finally showed me his problems I saw the tire had about twenty patches in it, meaning he'd had it on and off that many times. He was levering the tire with a screwdriver instead of a tire iron and each time he put it on he'd poke new holes in the tube.

I soap the other edge of the tire, lever it over, replace the valve and fill the tire. I look at Surly and, by golly, he doesn't look Surly anymore.

He finally says, "You don't see many of them changed like that anymore."

He must have had doubts about the quality of my work.

"Brings back memories," I say.

"That it does," he says.

The bell rings from a big Lincoln at the pumps, so he goes to take care of it. New York license plate. I see, as he puts the hose in, that his expression is surly again.

The wheel goes back on awfully hard. Something's wrong. I have to strain like hell to get the axle through it. That shouldn't be. I pull the axle out and try it again. No better. I pull the axle out a third time and try reversing it, putting it in from the other side. No better. I try shoving the wheel in really hard. Still no luck.

I stand up and bend backward to take the kink out of my spine.

Surly sees me and says, "All done?"

"No, something's stuck. I'm going to leave it and come back later."

"Sure," he says.

We start to walk around the block, with the leaves of the trees and the concrete of the sidewalk very vivid now, the way things sometimes are when you're suddenly required to do something you hadn't expected to do.

Chris asks, "Why is the wheel stuck?"

"I don't know."

"Maybe you got the tire wrong."

"No," I say disgustedly. "That couldn't possibly be the trouble."

He looks down at the sidewalk, and his silence tells me his feelings are hurt. He avoids the cracks with his steps. I forget he's eleven.

"The reason the tire can't cause the wheel to stick," I say, "is that there's no place the tire touches anything except the wheel rim. To make the wheel stick, the tire would have to touch some place on the motorcycle or touch the ground. You see that? The wheel's got to be binding at some place where it touches the machine. Do you see why that is?"

He doesn't say anything. This is part of the whole problem; the way his feelings get hurt so easily. I'm just trying to avoid a bad-mood trap of my own and he's helping to shove me into it. He doesn't see that, of course. Maybe he's just trying to avoid a bad-mood trap of *his* own and I helped shove *him* into it.

Bad-mood traps like this are inevitable when things go wrong. You think you're just about done and suddenly you discover you're nowhere near done and the natural reaction is anger. Until we can figure out what's binding that wheel, we're just going to have to stay here and work on it. That news, combined with the hot sun and all the out-of-position straining, got me for a second and that's why we now walk. The rule is you never work on a machine when you're mad. Back there I caught myself about to get a hammer to pound that wheel in place. That's the kind of idiot thing that can happen when the sun and the physical effort and the anger get to you. That would have damaged something for sure. Before you can

---

2 1 6

maintain any real control over the condition of the machine you have to have control over yourself. The two aren't ever separate.[9]

We get back to the machine now and I sit down, light a cigarette, and study the wheel.

Chris asks, "Aren't you going to do anything?"

"I *am* doing something," I say.

"What?"

"I'm *looking* at it."[10]

"What are you looking for?"

"I'm looking to see why the wheel won't go back far enough."

Chris looks for a while with me. Five drags later on the cigarette I hear him suddenly say, "The chain's too tight."

I look at the chain and see that it *is* too tight. I check the chain adjuster links to see if they're taken up too far but they aren't.

"It's caught," Chris says. "Down here."

Sure as hell, he's found it.[11] The chain passes *under* instead of *over* the muffler bracket. The bracket's taking up just enough of the slack in the chain to make the wheel hard to mount. I spent so much time trying to position the wheel, I unconsciously got a mental fixation that the trouble was in the axle assembly. We both push the wheel forward, bring the chain up over the muffler bracket, move the wheel in place again, and everything suddenly fits and moves freely.

In a few minutes we have it together. We start the engine to check the rotation of the wheel. It works.

Surly is out of the station, watching.

"Got her going, huh?"

"Finally."

"I was the one who found it," Chris says. He explains how he found it.

Surly smiles and says, "Think you'll be a mechanic when you grow up?"

Chris says he doesn't know.

"Like your Daddy here?"

Chris's expression lights up. "Yeah."

[9] Control over the machine and the self are not only inseparable but even identical, for "the real cycle you're working on is a cycle called yourself" (*ZMM*, p. 293). What was stuck in this episode was not so much the axle or chain as the narrator's mind.

[10] See the references to staring in *ZMM*, pp. 152 and 280.

[11] Chris's finding the solution to the problem in this omitted chapter resembles his "I told him to look at the gas tank" (*ZMM*, pp. 20 and 138) and his folding the rotisserie instructions (*ZMM*, p. 145). Chris's attention to and care for his father form together another ostensive definition of Quality.

A motorcycle usually has a single exhaust pipe on the opposite side from the chain. But the 1964 Honda Superhawk had twin exhausts, so there was one on the same side as the chain.

Surly laughs. He asks us where we're from and where we're going and when we tell him thinks that's fine.

As we roll out Chris waves good-bye to him and he waves back.

Now we head up the same street we walked down from the college on, just an hour ago.

Chris shouts, "Let's see our old house again."

I shrug and nod and turn onto a street going that way.

At the college we ride around to the other side where a new edge of town works its way back toward the mountains. Here there are no more trees. Up ahead the pavement ends and the road becomes gravelled and rutty, surrounded by cheap pre-fab houses probably used as temporary dwellings for new faculty. We stay in first gear along the ruts and gravel until the road ends.

"There's our house," Chris says.[12]

We stop. I'm glad he recognized it. I'm not sure I would have. But now, just seeing it like this, I can remember how it was.

Outside the bedroom window sometimes would be snowstorms coming in from the other end of the valley until they blotted out the dark green of the mountain forests, and within minutes the snow would be upon the house with a wind that shook it and howled through its many cracks. That sight of fields and upswept mountains is vivid.

Now the college has put up some new buildings on the alfalfa field between the house and the mountains and killed the view. It's now just another dingy pre-fab house, closed in by a parking lot and brick walls of other buildings.

Out the door comes a little girl about the age Chris was then. She looks at us for a long time. Soon her mother comes out, looks at us too, and then takes her back in. They must wonder why we stare at them and their house so.

I start the machine and we turn around and head back. To our left, behind a rusted fence, I recognize a peculiar old rusted boiler, five feet high, sitting in the weeds, with all sorts of sawed-off pipe ends sticking out of it. That's the "Army Boat," a name Chris and his brother gave it when they climbed up on it and sat, one at each end, making fantasies about trips to somewhere.

"Do you remember the 'Army Boat'?" I say to Chris. I look around. I see he does but he doesn't answer.

He and his brother would wave to Phaedrus as they sat there on the Army Boat like crewmen on a distant ship. They knew him as a familiar but distant figure in their lives and that was about all. Two lonely kids sitting on a magic Army Boat in the middle of the

[12] The Pirsigs lived at 19 Faculty Court.

weeds.[13] And now the fence around it announces that no children will ever sit there anymore.

We round a street corner, and now from this angle comes another fragment. He's screaming with a terrified wail that won't stop. I've seen this corner in dreams. A woman's holding his hand try to console him, but he won't be consoled, and the woman's looking at me angrily and she asks if I know who his parents are.

I explain that we were walking and that I must have forgotten about him;[14] as soon as I take his hand and walk with him again the wail slows down to a whimper and stops.

I stop the machine and turn and look at Chris now. The face has become elongated and his body has thinned out but it is still clearly an evolution from the child that stood at this corner and wailed years ago.

He wonders why we've stopped and a look of apprehension is there. It's the same frightened look. It matches. That's an evolution too.

I say seriously, "I think we're going to have a good trip from here on, Chris."[15]

"Why?" he asks. He's puzzled about my stopping to tell him this.

"It's just a feeling."

"Oh." He grins. "Are we going camping tomorrow?"

"Yes."

He grins some more. I grin back. He looks at me for a while. "Well then let's *go!*" he says.[16]

So I start up the engine and we go.

This next passage was not dropped outright, but was summarized instead by the last three lines on page 231 and the first ten lines on page 232 of *ZMM*. Pirsig rescued three paragraphs about

[13] The Army boat may refer to all the water motifs—see *ZMM*, pp. 55–56, 220, 246, 265, 360, 363, 364, 367.
[14] In another section that was cut, the narrator comes down from the mountain and says: "An hour later and we are out of the brush at last, and it's time for a rest. I'm drenched with sweat. Chris is too. He has been tagging along behind without a peep, and in my preoccupation with the Chautauqua and the underbrush I have forgotten all about him." Of course, during the whole of the bike trip until the last couple of pages, Chris is riding along behind while the narrator and the reader are preoccupied with the Chautauqua.
[15] The motif of feeling good is echoed at the end of the book; another cut section which would have occurred between the third and fourth to last lines of *ZMM*, p. 231, stated ". . . it'll be better going."
[16] The historical DeWeeses recall the historical Chris as having been less than enthusiastic about the prospect of the historical hike.

Jules Henri Poincaré and placed them near the beginning of Chapter 22, pp. 232–233. The material that is printed here for the first time provides a fuller description of the end of the descent from the mountains, the crossing of Hyalite Creek, and the return to Bozeman.

An hour later and we are out of the brush at last, and it's time for a rest. I'm drenched with sweat. Chris is too. He's been tagging along behind without a peep, and in my preoccupation with the Chautauqua and the underbrush I have forgotten all about him.

Ahead the forest is opened up with thousands of dead-falls which have open space and occasional standing trees between them. "It'll be better going now," I say.

"I hope so," Chris says. "That was awful."

We talk about getting down and I suggest that when we come to a road at the bottom of the canyon we should head into town. He is tired and the ego-stuff of proving himself seems gone temporarily. He says nothing.

He finally says, "Let's wait until we get down and see."

I agree.

For the remainder of the afternoon we climb down over grey weathered trunks of dead-falls and angle back and forth on the steep slope. The sky is still light when the sun goes behind our mountain and will remain light for many hours, I hope. It seems like we've just gone down for hours without much apparent progress.

"Are you sure there's a road down there?" Chris asks during a break.

"Yes."

"How do you know?"

"It's on the map." The dark green mat of the forest tree-tops drops steeply around us but there's no view anywhere of the road. I get out the map and show Chris where we are. "See," I say. "The only thing that bothers me is how we can get down. It's getting steep."

"Oh, we can get down," Chris says.

"Sure," I say. "Head-over-heels!"

"You're sure there's a road down there?"

"Yes."

"How do you know?"

"I just got through all that!"

"Well, I just hope there's a road down there."

"There's a road there," I say.

The slope is at about forty-five degrees and is slow going. On the map wavy isobars[1] come very close together on parts of this slope, indicating steepness. In places where they touch it means a cliff. The dusk is gathering now and I'm worried we may have to camp tonight on this slope before we reach the road.

We slide down from one fallen tree trunk to another. We must have climbed over two hundred of these trunks today. Some big storm must have knocked them all down years ago. . . .

In tomorrow's Chautauqua we will have a surprise guest visitor. He's a person whom Phaedrus never heard of, but whose writings I've studied quite extensively in preparation for this Chautauqua. Unlike Phaedrus, this man was an international celebrity at thirty-five, a living legend at fifty-eight, whom Bertrand Russell has described as "by general agreement, the most eminent scientific man of his generation." He was an astronomer, a physicist, a mathematician and philosopher all in one. His name was Jules Henri Poincaré. . . .[2]

We reach a cliff, angle along its edge in search of a way down, and eventually a narrow draw appears which we're able to climb down. It continues down through a rocky crevice in which there is a little rivulet. Shrubs and rocks and muck and roots of huge trees watered by the rivulet fill the crevice. Then we hear the roar of a much larger creek in the distance.[3]

"That's it," I say to Chris.

We stop and drink some of the water from the rivulet. I feel tired. Then I hear the sound of a truck engine on top of the roar from the big creek.

"Hear that?" I say.

Chris doesn't answer.

The draw opens onto the main stream between small cliffs on either side. The main stream is swollen from melted snows and rushes by with terrific speed. The noise is so loud I have to shout to Chris. "We have to cross that!"

"How?"

"I don't know!"

I decide to try for a small island of willows in the middle of the

[1] An isobar line is a line on a topographic or contour map marking a given elevation above sea level.
[2] In *ZMM*, the biography of Jules Henri Poincaré (1854–1912) follows this passage, which has been slightly rewritten, and appears on pp. 232–233.
[3] This is Hyalite Creek, lying northeast of Cottonwood Creek and flowing parallel to it toward the northwest into the Gallatin River.

main stream. I take off my boots and wade in. Soon the freezing water tries to push my feet out from under me. The stones under my feet are so slippery and so rounded I can't get any kind of a sure footing against the current. By the time the water is over my knees I see this could turn into a catastrophe and decide to turn back. It doesn't look so dangerous, but if my feet slip the current will pick me up and dash me against rocks farther down.

"What did you come back for?" Chris says impatiently.

"It's too hard."

"Well, how are we going to get across?"

"I don't know. Get my boots, will you?"

This seems to anger him. "No."

"What?!"

"I don't want to."

"Just get them!"

"NO!"

"Why?!"

"I'm tired!"

"So am I!"

With no choice, I go back and get the boots and put them on. It will be dark in not many minutes now. The knowing of this and not knowing of how to get across the stream together with Chris's attitude suddenly make me furious.

"You're some help!" I say.

"I don't care."

"Why?"

"I don't like this whole trip! I don't know what we came here for! I thought it was going to be fun!"

"Well, what the hell were you expecting!"

He sits on a big rock and says nothing. Then he says, "I expected we would have fun! I want to go home!"

"You can't get there fast enough for me!" is in my mind, but I don't say it.

I try picking my way upstream against the edge of the cliff. It's slow going, but after a few hundred yards I see the branch of a fallen tree around a bend where it should be easy crossing. The bright idea occurs to me that the tent rope can be used here. The biggest danger is from the current, and if I tie the rope to that branch, even if I fall I can still hang on. If I can get to the other side I can tie the other end of the rope and then Chris can use it to get across.

I try this, gingerly. The water rushes up over my knees, soon numbing my legs and feet, but the boots work better on the slippery stones than bare feet. I feel out pockets between the stones with the toe of my boot, jam the heel into the pocket and then find a new spot for the walking stick. I have to thrust the walking stick down quickly before the current washes it out. Step by step, one foot at a time, I make it across.

I tie my end of the rope to a large branch and tell Chris to come across. He tries to pick up a pack but I motion him to leave it and shout this but I don't think he hears me. I guess he does; there, he's leaving the pack.

He comes, hanging on to the rope. A couple of times his feet almost go out from under him but the rope saves him and he makes it.

Really exhausted now, I go back for the first pack and bring it back again. Then, agonizingly exhausted, I go back for the second pack and bring it back. I don't want to see this stream again for a long time. Chris takes one pack, I grab the other one and we climb up to the road.

It's about dark and Chris is shivering. The icy stream took the anger out of both of us. Some people walk by on their way to their truck farther down the road, and we bum a ride with them back to Bozeman. The driver is an electrical engineering professor at the college. They have just acquired a computer I helped write the manuals on. He asks a lot of questions about the computer but it turns out they're all software questions and I only worked on the hardware manuals so I can't tell him much.

Chris's shivering causes them to turn on the truck heater for us, but our clothes are so soaked this causes all the windows to fog up and the defroster has to be turned on too.

This next passage narrates the morning after the return from the mountain hike. It was the original beginning of Chapter 22, so it belongs after the chapter heading on page 232.

A hot shower feels good in the morning, but a hung-over depression about Chris, asleep in the next room, remains. I haven't learned much.

Back in the bedroom again, the boots still feel damp from last night and I have to tug hard to pull them on. When they're finally on I stand up and look out our fifth-story window. All across the town the morning sunlight makes rooftops look bright and clean. Off in the distance are the mountains where we were yesterday.

I shove Chris, on the next bed, to wake him up.

"I want to sleep," he says, so I let him. I try to find the De-Weeses' number in the telephone directory again, to tell them where we are. I look under *Gallatin Gateway* this time, and find it. I hear

Chris ask, "What are we going to do today?" and look up and see he is at the window, looking out.

I answer, "Get things in shape."

"What things?"

"Clothes, motorcycle . . . we've got a lot to do. We're going West. Take a shower."

"Why?"

"Why, why, why? Always why. It's the last shower you'll get for days. We'll be camping every night now."

"Whoopee!" He jumps out of bed for the shower and then, halfway across the room, bends, and stops. "My legs ache."

I smile. "Mine do too. Turn the shower on very hot, and exercise them."

On the phone Gennie answers, "Where are you?"

"We're camping on the south slope of the Baxter Hotel."[1]

She laughs and I describe our climb for a while and then we make arrangements for a ride out to the canyon.

When we get there, in the canyon, the motorcycle is under the eave of the house just as I left it. All over it though is a thin film of dirt which puzzles me. How could it get so dirty? Then I look up and see it is parked right under the drain opening of the roof gutter. There's no downspout. During the rainstorm the run-off from the entire roof must have come down right on top of it. Great.

From the saddlebag I get out a rag and clean off the seat, the handlebars and fenders. Then I wheel it over to where I can try to kick-start it. Rain isn't supposed to affect the operation but it does, somehow. Condensation gets into the points and rainwater sometimes shorts out the plugs. I turn the ignition and headlights on. Battery is good. I set the choke, give the throttle one-eighth turn and jump.

She starts, dies a little, and I lean out the choke and open the throttle and then she settles into a rough idle and I let her warm up. First kick! Not bad after two days and the equivalent of five hundred rainstorms. I see Chris smile too. We may quarrel about other things but our feelings about the cycle are identical. I tell him to gather everything so that we can pack it and leave, and to give DeWeeses our unused food. I'm itchy to be going.

While the machine's still running I go get the two oil cans I bought in town and bring them to a level spot in the corral back of the house near the creek. Then I wheel the running machine to the corral and shut it off. With a wrench I remove the drain plug under the crankcase.

[1] The Baxter Hotel, 105 West Main, was the biggest hotel in Bozeman during the 1960s.

While the oil drains DeWeese comes over to watch. Chris probably told him we're leaving. I see he's still a patron of the technologies, fascinated with mechanical things.

"Putting in oil," he says.

"Changing it."

He's a little surprised that we're leaving today, but I explain that all the way down the mountain I've been just suddenly restless to move on the road again. I'm sure too they've other things to do than entertain us. I explain that we got to a point where Chris saw what the climbing is all about and I didn't want to push it any further. Later, when he's bigger, he'll be back, I say. DeWeese nods.

He looks for a long time. "How often do you have to do that?"

"Every five hundred miles," I say. "It's a high-speed engine and the transmission and clutch both run in the engine oil so you can't let it get at all dirty."

"Oh," DeWeese says, and nods. He continues nodding, then squints a little, then nods some more, like a spectator in an art gallery. For his benefit I wish I could do a perfect job of pouring the oil in but the oil filler hole is located so that I can't quite get the can directly over it, and as usual, I spill a little.

"Someday," I say, "when I get really good at this, I'm going to pour a can of oil in there and not spill a single drop."

DeWeese sees I'm smiling and smiles too.

I look up and see that the sky is clear but that there is a pretty hefty north wind blowing. Too bad it's a strong north wind. Maybe it's just a canyon updraft, though. Can't really tell until we get out into the valley.

DeWeese sees me look around, and says, "Bet you've really missed the 'Happy Valley' all these years."

"I was just looking to see which way the wind was coming from," I say. "When you're riding it makes a lot of difference."

We say thank you and good-bye and talk for a while and have a cup of coffee and then are out on a road north to the U.S. highway. It's no canyon updraft. We can feel the headwind buffeting plenty. It's the kind that wears you down physically, particularly when you haven't got a windshield. We're going sixty but the headwind is probably at about thirty so that makes it a ninety-mile-an-hour wind. That's what it feels like too.

But exhilarating. Now the mountain we climbed yesterday drops away behind us and the old vibrant regeneration occurs. Sparkling sun, cool thin air and the open road.

At the junction of the road from the canyon with the main highway, U.S. 10, we stop for an arterial sign.

"Which way?" I ask Chris.

"I don't know."

"Home or the ocean?"

"I don't know."

"You don't *know*?" I'm teasing, but his answer displeases. "Home then?"

I turn to look at him. He shrugs his shoulders. I turn the front wheel for a right turn east, and he says sullenly, "The ocean."[2]

"Glad you said that," I say. "We almost went home."

We head north across the Gallatin valley. Off to the left alluvial fans of soil emerge from canyons of the Bridger mountains. They're covered with the green of farms. The outline of the Bridgers doesn't seem to change much while you look at it, but when you turn away and then look back a few minutes later you can see the difference.

Every so often out of habit I glance into the rear view mirror to see the other motorcycle, and then realize the Sutherlands are probably halfway home by now. The empty mirror produces a sudden lonesome feeling, and a feeling we're on our own now. Also a little happy because of the freedom from group decisions. No schedule to make anymore. No particular destination.

Poincaré. I suspect the real reason I've been so itchy to be back on the road again is to get the time and solitude to think and talk about him. When you live on the edge of insanity, the appearance of another mind that thinks and talks like yours is something close to a blessed event. Like Robinson Crusoe's discovery of footprints on the sand.

The following six paragraphs recollect the narrator's acquisition of the 1964 Honda Superhawk on which he and Chris make the trip. The fourth paragraph of *ZMM*'s Chapter 26, on page 270, is a fragment of what appears here:

The cycle looms silently over me, ready to start, as if it has waited all night like some silent guardian. From the ground up it looks very impressive. No frills. Everything with a purpose.

By my nose the little blocks of rubber tread are worn on a fore-and-aft bevel that looks peculiar. I worried about it until I was told by a filling station attendant that the free-running wheels on trucks wear the same way.

[2] The Buddha's father makes the choice for his son at some of the forks in his road; see p. 63 above.

Silver-grey and chrome and black—and dirty. Dirt from Idaho and Montana and the Dakotas and Minnesota. I bought it second-hand two years ago from a friend who had already ridden it from the East coast to the West coast and had memories of his own.

We went into the house and on the dining room table I wrote out the check and he folded it and put it in his billfold and put his billfold in his pocket and then we went outside where his wife was waiting. And after we talked for a while, to break the conversation he turned and patted it on the fender and said half-humorously, "Well good-bye, old motorcycle!"[1] And then he looked up at this wife and she looked at him and there was a flash of sudden recognition and hurt between them and then his lips tightened and they both looked sad.

"I'll take good care of it," I said, but that just seemed to make them sadder. "It'll have a good home," I added, and they smiled a little, but when they got in the car to leave, their expressions were downcast.

I don't think I'll ever sell it like that. No reason to, really. They're not like cars, with a body that rusts out in a few years. Keep them tuned and overhauled and they'll last as long as you do. Probably longer. Quality. It's carried us so far without trouble.

This final item, from Chapter 26 also, would have gone on page 280 of the 1979 Bantam edition of *ZMM*, between the eighth and seventh to last lines, to expand the commentary on successful motorcycle maintenance procedures.

If new facts are desperately needed to complete a harmony they are grabbed at and assimilated rapidly. These facts have high value but in a sense aren't really new. If the engine stops and we look in the gas tank and see there's no gas, that's a new fact whose meaning and value is assimilated rapidly. During the process we might actually have set our eyes on the underside of the gas cap and never noticed that the vent hole was clogged because that was a fact we weren't looking for. We won't notice it until we fill the tank with gas and discover that the engine *still* stops.[2] Genuinely new facts, the ones

---

[1] The previous owner's "Well good-bye, old motorcycle" recalls Billy Budd's "And good-by to you too, old Rights of Man." See *ZMM*, p. 39 and its note in Section 11 of this guidebook; see also earlier in this section, p. 213, "What the smooth sound of the engine really tells you is that it's responded to your care."
[2] The vent hole in the gas cap keeps the tank from developing a vacuum that would prevent gasoline from flowing down to the carburetor.

you not only aren't looking for but couldn't possibly *be* looking for, always appear as a wrench in the works. These can take centuries for acceptance because they don't satisfy a harmony. The fact that bodies of different weight all fall at the same speed was such a fact. The curvature of the earth was another. I'm afraid the reality of Quality is still another, because our intellects are just not culturally conditioned to deal with it.

But in cycle maintenance, if you ever get the idea beforehand that you *know* what's of value and what's not, you're sure as hell going to get gumption-trapped into bafflement on the first really tough problem you meet. On the tough ones, the facts that are going to save you have little or no value just before you "discover" them. That's why the problem is so tough.

S E C T I O N 7

ROBERT M. PIRSIG'S LETTER
TO ROBERT REDFORD

Movie actor and director Robert Redford has been interested in filming *ZMM*. It would join such famous Redford movies as *Butch Cassidy and the Sundance Kid* (1969), *The Sting* (1973), *The Great Gatsby* (1974), *All the President's Men* (1976), *Ordinary People* (1980), *The Natural* (1984), *Out of Africa* (1985), and *The Milagro Beanfield War* (1988).

While negotiations were going forward some years ago, Robert M. Pirsig wrote Redford detailing some of his ideas about how *ZMM* might be filmed. The letter holds a great deal of interest for its revelation of the author's understanding of certain central features of his book.

> Sas Van Gent,
> Netherlands,
> April 24, 1981

Dear Bob,

I think that now, while all the aftermath of *Ordinary People*[1] is being absorbed and before you arrive at firm decisions about *ZMM*, is the best time for me to set down all my thoughts about how it should be done. Putting them in a letter this way should enable you to think about them and change your mind back and forth at leisure in the normal creative way.

GENERAL

My overall feeling is that the film should be low key and low budget with lots of "space" in it. My idea at one time was to take about five people and a pick-up camper and a couple of motorcycles and some videotape equipment and see if, learning as we went, we could put together some footage that we could present to a producer for 35 mm production. I felt that the less slick and "artistic" the film looked the better it would be for the story, and I gather from the reviews of *Ordinary People* that that is exactly the attitude you took there and it worked.

Another idea I might have pursued if you had lost interest was to go to Sweden and talk to the representatives of the film industry there. Many of their films have exactly the kind of low key sensitivity and absence of theatrics that the book calls for. In many ways it's an extremely delicate story, particularly in the portrayal of Chris.

NARRATIVE

I think the dramatic force of the narrative is almost entirely dependent upon the mystery of the narrator, and if this mystery is lost the whole story goes with it. The narrative was constructed to remove a series of veils, one at a time, carefully and in sequence, from in front of the true nature of the narrator.[2]

In Chapter 1 the narrator is established as a rather normal, unexceptional fellow. The purpose of John and Sylvia was mainly to render this "ordinariness" of him. The reader has to buy in on him early, believe in him, want to keep him going because as the book progresses this narrator's ordinariness becomes more and more incredible and in the end is demolished completely.

In Chapter 3 the first veil is removed when Phaedrus appears in a storm. In Chapter 4 confidence is restored by John, Sylvia and Chris and a maintenance-oriented Chautauqua. In Chapter 5 another veil is removed and we learn that Chris shows signs of mental illness. Chapter 6 again restores sanity. In Chapter 7 we have one of the most difficult chapters, in which the reader is persuaded that Phaedrus is not the narrator, even though in a way he really is. This is absolutely essential to the construction of the plot, for the whole climax becomes flat and meaningless if this is not accepted.

In Part II, the mystery of the narrator becomes the mystery of Phaedrus, and the removal of a series of veils reveals more and more about Phaedrus. He was a teacher in Bozeman, Montana. He was in pursuit of something. What was he looking for? Quality. What was that? . . . To raise that single question was the purpose of the whole narrative. All the characters except Chris and the narrator are disposed of while a series of veils is removed about Quality in terms of Phaedrus' struggle with it up to his psychic death through shock treatment.

This is the end of the veils as far as the narrator can remove them, but there is still another veil that the narrator himself doesn't understand. Phaedrus, the enigmatic villain of the narrator's tale, is threatening to take over the narrator's whole personality. Chris is in danger, but from whom? From Phaedrus or from the narrator himself? Chris seems to reject the narrator and mourn for Phaedrus. How can the narrator do anything at all but give up and let things take their course? What can save the situation?

What saves the situation is one last veil, which was concealed back in Chapter 7. The narrator has made a mistake. The father Chris mourns for isn't dead after all. He is still alive and is the narrator himself.

Here the book ends for most readers, leaving them a little puzzled and a little haunted by it all, wanting to discuss it with someone and ask questions. A few perceptive readers and one lone British critic kept on going beyond the end of the book into a whole other interpretation which the narrator never really gives you. John and Sylvia, the bourgeois butts of the narrator's criticism, are now seen as tolerant friends. Chris, the troubled brat of the narrator's tale, now appears as almost saintly, and the benign, omniscient narrator, whose point of view the reader has *had* to accept as true until now is seen as Phaedrus himself, broken, his mind half-destroyed, struggling desperately to recover.

What really happened? In the end Phaedrus said he wasn't insane. But the court ruled that he was, and his symptoms through the book are classic textbook symptoms of schizophrenia. What is wrong here?

I think the effect of ending the book on this question rather than an answer to it is correct. Questions can be stories too. Even though the audience is not consciously aware of another possible story, something in their subliminal minds responds to it, and that is why the story lingers with them so. Subliminally they *know* Phaedrus was getting better, not worse. They *know* he was acting rationally, not irrationally. But they can find no words to justify this and that is what haunts them. It gives a kind of resonance to the book, a sense of sounds from out of the range of hearing that nevertheless affect the main sounds.

The book doesn't demand that the reader accept any other conclusion than the psychiatric one. It merely casts some question on this psychiatric conclusion and then stops. But there is an alternative, Zen explanation: What occurred in Chicago was not insanity but enlightenment as it has been understood for thousands of years in China, India and Japan.[3] The book never says this because to do so would sink it completely and would in fact be bad Zen to bring up. But the question of what really happened to Phaedrus is taken up again in the book I am now working on and will probably be taken up still again in the book after this one. This means that if the film script varies too much from the book there may be a continuity problem for my next book, which is another reason for not changing the ending.

There is yet one more veil that went not only beyond the narrator's perception but beyond the author's. I didn't begin to see it until long after I had written it, and after I saw it, I just left it there and never exploited it, but it helps explain the power of the final scene with Chris.

The psychiatrist Jung wrote that we all live in a world of values derived from ancient myths.[4] Old tribal experiences control our lives without our even knowing it, and when sometimes a story or a scene has a strong emotional impact it's because one of these ancient value-myths has been tapped.

In this narrative a son's father has lost contact with the world. No one believes in him anymore. The son is the only one. And his belief in his father is forcing him further and further from the world itself with only his father left to hang on to. Then his father seems to abandon him and he suffers a kind of death right before his father's eyes, and seems to cry out "My father, why hast thou forsaken me?" His father is transformed by this, and as a result of his son's sacrifice, returns to the world again.

I'm convinced that this unintended Christian value-myth was the real source of the power of that scene and that if it is left inviolate the same effect may be possible on film. I also think, however, that deliberately inserting allegories into stories is dangerous writing and usually creates a kind of overdramatized "theatrical" effect that kills everything. The secret, I think, is just to know it is there but leave it alone, not crush it, not exploit it, just let it be.

THE CHAUTAUQUA

To me, giving someone the *ZMM* narrative without the Chautauqua is like giving someone a diamond ring without the diamond. The Chautauqua is what came first, and at one time was intended to be the whole book. The narrative was originally intended to remove the "ex cathedra" effect, the "talking down," the pontification, which pure essays get into because they come from a disembodied speaker. The narrative puts the Chautauqua into the mouth of someone fallible. The reader is not quite so put off by all the high-flown talk about philosophy because he realizes the narrator is just trying to say something he believes in and *he* isn't perfect either. That was the original reason for the narrative.

Probably my greatest misgiving of all about this film is that because philosophy is so hard to film and narrative is so easy to film there will be an almost overwhelming pressure to subordinate the Chautauqua to the narrative—chopping it here and there, working it around here and there, slipping it in here and there into nooks and crannies of the narrative, hoping that somehow it will squeeze in. It won't. What will result is a slipshod, superficial intellectualism that will smell up the whole film with that slick commercial shallowness for which America and Hollywood have become so well known.

The problem, of course, is that if the Chautauqua is filmed in its entire complexity it will be too dull and too difficult for anyone to sit through. It has to be boiled way, way down. I think it can. It has to be dramatized and interrelated with the action wherever possible. This can also be done. But it must be subordinated to the narrative. Some of it may have to be done in a very dry, dreary dull way that will certainly weaken audience interest. If this has to happen, this has to happen. This isn't *Jaws*. The purpose of this book is to tell people something, not just entertain them, and if part of the audience is so dull they can't stand any kind of straight information whatsoever, the film will just have to lose that fraction of the audience. Otherwise things get into that lowest-common-denominator approach that destroys the integrity of the whole film effort and reflects on the book as well.

In my previous letter I said I had some ideas about how to solve the problem of making the Chautauqua interesting without cheapening it, and I guess now is the time for these.

POINT OF VIEW

To me this seems like the most important thing I have to say here so let me back way up for this.[5]

The teacher of composition who most affected my writing was the poet Alan Tate, who died a couple of years ago.[6] His name is usually associated with Robert Penn Warren, who wrote *All the King's Men*, and as Warren described him, "With Tate writing was a matter of life or death." You couldn't spend fifteen minutes in a class with him without understanding that.

I sat though three quarters of Tate's advanced composition classes during which he assigned Henry James's *The Turn of the Screw* as a story for analysis.[7] In the story, a governess, assigned to take care of two children, tries to protect them from a ghost of their former governess. She fails and the boy dies. At the end of the reading Tate astonished everyone by saying there really wasn't any ghost at all, it was all in the mind of the governess who was telling the story. I got upset by this and got into a ferocious argument. If there was anything that was obvious about that story it was that there really was a ghost. But, point by point, sentence by sentence, Tate argued me down and by doing so demonstrated what was the whole point of the assignment, the importance of point of view.

James believed that to make a story rise up from the page and come to life you must establish a specific point of view for the reader and never violate it except when absolutely necessary and then it must be changed only in the most careful and deliberate way. Tate said that *The Turn of the Screw* was a demonstration of this principle in which he deliberately tricked you into thinking the ghost was real by his use of first person point of view.

Tate said the first person point of view is by far the most powerful in its control of the reader but it is also the most hellish in its limitations upon the author. The author is in a straightjacket. He has no "meanwhile, back at the ranch" shifts to help him work the story along. He is locked inside the head of the narrator and must show only what the narrator can see in the order the narrator sees it. But the reward for this straightjacket punishment is that whatever the narrator sees becomes the reader's *reality*. That was why it was so hard to see that that ghost in *The Turn of the Screw* was an illusion in the mind of the narrator.

The first person point of view has never been popular with writers because of its mechanical difficulties, but as Tate's analysis showed, if you've got a fantastic, incredible tale to tell, and if the whole success of the story depends on the reader being convinced it is true, then the first person is the way to tell it. It was out of Tate's class and the argument about *The Turn of the Screw* that the ghost called "Phaedrus" was created.

My idea for making the Chautauqua bearable to a film audience without cheapening it and for solving some other extremely important problems as well, is to carry James's advice about point of view right on into the film. I think there are tremendous advantages to locating the camera right inside the head of the narrator and never letting it get out of there. In this first person point of view the audience should *never see the narrator's face*. That is the way to sustain his mystery, which is so important to the dramatic suspense of the story and, by God, that is the way to handle the Chautauqua. The dry, prosaic Chautauqua can flow and weave freely into the other elements of the story with a kind of symphonic intermingling because the audience knows that everything is part of the panorama of the narrator's internal point of view. You can move back and forth from highway to thoughts to Chautauqua to India to Bozeman to Chris to the Chautauqua again and to Chicago in any order you want with complete freedom and ease with no explanation needed because the audience will always know they are seeing just what the narrator sees and remembers and thinks about and that is the natural way his mind is working.

And that's really the way life is too; not just a series of external objects and faces but a mixture of these with memories and reflections and interruptions in a kind of endlessly changing kaleidoscope. The reality portrayed by this free-flowing mixture is *more* true to life than conventional presentations whose reality is based on limitations of the old theatrical stage. Once the audience gets used to it the screen can shift from Chautauqua to road scene with such ease no one will know it is happening, and all kinds of liberties can be taken. If the narrator has a hard point in the Chautauqua he wants to make he can visualize a blackboard and make a diagram. He can stop a motorcycle in action and do a strobe-lighted sequence to show how it works. He can do anything.

And there are other advantages:

1. The plot of the story only works if the audience accepts the idea that Phaedrus and the narrator are completely separate people. This separation will be impossible if you show both their faces. People will see right away they are the same. When you use first person, and show Phaedrus' face only, this problem is completely solved.

2. The first person point of view enables a peculiarly compelling intimacy between the narrator and the audience. In the book the narrator almost whispers in the reader's ear in such a confidential intimate tone that he sometimes breaks through the reader's own shell of isolation and transports him into the narrator's world as if in a dream. I think this could happen on film too.

3. The earlier statement that the narrator's face should never be shown can be amended for one exception: the dramatic climax. In doing so you give this climax a tremendous visual power that it couldn't achieve by any other means. The narrator, whom the audience has never seen, sits down beside Chris in the coastal fog and says, "Don't cry Chris. Crying is just for children." The camera shows his gloved hands from his internal point of view and then, as quietly and unobtrusively as possible, it shifts and shows the same gloves reaching up and wiping a tear from the narrator's face—which we see now for the first time. We see that his face is much older and tireder than before but it is Phaedrus all right, and we gradually understand the most important point of the whole story. He has come back.

In the final scenes where Chris and his father bank and turn down the ocean highway, talking freely back and forth, both faces are now shown in the conventional objective manner. The relief the audience feels at returning to this "normal" way of looking at things should parallel Phaedrus' own relief at this new perspective of himself. Now it is understood that the real ghost of the story—the unseen narrator—is gone. You never really saw his face because *he* never really saw his face. He never really *had* a face. He was a fiction, really, created by the courts and psychiatrists. Phaedrus had accepted this fiction after his shock treatment, but Chris had not. And that was the source of Chris's troubles.

In using the first person the film has traded off one kind of freedom for another, and the one that is given away wasn't needed anyway for this story, but the one that is gained allows a kind of film to be made in which intellectual concepts can be handled as freely as desert scenery, and a high dramatic power is gained through a single shift in point of view. It's an unusual way of showing things, but it's an unusual book, and an unconventional film technique is actually more appropriate to the book's style than a conventional one.

CASTING

Narrator

If the first person convention is followed and the narrator's voice is never associated with any face until the end, then I could read his lines myself and, you can be sure, say them exactly the way the author intended them. However my voice may be too thin and high for this part and I've noticed that authors reading their own works often don't do nearly as well as actors. Authenticity isn't necessarily Quality. That's for you to decide.

Phaedrus

One of the most interesting conversations I've had about this film was with Joseph Strick, who directed *Ulysses, Portrait of the Artist as a Young Man* and some other art films.[8] In his opinion, the acting of the narrator and Phaedrus roles would make or break the film. He thought the actor chosen should be unknown, so as not to compromise Phaedrus' mysteriousness. He thought there should be a long search by both of us together, auditioning as many as 100 or 200 actors to find the right one. "When you find him," he said, "I predict you will know it right away. There will suddenly be no doubt in your mind."

Strick's offer was rejected and I would have forgotten this except that his prediction was accidentally fulfilled. An actor appeared who gave me exactly the eerie feeling that he was talking about. I felt I was looking at a double.

His film name is Peter Coyote.[9] I haven't seen him act but got the feeling from his off-stage actions that he is probably very good, and some of the articles that I'm sending along here also seem to indicate this is so. When I told him I would mention him to you he sent this material so that you wouldn't think I was pushing "Sleazy Eddie, my brother-in-law who can't find a job." Peter has a two-level personality. On the surface he is bright and funny, but underneath there is an extreme seriousness that seems just right. He is a motorcyclist and a mechanic and was a friend of Chris. Chris used to fix cars for everybody but, as Peter told it, he always undercharged and lost money. The look of mixed anger and hurt on Peter's face as he told that about Chris was what suddenly produced the "double" feeling.

In one way it's irrelevant to his acting that he was one of the first to find Chris's body, and that he spent many weeks with the police trying to find the murderers, and actually found witnesses and got them to testify,[10] but in another way it is not irrelevant. I think his memory of Chris may have a very deep effect on his performance, and in the final critical dramatic scenes we may see from him a kind of ultimate effort that would be hard to get from someone else.

Casting is, of course, your decision not mine. But if his acting seems right to you then we are in great luck.

John Sutherland

One major disadvantage of the first person point of view is that if you don't show the face of a character you have lost one of your most important visual means of telling his story. I think this could be made up in part with a montage technique, where instead of showing the narrator's sadness by a baleful look on his face, you could show it by putting sadness in whatever he happens to be thinking about. If it is a motorcycle, for example, it could be shown on a cold rainy day, with some dents on it or mud on it, and an effect of sadness would be created. Getting along without the narrator's face, however, puts a huge burden on everyone else in the narrative, who, to some extent, will have to create him in *their* faces. John Sutherland's support in the opening chapters will be critical, I think, and I've been hoping you might consider this role. As was said earlier, the purpose of John and Sylvia is to make the narrator seem like a normal conventional American through his relationship to them. If you take the part of John that normality will be immediately conferred upon the narrator and the film will be off to a very strong start.

I've never been satisfied with the portrayal of John in the book (and neither, you can believe it, has John.) I kept him dull and two-dimensional because I worried that he would upstage the narrator. But with the first person I don't think this is anything to worry about. You can't upstage the narrator when the narrator *is* the stage. I could do a lot to enrich John's part if you are willing to take it.

PROPS

The Honda Superhawk[11] that made the trip is available, but it's a 1964 machine and might give an unintended obsolescence to the film. Also, I'm ashamed to say, it needs some maintenance. That's what success does for you.

CONCLUSION

That's about all the advice I have at this time and as I read back over it I can see you saying, "Well, God, I hope so!" It's quite a sermon, and is a kind I almost never make. I once compared a basic author to a mother-in-law and am reminded of that now. Everybody knows she gave birth to the desired one and you've got to be nice to her, but damned if she's going to run the marriage. Once you get going on the film I'm sure my influence will get weaker and weaker and I'll never have a clear field to run all these ideas through like I have now, so that's why I'm going on at such length. Certainly it's better to know all these ideas and reject them for good reason than never to know about them at all. Ultimately the only real mandate is the one contained in *ZMM* itself, "I don't care how you do it, just so it's good."

Good luck on your period of reflection. If it lasts past the first of July we may be seeing you in Norway. Plans will depend a lot on how our new passenger[12] likes the boat. If it becomes definite that a film will be made that will certainly take priority over the second book and we will move to whatever location suits best for as long as you need us. As a matter of fact the setting of the second book is in Manhattan, and I have to go there anyway to do some research on it.

Sincerely,
Bob Pirsig

NOTES

[1] *Ordinary People* was Redford's 1980 Oscar-winning movie featuring a troubled teenage boy.

[2] In a letter to Thomas J. Steele, S. J., of February 25, 1975, Pirsig wrote: "There are many comments of bafflement and befuddlement on the part of critical analysts who sensed something phony about the narrator, but confused him with the author, and waited all through the

book to pounce on him. Then at the end they discovered that, like a mouse escaped through a hole, he was no longer there to pounce on."

[3] Pirsig wrote in a letter to Ronald DiSanto, dated January 10, 1987: "I don't think all insanity is a form of enlightenment nor do I think all enlightenment is a form of insanity, but I think that there is an area of overlap between the two where identical phenomena can be interpreted either way depending upon which culture one is looking out of." For another view, see R. C. Zaehner, "Madness," in *Mysticism Sacred and Profane* (London: Oxford University Press, 1961) pp. 84–105; Zaehner wrote the anonymous London *Times Literary Supplement* review in 1974.

[4] Noted Swiss psychiatrist C. G. Jung (1875–1961) claimed that each person shares a "collective unconscious," a combination of the instincts and archetypes produced both culturally and biologically by previous generations and transmitted as the means by which a person's life can become a meaningful part of the development of all mankind. Myths (sacred stories) and rituals (sacred actions) particularize these instincts and archetypes and can make them a concrete part of a particular person's life. See his *Archetypes and the Collective Unconscious*, Vol. 9, Part 1 of *Collected Works* (New York: Bollingen, 1959), pp. 4–6, 67, 153–156.

[5] For the motif of backing up to find the right starting point, see *ZMM*, pp. 59, 97, 247, 353–354.

[6] Allen Tate (1899–1979) taught at the University of Minnesota from 1951 to 1968; he and Robert Penn Warren (1905–1989) were members of "The Fugitives," a group of southern literary men at Vanderbilt in the 1920s and 1930s. Warren's *All the King's Men* won the Pulitzer Prize for the novel in 1947 and won three Academy Awards as a movie in 1949.

[7] Henry James's *Turn of the Screw* has been called the best ghost story ever written. It can be interpreted as a literal account of ghosts, as a chronicle of the narrator's projected hallucinations (Tate's view), or as a tale that teases the reader between the first and the second interpretations without ever permitting a resolution.

[8] American-born director Joseph Strick's two ambitious movies *Ulysses* (1967) and *Portrait of the Artist as a Young Man* (1979) remain true to James Joyce's two novels.

[9] Peter Coyote, product of San Francisco State University and the San Francisco Actors' Workshop, has been actor, director, and writer of a half-dozen real movies and a dozen movies made for TV. He assisted in the development of guerrilla theater, was a serious student of Zen, and served by appointment of the governor as chairman of the California Councils for the Arts.

[10] Robert Pirsig tells the story of his son Chris's casual murder on the streets of San Francisco in "An Author and Father Looks Ahead at the Past," *New York Times Book Review* (March 4, 1984), pp. 7–8, used in a slightly different form as "Introduction" or "Afterward" in Morrow/Quill and Bantam editions of *ZMM* since 1986.

[11] The 1964 Honda Superhawk is still in Pirsig's garage.

[12] The Pirsigs' "new passenger" was daughter Nell, born April 24, 1981, four days before the letter to Redford.

CRITICAL RECEPTION OF *ZEN AND THE ART OF MOTORCYCLE MAINTENANCE*

"GOOD TRIP"

BY ROBERT M. ADAMS

Earnest, innocent, awkward, authentic—long on character and short on formal art (but that includes a blessed lack of artfulness)—Robert Pirsig's book is an ungainly piece of do-it-yourself American Gothic. It is a novel, a travelogue, a quest, a set of lectures, and a secular confession, with some sketchy information on motorcycle maintenance thrown in for good measure. In his subtitle the author describes it as "an inquiry into values," and it's that too. But anything you call it, it's also something else. They may seem silly, but these problems of nomenclature are symptomatic; the book is exasperating and impressive in about equal measure, which is to say greatly. It's a completely heteroclite performance.

The book can be simply outlined. A father and his eleven-year-old son are traveling by motorcycle from Minnesota to San Francisco. At home there is a mother with another son, but they are unimportant—I mean they are just *out* of it, no names, no characters, no histories. The travelers are accompanied as far as

Bozeman, Montana, by two friends on another motorcycle; but they are largely out of it too. (The narrator knows a lot about them, but says he doesn't want to exploit his personal friends, so he doesn't tell us anything, leaving us to wonder again what sort of book this is.) After Bozeman, father and son continue by themselves. Wearing motorcycle helmets and moving fast, the travelers are isolated not only from the outside world but from each other. They wave, point, and occasionally shout a word or two, but mostly they have to stop in order to talk, and even then they don't say much, being uncommunicative to start with; often sulky, and generally exhausted after long hours on the motorcycle.

Thus the book mainly consists of a series of monologues or imaginary lay-sermons (Pirsig calls them, only half-derisively, "Chautauquas") composed by the motorcycling father-author-narrator for delivery to a hypothetical reader. They are the book's inquiry into value, though "quality" is the word the author prefers, and "the good" would do almost as well. His illustrations are drawn chiefly from teaching freshman rhetoric (which the author has done in the past, though he is a writer of technical manuals) and from motorcycle maintenance. But as the lectures proceed, these somewhat limited and undramatic topics fade; and from behind them emerges the real subject of the book, which is a spiritual and intellectual autobiography.

The narrator forces his mind toward a reckoning with a shadowy, Platonically-minded alter ego named "Phaedrus," who is in effect the narrator himself, as he existed some three or four years ago before a nervous breakdown, electric shock therapy, and a spell in an asylum. Reliving this traumatic experience, trying to understand the threat that its continuing half-life poses to him and to his son, the narrator drives toward a new crisis, somehow surmounts it, and finally achieves (we are to understand) an affectionate relation with the scared, wretched, silent child on the saddle behind him. And so, with something like a sense of earned triumph, they at last enter San Francisco.

Thus crudely and no doubt unfairly reduced, the book (which defies one even to grasp it by its ungainly title: best, perhaps, to call it by an acronym, *ZAAMM*) must seem to consist of pieces held together with Scotch tape—yet this situation is responsible for one of its special and admirable effects. It is so precarious in every sense, so wobbly as a structure of either thought or feeling, that one is constantly expecting it to crash in the nearest ditch. The reader is lured on by the premonition of imminent disaster. When this anticipation for some reason comes to nothing, the lecturer seems too secure on his podium, or his spiel sounds camped, then in fact things get sticky in *ZAAMM*. There is more than a touch of the Ancient Mariner in Mr. Pirsig, who is apt to fix you with his glittering eye and go on about "quality" or "gumption" for many unbroken pages.

There are moments too when he seems confirmed in the familiar combination of paranoia and self-pity. But either he or his editor has been able to dodge or jump over most of these traps; and the book moves forward, reeling and tottering to be sure, but sustained by a rich and vehement eloquence, and above all by its refusal to be careful or self-protective. Like the picaresque saints who precede him in the long tradition of American Romance, the hero of *ZAAMM* is a chance-taker, an odds-beater; we follow him in fear and trembling, and finally with a kind of love.

The fabulist is of course bound to be "ego-oriented" to the point of making the word "Zen" in the title more than commonly misleading. In fact, there's precious little about Zen in the book. The title uses it as a twist on Herrigel's *Zen in the Art of Archery*, but the Zen approach to motorcycle maintenance doesn't seem to involve much more than the familiar instructions of common sense. Read the manual carefully, buy good tools, don't tighten the screws too much or you'll strip the threads. Well, sure. But this falls a bit short of Zen, if it's even heading in that direction. Indeed, it's the overflowing and expansive, not the absorbed or emptied personality that Mr. Pirsig's lecturer values. No particular surprises here; most Westerners seem to take what they call Zen in much this way, as Alka-Seltzer for a romanticism hangover. But the story rushes the narrator forward and backward, as a narration must—forward to his destiny, backward into the trauma that determined that destiny, always down, inside his character. As a novelist, Pirsig is more a rider than a repairer of motorcycles, with perhaps a streak of Evel Knievel in his disposition.

To say that the narrator's "Chautauquas" sound on occasion like L. Ron Hubbard on his way to discovering dianetics may sound like a putdown; but it's one source of his appeal. He wants a larger definition of reason than can be built out of merely reasonable materials, a technology of the heart, a unified field theory of man and the cosmos. Naturally our feelings are all with him. So the lectures out of which *ZAAMM* is largely constructed work like isometric exercises. Because they are abstract, remote from the child behind him who constitutes, after all, the narrator's only human environment, they are hateful. But because they represent an ideal, fragile vision of things after which, against expectation, we aspire, they are precious. I haven't very often seen this particular fictional dilemma spread its horns so disturbingly.

As a four-square, feet-on-the-ground thinker, Pirsig leaves us bemused and quizzical; as a teller of stories, he disturbs more than he ingratiates, but the way values now stand, that's all to the good. His work mainly depends on the quality of his writing, and about this I don't think there can be two opinions. He is a stunning writer of fictional prose. With a minimum of apparatus, he can evoke a landscape or intimate a deep sense of uneasiness, allow a mood to evaporate, or touch us with compassion. Yet there's very little overwriting.

For example, "Phaedrus" slowly impinges on the narrator from the murk of the past, with his obsessed and disturbing demand on the constitution of things, and this threat of the narrator's total breakdown is mirrored in the silent tensions of the boy Chris. Taking place as it does in a sealed social void, the novel depends heavily on Chris as an unspoiled source of value. But as he is a center of feeling, he is also a magnet for any lint of pathos or mawkishness that happens to be floating in the atmosphere. It is to Mr. Pirsig's credit that he has been able to keep the relationship of Chris to his father clean and strong. He can write dramatically even about ideas that strike one as sleazy; the "Chautauquas" at their best have a mobile and self-deriding way with the rhetoric of truth-telling that seems distinctively American, in the tradition of Huck Finn, Augie March, and the Dharma Bums.

Paradoxically, the novel has a sharper line as a stream of sensations than it does as an organized story. Zen and motorcycle maintenance dominate the earlier pages; but they represent the solution to a problem that is defined only in the last part of the book. That leaves them hanging out, so to speak: more like picturesque properties than working components. Or to put it another way, "Phaedrus" represents the ghost that the present mature narrator must track down and lay; yet "Phaedrus" also, as Platonist and Buddha-seeker, represents much of the answer to the narrator's monstrous problem.

"Phaedrus" contains all sorts of freaky ingredients. The narrator entertains a private notion that the name in Greek means "wolf" (which it doesn't); "Phaedrus" is associated not only with a timber wolf but with Goethe's Erlkönig: he is evidently felt as a real menace. Yet while his breakdown in the course of a head-on encounter with the University of Chicago is melodramatized nearly to the point of comedy, it is a muted reaffirmation of his sanity that opens the way in the last pages of the novel to the father's almost charmed reconciliation with his son. These oddities are not, perhaps, wholly Mr. Pirsig's. Throughout the latter part of the book particularly, the lighting is fitful and the sequences of thought and action spasmodic, as if from heavy cutting of a longer manuscript.

The real test of a prickly, rankling book like *ZAAMM* lies in its enduring power to disquiet. One can guess that even if the intense and confused metaphysics should pall (based as they seem to be on feverish interpretations of hastily read books), the wonder and fear of the novel would remain. These are loose, impressionistic words for an effect that grows, not simply out of effect making, but from quiet and deft prose on seemingly impersonal topics. Looking back to one of Mr. Pirsig's recent predecessors, one finds Jack Kerouac wielding a heavy prose hammer in a brief but typical scene from *On the Road*. Teresa, picked up on a bus to Los Angeles, has decided Sal Paradise is a pimp, and barricaded herself in the bathroom; he gets angry, throws her shoes against the door, and tells her to clear out:

> Terry came out with tears of sorriness in her eyes. In her simple and funny little mind had been decided the fact that a pimp does not throw a woman's shoes against the door and does not tell her **to get out**. In reverent and sweet little silence she took all her clothes off and slipped her tiny body into the sheets with me. It was brown as grapes. I saw her poor belly where there was a Caesarian scar; her hips were so narrow she couldn't bear a child without getting gashed open. Her legs were like little sticks. She was only four foot ten [p. 84].

By way of contrast, Mr. Pirsig:

A "mechanic's feel" implies not only an understanding for the elasticity of metal but for its softness. The insides of a motorcycle contain surfaces that are precise in some cases to as little as one ten-thousandth of an inch. If you drop them or get dirt on them or scratch them or bang them with a hammer they'll lose that precision. It's important to understand that the metal *behind* the surfaces can normally take great shock and stress but that the surfaces themselves cannot. When handing precision parts that are stuck or difficult to manipulate, a person with mechanic's feel will avoid damaging the surfaces and work with his tools on the nonprecision surfaces of the same part whenever possible. If he must work on the surfaces themselves, he'll always use softer surfaces to work them with. Brass hammers, plastic hammers, wood hammers, rubber hammers and lead hammers are all available for this work. Use them. Vise jaws can be fitted with plastic and copper and lead faces. Use these too. Handle precision parts gently. You'll never be sorry. If you have a tendency to bang things around, take more time and try to develop a little more respect for the accomplishment that a precision part represents [p. 292].

The theme of both passages is reverence; both use the vocabulary of exact observation to suggest an undercurrent of feeling, amounting to anxiety. But Kerouac bangs the English language around in those first two sentences, and falls into bathos in the last. He is incapable of a pair of sentences like "Use them," and "Use these too." Pirsig, with his severe, schoolteacherish tone and his clean, clear style, convinces us that we may have a kind of love for tappets and wonder over camshafts; and this conviction may very well give long life to his fine and peculiar book.

"A FINE FICTION"

BY W. T. LHAMON, JR.

Though the book jacket is too cagey to declare it, this book is a novel. It says nothing practical about choppers, and little more about Zen. But it says plenty about cycles writ large, and implies even more about art—particularly the fiction of the American '70s. *Zen* is a novel in need of maintenance because it chops and grinds its way along, truly humming only at the end—which is part of the point.

Or, I could begin this review like this: We've got ours! We've got our sweetly reasonable man of the people, our Paul Goodman out of Central Park riding his machine into Yellowstone and beyond! He likes his beer, his cigarettes, his steak, his eggs. He climbs tall mountains with his son. And he thinks. Thinks? Shucks, he conceptualizes. He's read Kant and Hume, Plato and Aristotle: we know he has because he shows how they all went wrong. Instead of watching TV, our man on the highway prefers to prop his feet on footrests and ponder. He's against suburbia, frenzy, competitiveness, shallow academics, and squareness. He's for Soul, Quality, the One, the Good, and selective capitalization. He even tells us that some of his best friends used to be Negroes. He admires Gumption.

Or, perhaps I should begin with Pirsig's ending—"there is a feeling now, that was not here before, and is not just on the surface of things, but penetrates all the way through: We've won it. It's going to get better now. You can sort of tell these things." This remarkable novel is part of the evidence that there is indeed an important new victory making itself felt now, a resurgence rivaling the one that seized America in the middle of the last century. Ideas in the outdoors: we haven't seen anything like it since Melville. If Melville and his contemporaries worried about the machine in the garden, Pirsig is one of many writers now worried about slipping the garden back into the machine—art back into artifice, romantic back into classical—and it's a telling moment when Pirsig rebukes Thoreau for "talking to another situation, another time, just discovering the evils of technology rather than discovering the solution. . . . No books can guide us anymore."

From *The New Republic* (June 29, 1974), pp. 24–26. Reprinted with permission. Copyright © 1974 The New Republic, Inc.

Not unlike Thoreau's and Melville's books, nevertheless, Pirsig's novel is by turns exasperating and profoundly exciting. *Zen* starts as a simple vacation trip across country—light tripping soon to turn heavy. The narrator is a 40-year-old technical writer who rides his motorcycle from Minneapolis through the Dakotas to Montana—up through Red Lodge, down through Yellowstone, over to Bozeman—then on to Oregon, and down the coast to the San Francisco Bay. He's riding west, as so many have before, through the incredible vastness and disparity of North America. Moving, as in the hymn, through the lonesome valley toward the Pacific: "No one else can cross it for you. You've got to cross it for yourself." With the narrator is his 11-year-old son, Chris, riding behind, also crossing a lonesome valley of his own. There cannot be much talking on a cycle, but there can be much thinking, and that's what the narrator tells us this book will be—thoughtful essays, a series of set pieces he calls Chautauquas, "intended to edify and entertain." But this novel is less about edification, besieged as it becomes, than about the relationship of edification to everything else in the world.

From the first day the Chautauqua is in trouble. The narrator wants to describe the division of Western thought into what he calls classical and romantic thought, one hierarchical and formal, the other immediate and recoiling from form. But how far back must he go to find its source? And he's haunted all the while by other problems. The landscape calls for attention, the motorcycle needs maintenance, women hover at vision's periphery—and Chris. Chris badly needs attention, which the narrator only gives grudgingly through the bulk of the book. Then there is Phaedrus (named for the victim of the famous Platonic dialogue), an earlier personality of the narrator himself.

As a college teacher Phaedrus became increasingly alienated from the ways of the Aristotelian classroom, then more and more Ahabian in monomaniacal pursuit of the source of the Western mythos, until hospitalization and electroshock therapy erased him years before this journey. Remembered fragments of that former life demand attention because Phaedrus had already been down the path of the romantic/classical division and found it led inevitably to madness: "To go outside the mythos is to become insane . . . Insanity is the *terra incognita* surrounding the mythos." Only in the unremembered and undiscovered territory beyond the mythos, Phaedrus believed, can fresh cultural springs flow. Back with the

Sophists, pre-Plato, existed true unity, the Godhead, the One, the Whole, Quality. The romantic and the classical modes, Phaedrus thought, have actually been trying to voice the same thing—Quality—but with less consciousness of doing so as the chasm widened between the present stutter and the mother tongue. One is left only with the two voices and no sense of the third, which contained them both.

Both voices are inadequate: two halves of one larger vision each arrogating all truth and reality to its own method. The major tone of all Western thought footnoting Plato has been this dialectic, his dialogue introjected and projected, his competitiveness, his sense of discovery as a heads-on fight so nervous that it was peripatetic, so destructive that it masked itself as Socratic innocence, so manipulative that we will study Plato's dialogues as we do famous chess games; dialogue and dialectic are displaced war. Small wonder that martial metaphor seems so pertinent to our lives, that so much seems like war to us even when it really is not. Merely by talking about things we wage war. The eternal polarities of American literature—romance to naturalism, round and round—are an instance of such a dialectical battle. In fact, one of the keener readings of Pirsig's as well as several other recent novels is as a recapitulation of this old fight. However, Pirsig and other new writers hope to surmount the battle neither by joining one side to vanquish the other, nor by staking out a golden mean, but by imagining, living and yoking the extremes. People who wake up starving in the middle of the night to make mile-high Dagwoods will know what this book is about.

Pirsig addresses all this less in the Chautauquas than in the back-ups. The narrator is reluctant to face the competition in his novel between essay and fiction, Chautauqua and Chris, edification and experience. These disturbing fragments, piling up, become the reader's greatest anxiety. At the expense of the boy who desperately needs to hear his father's voice, the discussions of philosophy sometimes grind on. The few times father and son talk early in the trip, the boy is eager, bright, inquisitive. But the trip is not so much across as it is farther and farther into the past's silence and toward Phaedrus' madness. The son goes quietly crazy with this—day after day sitting with helmet on head, staring at his father's back, obeying the man's benevolent routine, with no one to talk to, and mysteriously unable even to write his mother. Pirsig builds this beautifully, paradoxically. The Chautauqua is about the need to unify experience, but its clutching changes take the travelers out of experience, away from women; away from the land they meant to encounter; away from fiction, into Phaedrus' history and insanity, into fear and denial. The back-ups reluctantly reveal more and more of this difficulty until, finally, the narrator sees the reluctance as plain hypocrisy. Our sweetly reasonable guide has all along had a "mind divided against itself." He feels, "somehow we have arrived at the end of the world."

In the fog of the Mendocino coast the boy breaks down, suffers the silent inattention no longer, begins to wail "high-pitched and inhuman, like a siren in the distance." At an edge of his own, the father has seriously considered returning to the hospital, but decides to try talking to his son one last time. Yet as experience hounded the Chautauqua, now whining gear-changes from a straining truck punctuate the reaches of man and boy toward each other. Two sounds: the wail of a boy's totally acknowledged misery; the whine of machines. Maybe Pirsig means they are the same sound: some distant unity suddenly converging on the narrator. Subliminal whines and wails have been in the novel all along, but the father has chiefly ministered to the gears—of the cycle, of the Chautauqua—at the expense of Chris' needs. Now both voices are upon him. And Phaedrus is also upon him—talking through the man to calm the boy. That voice from territory beyond the dialectic, then, is possible: "It has all come together." The father encompasses it all, encompasses even mad Phaedrus when he tells the boy that Phaedrus was not insane. Father and son return to the cycle, more in tune with its drone and swings than ever before. They ride it to the water of the bay.

I'm inclined to accept the winning end because the narrator has so clearly gone through it all, has faced the pits of history, has spoken the tongues of his times. Like the Prufrock he almost becomes, the narrator has intimated he'd prefer to scuttle across the floors of silent seas, has wondered how to begin, how to presume, has feared himself a fool. But he has presumed and he has disturbed the universe and he has walked the *terra incognita* and declared that walk sane. When his son's human voice woke him, he did not drown. There will be a lot of people reading this novel and it may well become an American classic.

"UNEASY RIDER"

BY GEORGE STEINER

Told by the blurb that we have here "one of the most unique and exciting books in the history of American letters," one bridles both at the grammar of the claim and at its routine excess. The grammar stays irreparable. But I have a hunch that the assertion itself is valid. *Zen and the Art of Motorcycle Maintenance: An Inquiry Into Values*, by Robert M. Pirsig (Morrow), is as willfully awkward as its title. It is densely put together. It lurches, with a deliberate shift of its grave ballast, between fiction and philosophic discourse, between a private memoir and the formulaic impersonality of an engineering or trade journal. As it stands, it is a very long book, but report has it, and fault lines indicate, that a much longer text lies behind it. One hears of an eight-hundred-thousand-word draft and feels perversely deprived of it by the mere sanity and worldliness of the publisher. *Zen and the Art* is awkward both to live with and to write about. It lodges in the mind as few recent novels have, deepening its grip, compelling the landscape into unexpected planes of order and menace.

The narrative thread is deceptively trite. Father and son are on a motorcycle holiday, travelling from Minneapolis toward the Dakotas, then across the mountains, turning south to Santa Rosa and the Bay. Asphalt, motels, hairpins in the knife-cold of the Rockies, fog and desert, the waters dividing, then the vineyards and the tawny flanks of the sea. Mr. Pirsig is not the first ever to burst: Kerouac has been here before him, and Humbert Humbert, a clutch of novels, films, stories, television serials of loners on the move, lapping the silent miles, toasted or drenched under the big skies, motelling from one neon oasis to the next, and gliding at sundown through the nerve-wrenching sadness of the American suburb, honky-tonk town, and used-car crater. Pirsig is good on distance, windburn, and the uncomely occurrences in one's innards after too many hours on a cycle, after too many dusty snacks. But this would not make for the force of his book.

There are other pressures. The eleven-year-old passenger is called Chris. The weight of his nascent perceptions, of his endangered identity, grows fierce. There is a level at which this is the story of the great-shouldered ferryman of the Lord, of St. Chris-

From *The New Yorker* (April 15, 1974), pp. 147–150.

topher, guardian, talisman of travelers, his ribs bursting, his thighs shivering as the Child's weight almost overwhelms him in midstream. And Pirsig knows, perhaps senses with the somnambular erudition of a major artist, that the Christian image is itself a reflection of something much older—the centaur, a creature "motorcyclic" if ever there was, bearing the infant Hercules. A father and his child are riding through night and wind, enigmatically pursued, in receipt of eerie solicitations that seem to tear at the boy's soul. Yes, of course: the most famous of ballads, Goethe's "Erlkönig," some of whose multitudinous musical settings seem to resound from between the crotchets and plosives of the motorcycle engine. An erl-tale of nocturnal harrying, the human psyche being drawn back into an ancient slumber or possession, precisely as Chris may be if the cleansing Pacific is not reached in time. In short, we find a prodigality of pointers and echoes. There are the Wild Ones from Marlon Brando's pack, the Angels out of Hell (all theological inferences being allowed)—those outriders of Death whom Cocteau sheathed in leather and filmed long ago. A largesse of symbols, allusions, archetypes so spendthrift, so palpable, that only a great imaginer, shaping his material out of integral need, could afford it. A more professional contriver would have excised, he would have made his mythologies oblique, he would have felt embarrassed at the obviousness of the symbols offered. Mr. Pirsig allows himself a certain broad innocence. Everything is animate at the surface, contoured, casting exact shadows, as in the snowscape of an American primitive. Because the underlying design is covert and original to a degree.

Pirsig's work is, like so much of classic American literature, Manichaean. It is formed of dualities, binary oppositions, presences, values, codes of utterance in conflict. Father against son; the architectures of the mind against those of the machine; a modernity of speed, uniformity, and consumption (of fuel, of space, of political gimmicks) against conservancy, against the patience of true thought. But these confrontations are themselves ambiguous; they keep us off balance and straining for poise as do the swerves of the motorcycle.

Phaedrus is hunting the narrator. He is, at one level, the secret sharer, the intense questioner, the compaction of pure intellect. He has sprung directly out of the Plato dialogue that carries his name, and the device of having a living being pursued by a shadow out of Plato is by itself enough to certify Pirsig's strength, his mastery over the reader. But the chase is, to be sure, internal. It is the narrator himself who is a rent being, cloven nearly to his roots by alternate modes of identity. It is not the Demonking who is threatening the child's psyche, perhaps his life, but the father. Chris's dawning awareness of this fact, via nightmares, via the strangeness he hears in the penumbra of his father's voice, and the final duel between divided man and child on the verge of the healing sea, are of a numbing force. Chris perceives that his father has, at some dread point in the past, been out of his mind, literally ecstatic, as are the daemonically inhabited. The remembrance of a glass wall, in some hospital long ago, overwhelms him. Phaedrus, the lambent but ultimately anarchic agency of untamed thought, of speculative obsession beyond the constraints of love and of social life, is about to spring:

> His gaze fails in a sudden inward flash. Then his eyes close and a strange cry comes from his mouth, a wail like the sound of something far away. He turns and stumbles on the ground, then falls, doubles up and kneels and rocks back and forth, head on the ground. A faint misty wind blows in the grass around him. A seagull alights nearby.
> Through the fog I hear the whine of gears of a truck. . . .

Gears, points, engine-mounting bolts, the overhead-cam chain-tensioner, chain guards, fuel injectors play a major part. This is indeed a book about the art of motorcycle maintenance, about the cerebral concentration, about the scruple and delicacy of both hand and ear required to keep an engine musical and safe across heat or cold, tarmac or red dust. It is a book about the diverse orders of relation—wasteful, obtuse, amateurish, peremptory, utilitarian, insightful—which connect modern man to his mechanical environment. A motorcycle is "a system of concepts worked out in steel." Phaedrus and Plato, his master, believe that the steel fabric is but a shadow, necessarily inferior, of the idea of an engine generated by, perfect within, the mind. There is, the narrator allows, truth in this addiction to the ideal. But it is a perilous truth. It is the actual, the material we must endure and shape to our needs. Matter, too, has its exactitudes:

> If the fit is loose by a distance of only a few thousandths of an inch the force will be delivered suddenly, like a hammer blow, and

the rod, bearing, and crankshaft surface will soon be pounded flat, creating a noise which at first sounds a lot like loose tappets. That's the reason I'm checking it now. If it *is* a loose rod and I try to make it to the mountains without an overhaul, it will soon get louder and louder until the rod tears itself free, slams into the spinning crankshaft, and destroys the engine. Sometimes broken rods will pile right down through the crankcase and dump all the oil onto the road. All you can do then is start walking.

The two disciplines of apprehension, ideal and instrumental, are bodied forth in what is probably the wittiest, most ramified episode in the tale. The traveller returns to the college in Montana from which nervous collapse and Phaedrus's insistence on the absolute value of truth, on education as moral begetting, had driven him years before. His hosts dwell in the perfect house in the perfect canyon. Theirs is the very essence of the new American pastoral, of those chic serenities we now dress, build, and diet for. Robert DeWeese, artist-in-residence, brings out instructions for the assembly of an outdoor barbecue rotisserie which have baffled him. The discussion flows deep. It touches on the limitations of language in regard to mechanical procedure, on machine assembly as a long-lost branch of sculpture whose organic finesse is betrayed by the inert facility of commercial blueprints, on the ghost (O shades of Descartes) that inhabits the machine. Pirsig's timing and crafting at this juncture are flawless.

This is not always so. The westward journey is punctuated by lengthy meditations and lay sermons that Pirsig calls "Chautauquas." They are basic to his purpose. During these addresses to the reader, Phaedrus's insinuations are registered and diagnosed. The nature of quality, in conduct as in engineering, is debated and tested against the pragmatic shoddiness of a consumer society. Much of this discursive argument, the "inquiry into values," is finely shaped. But there are pedestrian stretches, potted summaries of Kant which betray the aggressive certitudes of the self-taught man, misattributions (it was not Coleridge but Goethe who divided rational humanity into Platonists and Aristotelians), tatters out of a Great Books seminar to which the narrator once took bitter exception. The cracker-barrel voice grinds on, sententious and flat. But the book is inspired, original enough to impel us across gray patches. And as the mountains gentle toward the sea— with father and child locked in a ghostly grip—the narrative tact, the perfect economy of effect, defy criticism.

A detailed technical treatise on the tools, on the routines, on the metaphysics of a specialized skill; the legend of a great hunt after identity, after the salvation of mind and soul out of obsession, the hunter being hunted; a fiction repeatedly interrupted by, enmeshed with, a lengthy meditation on the ironic and tragic singularities of American man—the analogies with *Moby Dick* are patent. Robert Pirsig invites the prodigious comparison. It is at many points, including, even, the almost complete absence of women, suitable. What more can one say?

"MAN AND MACHINE"

BY GEORGE BASALLA

Technology, one of the defining characteristics of mankind, has been a part of every human community that ever existed, no matter how primitive, and the influence of science has shaped the intellectual outlook and the style of life in Western society since the Renaissance. Nevertheless, it was not until the 20th century that the significance of these twin forces began to be studied in a systematic way, and we have yet to forge the intellectual and methodological tools necessary for the full comprehension of scientific and technical activity within a wider social and intellectual matrix. The "experts" on these matters—the sociologists, historians, and philosophers who write on the social implications of technology and science as their specialty, and the senior scientists and engineers who turn to the subject after having distinguished themselves in professional careers—have missed the mark. They have yet to make contributions commensurate with the complexity and range of their subject. The appearance of *Zen and the Art of Motorcycle Maintenance*, along with Studs Terkel's *Working* (Pantheon, 1974), has convinced me that some of the most original and imaginative books on technology and society are being written by authors who do not claim a professional expertise in the field. I believe that *Zen and the Art of Motorcycle Maintenance*, with its highly personal and yet analytical approach to technology and rationality, might open new paths for those specialists who see the scope of the problem but have yet to find creative ways in which to pursue its solution.

The author's note warning his reader that the book offers little factual information on either orthodox Zen Buddhist practice or actual motorcycle maintenance should quiet the fears of those who suspect this to be yet another counter-culture attack on science and technology. It was not written by a leather-jacket motorcyclist who obtained his knowledge of Eastern religion from a hasty reading of an Alan Watts paperback. Pirsig, a 46-year-old technical writer, is employed writing computer instruction manuals. He studied chemistry and philosophy at the University of Minnesota (B.A. 1950), having entered at age 14 with the intention of be-

From *Science*, Vol. 187 (January 24, 1975), pp. 248–250. Reprinted with permission from Dr. George Basalla and the American Association for the Advancement of Science. Copyright © 1975 by the AAAS.

coming a molecular biologist. After studying Oriental philosophy at the Benares Hindu University he taught English composition and rhetoric at the State University of Montana and did graduate work in ancient philosophy at the University of Chicago.

These facts are the structural elements upon which Pirsig builds his three-level autobiographical account of motorcycle travel and intellectual exploration. Taken at its simplest level, this is a story of a father and his 11-year-old son traveling by motorcycle, camping along back roads, from Minnesota to California. It extols the motorcycle as a vehicle that, by contrast with the automobile with its cushioned seat before the rectangular "TV screen" of the windshield, thrusts the rider into close contact with the physical environment through which he speeds. The book's description of natural scenes and the local people encountered in small-town restaurants and motels would earn its author recognition as a sensitive, if not original, writer of travel narrative.

Progressing to the next level of complexity we learn that the father has suffered a serious mental breakdown and that his son is showing early symptoms of psychotic illness. As they travel to the Pacific Coast, father and son are pursued by a ghost, Phaedrus, the remnants of the father's earlier personality. Phaedrus had been:

> Destroyed by order of the court, enforced by the transmission of high-voltage alternating current through the lobes of his brain . . . on twenty-eight consecutive occasions. . . . A whole personality had been liquidated without a trace in a technologically faultless act that has defined our relationship ever since. I have never met him. Never will.
>
> And yet strange wisps of his memory suddenly match and fit this road and desert bluffs and white-hot sand all around us and there is a bizarre concurrence and then I know he has seen all of this [p. 77].

Intense psychological analysis supersedes travel narrative and in turn reveals the metaphysical problem lying at the core of the book. How can the discordant worlds of the rational and the irrational, of logic and emotion, be reconciled? Phaedrus, a brilliant, abrasive man with a restless intellect, was exploring this problem when he lost his sanity. The narrator, who emerged from the technological act that annihilated Phaedrus, recalls the general lines along which Phaedrus had been thinking and gropes to find his own answer. The motorcycle, as technological reality and symbol of the rational order, figures largely in Pirsig's answer as it does in binding together travel narrative, psychological analysis, and metaphysical inquiry. And this is as it should be, because, according to the author,

> The Buddha, the Godhead, resides quite as comfortably in . . . the gears of a cycle transmission as he does at the top of a mountain or in the petals of a flower [p. 16].

The unified world view implied by this quotation is not in keeping with the Western intellectual tradition. Nor does it fit comfortably into the Eastern philosophical-religious outlook. True, the German philosopher Eugen Herrigel had written about sport and Zen Buddhism in *Zen in the Art of Archery* (Pantheon, 1953), but shooting an arrow at a target involves a traditional technology not to be compared with lubricating and tuning a motorcycle engine, welding a broken chain guard, or tracing a short circuit in the cycle's electrical system. Is it indeed possible to experience an Epiphany amidst the greasy clutter of a mechanic's workbench? Is the Godhead to be found among socket wrenches, spark plugs, speedometer cable, and handlebar shims? Yes, says Pirsig, but first you must make a critical attack on some of the central ideas of Western culture.

As an undergraduate Phaedrus discovered that science was not the source of final truths; he learned that it was but one of many branches of philosophy. Like any other intellectual venture science existed as a "ghost," an idea, in the minds of the men who first conceived it and then perpetuated it.

Science and rational inquiry in general gained status in the West from our acceptance of the bifurcated world created by subject-object dualism. This dualism made objective knowledge, at most, superior to subjective knowledge and, at least, its copartner in an antagonistic relationship constantly generating paired dichotomies: mind and matter, feeling and reason, art and science, life and technology. Phaedrus's battle against subject-object dualism began in Bozeman, Montana, where he was searching for new ways to teach his undergraduates the meaning of good writing. It ended in Chicago when he pursued dualism to the very edge of Western thought, closely reading Aristotle and Plato, and to the limits of sane inquiry, lying in a pool of his urine with fingers blistered by burning cigarettes about to be committed to a mental hospital.

Phaedrus-Pirsig first transformed subject-object dualism into a trinity by the inclusion of value judgments associated with the words "excellence," "worth," and "goodness." These he called Quality. A subsequent transformation reduced the original duality to a secondary role and placed Quality alone at the top. Quality became "the *parent*, the *source* of all subjects and objects" (p. 222). It is "so simple, immediate and direct" (p. 225) that it defies definition and yet it remains "the continuing stimulus which our environment puts upon us to create the world in which we live" (p. 225). With the supremacy of Quality Pirsig resolved the inconsistencies he found in Western philosophy and aligned himself with the great minds of the Orient, especially Lao Tzu.

What is the place of Quality, Tao, or Zen in 20th-century industrial civilization? A question of this sort is typical of the queries encountered in the bifurcated Western world, where the mechanic has been carefully set apart from the machine. Western man has been taught to divide reality into the subjective and the objective and then to exclude Quality from the objective knowledge upon which science and technology are based. Consequently, he cultivates a value-free, uninvolved attitude toward machines. Technology is something "out there" that he manipulates for profit or pleasure without caring to understand.

Pirsig's commentary on these matters reveals the holistic nature of his philosophical approach:

> The real cycle you're working on is a cycle called yourself. The machine that appears to be "out there" and the person that appears to be "in here" are not two separate things. They grow toward Quality or fall away from Quality together [p. 293].

This is similar to the thought Pirsig found printed on an instruction sheet accompanying a foreign-made bicycle, "Assembly of Japanese bicycle require great peace of mind" (p. 146). To confront successfully the assembly of a bicycle, the maintenance of a motorcycle, or the care and understanding of any other manifestation of modern technology requires a series of acts of value judgment accompanied by a mental predisposition to view subject and object, mechanic and mechanism, as a unity.

Pirsig hopes that the introduction of Quality into technology will carry us back into a "craftsmanlike self-involved reality" (p. 253) where the mechanic *cares* about his work.

Some of the issues raised here have been discussed in a similar vein elsewhere in philosophical literature, but never with such intensity and never with such close attention paid to the details of the machine. What academic philosopher would claim that a motorcycle is primarily a mental phenomenon and that the study of its maintenance "is really a miniature study of the art of rationality itself" (p. 84), or could write a serious philosophical discourse about Aristotle, Plato, Kant, and Hume in terms of Harley-Davidson and BMW?

Pirsig has done much in helping us to understand better the nature of science and technology and to appreciate machines and the men who work closely with them. He is at his best when dealing with the relationship between one man and one machine. Unfortunately, he does not systematically extend his analysis from personal mechanical maintenance to the manufacture of mass-produced items on an assembly line by large numbers of workers.

In writing his book *Working* Studs Terkel interviewed a wide variety of workers and allowed them to speak for themselves on the meaning of work. One of the constant complaints of the industrial worker was that he was unable to identify with the product he built and that slovenly workmanship went unnoticed. What does Pirsig's Quality mean in a factory situation where it has been distorted into quality control which is concerned with maintaining the barest minimum standards, not the highest ones? Why should the worker show care in his daily work routine when his job has been designed to rule out caring? In the words of a spot welder at an automotive assembly plant:

> Proud of my work? How can I feel pride in a job where I call a foreman's attention to a mistake, a bad piece of equipment, and he'll ignore it. Pretty soon you get the idea they don't care. You keep doing this and finally you're titled a troublemaker. So you just go about your work [*Working*, p. 162].

Between Terkel's record of job dissatisfaction and Pirsig's philosophical insights into the man-machine relationship lies an important, but relatively unexplored, area of industrial civilization. *Zen and the Art of Motorcycle Maintenance* might well serve as a preliminary guide for those who in charting this territory will aid man's attempt to redirect technology toward the realization of broadly based social goals.

"ZEN AND THE ART OF MOTORCYCLE MAINTENANCE"

BY UNA ALLIS

I

It is four years since *Zen and the Art of Motorcycle Maintenance* was first published and enthusiastically received. The novel is already in its fifth edition, and there is no evidence of demand waning. Its title causes ripples of excitement wherever it is mentioned, and, it seems, it is mentioned everywhere. It has gripped the imaginations of all strata of society. By any standards it is a success, and this, coupled with the fact that the book runs contrary to the twentieth-century literary trends, invites explication. For the unmistakable response of modern literature to the growth of relativism has been to retreat from representationalism. Realism, with its confidence in the continuity between man and the world, language and object, is clearly an inappropriate medium for an age racked by insecurity and alienation. Abstraction is intrinsically disjunctive, and hence congenial to the modern imagination. "Modernism marks the inception of a new era of high aesthetic selfconsciousness and non representationalism, in which art turns from realism and humanistic representation towards style, technique and spatial form."[1] It is in this context that Pirsig emerges with his unequivocally realistic and optimistic novel. Instead of being rejected for its naivety or conservatism, the novel receives a standing ovation. Why? Is this a confirmation of Zeraffa's observation that "innumerable novels, often by very gifted authors, gain favour from the mass of middle-class readers because of their realism and humanism"?[2] Is Pirsig's aesthetic, his appropriation of realism, purely pragmatic, designed to appeal to a mass audience? Or is it functionally related to the novel's content? Is Pirsig retreating to realism, or redeeming it? This is an important issue, for unless one can establish whether the novel is reactionary or radical, one cannot assess its implications for contemporary literature. The answer to these and related questions will only be revealed by careful analysis of the philosophical contents. The central section of this essay is therefore devoted to explication.

From *Critical Quarterly*, Vol. 20 (Autumn 1978), pp. 33–41. Reprinted with permission from Dr. Allis and *Critical Quarterly*.

The novel records the journey of Pirsig, his eleven-year-old son, Chris, and two friends, John and Sylvia Sutherland, as they travel across America on motorcycles. Although the physical events are vividly and sensuously described, the significant action occurs at the reflective and emotional levels. As in Romantic epics, the drama is internalised, the real arena being the consciousness of the artist. The movement is inwards and retrospective as Pirsig struggles to comprehend and assimilate his traumatic past, details of which are sporadically revealed. Some years prior to this trip, Pirsig suffered a nervous breakdown and was hospitalised as insane. Eventually he was discharged, but only after intensive ECS treatment had obliterated his memory of the past and of his former personality, whom he refers to as "Phaedrus." His attitude towards this prior self, this Phaedrus, is not one of morbid curiosity, but of terror and bewilderment. "Evil spirit," he calls him. "Insane, from a world without life and death." Intrigued by Phaedrus's philosophy notes, now in his possession, and from which it is clear that Phaedrus believed he had a "new and shattering and world-shaking truth" to deliver, which would revolutionise our understanding of reality, Pirsig cautiously attempts to reconstruct them. This has unforeseen and terrifying consequences, as his investigations exhume the past, and memories begin to erupt into consciousness. These freakish moments produce sudden coalescences of vision when Phaedrus and Pirsig merge together:

> . . . And yet strange wisps of his memory suddenly match and fit this road and desert bluffs and whitehot sand all around us and there is a bizarre concurrence and then I know he has seen all of this . . . And in seeing these sudden coalescences of vision and in recall of some strange fragment of thought whose origin I have no idea of, I'm like a clairvoyant, a spirit medium receiving messages from another world . . . [p. 77].

Phaedrus begins to haunt and terrorise him. The situation is exacerbated by Pirsig's inability to communicate with his son, Chris, who is showing signs of mental disturbance. As Phaedrus occupies more and more of his consciousness, one senses that Pirsig is losing control and heading towards another collapse. In the final pages, in a crucial confrontation of Pirsig and Chris, the dreaded event occurs—Phaedrus breaks through and assumes complete control of the situation. To our relief this does not precipitate the expected collapse, but frees Pirsig from an intolerable burden, and evokes Chris's recognition and response. The tension is resolved as Pirsig and Phaedrus are reintegrated, and father and son are reconciled.

This then is the skeleton of the novel. It is a compelling narrative, brilliantly executed and profoundly moving. But its aim is to instruct as well as to delight. Phaedrus's philosophical thesis is not merely an hypothetical construct around which to drape the narrative—on the contrary, it informs every detail of the novel. His interest in philosophy is ethically motivated, stimulated by his growing conviction that the deplorable quality of life in Western society is contingent upon its dualistic bias. Pessimism is an intelligible response to the intolerable schism between fact and value and the consequent tyranny of Science. Reason has installed itself as the absolute arbiter of truth, thereby trivialising all it does not accommodate: "Reason becomes an inhuman, mechanical, lifeless and blind force, a death force giving rise to science and technology and which somehow makes you a stranger in your own land." It becomes Phaedrus's passionate, even fanatical desire, to depose reason and close this breach. His strategy is not to retreat into subjectivity or irrationality, but to discover when and how reason first gained such power, for that will coincide with the inception of dualism . . . "the solution to the problem isn't that you abandon rationality, but that you expand the nature of rationality so it is capable of coming up with a solution." Thus begins his long philosophical quest, a quest which, after leading him through as many cultures as professions, all of which help him clarify his goals, brings him to the threshold of ancient Greek philosophy. Here the missing link is found, and the final "wave of crystallization" takes place. His analysis focuses on the relationship between dialectic and rhetoric in Plato's dialogues, his contention being that while Plato's explicit aim is to understand universal terms (such as "Goodness," "Love," "Beauty"), in actual fact he is using dialectic not to comprehend, but to *subjugate* these concepts. Plato's arguments are captious, a series of word traps, designed to throw the rhetorician by the force of the dialectic, rather than to unveil the intrinsic meaning of the words being investigated. Thus dialectic usurps the throne it should serve, installing itself as an end instead of a means. This then is when reason and value, truth and goodness were sundered, and dualism inaugurated. Phaedrus is frenetic with excitement when he discovers that this development can be attacked on logical grounds. For Plato's covert assumption is that dialectic (or reason) "comes before everything else," and this premise is demonstrably erroneous. Dialectic *presupposes* knowledge of what is valuable and good, else why, one might ask, choose dialectic as a method and not, say, tossing of a die? Value, or to use Pirsig's term Quality, is the source of reason. Reason does not exist in opposition to Quality, but as an extension of it. Thus a recognition of Quality's ultimacy does not invert dualistic tyranny but transforms the traditional dichotomy into a continuum: "Value is no longer an irrelevant offshoot of structure. Value is the predecessor of structure."

Although Quality is an elusive and indefinable concept, Pirsig insists that we can recognise it if we are "quiet long enough to see and hear and feel the real universe, not just one's own stale opinions about it." Having silenced ourselves, we will recognize Quality as being the underlying propulsion of the universe, of which we are a part, towards harmony and integration. The person who aligns himself with this principle will experience liberation. For he will no longer be striving to meet external criteria of excellence, or objectified goals, but will be evolving in accordance with the inner structure of his being, which is simultaneously the structure of reality. To be "at one with goodness" is to be true to oneself. What Pirsig is advocating is an internalisation of goals, a transference of authority from inner to outer domains. "We need a return to individual integrity, self reliance," he says. Clearly this is not a licence for subjectivity and waywardness. On the contrary, Quality intensifies one's sense of responsibility, throwing the individual back upon his inner resources. "The social values are right only if the individual values are right. The place to improve the world is first in one's own heart and head and hands, and then work outward from there." Quality is the very opposite of capriciousness. It does not involve the slavish submission of self to other, or the assertion of self against other—it is a sympathetic and respectful attentiveness to the other on its own terms. Confrontation is replaced by cooperation. Qualitative perception attempts to assimilate and integrate the other rather than reject it.

The novel is full of examples of the alternative modes of perception, a key passage being the analysis of mountaineering. Phaedrus was forced to abandon a pilgrimage in an Himalayan mountain after three days, because he was trying to use the mountain for his own purposes and the pilgrimage too. He regarded himself as the fixed entity, not the pilgrimage or the mountain, and thus wasn't ready for it. He speculated that the other pilgrims, the ones who reached the mountain, probably sensed the holiness of the mountain so intensely that each footstep was an act of devotion, an act of submission to this holiness. The holiness of the mountain infused into their own spirits enabled them to endure far more than anything he, with his greater physical strength, could take [p. 189].

Chris repeats Phaedrus's mistake: "Every step's an effort, both physically and spiritually, because he imagines his goal to be external and distant." Dualism thus projects values into external receptacles, leaving life sadly depleted. The liberation qualitative vision precipitates is amply demonstrated by Pirsig's response to motorcycle maintenance. His friend John scorns technology and asserts himself against it. By doing so, he throws himself at its mercy, since he is dependent, for example, on his motorcycle's effective functioning, and has no resources for coping with it should he break down. He thus allows technology to determine the boundaries of his freedom. Pirsig's response to assimilate and redeem technology by mastering the art of motorcycle maintenance. He develops a craftsmanlike attitude to his machine. His response to a possible source of alienation is to transform it from within, and use it to promote his freedom. Hence Quality establishes continuity between man and his environment and enables him to experience "what it is like to be a part of the world and not an enemy of it."

Quality is also the generator of all intellectual activity—both artistic and scientific. Since few are likely to dispute the relationship between Quality and art, it is to the less familiar correlation of Quality and science that Pirsig devotes most of his attention. It is Quality, he says, that informs the scientist's selection of facts from the infinite number available to him. Quality, beauty and harmony are the centre of scientific endeavour. "It is the sense of harmony of the cosmos which enables us choose the facts most fitting to contribute to this harmony." On the basis of Quality the mechanic is able to select good facts from bad facts. Harmony structures what would otherwise be only ephemeral. It would be wrong to infer from this that Quality is the search for permanent, enduring hierarchies and structures. For in fact the scientist's task is never completed. Once a theory or paradigm has established itself beyond doubt, the facts in conformity with it become dull, because they no longer teach us anything new. Then it is the exception, which can't be accommodated by the theory, that becomes important. Those little facts which "tug at the line, nagging for attention, asking if we'll be interested in them," turn out to be the growth points. Gradually they accumulate evidence, amass support, intimating our paradigm is too narrow and needs reconsideration. This eventually effects a scientific revolution. What was an anomaly becomes the focal point of the developing analogue.

Quality, therefore, always lures us on, "going in front of the track," inviting us to supersede existent harmonic structures. "Even if at times we fall into traps and seem to be irredeemably stuck, no matter how hard you try to hang on to it, this stuckness is bound to disappear. Your mind will naturally and freely move towards a solution. Quality gets you unstuck every time." Thus reality is not static but dynamic. It is a process (of which we are an extension), not an entity existing "out there" in opposition to us. There are no neutral facts to be discovered: "the whole history of science is a clear story of continuously new and changing explanations of old facts." The validity and significance of a "fact" is determined by the context of beliefs in which it is embedded. Hence in an (American) Indian "context of thought, ghosts and spirits are quite as real as atoms, particles, photons and quants are to a modern man." Pirsig, then, is not a naive realist or positivist. Neither is he a relativist, assuming reality is "what you will." He believes we have knowledge, not of the constituents of reality, but of its underlying structure. The *principle* of Quality/harmony is ultimate; the material it operates with is continually changing: "It is not the facts but the relation of things that results in the universal harmony that is the sole objective reality." Thus our predilection for consonance is not an imposition on reality but a response to it and an extension of it.

III

This synopsis of the novel's philosophical content may suggest that the book is dull and pedantic. Nothing could be further from the truth. Yet clearly the proposed philosophical emphasis did pose difficulties. As Pirsig remarks "the problem has been how to get off the generalities." That he triumphs over this "trap" is indubitable. The key to his success lies in his ingenious and subtle interweaving of philosophical speculation with the narrative structure. An author's most difficult task is to win the reader's "willing suspension of disbelief." Pirsig gains our assent from the opening lines:

> I can see by my watch, without taking my hand from the left grip of the cycle, that it is eight-thirty in the morning. The wind, even at sixty miles an hour, is warm and humid. When it's this hot and muggy at eight-thirty, I'm wondering what it's going to be like in the afternoon [p. 3].

He is a master of realism. His choice of the present tense, the first person, and his calculated transparency of style are skilfully manipulated to promote an atmosphere of casualness, naturalness, and to forge a bond of complicity and trust between reader and narrator. We are projected straight into his mind, *in medias res,* and experiences are filtered to us through his eyes. In accordance with the theories enunciated above, he is immersed in his experience, rather than reflecting on it from a privileged perspective:

> You see things vacationing on a motorcycle in a way that is completely different from any other. In a car you're always in a compartment, and because you're used to it you don't realize that through that car window everything you see is just more TV. You're a passive observer and it is all moving by you boringly in a frame.
> On a cycle the frame is gone. You're *in* the scene, not just watching it anymore, and the sense of presence is overwhelming [p. 4].

The reader is struck by the vivid concreteness with which the journey is portrayed. The descriptions, with their particularity and freshness of detail convey, in his words, "the overwhelming sense of presence":

> My watch says nine o'clock. And it's already too hot to sleep. Outside the sleeping bag, the sun is already high into the sky. The air around is clear and dry.
> I get up puffy-eyed and arthritic from the ground.
> My mouth is already dry and cracked and my face and hands are covered with mosquito bites. Some sunburn from yesterday morning is hurting.
> Beyond the pines are burned grass and clumps of earth and sand

so bright they are hard to look at. The heat, silence, and barren hills and blank sky give a feeling of great, intense space [p. 57].

The sensuousness of his remarks, his receptivity to the world around him, anchor the novel unequivocally in the physical world and carry the conviction of lived experience. Moreover these descriptions are peppered with acute and penetrating observations, observations based on massed evidence, on reflection and introspection. They are startling because his vision is so fresh and uncluttered. He assumes responsibility for what he perceives rather than reiterating stock responses and this shows a concern for, a patience and interest in, the people and world around him. And these observations generate a context for the narrative, spreading out roots, providing a sense of community and continuity. They implicate the past in the present, hinting a network of established relationships. This careful diffusion of attention saves the novel from lapsing into obsessive self-preoccupation.

In the opening pages Pirsig portrays himself as a stable, accommodating and generous person, and this creates an atmosphere of security: the reader settles down in confident expectation, savouring the leisurely pace of the narrative, looking forward to the gradual unfolding of events. It is into this atmosphere of well being and stability that the ghost of Phaedrus first bursts:

> We whizz through the flat open land, not a car anywhere, hardly a tree, but the road is smooth and clean and the engine now has a "packed," high rpm sound that says it's right on. It gets darker and darker.
>
> A flash and *Ka-wham!* of thunder, one right on top of the other. That shook me, and Chris has got his head against my back now. A few warning drops of rain . . . at this speed they are like needles. A second flash—*WHAM* and everything brilliant . . . and then in the brilliance of the next flash that farmhouse . . . that windmill . . . oh, my God, he's *been* here! . . . throttle off . . . this is *his* road . . . a fence and trees . . . and the speed drops to seventy, then sixty, then fifty-five and I hold it there [p. 26].

We have no point of reference for establishing the identity of "he" and our passivity is shattered by this intrusion of the inexplicable, the mysterious, the supernatural. Pirsig makes skilful use of an impressionistic style to convey the sense of intensity and shock. The experience is too immediate to be filtered syntactically. We are bewildered and have no means of comprehending this event except by *reading on*. This single occurrence is at once of more interest to us than anything else in the novel, precisely because it *doesn't fit*. From then on we are gripped by the narrative and propelled onwards in pursuit of the ghost who has so unceremoniously punctured our world, creating an intolerable gap in our framework of understanding. The tension thus generated entices the reader through the labyrinths of philosophical speculation in search of a satisfying explanation. It is wonderfully sustained. At no stage do we feel duped, since the narrator shares our predicament and is as exposed as we are to the unpredictability of events. As we advance in our search, evidence begins to accumulate around the anomaly, expanding, reinforcing and consolidating it. In the final confrontation between Pirsig and Chris a "wave of crystallization" occurs, and hitherto disconnected parts slide together into a coherent whole. In fact there is a complete reversal of roles: the anomaly becomes the norm, the dream becomes the reality, the insane becomes the sane. We are relieved and satisfied by the propriety of the resolution. The missing facts were always present, but as Pirsig observes, one is always blinded to them by "value rigidity": "Truth knocks on your door and you say 'go away. I'm looking for the truth,' and so it goes away." What is required is a change in our perception in order for us to "become unstuck." This occurs slowly and inevitably as ambiguity after ambiguity is resolved.

Quality, I have said, lures us towards harmony and resolution. The book expounds this and enacts it in its structure. Quality also invites us to resolve the dichotomy between self and other by a process of assimilation. This is precisely what Pirsig achieves by immersing himself in the past. By recreating and reliving Phaedrus's history, he eventually dissipates the fear that has crippled him and emerges from the experience healed. Dualistic perception encouraged him to reify and externalise part of himself. Quality lures him to absorb and reintegrate that which he has alienated. Quality is the instrument of at-one-ment.

IV

The appeal of *Zen and the Art of Motorcycle Maintenance* is obvious: not only is it a triumph of artistic skill, it is an affirmation of heroic, humanistic ideals. It is Chris's dumb, uncomprehending love that sustains Pirsig throughout his worst ordeals. "I haven't been carrying him at all. He's been carrying me," he recognises at the end of the book. Suffering and evil are redeemed, not through resistance and reaction, but by being absorbed and transcended. His is not a facile, cheap optimism—it has been earned.

But has Pirsig earned the right to appropriate realism as his artistic medium? Realism is, after all, the minion of dualism, and presupposes a positivism of objects, which Pirsig has explicitly denied. Is he compromising his beliefs and failing to follow through the implications of monism? Weight is given to this conjecture by the fact that Blake, whose epistemology coincides almost exactly with Pirsig's, eschews realism. For Blake, structures are only contingent, pragmatic devices, subservient to the "shaping spirit of the imagination." The imagination is the instrument of permanent revolution, a power which inexorably propels one into the future, into the unknown, "going forward, forward— irresistible from eternity to eternity." Realism conceals this. By presupposing a one to one correspondence between word and object, it consolidates these structures into "mind-forged manacles." Art, for Blake, should be a process, not an object, and for this reason he rejected realism and retreated to abstraction. Is this a major inconsistency in Pirsig's work? Or does analysis reveal a discrepancy between Blake's profession and practice? Might one not reasonably argue that Blake's peremptory imagination, in reacting so uncompromisingly against dualism, sets up an alternative tyranny—that of the subjective? Dualism is kicked out of the front door only to reappear at the back. Blake's later art is, after all, visionary at the expense of the visual. It is the significance of things, their "underlying form," that he emphasises—their "romantic surface," or concrete particularity is glossed over. Pirsig, on the other hand, achieves a delicate balance between the concrete and the abstract. The two are mutually dependent—the philosophy determines what details are included, and bestows on them a "halo of presence":[3] the narrative determines how the philosophy unfolds. To reject realism would be to set up an external enemy, to reify and exclude it. By incorporating and assimilating realism, Pirsig redeems it. He is thus scrupulously consistent with his principles.

Pirsig is a writer of the highest integrity. He has produced a work of power and originality, a work which challenges contemporary assumptions and demands a careful revaluation of objectives. After such an injection of optimism and vitality one wonders whether the direction of contemporary art is not soon destined to change.

NOTES

[1] *Modernism 1890–1930*, ed. M. Bradbury and J. McFarlane (Penguin, 1976).
[2] *Fictions—The Novel and Social Reality* by Michel Zeralla (Peregrine, 1976).
[3] *The Sovereign Ghost—Studies in Imagination* by Denis Donoghue (Faber, 1978).

"RINGER TO SHEEHY TO PIRSIG: THE 'GREENING' OF AMERICAN IDEALS OF SUCCESS"

BY JOHN G. CAWELTI

One of the most widely read books of the late 1960s, Charles A. Reich's *The Greening of America*,[1] looked at American culture in terms of a succession of what Reich called "consciousnesses." As Reich defined it, a consciousness is a socially shaped "total configuration" of attitudes, values and opinions which makes up an individual's perception of reality, his whole world view" (p. 14). In Reich's view, American society in the course of the nineteenth and twentieth centuries had generated three different consciousnesses. Consciousness I centered on the traditional ideal of the American dream and individual success. It was predominantly an ethic of work and it embodied the belief that all Americans had the opportunity to better themselves through "character, morality, hard work and self-denial" (p. 25). It assumed that "invention and machinery and production are the equivalent of progress; material success is the road to happiness; nature is beautiful but must be conquered and put to use" (p. 25). Its central model of human virtue was the independent entrepreneur, the self-made man. However, though Consciousness I was a more or less appropriate response to the social realities of early nineteenth century America, by the end of the nineteenth century this perception of reality had become increasingly out of touch with the actualities of a large industrial corporate state.

Consciousness II, as Reich portrayed it, grew out of a world in which the most important social realities were large organizations: "One of the central aspects of Consciousness II is an acceptance of the priority of institutions, organizations and society, and a belief that the individual must tie his destiny to something of this sort, larger than himself, and subordinate his will to it" (p. 67). While Consciousness II still placed a primary emphasis on the material success of the individual, the conception of the way to success which it reflected differed markedly from that of Consciousness I: "The man of Consciousness II sees his life and career in terms of progress within society and within an institution. An established hierarchy and settled procedures are seen as necessary and valuable. Achievement by character and hard work is translated into achievement in terms of a meritocracy of education, technical knowledge, and position. When he speaks of the vitality and challenges of his life, this is likely to be in terms of 'his part' in the challenges of organized society" (pp. 67–68).

However, Reich's major point was that, in our own time of social and cultural crisis, Consciousness II was itself becoming rapidly obsolete. Responding to such concerns as the destruction of the environment by runaway technology, the corporate state's tendency toward permanent warfare, and the lack of political and social responsibility in a world of multi-national corporations, many young people rejected the professional rationalism and dependence on organization and technology characteristic of Consciousness II. Out of their protest against the existing system and their experimentation with new life styles, a new consciousness was emerging. Consciousness III, Reich argued, was a new and better world view, more consonant with the deeper idealism of the "American dream." This new world view, which involved the rejection of the material success ethic of Consciousness II, was based on "liberation." "It comes into being the moment the individual frees himself from automatic acceptance of the imperatives of society and the false consciousness which society imposes" (p. 225). The new consciousness "starts with self." Unlike Consciousness II, "which accepts society, the public interest, and institutions as the primary reality, III declares that the individual self is the only true reality" (p. 225). But Consciousness III is the antithesis of selfishness because it "postulates the absolute worth of every human being" and rejects the "antagonistic or competitive doctrine of life" (p. 226). Thus, according to Reich, Consciousness III propounds a different standard of individual success, based not on the accumulation of wealth or the achievement of status within a large organization but on the integrity and wholeness of the self and meaningful work of a kind that is valuable rather than destructive to the human community.

Reich's book offered a sympathetic account of the student movement of the 1960s. He pictured the rebellion and the radicalism which so upset many older Americans as signs of a new and more meaningful understanding of the American dream and prophesied that this new consciousness would spread rapidly until it brought about a fundamental revolution in American society: "It will not be like revolutions of the past. It will originate with the individual and the culture, and it will change the political structure only as its final act. It will not require violence to succeed, and it cannot be successfully resisted by violence. . . . It promises a higher reason, a more human community, and a new and liberated individual. Its ultimate creation will be a new and enduring wholeness and beauty—a renewed relationship of man to himself, to other men, to society, to nature, and to the land" (p. 4).

From the perspective of the anxious and inflationary 1970s, when the younger generation seems more concerned with finding remunerative employment than with changing the world, Reich's analysis seems prematurely apocalyptic. *The Greening of America* along with other major statements of the late 1960s like Theodore Roszak's *The Making of a Counter-Culture* has so rapidly become a dated, almost forgotten work that one is half inclined to dismiss Reich's analysis as the sort of prophetic wishful thinking which usually accompanies movements of messianic enthusiasm, such as the American student movement of the 1960s or the popular front excitement of the late 1930s. Yet, though Reich carried his analysis to extremes of optimistic simplicity, his delineation of a sequence of changing perceptions of the individual quest for significance and fulfillment was similar to the conclusions reached by many American social and cultural historians. Reich's Consciousness I is the traditional ethic of individual success, while his Consciousness II relates to the world view of the organization man, or what a more recent historian has analyzed as the "culture of professionalism."[2] The Reichian analysis also parallels in many ways David Riesman's famous description in *The Lonely Crowd* of "inner directed" and "other directed" personality types. Indeed, Reich's analysis of Consciousnesses I and II can be seen as a synthesis and popularization of the basic cultural differences between early and late industrial society perceived by a slightly earlier generation of historians, sociologists, and social psychologists.

But the real issue of *The Greening of America*, and probably the source of both its great influence in the late 1960s and its present obscurity, is that of Consciousness III. Did the 1960s result in any basic changes in American world views, particularly as involving the definition of individual success and temperament, or were the alarums and excursions of that period only temporary responses to a particular historical situation? To explore this question I propose to look at what has happened to some of the central traditions of American self-help and success literature as they have manifested themselves in the 1970s. In particular, I shall examine three best sellers, *Winning Through Intimidation*,[3] *Passages*,[4] and *Zen and the Art of Motorcycle Maintenance*. . . .

[The treatments of the Ringer and Sheehy books, *Winning Through Intimidation* and *Passages*, are omitted.]

Though the two strands of advice on business success and of moral and psychological self-help have been the predominant literary manifestations of the ideal of success, there has been a third strand of considerable importance. Exemplified in works like Thoreau's *Walden* and Emerson's *Essays*, this tradition has always engaged the ideal of success from a critical and transcendent perspective, while at the same time invoking the imaginative landscape of individualism and the quest for the American dream. Thus, Thoreau's *Walden* has so many formal and thematic connections with the literature of success and self-help that in one of its dimensions it can be read as an ironic parody of the typical advice to young men guidebook. Emerson, as one of the most popular lecturers of his day, often spoke of success, and the self-made man was one of his archetypal figures. Yet both Emerson and Thoreau sought to transform the cultural ideals of individual accomplishment and psychological fulfillment into a higher vocation. Rejecting both the material definition of success and the conventional religious association between business achievement and godliness, they saw in the quest for the American dream a metaphor for spiritual transcendence. It was a self-making of the soul rather than the accumulation of property and rising in society which they sought to define in their writings. Though Thoreau was more sharply critical of conventional ideas of success than Emerson, both understood that the transcendence they sought as the ultimate goal of life could not be achieved by an outright rejection of the ideal of success. Even Thoreau's famous experiment at Walden Pond was not an escape into nature but a simplification of life in order to achieve individual autonomy. With his cottage and bean field, Thoreau tried to create an economic self-sufficiency through which he might transform the conduct of life into a process of spiritual regeneration.

The importance of Emerson and Thoreau to the development of American ideals was twofold. First of all, they were among the most powerful and influential critics of the narrowly social and economic definition of success which Americans tended to pursue. But even more important than their criticism and rejection of conventional conceptions of success as the accumulation of wealth and status was their insistence that the ideal of success symbolized and prefigured a higher truth. It was the possibility of an ongoing dialectic between Emersonian ideas of spiritual transformation and the conventional idea of success that was probably responsible for much of Emerson and Thoreau's later influence, for their writings suggested that hard-driven Americans, frustrated by the anxieties generated by their business pursuits, might imagine themselves on the verge of a spiritual breakthrough which would finally legitimate the conduct of their lives and resolve its contradictions.

This tradition, most powerfully embodied in the Transcendentalists, has always been an important strand in American writings on success. Its chief function seems to be the criticism of conventional definitions of success and individualism in order to affirm a more transcendent vision of the American dream. One would expect to find such treatments of the success ideal particularly prominent in times of crisis. This was the case in the 1960s which did in fact produce a considerable literature of this sort. Indeed, one might view Charles Reich's *The Greening of America* as an Emersonian essay for the 1960s, as Reich's criticism of Consciousnesses I and II do resemble Emerson's treatment of conventional ideas of success while the enthusiastic portrayal of Consciousness III is an attempt to define a more transcendent ideal of individualism. Perhaps the striking immediate popularity as well as the current obscurity of Reich's book resulted from its being little more than a slightly Marxian updating of Emerson. That the general thrust of his argument was quite familiar made its apparent novelty all the more exciting to the reading public at first. As this public came to realize that he had little to add to a perception of American culture which had been often urged since Emerson articulated it over a hundred years ago, interest in *The Greening of America* quickly dissipated.

More significant as a "transcendental" critique of the American dream was another work growing out of the experience of the 1960s. If Reich might be (generously) called the Emerson of the 1960s, Robert Pirsig was the Thoreau of the early 1970s. His remarkable book *Zen and the Art of Motorcycle Maintenance*, though not as immediately successful as *The Greening of America*, already shows signs of having struck deeper roots in the American imagination. The way in which the book has been read and reread, without losing its fascination, suggests that it is the best possible text for an exploration of the impact of the 1960s on the transcendental tradition of individualism and success. Because the book is obviously modeled in many ways on Thoreau's *Walden,* it provides us with an excellent opportunity for controlled comparison.

The central theme of *Zen and the Art of Motorcycle Maintenance* is the quest for wholeness in a culture that has become intellectually, spiritually and emotionally fragmented. The importance which the author places on this quest and the intensity of his claim to have diagnosed and sought a cure for the divided psyche of modern man, is manifest in the striking set of antitheses coupled in his title: religion versus technology; spirit versus matter; mysticism versus mechanism; mind versus machine; art versus engineering; East versus West: Buddhists versus Hell's Angels. This title seized on the imagination of many readers precisely because it suggested the possibility of a linkage between aspects of our culture which are ordinarily felt to be in opposition to each other. This, as it turns out, is the basic problem which Pirsig explores in his narrative. Our culture has intensified divisions in the basic unity of human action and thought which go back, Pirsig believes, to the very foundations of Western civilization in classical philosophy—Plato's attack on the sophists and Aristotle's philosophy of classification and differentiation. As Pirsig portrays it, the Western world has become hopelessly entangled in the conflict between two forms of basic human understanding—which he calls the "classic" and the "romantic"—which have been extended into opposing philosophical principles and have thereby lost their true character as parts of a complex and unified dialectic. The modern split between what C. P. Snow labelled "the two cultures," the world as defined by the arts and humanities and the world as treated by science and technology, is for Pirsig a particularly virulent contemporary form of the divided human psyche which arose in history when Plato and Aristotle created the Western concept of knowing. This basic disjunction in modes of knowledge released vast human energies and made possible the unprecedented evolution of Western technology and its associated forms of social and cultural organization. But we have now reached a point in history when the gulf between ways of understanding has become destructive. Modern culture has become lost in its own fragmentation and spiritual confusion. Our culture and its most sensitive individuals have become cut off from the unity of self which is the true state of humanity. Significantly, the protagonist of *Zen and the Art of Motorcycle Maintenance* is a schizophrenic in quest of the unification of his divided self.

Like *Walden*, Pirsig's book is an exploration and a quest. Where Thoreau went into the woods alone, though, Pirsig's protagonist embarks on a motorcycle trip across the country with his son and two friends. His narrative of this trip combines, like *Walden*, a very specific account of the places he visited and the people he met with the general reflections on history, philosophy and culture which these immediate experiences stimulate. His debt to Thoreau is quite specific. He tells us that the one book he carries with him, along with clothing, is *Walden*. But *Zen and the Art of Motorcycle Maintenance* differs from the earlier work in one striking manner. As Pirsig proceeds, we become increasingly aware of the hovering presence of the protagonist's former self, whom he calls Phaedrus, after the title character in one of Plato's dialogues. As his Phaedrus-self becomes more articulate, we learn the past history of the protagonist. He had been a promising student of philosophy and a teacher of rhetoric, but his emerging philosophy of life had been so much in conflict with the world view of his culture that he had undergone a profound psychological breakdown and had been institutionalized. Released after shock treatments which had obliterated many of his former memories and perceptions, he has embarked on a new career as a computer technician. The cost of his new stability and status has been a total rejection of his Phaedrus-self, and thus of the totality of his being. Yet he has never been fully satisfied with his partial being and has found in the riding and repairing of motorcycles some expression of his yearning to escape from the narrowness and restrictiveness of his "sane" but partial self. His present trip is a desperate attempt to escape from the confinement of his new life. Through a complex process of experience and reflection it turns into a confrontation with his former self, and ultimately, to a tentative restoration of his soul.

Like Emerson and Thoreau, Pirsig sees the problem of individual fulfillment in broader terms much loftier than material success or status within an organization. Also, like his predecessors, he looks beyond the traditions of Western civilization to oriental mysticism and tries to adapt some elements of this alternative world view as a guide to seeing beyond the restrictive perspective on life he feels he has inherited as an American. Of course, the symbols he develop to express his insights are distinctly contemporary. The centrality of the motorcycle as a vehicle of transcendence, and of madness as a symbol of both alienation and the quest for escape from a repressive culture ties Pirsig's work to some of the most important novels and films of the 1960s—Kesey's *One Flew Over the Cuckoo's Nest* and Hopper's *Easy Rider*, for example. There are clear analogues to these symbols in Thoreau's treatment of walking as a transcendent activity and of individual isolation in nature as a mode of cultural escape. However, despite its clear affiliation with the transcendentalist tradition, there is, I think, a difference in Pirsig's work which reflects the impact of the 1960s. I would characterize this generally as Pirsig's emphasis on integration rather than transcendence.

Zen and the Art of Motorcycle Maintenance moves from an analysis of the character and sources of the fragmentation of life in modern American culture to a quest for reunification and integration. As Pirsig presents it, his protagonist must struggle with this problem on several different levels. At the beginning of the narrative, he feels alienated from nature, from his country, from his heritage, family and friends and above all, from himself. It is this sense of division and separation that drives him forward on his trip and this condition is reflected in the structure of the book which is, from the beginning, divided between thought and experience. His generalized reflections on the divisions between art and technology, classicism and romanticism, the mind and the machine are counterpointed with experiential descriptions of the country he passes through, of the feeling of riding and working with motorcycles, and of his mixed feelings toward the people travelling with him—in particular, his problematic and anxious relationship with his son. As his trip moves into the heart of the country, he also moves into his own personal past, and begins to understand how his personal breakdown and the destruction of his former self are related to the spiritual fragmentation of modern American culture. Finally, Pirsig's protagonist is able to bring his lost self through a return of repressed memories, gaining a new relationship with his son, his friends and the world around him. Thought, memory and present experience come together for him. He begins to see how he can make unity of his life just as earlier he had found an intimation of harmony between thought and action in the practice of working on his motorcycle.

It is this emphasis on an image of integration among different aspects of experience which the development of modern technological and industrial culture has increasingly separated which dominates *Zen and the Art of Motorcycle Maintenance*. This image differs markedly from the concept of transcendent experience envisioned by Emerson and Thoreau. At the end of *Walden,* the coming of spring fills the protagonist with intimations of regeneration and new possibility which will come from the development of our capacity for higher and richer knowledge. Because the protagonist has been able to transcend the limits of his imagination, the regenerative powers of spring can work in his soul and lead him to a new sense of the world:

> These may be but the spring months in the life of the race. If we have had the seven-years' itch, we have not seen the seventeen-year locust yet in Concord. We are acquainted with a mere pellicle of the globe on which we live. Most have not delved six feet beneath the surface, nor leaped as many above it. We know not where we are. . . . As I stand over the insect crawling amid the pine needles on the forest floor, and endeavoring to conceal itself from my sight and ask myself why it will cherish those humble thoughts, and hide its head from me who might, perhaps, be its benefactor, and impart to its race some cheering information, I am reminded of the greater Benefactor and Intelligence that stands over me the human insect. . . . The light which puts out our eyes is darkness to us. Only that day dawns to which we are awake. There is more day to dawn. The sun is but a morning star.

In contrast to this rhapsodic invocation of man's potential passage to higher and higher levels of understanding, experience and knowledge, the end of *Zen and the Art of Motorcycle Maintenance* seems more like the attainment of a precarious balance between conflicting forces, just as the riding of a well-tuned motorcycle involves a complex act of integrating natural, mechanical and mental energies which, if not properly balanced, can destroy the rider. Once one has learned the balancing act, the chance of survival and improvement exists. Since, however, the illumination has resulted from a period of crisis and breakdown, the protagonist is too aware of its tentativeness and fragility to reach for the transcendent potential expressed by Emerson and Thoreau. "Trials never end, of course. Unhappiness and misfortune are bound to occur as long as people live, but there is a feeling now, that was not here before, and is not just on the surface of things, but penetrates all the way through: We've won it. It's going to get better now. You can sort of tell these things" (pp. 372–73).

Pirsig's version of the quest for a higher success, the experience of significant selfhood, is, like the nineteenth century inspirational essays of Emerson and Thoreau, an enrichment and broadening more than a fundamental attack on the narrower traditions of business and psychological self-help. Though it reaches toward a more complex and richer ideal of individual autonomy and achievement than that of the successful intimidator proposed by Robert Ringer or of the passenger through the complicated cycles of life described by Gail Sheehy, Pirsig's vision does share with these other two contemporary works a rather different world view from that of either the traditional success literature of the nineteenth and early twentieth centuries or the positive thinking so prevalent in the forties and fifties. First of all, the image of the successful individual in all three of these works is more that of a survivor of crises than of a center of infinite and ever-expanding possibility. A sense of deep anxiety and fear of personal crisis was latent in the positive thinkers. The incessant invocations to confidence and optimism of self-help writers like Norman Vincent Peale reflected an underlying fear of failure and breakdown. However, the positive thinkers would never admit openly, as Ringer, Sheehy and Pirsig do in different ways, that the conditions of modern life make anxiety and crisis a recurrent experience. Second, these writers all reject the idea of a transcendent reality, the energy of which the individual can draw on to achieve either material success or a higher level of individual autonomy. Instead, they view the problem of individual development either, like Ringer, in terms of economic, legal and psychological strategems, or like Sheehy and Pirsig, as a problem of the integration of psychological needs and drives which the culture tends to fragment or set into conflict. Finally, none of these writers affirms the ideal of the American dream, the conception of America as a unique land of opportunity in which the achievement of individual success is not only a possibility, but an obligation. Pirsig and Sheehy both portray the traditional ideal of the American dream as an obstacle to true individual fulfillment and a source of inner conflict, while Ringer satirizes this theme as a delusion which interferes with realistic thinking about the conduct of business.

This sampling of the contemporary literature of success, self-help, and the quest for individual fulfillment seems to indicate that the American public retains much of its long-standing interest in the problems of getting ahead in life, in finding individual fulfillment, and in creating an ideal of individualism which will give a fuller sense of significance to life. The continuation of these traditional genres of self-help literature casts doubt on the Reichian idea that the younger generation of the 1960s heralded the emergence of a new consciousness or world view in American life. However, if we cannot perceive an apocalyptic transformation, there are distinctive signs of new emphases and of the decline of traditional themes in this literature which suggest that the social and cultural turbulence of the 1960s reflected some basic and long-term changes in American world views.

NOTES

[1] Charles A. Reich, *The Greening of America* (New York: Random House, 1970). All quotations are from this edition.

[2] Burton J. Bledstein, *The Culture of Professionalism* (New York: W. W. Norton & Co., 1976).

[3] Robert J. Ringer, *Winning Through Intimidation* (Greenwich, Conn: Fawcett Publications, Inc., 1974).

[4] Gail Sheehy, *Passages* (New York: Bantam Books, 1977).

"ZEN AND THE ART OF MOTORCYCLE MAINTENANCE: THE IDENTITY OF THE ERLKÖNIG"

BY THOMAS J. STEELE, S.J.

During the evening of the second day of the cross-country bike trip in Robert M. Pirsig's *Zen and the Art of Motorcycle Maintenance,* the narrator is trying to explain to John and Sylvia why he won't let his son Chris see a psychiatrist: " 'I don't know . . . they're not *kin*.' " Then his mind begins to free-associate the word "kin":

> Surprising word, I think to myself, never used it before. Not of *kin* . . . sounds like hillbilly talk . . . not of a *kind* . . . same root . . . *kind*ness, too . . . they can't have real *kind*ness toward him, they're not his *kin*. . . . That's exactly the feeling. . . .
>
> It goes over and over again through my thoughts . . . *mein Kind*—my child. There it is in another language. *Meine Kinder. . . "Wer reitet so spät durch Nacht und Wind? Es ist der Vater mit seinem Kind."*
>
> Strange feeling from that.
>
> "What are you thinking about?" Sylvia asks.
>
> "An old poem, by Goethe. It must be two hundred years old. I had to learn it a long time ago. I don't know why I should remember it now, except . . ." The strange feeling comes back.
>
> "How does it go?" Sylvia asks.
>
> I try to recall. "A man is riding along a beach at night, through the wind. It's a father, with his son, whom he holds fast in his arm. He asks the son why he looks so pale, and the son replies, 'Father, don't you see the ghost?' The father tried to reassure the boy it's only a bank of fog along the beach that he sees and only the rustling of the leaves in the wind that he hears but the son keeps saying it is the ghost and the father rides harder and harder through the night."
>
> "How does it end?"
>
> "In failure . . . death of the child. The ghost wins."[1]

The Goethe poem cited is "Erlkönig," a Gothic ballad dating from 1782. A narrator, the child, the father, and the "alderking," a goblinlike "king of the alder grove," tell the tale:

A slightly different version of this article was first published in *Ariel*, Vol. 17, No. 4 (1979), pp. 83–93. Reprinted with permission from University of Calgary Press. Copyright © 1979 University of Calgary Press.

"THE ERL-KING"

Who rides so late through night and wind?
It is the father with his child;
He holds the boy safe in his arm,
He holds him close and keeps him warm.

"My son, why do you hide your face in fear?"
"Don't you see, father, the Erl-king there?
The Erl-king with crown and robe?"
"My son, that is only a wreath of the mist."

"My pretty child, come, come with me!
Some pretty games I'll play with you.
Many a bright flower grows on the shore,
And my mother has many golden robes."

"My father, my father, now do you hear
What the Erl-king is promising me?"
"Be calm, remain calm, my child,
The nightwind is rustling the dry leaves."

"Will you, sweet boy, now come with me?
My daughters will wait on you,
My daughters will lead the nightly round
And rock you and dance you and sing you to sleep."

"My father, my father, don't you see there
The Erl-king in the gloomy place?"
"My son, my son, I see it clearly;
It is merely the old willows so gray."

"I love you, I'm charmed by your lovely appearance,
And if you're unwilling, I will use force."
"My father, my father, he's seizing me now!
The Erl-king has done me terrible harm!"

The father shudders, and now he rides fast,
In his arms he holds the moaning boy;
He reached his farm all troubled with need,
In his arms his dear child was dead.[2]

This ballad provides perhaps the best entrance into Pirsig's novel. First of all, it provides a model for the emotions of the reader as he accompanies the narrator and Chris on their cross-country ride and experiences with them the memory of past insanity and the dread of its onset in the son, its recurrence in the father, or both. Secondly, it offers a root metaphor which is worked over again and again, finally to be stood on its head by the happy ending of the book. Thirdly, and incidentally, the reader should note that the ocean does not appear in Goethe's poem, though it does in the narrator's relation of it and in his subsequent dream; it is read in—or dreamed in—from the end of the book.

That very night, for example, the narrator dreams:

> The moon is shining and yet there is a bank of fog and I am riding a horse and Chris is with me and the horse jumps over a small stream that runs through the sand toward the ocean somewhere beyond. And then that is broken. . . . And then it reappears.
>
> And in the fog there appears an intimation of a figure. It disappears when I look at it directly, but then reappears in the corner of my vision when I turn my glance. I am about to say something, to call to it, to recognize it, but then do not, knowing that to recognize it by any gesture or action is to give it a reality which it must not have. But it is a figure I recognize even though I do not let on. It is Phaedrus.
>
> Evil spirit. Insane. From a world without life or death [pp. 56–57].

And throughout most of the rest of the book the reader will be persuaded by the narrator's identification of the Erlkönig with Phaedrus, his own past identity before he underwent electroshock treatment.

The external framework of the plot is a journey by motorcycle. Eleven-year-old Chris and his father travel on one bike, John and Sylvia Sutherland on another, from Minnesota westward to visit friends near Bozeman, Montana, where the father had taught college English some years before. While John and Sylvia return home, the narrator and his son continue west across the mountains to the Pacific, eventually arriving in California. The entire journey of son and father westward is a double allegory. It is an intellectual journey, for the narrator attempts to retrieve his former personality's speculations about Quality in the reminiscences he calls "the Chautauqua"; the narrator's search for Phaedrus amounts to an obsessive fascination. It is secondly a personal and interpersonal odyssey, for the narrator is seeking his own integration and that of his son, Chris is trying to find himself and is seeking his father, and both Chris and the narrator are seeking a satisfactory meeting with each other. Neither Chris nor the narrator is ready for integration or meeting at any time early in the book; indeed, if the reader looks carefully he will find that the Phaedrus-dreams occur after the narrator has failed to provide paternal support for his son.[3]

Even by Chapter 19, when the narrator has another dream, he is not prepared to interpret it for what it really is:

> In the dream I was standing in a white-painted room looking at a glass door. On the other side was [sic] Chris and his brother and mother. Chris was waving at me from the other side of the door and his brother was smiling, but his mother had tears in her eyes. Then I saw that Chris's smile was fixed and artificial and actually there was deep fear.
>
> I moved toward the door and his smile became better. He motioned for me to open it. I was about to open it, but then didn't. His fear came back but I turned and walked away.
>
> It's a dream that has occurred often before. Its meaning is obvious and fits some thoughts of last night. He's trying to relate to me and is afraid he never will [p. 203].

As will appear as the book proceeds, this dream is not the usual projection of the concerns of the present but a fragment of past memory—of Phaedrus' memory—which Chris shares, so that the "I" of it is not the narrator as we know him and as he knows himself but instead Phaedrus. The narrator is correct about Chris's concern but wrong about the object of it; his mistake is the foundation for the ironic and optimistic unfolding of the real answers to three questions: Who is seeking whom? Who is fleeing from whom? Who, in Goethe's terms, is the father, who the son, and who the unholy ghost?

When Chris wakes, he claims that the narrator talked all night long about the mountain: " 'You said at the top of the mountain we'd see everything. You said you were going to meet me there.' I think he's been dreaming. 'How could I meet you there when I'm already with you?' 'I don't know. *You* said it. . . . You sounded like you were drunk or something' " (p. 204).[4] But as the plot continues, Chris and the narrator do not go to the top of the mountain; after mentioning the Yellowstone earthquake of August 1959, the narrator refuses to try for the summit:

> "I think we'd be very smart if we let that mountaintop go for now and try it another summer."
> He silent. They he says, "Why?"
> "I have bad feelings about it" [p. 219].

He refuses to take the risk of going to the mountain top—the physical risk of rockslides, the psychological risk of meeting Chris there as the dream had promised. The narrator refuses the journey to the point where earth meets sky, so the quest will turn toward another ultimate, that margin where earth meets sea, though it is spoken of as the bottom of the ocean.

Another of Phaedrus' dreams points clearly to this farther journey to a true meeting. It begins in the same way as the earlier dream, with the corridor and the glass door separating Phaedrus from his family; but then:

> And now I see what the glass door is. It is the door of a coffin—mine.
> Not a coffin, a sarcophagus. I am in an enormous vault, dead, and they are paying their last respects.

As he tries to communicate to Chris, a shadowy figure warns him not to do so, but he calls out anyway:

> "CHRIS!" I shout toward the door. "I'LL SEE YOU!!" The dark figure moves toward me threateningly, but I hear Chris's voice, "Where?" faint and distant. He heard me! And the dark figure, enraged, draws a curtain over the door.
> Not the mountain, I think. The mountain is gone. "AT THE BOTTOM OF THE OCEAN!!" I shout [pp. 245–46].

So the quest continues, despite the threat of the shadowy figure, the Erlkönig. But the problems continue as well, especially the problem of the narrator's inability to form an accurate notion of whom Chris will meet at the bottom of the ocean. After thinking that at certain times Chris "seems very far away and sort of watching me from some vantage point I don't see" (p. 269), the narrator goes on to speculate in a Bradleyan manner about the dividedness of any human mind from any other:

> I thought that the idea that one person's mind is accessible to another's is just a conversational illusion, just a figure of speech, an assumption that makes some kind of exchange between basically alien creatures seem plausible, and that really the relationship of one person to another is ultimately unknowable. The effort of fathoming what is in another's mind creates a distortion of what is seen [p. 269].

And yet the next appearance of the dream suggests that there is a great deal more shared experience of vital and central importance between Chris and his father than the narrator has yet suspected. Here, the dreamer confronts the ghost, the Erlkönig, and sees its face; Chris wakens him from the nightmare, and they talk:

"What were you dreaming about?"
"I was trying to see someone's face." ~
"You shouted you were going to kill me."
"No, not you."
"Who?"
"The person in the dream."
"Who was it?"
"I'm not sure."
Chris stops crying, but he continues to shake from the cold.
"Did you see his face?"
"Yes."
"What did it look like?"
"It was my own face, Chris, that's when I shouted."

But after he sends Chris back to sleep, the narrator realizes that "The dreamer isn't me at all. It's Phaedrus. He's waking up. *A mind divided against itself* . . . me . . . I'm the evil figure in the shadows. I'm the loathsome one. . . ." (p. 298). In Phaedrus' dream, then, the narrator is the Erlkönig; but what does that make Phaedrus? Is he still the madman that the narrator has told us of—indeed, keeps telling us of as the story proceeds?

The first hint that we need to reassess Phaedrus completely comes when the narrator and Chris have arrived at the Pacific, have come, that is, as near as literally possible to the bottom of the ocean. Chris is complaining about the trip in a general kind of way: " 'When I was little it was different. . . . We always *did* things. That I wanted to. Now I don't want to do *any*thing,' " and the narrator comments that Chris seems to have returned "to somewhere that I don't know about . . . the bottom of the ocean" (p. 360). The dialogue proceeds:

Then I ask Chris, "Was it better before we left Chicago?"
"Yes."
"How? What do you remember?"
"That it was fun."
"*Fun?*" . . .

"Sure," he says, and is quiet for a long time. Then he says, "Don't you remember? You made me find all the directions home. . . . You used to play games with us. You used to tell us all kinds of stories and we'd go on rides to do things and now you don't do anything."

"Yes, I do."

"No, you *don't*! You just sit and stare and you don't *do anything*!" I hear him crying again.

Outside the rain comes in gusts against the window, and I feel a kind of heavy pressure bear down on me. He's crying for *him*. It's *him* he misses. That's what the dream is about. In the dream . . . [pp. 360–361].

So suddenly Phaedrus becomes a source of value, though he is validated or guaranteed only by Chris, whom the narrator and therefore the reader have perceived as a spoiled and troubled kid. The dream is Phaedrus', and the resentment is the narrator's: "He wants to hate me. Because I'm not *him*." But then the honesty of the narrator comes to his aid, the honesty that has made his total intellectual and psychological history with all its self-destructive turnings and contradictions the main substance of the book; and with all his honesty, he turns on himself—and the reader—and says, "In all this Chautauqua talk there's been more than a touch of hypocrisy. Advice is given again and again to eliminate the subject-object duality, when the biggest duality of all, the duality between me and him, remains unfaced. A mind divided against itself" (p. 363). So there is hope, for the difference *is* between his two selves.

The overt reversal of the narrator's consciously-held role occurs in the same chapter, the second-last of the book. It is a fairly long process, because for one thing the narrator and Phaedrus have drawn closer, have depolarized; the man who bought his release from the mental hospital at the price of Phaedrus' "death" is no longer willing and therefore no longer able to destroy him. He can destroy Chris, however, and the possibility confronts him insistently if briefly:

He looks at me so strangely. I think he still doesn't understand. That gaze . . . I've seen it somewhere . . . somewhere . . . somewhere. . . .

In the fog of an early morning in the marshes there was a small duck, a teal that gazed like this. . . . I'd winged it and now it couldn't fly and I'd run up on it and seized it by the neck and before killing it had stopped and from some sense of the mystery of the universe had stared into its eyes, and they gazed like this . . . so calm and uncomprehending . . . and yet so aware. Then I closed my hands around its eyes and twisted the neck until it broke and I felt the snap between my fingers [p. 367].

He spares Chris; but he is drained as well of the ability either to oppose the enemy or defend himself. Chris, though, is equally unable to cope with any problem; he dithers about, incapable of accepting sympathy; but since the sympathy is baseless, for all his weakness he is on the right track; accepting this sympathy would be the end of it all, the final frustration of the quest for the meeting at the bottom of the ocean. Chris continues to rock back and forth on the ground, without aim or progress; the narrator briefly contemplates suicide, but then the Phaedrus-personality speaks (in italics, not in quotation marks) and encourages the boy to get up:

> *Everything is all right now, Chris.*
> That's not my voice.
> *I haven't forgotten you.*
> Chris's rocking stops.
> *How could I forget you?*

But Chris still has to question this voice:

> "Why did you leave us?"
> *When?*
> "At the hospital!"
> *There was no choice. The police prevented it.*
> "Wouldn't they let you out?"
> *No.*
> "Well then, why wouldn't you open the door?"
> *What door?*
> "The glass door!"
> A kind of slow electric shock passes through me. What glass door is he talking about?
> "Don't you remember?" he says. "We were standing on one side and you were on the other side and Mom was crying."
> I've never told him about that dream. How could he know about that? [pp. 368–369].

And so it is simply untrue that "the idea that one person's mind is accessible to another's is just a conversational illusion," that "really the relationship of one person to another is ultimately unknowable." The father's abiding nightmare is his son's as well; and now the narrator needs only realize that this is Phaedrus' dream ("I am Phaedrus, that is who I am, and they are going to destroy me"); realize that the leading figure among the "they," the shadowy Erlkönig, is the narrator himself, the new personality which will cooperate in Phaedrus' destruction in order to be let out of the institution; and reassure Chris that everything is all right:

> "Were you really insane?"
> Why should he ask that?
> *No!*
> Astonishment hits. But Chris's eyes sparkle.
> "I knew it," he says [pp. 369–370].

The main reassurance, however, is what the father himself receives from his son. " 'I knew it,' he said," the father repeats to himself several times. The father's "I" clarifies itself ("Phaedrus always said—*I* always said") and finally comes to the realization that "I haven't been carrying him at all. He's been carrying *me*!" (p. 370). Indeed, both physically, sitting behind him on the motorcycle all those miles, and metaphorically, keeping the idea of Phaedrus intact, Chris has been carrying his real father, the personality that the narrator has rejected. But why else is his name Chris—Christopher—the carrier of the Christ? And so, evidently, Chris occupies the place of the father in Goethe's poem, Phaedrus the place of the son, and the narrator the place of the Erlkönig; and the story ends this time not "in failure . . . death of the child. The ghost wins," but in victory: "For God's sake relieve him of his burden! Be one person again!" (p. 370). The last few pages of the book are full of positive happenings. Father and son remove their helmets and are for the first time able to converse in ordinary tones. Chris stands up so that he can see better and begins to enjoy the scenery along the road. He asks about having a motorcycle when he gets older, and his father can promise him not only the bike and instruction in how to take care of it but "the right attitudes" as well: " 'Will I have the right attitudes?' 'I think so,' I say. 'I don't think that will be any problem at all' " (p. 372). So the book ends with a deep and abiding assurance of victory: "We've

won it. It's going to get better now. You can sort of tell these things"
(p. 373).

So at the end the former personality has successfully won through to the light by the kind of resurrection a sun-god might undergo; and this is appropriate enough, for "Phaedrus" really means "bright," "shining," "cheerful," "radiant with joy," and it names such a figure as the bright, shining sun-god Apollo who serves in Milton's "Lycidas" as a stand-in for Christ. As such, Phaedrus may fittingly be thought of as a Christ-figure indeed, in fact the very Christ that his son Christopher, "the Christ-bearer," has faithfully borne during all the miles of the journey.

The retrieval of Phaedrus, the reintegration of the personality that had been purged, establishes the book as an existential work of literature. Meursault in Camus' *Stranger* and Bigger Thomas in Wright's *Native Son* would have suffered a loss of being if they had rejected their acts of killing. Just so, Chris's father would have suffered an even more obvious loss of being if he had not, with the help of his son and his own reliving his intellectual autobiography in the Chautauquas, managed to "be one person again" by integrating his Phaedrus and narrator personalities. But Chris's father overcomes, with the help of his son, the electrically-induced loss of being at the hands of psychiatric technology and persists in his pursuit of a truth which goes beyond the usual meaning of the term as the Greeks and their cultural heirs have understood it. Chris loved the person who pursued Quality, and the Erlkönig personality who had rejected the quest and participated instead in the attempted murder and burial of Phaedrus was existentially inauthentic.

Paradoxically, the success of such existential novels as *The Stranger* and *Native Son* is that, at the same time that they repudiate archetypal models and find being and authenticity only in individual life-history, they stand as archetypal patterns for their readers: this is how the hero of the age of the absurd achieves and maintains essence, how he becomes and remains authentic. For whatever the "real" world of voluntaristic philosophy may be, the world of art by its very nature produces patterns and creates archetypes even as it perceives and proclaims the death of archetypes. I believe that Robert Pirsig has created for serious readers of American literature a powerful and enduring archetype of personal integration in this technological society.

NOTES

[1] Robert M. Pirsig, *Zen and the Art of Motorcycle Maintenance* (New York: Bantam Books, 1979), pp. 54–55; subsequent references will be in the text. Steele's article originated as a presentation for the Tuesday Book Club in January 1976; it then became a paper for the Rocky Mountain Modern Language Association Convention in October 1976; it next appeared in *Ariel,* Vol. 10 (1979), pp. 83–93. It has been slightly revised for republication here.

[2] The translation given borrows from many previous versions. Johann Wolfgang von Goethe (1749–1832) wrote "Erlkönig" in 1782. The setting of the text by Franz Schubert (1797–1828, D. 328d) is a monument of German romanticism, especially as performed on an out-of-print Deutsche Grammaphon recording by Dietrich Fischer-Dieskau with Gerald Moore as piano accompanist.

[3] The narrator's failings as a father appear on pp. 29–31, 52, 121, 202–203, 217, 229, 244–245, 290, 362–363, and 367–368.

At least on the surface, the narrator and his son usually relate to each other well enough; otherwise the narrator would not have proposed the trip they are taking and Chris would never have acquiesced. Like Telemachus and Stephen Dedalus, Chris makes the journey as a quest for the lost father. By contrast, the narrator is no Odysseus, no Leopold Bloom; he is perhaps more like J. Alfred Prufrock. The narrator thinks only that the trip will be an opportunity for Chris to find himself. But we should probably understand that the Phaedrus side of that total personality, from beyond consciousness, has elicited the trip so that he can make contact with his son and force the narrator to reconstitute his authentic self.

[4] When Chris says that the voice from the dream sounded "Like you used to sound a long time ago. . . . When we lived here [in Montana]," he might have said that he sounded as if he was talking in italics, which are the typographical signal for the Phaedrus voice; see pp. 245–246, 297–298, 368–369, and the top line of 370.

"IRONY AND EARNESTNESS IN ROBERT PIRSIG'S *ZEN AND THE ART OF MOTORCYCLE MAINTENANCE*"

BY RICHARD H. RODINO

Just after he declines to climb with his son to the top of a mountain in Montana, the narrator of *Zen and the Art of Motorcycle Maintenance* (1974) ingratiatingly declares: "I think metaphysics is good if it improves everyday life; otherwise forget it."[1] The remark is profoundly and unwittingly ironic in context. Following the scene the narrator begins a new wave of dazzling metaphysical theorizing, but the single most important part of his everyday life—his relationship with his son, Chris—deteriorates steadily and painfully. Such ironic friction between action and commentary is precisely the principal strength of the book as well as the cause of much confusion over it.

After Pirsig's work was greeted by being compared to *Moby Dick* ("the narrative tact, the perfect economy of effect defy criticism"),[2] it received a predictable critical backlash, mostly patronizing remarks about Pirsig's schoolboy solemnity, "flat, Midwestern voice," and almost autistic insensitivity toward his son. With the benefit of a few years' hindsight, we can see that this kind of blame is itself often based on naive critical assumptions, as if we had special difficulty distinguishing between the narrator of the book and the author or were reluctant to admit there might be anything artful or fictional in *Zen and the Art of Motorcycle Maintenance*. Of course, the work practically invites the discourtesy by refusing to be categorized either as fiction or as autobiography— one of the dualities the book determinedly sets out to break down.

We need some basic clarifications. As in *Moby Dick* or other significant novels, the narrative voice in *Zen and the Art of Motorcycle Maintenance* gives its readers only a limited and partial perspective. We must deal with at least three versions of Pirsig: the character who tells the story; Phaedrus, his alter ego; and the author of the book—and we should not confuse them. Just as the narrator understands the weaknesses and obsessive solipsism of Phaedrus' thinking, so does the reader eventually come to see the awkwardness and emotional confusion of the narrator. A substan-

From *Critique: Studies in Modern Fiction*, Vol. 22 (1980) pp. 21–31. Reprinted with permission of the Helen Dwight Reid Educational Foundation. Published by Heldref Publications, 4000 Albemarle St., N.W., Washington, D.C. 20016. Copyright © 1980.

tial difference exists between the mind of the author who finished writing the book a decade after the events took place and the mind of the character he invents to tell the story (conspicuously in the present tense). The distance between the two keeps everything that is said dynamically alive—pregnant with misunderstanding, ironies, partial angles of vision. The biggest block to reading the work adequately is the facile assumption that the voice talking to us represents the normative values of the book.

Such a statement may seem a pretty serious thing to say about a book which is primarily (and very solemnly) concerned with values, and which spends much of its time lecturing the reader. No one is going to argue that Pirsig does not endorse most of what his first-person narrator says, but the tension between the sweeping meliorism of his assertions and the painful inadequacy of his actions in "everyday life" make *Zen and the Art of Motorcycle Maintenance* much more than a bit of successful popular sermonizing. The book as a whole is highly conscious of its own limitations; like many great works of art, it is quite skeptical about its own procedures.

The essential motive of Pirsig's Chautauquas is to dissolve all the dualities, both metaphysical and workaday, that he sees as the roots of civilization's problems: hip and square, subject and object, romantic and classic, mind and machine, thought and action—the book is stuffed with them. What electrifies the schoolmasterly pursuit of solutions, though, is Pirsig's peculiar inability to see that his own present personality is part of a divisive duality with his former self, Phaedrus. Even as he rambles on, reconciling extremes at a snappy pace, Pirsig remains, ironically, blind to the need to reconcile himself to Phaedrus: he fights a continuous battle of repression. We come to see—much sooner than Pirsig—that neither his present nor his former self is really adequate; each alone is doomed to failure. Even near the end of the journey, Pirsig still routinely divides the world up between Phaedrus and himself:

> I think it was Coleridge who said everyone is either a Platonist or an Aristotelian. People who can't stand Artistotle's endless specificity of detail are natural lovers of Plato's soaring generalities. People who can't stand the eternal lofty idealism of Plato welcome the down-to-earth facts of Aristotle. Plato is the essential Buddha-seeker who appears again and again in each generation, moving onward and upward toward the "one." Aristotle is the eternal motorcycle mechanic who prefers the "many." I myself am pretty much Aristotelian in this sense, preferring to find the Buddha in the

quality of the facts around me, but Phaedrus was clearly a Platonist by temperament [pp. 331–332].

Aside from giving Coleridge credit for something Goethe said, the passage is so convincingly neat and matter-of-fact, even pedantic, that we may not register the significance of its appearance in the middle of a rather thoroughgoing repudiation of both Plato and Aristotle. Pirsig has been arguing that the separation of Platonic and Aristotelian ways of thinking from each other has had a heavy hand in making the present mess of civilization. He persists in thinking of Phaedrus as the "other," irretrievably separated from Pirsig, and we readers are apt to follow him in this thinking, if we are not careful, for our great intimacy with the narrator (present tense, continuous access to his thoughts) makes him seem a sane alternative to the loony and dangerous Phaedrus, who is introduced as a frightening, ominous doppelganger. The problem is that Pirsig's droning didacticism and "safe" ordinariness are not an alternative at all. By the end of the book we learn that there are no options—it is all or nothing, just as with every other duality in the book—and the ending mocks the choices we thought we were making correctly along the way.

From the narrator's point of view, especially early in the work, Phaedrus seems so radically abstract that, if Pirsig is to have any real-life experiences, Phaedrus must be totally repressed. Of course, repression turns out to be a dreadfully bad tactic, and Pirsig comes to realize it, though he can do very little about the problem. By the end of the book the narrator and the reader know that he must aim not for exclusion and retrenchment but for inclusion and some sort of accommodation of both Pirsig and Phaedrus. In spite of Phaedrus' crippling indifference to "everyday life" (what could be more graphic than the picture of Phaedrus sitting in a darkened room, face to the wall, in his own urine), he has the exulting courage of his convictions and the sheer intellectual excitement (which Chris calls "fun") that Pirsig sadly lacks. The lack is felt most keenly in his unsuccessful relations with Chris, though we gather from Pirsig's detachment from and reticence about his marriage that it is not going along swimmingly, either. That the note of hope at the end of *Zen and the Art of Motorcycle Maintenance* comes when Chris senses the possibility that his father's personality may contain both Pirsig and Phaedrus is not at all trite. Pirsig badly needs Chris's help to have any chance of coalescing his fragmented self—becoming a whole person again is inseparable from recovering the love and understanding between father and son. Breaking down dualities inevitably becomes a chain reaction, a concept Pirsig explains in his lectures but cannot quite get hold of in his personal life.

The narrative technique seems, on the surface, to give something like equal weight to abstract formulations and to concrete impressions (snacks consumed in roadside taverns are recorded with scrupulous attention), which gives the impression that the narrator has a sane and wholesome equilibrium between thinking and experiencing. All this is critically deceptive: as the narrator talks more and more articulately about Quality, one forgets that all the while Chris is hunched on the back of the motorcycle, seeing little, saying nothing.

Certainly, the narrator forgets about Chris during his long metaphysical sessions. Right at the beginning of the book and the journey, he makes an *a priori* acceptance of the limitations of motorcycle travel that becomes a staggering threat to the Quality of his everyday life:

> Unless you're fond of hollering you don't make great conversations on a running cycle. Instead you spend your time being aware of things and meditating on them. On sights and sounds, on the mood of the weather and things remembered, on the machine and the countryside you're in, thinking about things at great leisure and length without being hurried and without feeling you're losing time [pp. 6–7].

Lost in the cottony silences of his own thoughts, Pirsig does not realize until the end of the journey that all his thinking about Quality is solipsistic, cutting him off from Chris, ruining his chance for what he would call a high-Quality life. His points about Quality are not any less true or any less urgent, but the last few pages of the book express what we come to see as the only real chance for Pirsig by making point-by-point repudiations of Pirsig's assumptions in the beginning. Chris and Pirsig remove some of the insulation between them and begin to learn to make "great conversations" on a running cycle. Throughout the book, Pirsig unconsciously abandons the experiential for the abstract, surrendering basic empathy with his son in favor of getting his thesis right. The choice is not one Pirsig would consciously make, and as

an epistemologist and theorist of rhetoric, Pirsig is abstractly convinced that conceptualizing can be the enemy of Quality. From
time to time he says as much: "All this classical talk about Quality
isn't Quality." Since his great thesis is that abstraction, inherited
from classical reason, is dangerous, the dramatic irony of Pirsig's
own abstraction raises questions and insists on complications that
Pirsig—the great problem solver—is only dimly conscious of.

Anyone who has waded through some of the "post-modernist"
writing that is so fashionable now will be struck by the same kind
of irony: the discourse is determinedly abstract, yet its lesson is
that abstraction itself is at the heart of all that is wrong with our
civilization.[3] Of course, one may argue that the human mind is
inevitably a sense-making machine, that eventually it will rational-
ize any sensory experience and force it into a place in some conceptual order. Abstraction, too, is an indispensable part of all
communication; all forms of language are processes of abstraction.
Pirsig accepts this, too, but wants to warn us of the dangers of
being complacent about the inevitability. Abstraction may be un-
avoidable, but the most valuable effort we can make in our lives is
to resist concepts and stereotypes for the brief time we are able:

> You can't be aware that you've seen a tree until *after* you've seen the
> tree, and between the instant of vision and instant of awareness
> there must be a time lag. We sometimes think of that time lag as
> unimportant. But there's no justification for thinking that the time
> lag is unimportant—none *whatsoever*.
>
> The past exists only in our memories, the future only in our
> plans. The present is our only reality. The tree that you are aware
> of intellectually, because of that small time lag, is always in the past
> and therefore is always unreal. *Any* intellectually conceived object is
> *always* in the past and therefore *unreal*. Reality is always the mo-
> ment of vision *before* the intellectualization takes place. *There is no
> other reality* [pp. 221–222].

This is exactly what Pirsig means by "Quality": not at all some
form of "merit," but a "preintellectual reality" that may give us
the chance to experience the essence of an object, person, or event.

Pirsig is no fool about rhetoric or about epistemology. He
knows that Quality is a process and that making it into an idea,
especially into a definition, destroys something about it—thus his
famous insistence that Quality cannot be defined. Most readers are
stimulated to do a little thinking about it themselves, but Pirsig

also knows that withholding a definition from his readers is bound to annoy them, even if it stimulates them for a time. We do not really enjoy being deprived of our rational categories and always wind up irritably reaching after facts and certainties anyway. Denying that "Quality" can be defined will serve a positive purpose only for a limited time. Readers will short-circuit the constant provocation Pirsig tries to provide or else they will trivialize it by not caring. Knowing this, Pirsig eventually provides a definition (which he was beginning in the quotation above): "Quality is the continuing stimulus which our environment puts upon us to create the world in which we live. All of it. Every last bit of it" (p. 225).

Obviously, Pirsig knows that communication depends on shared definitions; even the undefinable has to be categorized to some extent if the narrator is ever going to share his understanding with his reader. At the same time, the structure of *Zen and the Art of Motorcycle Maintenance* makes the experience of reading the book much more complicated than learning definitions or paying attention to answers. We also learn to look critically at our usual ways of receiving, organizing, and expressing experience. Take, for example, the earnestness of Pirsig's Chautauquas. He means everything he says in them, and we are meant to take them straightforwardly, as valuable lessons. So believable, indeed, is this method of discourse that even when Pirsig switches from motorcycles and Quality to the matter of Chris and himself, we are apt to accept that his judgment is still sound—an acceptance we are ultimately made to see as dangerous. For example, three-quarters of the way along, Pirsig remarks in his typical manner:

> I wish I knew what to say to him. Or what to ask. He seems so close at times, and yet the closeness has nothing to do with what is asked or said. Then at other times he seems very far away and sort of watching me from some vantage point I don't see. And then sometimes he's just childish and there's no relation at all [p. 269].

This sort of comment is intelligently pathetic (sounds "human," we say), seems based on sensitive and sympathetic observation, and sounds as if Pirsig is trying so sincerely that we readers may unwittingly get absorbed in Pirsig's well-intentioned rhetoric. But, as the ending of the book makes very plain, a good part of Pirsig's difficulty with Chris is caused by the former's silence and self-absorption. Even when Pirsig is thinking about Chris, worrying about him, he comes across as indifferent to the boy sitting behind him. In the above paragraph, as in countless others, Pirsig moves persuasively away from "I" and arrives at "He," rationalizing away his own responsibility: "the closeness has nothing to do with what is asked or said."

If we are careful readers, by this point in the novel (or at least on a second reading) we should be grappling with a serious, continuous problem of interpretation. The narrator is completely concerned, highly intelligent, perfectly sincere—and he is a very talented communicator, but much of what he tells us about Chris (and himself) is wrong or misguided in subtle but parlous ways. What are the rules of this narrative game? Even if we are old hands at dealing with deceptive or limited narrators—veterans of Swift or Conrad, say—we may have a good deal of trouble making sense of a narrator who believes he is telling us the truth, wants to tell us the truth, but sometimes cannot, and who is contradicted only by subtle shifts in a relationship we learn about only through him.

One way of describing the process of reading *Zen and the Art of Motorcycle Maintenance* is to point out that the dramatic action continuously provides critiques of the usual, well-meaning ways we unknowingly trivialize what is most important to us. The tone of the passage quoted above is a brand of self-defensiveness that should be familiar to almost everyone ("nothing I can say or ask will do any good"), disguising ineffectiveness as faithfulness to profundity. Almost every scene in the book establishes an attractive and convincing rhetoric and then subverts it. One early scene in particular sets up the procedure: at their first campground, Chris decides he hates camping and a whole lot more.

"Do you suppose he's just *punishing?*" Sylvia asks.
"I suppose," I say, "although it doesn't sound quite right." I think about it and add, "That's a child-psychology term—a context I dislike. Let's just say he's being a complete bastard" [p. 53].

Almost every reader gives a little silent cheer the first time he reads this passage, for Pirsig chooses the seemingly blunt, "everyday" term over clinical jargon, and most of us applaud the choice. We may even be tempted to think pompously that less sophisticated readers are getting a little lesson in rhetoric, but the lesson is for all of us—and it is much more profound and difficult. If Sylvia's "punishing" is abstract and categorical, Pirsig's "complete bastard" is deceptively glib and falsely cheerful. Pirsig would like to leave the matter buried there, but under prodding from Sylvia he tells of Chris's incipient mental illness, which ought to make us sorry for our satisfaction with "complete bastard" as a description.

The sequence of thoughts and events in the next three pages is typical of the process of continuous undermining in the book and worth examining in detail. Pirsig denies the suitability of reasoned investigation into Chris's instability:

> Sylvia says, "What do you suppose the cause is?"
> John's voice rasps, as if to cut it off, but I answer, "I don't know. Causes and effects don't seem to fit. Causes and effects are a result of thought. I would think mental illness comes before thought." This doesn't make sense to them, I'm sure. It doesn't make much sense to me and I'm too tired to try to think it out and give it up [p. 54].

After a little while, he suddenly finds a language for this that is better than either Sylvia's child-psychology jargon or his own earlier attempt to put the matter outside the bounds of discourse:

> "I don't *know* why . . . it's just that . . . I don't know . . . they're not *kin*." . . . Surprising word, I think to myself, never used it before. Not of *kin* . . . sounds like hillbilly talk . . . not of a *kind* . . . same root . . . *kind*ness, too . . . they can't have real *kind*ness toward him, they're not his *kin* . . . That's exactly the feeling.

But finding the exact language for thinking to oneself may be itself an act of retreating from communication. After the first sentence, and continuing for the next three paragraphs, Pirsig is no longer sharing his thoughts with the Sutherlands. The special rightness of the word remains in his own head. As he goes on thinking, Pirsig vibrates to private meaning with a special inner sensitivity:

> Old word, so ancient it's almost drowned out. What a change through the centuries. Now anybody can be "kind." And everybody's supposed to be. Except that long ago it was something you were born into and couldn't help. Now it's just a faked-up attitude half the time, like teachers the first day of class. But what do they really know about *kind*ness who are not *kin*? [p. 55].

Throughout the book, Pirsig relies heavily on this sort of inner understanding in dealing with Chris. A poem by Goethe comes into his head now, for his thoughts about Chris have become feelings and are best expressed in metaphors or in dreamy symbols—not very good for purposeful action:

> "How does it end?"
> "In failure . . . death of the child. The ghost wins."
> The wind blows light up from the coals and I see Sylvia look at me startled.
> "But that's another land and another time," I say. "Here life is the end and ghosts have no meaning. I believe that. I believe in all this too," I say, looking out at the darkened prairie, "although I'm not sure of what it all means yet . . . I'm not sure of much of anything these days. Maybe that's why I talk so much" [p. 55].

Though Pirsig values communication fiercely, his talking usually induces silence in his companions—only Sylvia and DeWeese understand him much at all—and he speaks out loud less and less.

Lost in his thoughts about "kindness" and Goethe's poem about kinship—and very anxious about Chris's welfare—Pirsig is dismayingly silent and distant when Chris himself returns:

> "There's a great big sandpile over there," he says, crunching around on the pine needles.
> "Yes," I say. "Get to sleep."
> "You should see it. Will you come and see it tomorrow?"
> "We won't have time."
> "Can I play over there tomorrow morning?"
> "Yes."
> He makes interminable noises getting undressed and into the sleeping bag. He is in it. Then he rolls around. Then he is silent, and then rolls some more. Then he says, "Dad?"
> "What?"
> "What was it like when you were a kid?"
> "Go to *sleep*, Chris!" There are limits to what you can listen to [p. 56].

In spite of his sleepiness, Pirsig has rather self-destructive limits. Distrusting the triviality of words and the congealing effect of thinking about his son in a category, Pirsig leaves his love unexpressed:

> Later I hear a sharp inhaling of phlegm that tells me he has been crying, and though I'm exhausted, I don't sleep. A few words of

consolation might have helped there. He was trying to be friendly. But the words weren't forthcoming for some reason. Consoling words are more for strangers, for hospitals, not kin. Little emotional Band-Aids like that aren't what he needs or what's sought . . . I don't know what he needs, or what's sought [p. 56].

Perhaps he should have told Chris a poem, perhaps poems put things properly without distorting or falsifying, but Chris would have understood Goethe's poem no better than the Sutherlands did—and surely he would have been as depressed by it. Pirsig does not think to tell a poem, and Chris goes to sleep crying because Pirsig believes that comforting words are banal—everyday life sacrificed again to the thinker's conclusions. With perfect, unknowing irony, Pirsig "tells" the poem in a specially profound way, too— he and Chris are in it now—but only after Chris is asleep.

The passage can be seen as series of attempts to understand Chris's problems. Each attempt is an improvement in some way on the one before it, but as the passage goes on, a counterprocess takes place as well. Pirsig becomes less and less able either to share his growing insight or to act profitably on it. The climax of the double-edged process occurs when Chris returns to the campsite, interested finally in what is around him and even seemingly happy. Pirsig's brusqueness is no longer merely unhelpful; it now causes Chris's continued problems.

The irony in *Zen and the Art of Motorcycle Maintenance* is continuous and unremitting. In no passage in the book does Pirsig not both advance and recede in some way, losing to Phaedrus and gaining valuable control over his ideas, climbing the mountains in the "high country of the mind" and retreating from them. Pirsig's personal failures qualify the way we read the aggressive optimism of his inquiries into universal values, and the irony is not only of the "physician-cure-thyself" variety. Pirsig's personal downward spiral is not *in spite of* his metaphysical successes but really *because of* them. When we read the book carefully, it demands from us a self-conscious awareness of how we respond to ordinary-sounding words and tonalities, and especially how we learn from precepts and from examples. *Zen and the Art of Motorcycle Maintenance* warns us that "thinking things through" is not the same as making everyday life better, nor do Pirsig's sample solutions provide adequate—let alone automatic—guides for his own most heartbreaking problems.

The book shows the sheer difficulty of accomplishing what it urges, not didactically but by the mutual modifications of commentary and action. For a book that lectures about solutions to the most profound problems of civilization, *Zen and the Art of Motorcycle Maintenance* is profoundly suspicious of all rhetoric. Words are apt to trap us at any time in an illusion of success; the world of words is not the world of Quality. At the same time, language is indispensable, the most potent tool for change. The book is self-consciously "post-modern," especially in its language, endorsing a sensible, plain style and reasoned argument. At the same time, it is highly conscious that logical concatenation, nononsense tones, and continuous sincerity are attractive and induce rationalizing, even when they are not meant to. They are always threats to make us complacent about our human ability to design answers, to package answers for convenient consumption, and to look outside ourselves for manufactured solutions. The problems themselves may come to seem universal, uniform, and so external.

Without its present-tense narrative, *Zen and the Art of Motorcycle Maintenance* would be a combination of folk philosophy and popularized doctoral thesis. With the narrative added, it becomes a complicated artistic structure, providing criticisms of its own official assertions and manner of proceeding. Reading the book is an experience of making constant adjustments and reservations, valuing what one is taught, yet being alert to the dangers of being taught. The difficulties of accommodating the ironies and earnestness of *Zen and the Art of Motorcycle Maintenance* are rewarded by new discoveries the narrator himself only begins to understand, by a highly intelligent and critical attitude of mind.

NOTES

[1] Robert M. Pirsig, *Zen and the Art of Motorcycle Maintenance* (New York: Bantam Books, 1979), p. 221. Subsequent references are to this edition.

[2] George Steiner, *The New Yorker*, Vol. 50 (15 April 1974), p. 147.

[3] After a distinguished series of papers had been read at a "postmodern" conference on the Humanities in Los Angeles in 1977, Benjamin DeMott stood up on the last day and told a long story about a friend whose wife had died suddenly. The audience, which had been measured in its approval of the brilliant theorists who spoke previously, gave DeMott a fifteen-minute standing ovation—presumably out of sheer relief at hearing something concrete.

"THE MATRIX OF JOURNEYS IN
ZEN AND THE ART OF MOTORCYCLE
MAINTENANCE"

BY RICHARD H. RODINO

> "Well," I say, "we can stop here, or we can go ahead, or we can
> go back. Which do you want to do?" . . .
> "I don't like this trip," he says. "It isn't fun. I thought it was
> going to be fun."
> . . . "That may be true," I reply, "but it's a hell of a thing to say"
> [pp. 192–193].

Zen and the Art of Motorcycle Maintenance has been fairly consistently misread.[1] After George Steiner's extravagant praise in *The
New Yorker* ("the narrative tact, the perfect economy of effect
defy criticism"), there was a predictable critical backlash, mostly a
lot of patronizing remarks about Pirsig's schoolboy solemnity and
his potted summaries of the history of philosophy.[2] But it seems
myopic to criticize *Zen* for its rhetoric, since the book as a whole,
by systematic undercutting, makes a highly critical statement about
the narrator's naively aggressive confidence in theoretical formulations. The narrative structure of the entire book continually reminds us that "thinking things through" is not necessarily the same
as "improving everyday life," a notion that Pirsig is careful to
explain in his lectures but cannot quite get hold of in his personal
life.[3] Throughout the book, Pirsig's great thesis is that conceptualizing itself is the enemy of Quality responses to experience. From
time to time he warns that "all the classical talk about [Quality]
isn't Quality" (p. 200) and insists on the superior claim of actual
life over theory: "I think metaphysics is good if it improves everyday life; otherwise forget it" (p. 221).[4] But there is crucial
dramatic irony in the way Pirsig's own habits of abstraction and
talking (to himself) about Quality cause constant crises in his own
"everyday life." This irony raises questions and complications concerning "Quality" for readers of the book that the narrator is only
dimly aware of.

The basic narrative structure is a motorcycle journey on which
the narrator thinks his way to a concept of what he calls "Qual-

From *Journal of Narrative Technique*. Vol.11 (1981), pp. 53–63. Reprinted with permission
from Richard H. Rodino and *Journal of Narrative Technique*. Copyright © 1981.

ity," thereby reawakening an ominous part of his personality that had been annihilated by electroshock treatments and thereby also alienating himself from his son. Now, there is little doubt that we are meant to endorse in theory most of the narrator's conclusions. But *Zen* is not only a series of lectures, nor is it a single, unified journey. One way to understand how it creates its meaning is to think of the different plot developments as three simultaneous journeys, which create constant tensions between the grand and exciting progress of Pirsig's theorizing and the accelerating failure of his motions towards sanity and fatherliness. The book as a whole is greater than the lectures it contains; Pirsig's trip is much more complicated than just following the road to a concept of Quality.

The literal traveling in the book is the motorcycle journey of Pirsig and his son Chris from Minnesota, to the mountains of Montana, down to the sea-level of California. At the very beginning of the trip, Pirsig describes his plans for this trip as a sort of *quest*, an indeterminate search for a dimly perceived, but nonetheless urgent, goal: "Plans are deliberately indefinite, more to travel than to arrive anywhere" (p. 4). Nearly a third of the way through the book, he is still making the same claim: "To travel is better than to arrive" (p. 136). But this definition of the trip, like so many of Pirsig's definitions, is only partially true at best, misleading in the main, accurate mostly in unforeseen ways. By the time he makes the latter remark—a split second before he pulls into the dangerous terrain of his Montana past—Pirsig's tone is already more than a little unconvincing.

The literal cross-country movement metaphorically represents at least three other, more abstract, plots involving Chris, Pirsig, and Phaedrus, the ghost of Pirsig's former self. The narrator routinely refers to each of these other plots in images of directions taken, progress made or thwarted, destinations reached or missed. In addition, the narrative technique of the book—the plots constantly interrupting one another—keeps us thinking of all these plot developments in metaphors of spatial dimensions. I want to call attention to some of the travel metaphors that define each of the plots and then to describe each as a different, familiar pattern of journey: a pilgrimage, a quest, and a progress. This should make the essential ironies and tensions of the book more clear.[5]

First of all, there is Pirsig's strenuous effort to work out his theory of Quality, to explain the concept without (as he quite inaccurately claims) having to define it. For a while, Pirsig retraces Phaedrus's thoughts and uses metaphors of travel consistently to describe Phaedrus's metaphysical progress: "It always seemed incredible to me, and still does, I guess, that Phaedrus should have traveled along a line of thought that had never been traveled before" (p. 233); "In his pursuit of a concept of Quality, Phaedrus kept seeing again and again little paths all leading toward some point off to one side" (pp. 301–302). When Pirsig eventually decides to break off and think along lines of his own, he uses travel metaphors also: "I think we've gone as far along Phaedrus's path as we want to go . . . I want to leave his path now" (p. 220). Pirsig's categorical name for his thinking towards a concept of Quality is, significantly, "Chautauqua"—"like the traveling tent-show Chautauquas that used to move across America" (p. 7).

A second development is the re-emergence of Phaedrus, a process Pirsig fears is incipient insanity. This plot is full of suspense (is he really going insane?) as well as full of wrong turns, and it rewards our interest by a twist at the end of the road. Rather than threatening Pirsig's mental health, Phaedrus's re-emergence and co-existence is actually indispensable for Pirsig's sanity. Again, Pirsig regularly defines his resistance to Phaedrus by metaphors of physical movement and repose: "In pursuit of this ghost he went on to wider meanings of Quality which drew him further and further to his end. I differ from him in that I've no intention of going on to that end. He just passed through this territory and opened it up. I intend to stay and cultivate it and see if I can get something to grow" (p. 200). But there is an almost pathetic self-deception in this. Although Pirsig begins by distinguishing strictly between Phaedrus's route through "the high country of the mind" (p. 111) and his own settlement in the "valleys" of Quality (p. 220), his retracing of Phaedrus's metaphysical trail inevitably accelerates into a quest for and pursuit of his former identity. If Phaedrus seems to dog Pirsig during the first half of the book, Pirsig ends up finding that his compulsive pilgrimage to the shrine of Quality has caused him to go chasing after Phaedrus. The emblems Pirsig uses initially to define the difference in their destinations and modes of travel ("passing through," "staying to cultivate") devolve into metaphors of flight and pursuit: "I want to clear out of here as fast as possible . . . These damned heights get eerie after a while. I want to go down, way down; far, far down" (p. 220).

The third plot consists of Pirsig's progressively more desperate attempts to create a healthy, fatherly relationship with Chris. From the beginning of the trip, Pirsig gives indirect reports on the Quality of their relationship by describing their progress together as travelers. Chris, who misses Phaedrus, is naturally happy when they begin their climb *up* the mountain in Montana (the "high country," physical and metaphysical, is always associated with Phaedrus). In fact, the first conversation they have on the trail is one of the best they have at any time before the end of the book and, notably, it consists of a kind of reversal of the disastrous non-dialogue with which their journey together started at the very beginning of the book:

> . . . There's a red-winged blackbird.
> I whack Chris's knee and point to it.
> "What!" he hollers.
> "Blackbird!"
> He says something I don't hear. "What?" I holler back.
> He grabs the back of my helmet and hollers up, "I've seen *lots* of those, Dad!"
> "Oh!" I holler back [pp. 3–4].

> A whirr sounds and a partridge disappears through the trees.
> "Did you see it?" says Chris.
> "Yes," I say back.
> "What was it?"
> "A partridge."
> "How do you know?"
> "They rock back and forth like that when they fly," I say. I'm not sure of this but it sounds right. "They stay close to the ground too."
> "Oh, says Chris [pp. 169–170].

On the mountain, Chris asks real questions and listens to the answers—not something he does very often in this book. The two of them share a moment of naturalist observation—a kind of observing that Pirsig himself does alone very regularly, but in which Chris is almost never interested. For his part, Pirsig is willing to communicate with his son even though he is "not sure" about what he is saying: most of the time Pirsig clings fast to his reasoned principle that words should not be used as emotional sops. All this makes us hopeful that there will be real progress shared by the two of them on this mountain climb, this journey upwards. But it is a deceptive and temporary accord. Not until the final chapter of the book will the two travel in anything like harmony, nor, until then, will observation and communication begin to coincide.

Climbing the Montana mountain, Pirsig's manner of travel—his unwillingness to take any risks at all; his fear of climbing too high; his extreme deliberateness of movement—is soon radically at odds with Chris's way of climbing. Pirsig's smugness about the "correctness" of his own well thought-out method of travel makes him severely insensitive to his son. As always, their deteriorating relations are described by talk of travel:

> "Well," I say, "we can stop here, or we can go ahead, or we can go back. Which do you want to do?"
> "I don't care," he says, "I don't want to . . ."
> "You don't want to what?"
> "*I don't care!*" he says angrily.
> "Then since you don't care, we'll keep on going," I say, trapping him.
> "I don't like this trip," he says. "It isn't fun. I thought it was going to be fun."
> Some anger catches me off guard too. "That may be true," I reply, "but it's a hell of a thing to say."
> I see a sudden flicker of fear in his eyes as he gets up [pp. 192–193].

The two do achieve another momentary harmony of movement during the mountain climb, but this is, typically, based on a misunderstanding by Chris. Wishing to climb as high as possible, like Phaedrus, always reaching for a summit, Chris has his happiest moment of the trip when Pirsig gives the appearance of sharing Chris's goal:

> When the summit is about fifty yards away I say, "Let's go!" and start to dash for it, throwing into the effort all the reserves of energy I've been saving.
> I give it everything I have, but Chris gains on me. Then he passes me, giggling. With the heavy load and high altitude we're not setting any records but now we're just charging up with all we have.
> Chris gets there first, while I just break out of trees. He raises his arms and shouts, "The Winner!"
> Egotist.

I'm breathing so hard when I arrive I can't speak. We just drop our packs from our shoulders and lie down against some rocks. The crust of the ground is dry from the sun, but underneath is mud from last night's rain. Below us and miles away beyond the forested slopes and the fields beyond them is the Gallatin Valley. At one corner of the valley is Bozeman. A grasshopper jumps up from the rock and soars down and away from us over the trees.

"We made it," Chris says. He is very happy. I am still too winded to answer. I take off my boots and socks which are soggy with sweat and set them out to dry on a rock. I stare at them meditatively as vapors from them rise up toward the sun [pp. 215–216].

Details of this passage are worth noting, because they document the essential fraudulence of any "progress" Pirsig may seem to be making with Chris. The scene begins with Pirsig's keen awareness of the competition now between them—which, he has theorized, is very bad—then briefly the first-person plural pronouns record a moment of shared motion and mutual effort. But by the last paragraph of the scene, only Chris is using "we" to describe their journey upwards; Pirsig's use of pronouns marks their separateness in his mind. Pirsig's way of traveling is very different from Chris's: (1) he is less willing and less able than Chris to climb in the "high country"; (2) he does not answer a remark by Chris, as is his increasing habit; (3) he drifts off into thinking about "valleys" ("miles away"), while Chris is excited about attaining a peak; (4) he is silently critical, almost bitter, about Chris's "YMCA-camp ego-climbing," which reminds him of his own former personality; (5) he falls into his now-compulsive habit of meditation, which is a major cause of his growing alienation from Chris, though he seems not to recognize this. In addition, an instant of naturalist observation, unshared by Chris, signifies the distance between them, as it does so often in the book: "A grasshopper jumps up from the rock and soars down and away." The "blackbird" and "partridge" episodes quoted above are other examples of how pointedly Pirsig uses these moments of observation; so is the very late scene in which Pirsig "really looks at" a "green slug on the ground." He shows one to Chris, but the boy "has no comment" (p. 361). This is probably the lowest point in their relationship. Throughout the book, Pirsig "sees" in high-Quality ways, but he seldom can help Chris to do the same. (Not incidentally, Phaedrus was—by Pirsig's report at least—a phenomenally successful teacher; certainly he succeeded with Chris in a way that Pirsig cannot.)

Ironically, immediately before their brief sprint up the hill (at Chris's speed and in Chris's direction, for once), Pirsig rather complacently notes of Chris: "His mood seems much better than yesterday. I think he'll be a good traveler from here in" (p. 214). But at this stage of their journey together, Pirsig's idea of "good travel" is so fundamentally alien to Chris that Pirsig actually becomes chagrined when Chris finally manages to move along in a way that is pleasing and exciting to himself.

These three plots develop simultaneously, of course, and with enormous effect on one another. A summary of some of these mutual developments will be useful. For one thing, as Pirsig really does get somewhere in his Chautauqua, really does illuminate his concept of Quality, his schizophrenia accelerates. Dredging over the thought processes of Phaedrus inevitably awakens memories that seem to threaten the unity of Pirsig's consciousness. For another thing, as a direct result of Pirsig's improvement in metaphysicking, his relations with Chris practically fall apart. Not only is Pirsig more and more abstract and remote—Chris sits behind him, insulated by a helmet, staring at his back—but Pirsig's enthusiasm for his version of "Zen" acceptance and peaceful states of mind makes him less and less capable of tolerating Chris's natural childish interest in winning victories, climbing mountains, experiencing pungent external stimulation generally. Pirsig's only excitement is internal, mental, essentially private and not easily shared. When a cafe waitress eyes him carnally, he reacts as a mere observer, detached and virtually solipsistic.

Ironically enough, the fragmentation of the technical writer/ motorcycle mechanic into two conflicting selves is ultimately *not* insanity but rather the very means by which he becomes reconciled to Chris and perfects a harmonious way of traveling with him, recorded in the last chapter. In spite of Phaedrus's crippling indifference to "everyday life" (what could be more graphic than the picture of Phaedrus sitting in a darkened room, face to the wall, in his own urine?), he has the exulting courage of his convictions and the sheer intellectual excitement (Chris calls this "fun") that Pirsig sadly lacks.

I mentioned above that the three plots may all be thought of as conspicuously different kinds of journeys. Pirsig's movement towards a concept of Quality is a version of *pilgrimage*; Pirsig's pursuit of Phaedrus is a *quest*; and Pirsig's journey with Chris is a variation of a *progress*. As he makes his way along the three paths, his three simultaneous but often contradictory styles of movement dramatically suggest the wholeness of experience—its paradoxes and tensions—that Pirsig's lectures alone only talk about and perhaps falsify.

A *pilgrimage* is travel to a foreseen destination; the traveler's purpose in going seems relatively sure; and the traveler possesses all the necessary means of arriving—he does not have to learn how to make his way—though he encounters obstacles that test, and allow him to express, his commitment and perseverance.[6] Pirsig's Chautauqua is a kind of pilgrimage to the shrine of Quality. More accurately, it is a pilgrimage to an adequate understanding of and way of talking about Quality. Pirsig's Chautauqua tests his endurance and saps his emotional strength (he starts falling into "gumption traps" himself), but his movement to an account of Quality is steady, deliberate, and—to my mind, at least—notably successful.

It would take a considerably longer essay to do any sort of justice to Pirsig's philosophizing on the subject of Quality. Put very briefly, he is troubled by a pervasive sense of dichotomies—subject vs. object, romantic vs. classical, mind vs. machine, hip vs. square, and so on—all of which seem irreconcilably disjunct. Pirsig begins by rehearsing Phaedrus's pursuit of an understanding that will transcend these dichotomies, finding that Phaedrus took a lot of wrong turns on his way. For instance, Phaedrus denied that Quality can be defined (or even discussed), though eventually Pirsig does pretty much define it as an event, a "preintellectual awareness" that precedes subject and object and actually creates them. At one point Phaedrus speciously declares that Quality is "whatever you like" (purely subjective), then realizes that Quality is opposed to subjectivity. At another point, he decides that it is part of a metaphysical trinity with subject and object, eventually discovering this is not so.

Pirsig retraces, corrects, and extends Phaedrus's pilgrimage to Quality. By the end of Part III (ch. 26), he has arrived, ending with a note of anticlimax, but making a real finish nonetheless. Pirsig not only reaches a definition of Quality—"preintellectual reality" (p. 222); "the continuing stimulus which our environment puts upon us to create the world in which we live. All of it. Every last bit of it" (p. 225)—he also achieves a successful conversion of theoretical concepts into the practical, "everyday life" example of motorcycle repair.

However, finishing his pilgrimage only means that Pirsig is inexorably drawn in to give fuller energy to the quest for Phaedrus he has simultaneously been undertaking: "But now I want to shift into another direction, which completes *his* story. I never really completed it because I didn't think it would be necessary. But now I think it would be a good time to do that in what time remains" (p. 301).

The *quest* is a more familiar journey form to readers of modern literature—we are accustomed to unknown destinations, vague but urgent purposes—but it is worth noting that the quest as a structural metaphor probably evolved as a criticism of or corrective to the form of pilgrimage. (Think of the surprise of Spenser's Redcrosse Knight, at the end of *Faerie Queene*, Book I, when the destination he had automatically regarded as final and conclusive turns out to be just another temporary stopping place.) In a quest, destination and outcome are usually unforeseeable; the traveler's purpose in going is mysterious, though crucial; and obstacles of all varieties arise. At first Pirsig tries to deny that he is seeking Phaedrus at all; for a time Pirsig even seems to be pursued by Phaedrus, doppelganger-fashion. But, as the book goes on, Pirsig begins to understand that the intermittent appearances of Phaedrus are his own responsibility, the inevitable consequences of his own successful procession to the truth about Quality. He also begins to perceive that he himself has half-consciously set out to search for this lost part of himself. When they arrive in Montana, Pirsig deliberately seeks out "the school" where Phaedrus taught and thought. Chris repeatedly asks (a sensible question): "Why are we *here*?" (p. 157), but Pirsig cannot answer this question, either for Chris or for himself: "I just shake my head" (p. 157).

Compared with his pilgrimage to Quality—a goal Pirsig deliberately sets out for and reaches, more or less on schedule—his quest for wholeness of personality is powerfully motivated but entirely subjective and intuitive. Pirsig has no clear idea of what the result will be and feels menaced until the very last pages of the book. Chris, who has to suffer through his father's questing, and whose own idea of worthwhile traveling is very different, is dismayed by the lack of certain destination and clear direction inherent in the quest:

> "Dad?"
> "What?"
> "Why are we doing this?"
> "What?"
> "Just riding all the time."
> "Just to see the country . . . vacation."
> The answer doesn't seem to satisfy him. But he can't seem to say what's wrong with it.
> A sudden despair wave hits, like that at dawn. I *lie* to him. That's what's wrong.
> "We just keep going and going," he says.
> "Sure. What would you rather do?"
> He has no answer.
> I don't either [p. 304].

A *progress*, the journey pattern that I think best describes Pirsig's motions towards being a real father to Chris, resembles a pilgrimage in that the traveler knows his destination and knows why he wants to go there. But in a progress the journeyer lacks some crucial capacity for making his way. A progress is, therefore, an empirical kind of journey story, a story of learning from experience how to deal with circumstances. Pirsig wants the very best quality life possible for Chris and wants to be the best possible father to him—there is never the least question about his dedication to his son. But he is woefully ill-equipped to make the right movements in this direction, loaded down as he is with metaphysical baggage. He has to learn how to overcome the obstacles between Chris and himself, to absorb from experience—not from systematic theory—how to be a whole father. Any progress story (think, for example, not only of Bunyan, but of Fielding's *Joseph Andrews*) is primarily concerned with the social effects of learning. The character's values, purposes, and sense of destination do not change, but he does need to undergo a (sometimes slow and painful) course in learning how to enact his values, achieve his purposes, get to where he already knows he wants to go. Pirsig's progress to fatherliness is very much complicated and interfered with by the goals of his other "journeys." In fact, right at the beginning of the book he makes an *a priori* decision about the limitations of his chosen way of travel that become a staggering threat to the Quality of his relationship with Chris. Pirsig decides that motorcycle travel is perfect for his meditative pilgrimage to the concept of Quality:

> Unless you're fond of hollering you don't make great conversations on a running cycle. Instead you spend your time being aware of things and meditating on them. On sights and sounds, on the mood of the weather and things remembered, on the machine and the countryside you're in, thinking about things at great leisure and length without being hurried and without feeling you're losing time [pp. 6–7].

Lost in the cottony silence of his own thoughts—complacent about the transcendent value of contemplation—Pirsig does not realize until the end of the journey that he really *is* losing time, at least as far as being an adequate father to Chris. All his thinking about Quality is solipsistic, cutting him off from his son, ruining the chances of both for what Pirsig would call a high-Quality life. This does not mean, of course, that his "points" about Quality are any less true or valuable or that his pilgrimage could or should have been any less urgent. But some kind of compromise is indispensable, and the very last pages of *Zen and the Art of Motorcycle Maintenance* express what we have come to see as the only real chance for Pirsig and Chris by making a thorough point-by-point repudiation of all Pirsig's assumptions about motorcycle travel and contemplation at the beginning. Compared to the solipsism, non-dialogue, and myopia of travel at the beginning, the ending describes social, harmonious, and farsighted journeying (with a touch of the sensory excitement Chris loves):

> The cycle swings into each curve effortlessly, banking so that our weight is always down through the machine no matter what its angle is with the ground. The way is full of flowers and surprise views, tight turns one after another so that the whole world rolls and pirouettes and rises and falls away [p. 370].

The two are now traveling together, moving, pausing, progressing, and experiencing at the same pace and with perfect mutual economy of motion ("our weight is always down through the machine no matter what its angle is with the ground"). It is exactly what Pirsig had wanted for the two of them from the beginning but did not know, until near the ending, how to reach.

The three separate "journeys" that Pirsig undertakes, simultaneous epistemological metaphors for different facets of one man's life, enact the sheer contradictoriness of a single life, its cross-purposes and counter-impulses. At the end of the book, Pirsig, perhaps paradoxically, has to compromise his ideals of Quality to achieve any semblance of Quality in his "everyday life." "Peace of mind" grows best, peculiarly, when it is not systematically cultivated. Metaphysics must make continual accommodations to "everday life," especially its social responsibilities. Life is not "like a journey" so much as it is like several journeys, all different, all necessary, undertaken all at the same time.

NOTES

[1] I have discussed the obstacles to an adequate reading in "Irony and Earnestness in Robert Pirsig's *Zen and the Art of Motorcycle Maintenance*," *Critique: Studies in Modern Fiction*, Vol. 22 (1979), pp. 21–31.

[2] *The New Yorker*, Vol. 50 (April 15, 1974), p. 147.

[3] Throughout this essay I use "Pirsig" to refer to the character in the book who is also our first-person, present-tense narrator. It is a mistake to confuse this character, "Pirsig," with the author of the book. Just as Pirsig the narrator understands the weaknesses and obsessive solipsism of Phaedrus, an earlier version of himself, so does the author see and make us come to see the debilitating awkwardness and emotional confusion of the narrator. There is a substantial difference between the mind of the author who finished writing the book a decade after the events took place and the mind of the character he invents to tell the story. The distance between the two keeps everything that is said alive with misunderstandings, ironies, incomplete angles of vision. The biggest block to reading the book (not "novel," for it defies our generic categories) adequately is a facile assumption that the voice talking to us represents the normative values of the book.

[4] Robert M. Pirsig, *Zen and the Art of Motorcycle Maintenance* (New York: Bantam Books, 1979). (All quotations are from this edition.)

[5] Part of my thinking about types of journey metaphors derives from J. Paul Hunter's *Occasional Form: Henry Fielding and the Chains of Circumstance* (Baltimore: Johns Hopkins University Press, 1975), especially pp. 143–65.

[6] The archetypal pattern of "life as a pilgrimage" is, of course, not *Canterbury Tales* at all, but the New Testament, the Life of Christ, with its stress on certainty, preordination, but also endurance and sacrifice. As a model, its importance has always been chiefly internal and private, stressing the fulfillment of a plan and the resources of virtue and grace.

"CREATIVITY, RATIONALITY, AND METAPHOR IN ROBERT PIRSIG'S ZEN AND THE ART OF MOTORCYCLE MAINTENANCE"

BY JEROME BUMP

As American industry loses more and more ground to foreign competition, the need for more creative thinking in American science and technology becomes increasingly apparent. The popularity of pop psychology books and movements testifies to our desire for more creativity in our thinking about ourselves and our relationships with others as well. Yet attempts to make our thinking about such topics more innovative are stymied again and again by reductive definitions of thinking as logic and of science as a rigid, step-by-step approach to problem-solving.

The need for an expanded definition of rationality was recognized as early as the eighteenth century, most obviously in George Campbell's *The Philosophy of Rhetoric* (1776). Campbell rejected the traditional association of thinking with Aristotelian syllogisms and began to move toward a definition of rationality based more on the inductive approach of modern science. In 1870 John Henry Newman went further, including some elements of instinct, intuition, common sense, imagination, taste, judgment, and even emotion in the new *organon* of the mind outlined in his *An Essay in Aid of a Grammar of Assent*. Newman based his definition of "ratiocination" on inductive psychology, that is, on observations of actual persons and appeals to the reader's own experience and knowledge of others. The attempt to redefine rationality on this basis continues to this day in works such as Steven Toulmin's *The Uses of Argument*, Chaim Perelman's *The New Rhetoric: A Treatise on Argument*, Paul Feyerabend's *Against Method*, T. S. Kuhn's *The Structure of Scientific Revolutions*, Wayne Booth's *Modern Dogma and the Rhetoric of Assent*, and Michael Polanyi's *Personal Knowledge* and *The Tacit Dimension*.

Nevertheless, although such titles may be familiar to scholars, they have attracted relatively few readers. Robert Pirsig's *Zen and the Art of Motorcycle Maintenance*, on the other hand, has sold almost two million copies since it first appeared in 1974. The secret

From *The South Atlantic Quarterly*, Vol. 82, No. 4 (1983), pp. 370–380. Reprinted with permission from *The South Atlantic Quarterly*. Copyright © 1983 Duke University Press.

to the extraordinary popularity of this apparently naive Minnesota autobiography, it seems to me, is that it has helped hundreds of thousands of readers articulate their own need to redefine rationality and to discover more creative ways of thinking about themselves and their relationships.

Creativity is an issue throughout the book, ranging from the account of the creative process in an acknowledged genius like Henri Poincaré (chap. 22) to the representation of creative students as rebels who often drop out of school (chap. 16) to the story of the student who apparently had no creativity at all (chap. 16). Moreover, eventually, motorcycle maintenance becomes a metaphor for all kinds of problem-solving situations. However, the primary focus is, of course, on the narrator and on his recollections of the person he had been before he was subjected to electric shock therapy.

The narrator represents his prior self, Phaedrus, as potentially a very creative person, with an I.Q. perhaps high enough to classify him as a genius (chap. 7). Moreover, both Phaedrus and the narrator possess many of the traits traditionally associated with creative people. Otto Rank and many other psychologists associate creativity with the private inspirations of very individualistic people, usually rebels against society, a description which certainly fits Phaedrus and, to a considerable extent, the narrator. The case history of Phaedrus also fits the models of creativity of Cesare Lombroso and others since who stress a connection between psychopathology and genius.

Perhaps the most persistent trait of creative people, however, is revolt against simplistic dualisms. Arthur Koestler, Abraham Maslow, and Albert Rothenberg emphasize that a key element of creativity is replacement of "either/or" with "both/and" thinking. Instead of taking literally the simplistic "logical" partition of a subject into "either" the first "or" the second of two categories, creative breakthroughs are often achieved by perceiving that in reality the subject consists of "both" the first "and" the second parts. The most famous example of the replacement of either/or with both/and thinking in our century is Einstein's rejection of the absolute dualism of matter and energy. Revolt against dualism is also apparent in the theory of the complementarity of the wave and particle models of electromagnetic fields. The behavior of such fields can be understood fully only if they are considered "metaphorically" as both "waves" (at low frequencies) and "particles" (at high frequencies). Generally, both/and thinking is evident in love of paradox, ambiguity, irony, and tension; in integration of the abstract and the concrete; and in that sense of the permeability of boundaries that permits interdisciplinary thought.

Perhaps the ultimate revolt against simplistic dualisms, however—and thus a key to creativity according to theorists from Aristotle to the present—is metaphor. The apparent fusion of two things into one in metaphor epitomizes and, in many respects, is itself the most concise and effective linguistic revolt against dualism. Robert Frost in his 1930 lecture, "Education by Poetry," pointed out that to learn the powers and limits of metaphor was to grasp the essence of thinking itself. He emphasized that Einstein's "In the neighborhood of matter space is something like curved" is a metaphor and that even mathematics is based on a metaphor ("Pythagoras's comparison of the universe to number") as are mechanistic models of the world ("the universe as machine"), the theory of evolution ("the metaphor of the growing plant"), and the Heisenberg uncertainty principle ("a thing they say is an event").

Such metaphorical models are in fact indispensable tools for the generation of creative hypotheses and effective explanations in science. In *Models and Metaphors* Max Black has shown that "the use of a 'subsidiary subject' to foster insight into a 'principal subject' " through metaphor "is a distinctive intellectual operation . . . demanding simultaneous awareness of both subjects but not reducible to any comparison between the two." Metaphors thus enable us to make new connections and see things in a new way. Moreover, "the extended meanings that result, the relations between initially disparate realms created, can neither be antecedently predicted nor subsequently paraphrased in prose . . . Metaphorical thought is a distinctive mode of achieving insight, not to be construed as an ornamental substitute for plain thought."

Hence metaphorical thought is a crucial ingredient in Pirsig's expansion of our sense of rationality and his exploration of the wellsprings of creativity. The increasing reliance on metaphor in his book is also a clue to the puzzling question of its genre. Many critics insist on classifying his book as either an autobiography or a novel, but a third possibility is to regard it as a "prophetic book," incorporating elements of both autobiography and fiction as well as philosophy, in the tradition of Thomas Carlyle's *Sartor Resartus*, Benjamin Disraeli's *Coningsby*, George Eliot's *Middlemarch*,

John Henry Newman's *Apologia Pro Vita Sua*, and Thomas Hardy's *Jude the Obscure.* What distinguishes these books is that they are concerned, like Pirsig's, with "ultimate questions," as John Holloway puts it in *The Victorian Sage:* "They learn by a kind of trustful meditation that supplements reason with imagination; and the understanding to which they finally come is something concrete and particular which abstract formulae cannot express," something which "must come gradually alive in our minds."

Holloway's guide to books of this kind—and a good guide to Pirsig's book as well—is Newman's *Grammar of Assent.* Newman distinguishes "notional assent" to abstractions and propositions in logic from what he calls "real assent" directed, as Holloway puts it, toward assertions whose "meaning is too rich to be sharply limited, always liable to be unfolded further . . . a meaning which arises for the individual out of his own history and exists for him in vivid particular images that bring his belief to life. . . . For real assent the formal arguments of logic must be supplemented by something richer, more varied, more personal; . . . Certainly we may begin in our proof with mechanical logic but we are obliged to supplement it with the more subtle and elastic logic of thought."

The plot of *Zen and the Art of Motorcycle Maintenance* is essentially the movement of the narrator from a notional to a real assent to the proposition that what he calls "the desiccating lifeless voice of dualistic reason" (chap. 29) should no longer be his exclusive preoccupation. This movement is too complex to be sharply limited to any easily defined goal, as he eventually discovers. Arising out of his own history and existing for him in vivid images of what he is trying to escape, such as the wolf, the glass door, and the ghost, the meaning of his life is always liable to be unfolded further, as the ending of the book suggests. He began with proof, mechanical logic, formal arguments about the inadequacy of logic itself, but to realize the alternative, he had to supplement his arguments with a richer, more varied, more personal mode of thought, something not reducible to any mechanism or pattern.

Metaphorical meaning, the sense beyond the letter, plays an important role in this more subtle and elastic logic of thought. According to Newman: "Methodical processes of inference, useful as they are, as far as they go, are only instruments of the mind and need . . . that real ratiocination and present imagination which gives them a sense beyond their letter, and which . . . reaches to conclusions beyond and above them. Such a living *organon* is a personal gift and not a mere method or calculus." The "sense beyond the letter" is in fact a recurrent phrase throughout the *Grammar of Assent,* emphasizing the importance of figurative language. "Figurative language plays a most significant part" in prophetic books, according to Holloway: "Above all, figurative language is largely what sustains the outlook of a book through its entire length and throughout those parts of it which seem at a glance to contribute nothing to the whole."

A focus on Pirsig's figurative language enables us to perceive more clearly one source of his popularity, one way in which his book contributes to our attempts to generate a new, expanded definition of rationality which can assimilate and encourage creativity. Ultimately, the narrator concludes that his goal, Quality, or "the One can only be described allegorically, through the use of analogy, figures of imagination and speech" (chap. 30), that is, not in logic as we now know it, but through an expanded sense of rationality which includes metaphor, the kind of thought more typical of the humanities and religion. It is true that Phaedrus had said, "All this is just an analogy"; but he added, "Everything is an analogy, but the dialecticians don't know it" (chap. 30). The rejection of simplistic dualisms and their replacement by the way of thinking represented by analogy and other forms of metaphor—a way rarely traveled by dialecticians—is one of the chief goals toward which the narrator and the reader are journeying throughout the course of the novel. By becoming more aware of Pirsig's metaphors, we as readers can participate in the author's creative process, overcoming with him some of the dichotomies that plague him. Ultimately, the hope is that, just as the kind of holistic thinking and feeling epitomized by metaphor led the narrator to see himself and his son in a new way, we as readers, by this conscious calisthenics of metaphor, can begin to see ourselves, our problems, and our relationships in more creative ways.

One of the first simplistic dualisms we learn to reject is that between "primitive" and "medieval" thought and science, or, metaphorically, between "ghosts" and the "laws of science" (chap. 3). The narrator demonstrates that the "law of gravity exists *nowhere* except in people's heads!" that is, the law of gravity, like all laws of science, is only one of the ghosts of modern man.

The ghost metaphor, moreover, soon takes on another set of meanings. The narrator tells his son, "I knew a fellow once who spent his whole life doing nothing but hunting for a ghost, and it was just a waste of time." He goes on to reveal that this fellow found the ghost, thrashed him, and "Then he became a ghost himself . . . His name . . . is Phaedrus. It's not a name you know" (chap. 3). The ghost that Phaedrus sought, we eventually learn, was the ghost of rationality; ironically, though he thrashed him, Phaedrus himself still became a ghost of rationality (chap. 7). This ghost lives on in people's heads also—in Pirsig's book particularly, in the narrator's head and in his son's.

Calling the ghost "Phaedrus" is an especially powerful kind of metaphor—a metaphorical allusion (as distinguished from a topical or personal allusion). By using this one word a host of possible meanings are evoked in the reader's mind, all of which the reader must hold in suspension, in creative ambiguity, throughout the novel. Phaedrus is the Socratic foil whose name is given to one of Plato's dialogues. Phaedrus is usually considered an enthusiastic and rather naive friend of Socrates. While the narrator and Pirsig's Phaedrus often appear enthusiastic and rather naive, the narrator emphasizes the rebellious connotations of the word "Phaedrus": "He is unallied to any particular group. He prefers the solitude of the country to the city. He is aggressive to the point of being dangerous. At one point he threatens Socrates with violence. *Phaedrus,* in Greek, means "wolf" (chap. 30). The narrator admits, however, that in Plato's dialogue "he is carried away by Socrates' discourse on love and is tamed." In Plato's *Symposium* Phaedrus himself distinguishes between physical and spiritual love. Hence the allusions to Phaedrus immediately become potentially ironic in Pirsig's context because neither Pirsig's Phaedrus nor the narrator seems at first much interested in or capable of love. However, toward the end of the book the narrator's eyes finally begin to open and at last he begins to see his relationship to his son in a new way, a way that might lead him also to be tamed by that greatest of all revolts against dualism, love.

In Plato's *Phaedrus* Socrates, who frequently employs figurative language, creates a metaphorical model of the soul as a pair of winged horses and a charioteer. One horse is noble; the other, ignoble and troublesome because he is insolent and proud. Zeus in a winged chariot from heaven leads the noble horse, but the untrained, ignoble horse, hardly yielding to whip or spur, weighs the charioteer to earth. The result is that "after fruitless toil, not having attained to the mysteries of true being," the charioteer goes away and feeds "upon opinion." The dualistic horse imagery of this metaphorical allusion invites many potential meanings in Pirsig's book, such as the two motorcycles on their journeys; the two riders, father and son; and the two halves of the author's soul, Phaedrus and the narrator.

Other aspects of the Platonic dialogue, *Phaedrus*, are also relevant to Pirsig's novel, such as the discussions of rhetoric and the relation between creativity and madness. Socrates' assertion of the immortality of the soul may even be read as predictive of the persistence of the soul of Phaedrus in the narrator despite the electric shock treatment. Socrates' suggestion that the secret of the soul's immortality is constant motion also recalls the steady movement of the two motorcycles on their journey, a movement which keeps revealing different aspects of the Phaedrus who had been there before them. But the most important aspects of the allusions to Plato's *Phaedrus* are the suggestions that love is the goal and highest form of madness and that as long as the soul's two horses fail to work together the charioteer will fail, that is, as long as the charioteer is incapable of overcoming his antagonistic dualisms he will not attain to the mystery of true being.

The narrator first becomes aware of the obvious dualism of the two motorcycles, his and John's, and the opposition between his scientific, protechnological views and John's antitechnological feelings. He soon begins the task of transcending this dichotomy, however: John's is "a very serious and important way of looking at things that *looks* incompatible with reason and order and responsibility but actually is not. . . . The world as you see it right here, right now, *is reality*, regardless of what the scientists say it might be. That's the way John sees it. But the world as revealed by its scientific discoveries is also reality, regardless of how it may appear" (chap. 5).

The narrator's philosophy begins to expand in order to assimilate both scientific and antiscientific visions of reality, and that seems a step toward overcoming such basic human dualisms as himself versus John and, ultimately, himself versus his son Chris. But, as Newman pointed out, there is a great difference between abstract or notional assent to a proposition (such as the need to transcend the dualisms that divide one person from another) and real, emotional assent to it. The latter is often achieved in language only by repeating the basic theme in a number of ways, including a number of metaphorical contexts.

For instance, the ghost motif is soon repeated in another context of allusion, a recollection of Goethe's poem about a father, a son, and a ghost. The son sees a ghost in the landscape and the father pretends it is not there, with the result that the ghost wins and the child dies (chap. 5). The relevance of the tale to Chris, now revealed as having symptoms of the same mental illness that Phaedrus suffered from, seems to be that, if the father does not recognize the persistence of the ghost of reductive rationality in himself, it will claim his son the way it claimed Phaedrus.

After a philosophic discussion of the dichotomy between the romantic and the classic (that is, the scientific or rational) approaches, the narrator begins thinking again about "the rational, analytical, classical world of Phaedrus . . . a totally classic person" (chap. 6). Clearly drawing on his own experience as a technical writer in American industry, Pirsig emphasizes that Phaedrus's analysis of a motorcycle would be "duller than ditchwater" and dehumanized: "The observer is missing . . . no real subjects . . . Only objects exist that are independent of any observer" (chap. 6). And, of course, "no value judgments have been expressed anywhere, only facts." However, the narrator best conveys the quality of Phaedrus's approach in a metaphor, for metaphor combines emotional and philosophical connotations: "There is a knife moving here. A very deadly one; an intellectual scalpel so swift and so sharp you sometimes don't see it moving." The narrator then stresses what happens when this reductive version of rationality is used exclusively: "The knife he used was less that of an assassin than that of a poor surgeon. Perhaps there is no difference. But he saw a sick and ailing thing happening and he started cutting deep, deeper and deeper to get at the root of it . . . he used the knife because that was the only tool he had. But he took on so much and went so far in the end his real victim was himself."

More metaphors are needed to describe the knife-wielder, Phaedrus, the ghost of rationality. The lone wolf metaphor implied in his name is invoked: "There's no record of his having had close friends. He traveled alone. Always. Even in the presence of others he was completely alone . . . His wife says those who tried to go beyond the barriers of reserve found themselves facing a blank. My impression is that they were starved for some kind of affection which he never gave" (chap. 7). The narrator then recalls the moment when Phaedrus actually saw a timber wolf "and the memory of this incident stayed with him a long time . . . because he had seen a kind of image of himself" (chap. 7). An image of the narrator too, we might add, for ironically the narrator remembers this image while traveling with close friends and sharing the same motorcycle with his son, but most of the time he seems to be still traveling alone, still cut off from the son who remains starved for the kind of affection it seems that the narrator also rarely gives.

In other words, the narrator remains a worshipper in the old church of reason, to cite another of the metaphors he employs. He stops to adjust the tappets of the motorcycle, for instance: "I always feel like I'm in church when I do this . . . The gauge is some kind of religious icon and I'm performing a holy rite with it" (chap. 8). Soon he cites the chief priest of twentieth-century science, Albert Einstein, but it is significant that Einstein is more capable of combining reason and metaphor than either the narrator or Phaedrus:

> In the temple of science there are many mansions . . . [for many scientists] science is their own special sport . . . many others are to be found in the temple who have offered the products of their brains on the altar for purely utilitarian purposes. Were an angel of the Lord to come and drive all these people . . . out of the temple, it would be noticeably emptier but there would still be some men. . . . If [these] were the only types there were, the temple would never have existed anymore than one can have a wood consisting of nothing but creepers . . . those who have found favor with the angel [were brought] to the temple [to escape] from the fetters of [their] own shifting desires . . . escape from . . . noisy cramped surroundings into the silence of the high mountains where the eye ranges freely through the still pure air and fondly traces out the restful contours apparently built for eternity [chap. 10].

Because Einstein's subject is the emotional wellsprings of scientists, his primary technique is not logic but metaphor.

With this model before him, the narrator begins to develop the metaphor of the landscape of the mind—"in the high country of the mind one has to become adjusted to the thinner air of uncertainty"—and the temple, or the "Church of Reason" (chap. 13). Any detail of the landscape can be endowed with symbolic significance. For instance, the narrator speaks with his friend DeWeese and: "A rush of wind comes furiously now, down from the mountaintop. 'The ancient Greeks,' I say, 'who were the inventors of classical reason, knew better than to use it exclusively to foretell the future. They listened to the wind and predicted the future from that' " (chap. 14).

Sometimes the narrator explicates this kind of landscape symbolism, as in his explanation of Quality, his term for the transcendence of dualisms, as a "route through the mountain of the spirit. . . . For more than three centuries now the old routes common in this hemisphere have been undercut and almost washed out by the natural erosion and change of the shape of the mountain wrought by scientific truth. The early climbers established paths that were on firm ground with an accessibility that appealed to all, but today the Western routes are all closed because of dogmatic inflexibility in the face of change" (chap. 16). At the same time that he is developing metaphors in this manner, the narrator is literally hiking up a mountain and generating related imagery, as in his observation: "The rays of the sun create a cathedral effect through the pines."

The mere fact that the narrator is climbing a mountain with religious connotations suggests differences between himself and Phaedrus. Phaedrus "never reached the mountain," at least the mountain in India he sought on which "each footstep was an act of devotion, an act of submission to his holiness" (chap. 17). The narrator begins to be explicit about these differences: "I'm making a big thing out of all this, these classical-romantic differences, but Phaedrus didn't. He wasn't really interested in any kind of fusion of differences between these two worlds. He was after something else—his ghost. . . . I differ from him in that I've no intention of going on to that end. He just passed through this territory and opened it up. I intend to stay and cultivate it and see if I can get something to grow" (chap. 18).

Yet we are reminded that when he passed through science's high country of the mind, Phaedrus managed at least a notional assent to the proposition that the subject-object dualism must be overcome. Phaedrus realized that Quality could be found only in the relationship of the two with each other, that it was independent of the two. Like Kepler, he even began to see analogies with the Trinity and to incorporate metaphor into his thought: " 'The sun of quality,' he wrote, 'does not revolve around the subjects and objects of our existence. It does not just passively illuminate them' " (chap. 19). Metaphor, however, plays a much greater role in Pirsig's book than it did in Phaedrus's thought. Just after this quote from Phaedrus, for instance, we read: " 'Blue sky!' shouts Chris. There it is, way above us, a narrow patch of blue through the trunks of the trees." The technique may seem naive at times, but virtually every detail of their journey across the landscape becomes charged with symbolic significance.

Finally, the narrator recalls that Phaedrus eventually realized that what he was talking about was the "Tao, the great central generating force of all religions" (chap. 20). Yet his continuing obsession with logical dualisms and his simplistic application of the knife of analysis to his own mind made his own position precarious: "The internal parting of his mind suddenly gathered momentum, as do the rocks at the top of a mountain. Before he could stop it, the sudden accumulated mass of awareness began to grow and grow into an avalanche of thought and awareness out of control; with each additional growth of the downward tearing mass loosening hundreds of times its own volume, and then that mass uprooting hundreds of times its volume more, and then hundreds of times on that; on and on, wider and broader, until there was nothing left to stand" (chap. 20). This landscape of the mind echoes some of the most powerful archetypes in literature, including falling from the ledges of Dante's hell, from the cliffs of Dover in *King Lear*, and especially from the great precipices of the mind in Hopkins's "No worst, there is none":

> O the mind, mind has mountains: cliffs of fall
> Frightful, sheer, no-man-fathomed. Hold them cheap
> May who ne'er hung there. Nor does long our small
> Durance deal with that steep or deep. . . .

With the example of Phaedrus's downfall so vividly before him, the narrator begins to turn more and more to that basic dualism of his own everyday life that has been haunting him—and the reader—throughout the book: "I keep feeling that the facts I am fishing for concerning Chris are right here in front of me too, but that some value rigidity of my own blocks me from seeing it. At times we seem to move in parallel rather than in combination, then at odd moments collide. . . . I'm forever on the other side of the glass door from him which I don't open. He wants me to open it and before I always turned away. But now there's a new figure who prevents me" (chap. 26). The "new" figure is Phaedrus (chap. 27), and the meaning of the basic metaphor of the book becomes increasingly explicit: "The real cycle you're working on is a cycle called yourself" (chap. 26).

The narrator's eyes begin to open: "In all this Chautauqua talk there's been more than a touch of hypocrisy. Advice is given again and again to eliminate subject-object duality, when the biggest duality of all, the duality between me and him, remains unfaced. A mind divided against itself" (chap. 31). Finally, to save Chris, the narrator begins to reject the false division between him and Phaedrus, along with the sanity/insanity dualism (chap. 31).

Chris's response that he "knew" his father was not really insane then leads to an initial resolution of the dichotomy between father and son, a resolution expressed most effectively by the metaphor of "our" cycle journey: "The cycle swings into each curve effortlessly, banking so that our weight is always down through the machine no matter what its angle is with the ground. The way is full of flowers and surprise views, tight turns one after another so that the whole world rolls and pirouettes and rises and falls away" (chap. 32). They begin to transcend the dualism: "We're related to each other in ways we never fully understand. . . . He was always the *real* reason for coming out of the hospital. . . . I haven't been carrying him at all. He's been carrying *me*. . . . Be one person again! Rich air and strange perfumes from the flowers of the trees and shrubs enshroud us. . . . Chris hangs onto my shoulders now and I turn a little and see that he stands up on the foot pegs. . . . Chris says 'I never could see over your shoulders before.' The sunlight makes strange and beautiful designs through the tree branches on the road. . . . That's true. I never realized it. All this time he's been staring into my back" (chap. 32).

The narrator begins to relate two poles of a dualism to each other in ways no mere logical or metaphysical system could: "We're related to each other in ways we never fully understand." The two horses, representing the father's two selves as well as both father and son, begin to work together and the charioteer begins to take aim at the mystery of true being. In short, Phaedrus at last begins to let himself be tamed by love.

The strange and beautiful designs made by the sunlight at this point as the riders continue their journey on their spinning wheels with a new desire and will recall the final illumination of Dante's journey taken centuries before: "My high imagination failed/But like a spinning wheel/ My desire and will were carried along/By the Love that moves the sun and all the stars." This, the final discovery of so many of the great texts, remains curiously unacknowledged by most theorists of human creativity. By rediscovering his family, Pirsig's narrator joins Dante and countless predecessors in reminding us that the ultimate expression of human creativity may well be love.

Until this possibility is more fully assimilated in our models of mental health and creativity the ghost of rationality Pirsig so effectively describes will claim other victims. Moreover, until the need to transcend simplistic dualisms, epitomized so well in metaphor, is recognized in a new, expanded definition of rationality, our potential for innovation in other fields such as science and technology will remain limited.

"VISUAL IMAGERY AND INTERNAL AWARENESS IN PIRSIG'S *ZEN AND THE ART OF MOTORCYCLE MAINTENANCE*"

BY FORREST B. SHEARON

Pirsig's *Zen and the Art of Motorcycle Maintenance* is a deceptively complicated book that seems to say something about everything from universities to technology to Western philosophy to Eastern religions—to a madman who taught freshman composition. It is also an autobiographical book that places much emphasis on "seeing" and on that which is seen; and Pirsig seems to have manipulated his materials in such a way as to suggest "seeing" on at least four levels: external seeing (or visual imagery), philosophical understanding, spiritual perception, and finally emotional or internal awareness. When I first planned this paper, I had hoped to discuss all four of these levels, suggesting how Pirsig had used external seeing in relation to Phaedrus' metaphysical discoveries, to the narrator's Zen beliefs, and to his internal and relational problems. But I soon discovered that I could not develop all of these points in a brief paper, so I have limited myself to two of them—external imagery and emotional awareness.

The first three words of the book are "I can see . . ."[1] Approximately sixteen days[2] later, after traveling with his son Chris from near Minneapolis to the San Francisco Bay area, the narrator ends with a paragraph suggesting both external seeing and, more significantly, internal understanding: ". . . there is a feeling now, that was not here before, and is not just on the surface of things, but penetrates all the way through: We've won it. It's going to get better now. You can sort of tell these things" (p. 373). Clearly the narrator has gone from the external to the internal.

When we look closely at the imagery in *ZMM*,[3] however, we begin to realize that the narrator cannot see nearly so well as he assumes. In fact, throughout most of the book, he is rather blind to the emotional dimensions of his life even when he sees the external world clearly. This blindness is not a weakness in the book itself, but is rather a part of its overall plan. Since we are told that the story "must be regarded in its essence as fact," we are tempted to forget that Pirsig also said that "much has been changed for

From KPA Bulletin (1983), pp. 53–62. Reprinted with permission from Forrest B. Shearon, Department of Humanities, Eastern Kentucky University, Richmond, Ky.

rhetorical purposes." A part of his rhetorical—or artistic—design is to tell his autobiographical story by using a limited narrator, one who cannot see, until the end, the entire picture. Thus, it is important, as Richard Rodino has pointed out, to separate the "three versions"[4] of Pirsig—the narrator who has been given partial vision, Phaedrus who is presented from the narrator's point of view, and Pirsig himself who as the shaping artist sees the entire story and arranges it for his own rhetorical purposes. With these complications, it is small wonder that readers have trouble classifying the book. Is it a novel,[5] an autobiography, a quest narrative, a philosophical discussion, or what?[6] It bears resemblances to all of them. For the purposes of this paper, however, I am treating it more like a fictional work in its handling of selected visual imagery—including that of the sun—as the beginning step toward seeing and as an external reflection of internal and personal matters.

The narrator's own emphasis on visual imagery starts with the first sentence: "I can see by my watch, without taking my hand from the left grip of the cycle, that it is eight-thirty in the morning" (p. 3). A few sentences later, he says: "Here and there is a stretch of open water and if you look closely you can see wild ducks at the edge of the cattails. And turtles. . . . There's a red-winged blackbird" (p. 3). These two quotations almost epitomize the kinds of things the narrator sees—or, to put it another way, his visual images; he see the world of technology (the watch, the motorcycle) and the world of nature (the water, the blackbird). In addition, he gives us daily weather reports and much information about time and place, and these reports contribute to the visual quality of the book.

Like the narrator, Phaedrus (the name given the narrator's former personality) had also been interested in seeing, but the visual imagery associated with Phaedrus is often different from that of the narrator. For one thing, Phaedrus apparently did not have a motorcycle. Thus we never hear about his tinkering on his bike or analyzing it, as the narrator often does. Much of what Phaedrus sees, physically at least, seems to revolve around mountains (his real element) and isolated animals (a timber wolf, a moose, a small duck) or to be associated with his teaching or learning (the sights and sounds of his classroom at Montana State; the wall he saw in Korea; the round, cracked table at the University of Chicago).

Not only do the narrator and Phaedrus see the external world themselves, but they also try to teach others to look for themselves. The narrator mentions that people seem "trained *not* to see" (p. 5) shortly after he has pointed out some red-winged blackbirds to his son Chris, who shows no enthusiasm for them. Later, he tells a gloomy Sylvia about the blackbirds: "I was happy to see them again. They tie things together, thoughts and such. You know?" She finally responds with a smile, and the narrator thinks, "She understands a peculiar language which has nothing to do with what you are saying. A daughter" (p. 9). Even if his son does not early respond to this teaching, his "daughter" seems to begin grasping the initial stage of "seeing." Still later on this first day of the trip, the narrator is again thinking about Sylvia: "In my mind, when I look at these fields, I say to her, 'See? . . . See?' and I think she does" (p. 18).

As a rhetoric teacher, Phaedrus too had tried to make his students see for themselves. A vivid illustration involves a girl "behind . . . thick-lensed glasses" who could not think of anything to write about. He forced her to narrow her topic from "the United States" to Bozeman, Montana. When she still had writer's block, he became furious. " 'You're not *looking*!' he said. . . . 'Narrow it down to the *front* of *one* building on the main street of Bozeman. The Opera House. Start with the upper left-hand brick.' " (pp. 170–171). The method worked, and the amazed student turned in a five-thousand-word essay. She had been forced "to do some original and direct seeing"—and not to imitate what others saw.

While he has his narrator and Phaedrus put much emphasis on "direct seeing," Pirsig lets his readers know the ultimate source of the light that makes all visual imagery possible. This light, of course, is from the sun. Pirsig allocates the sunlight to his other selves in a manner generally befitting their emotional states. He has the narrator associate Phaedrus with gloomy weather or dawn or twilight or darkness. From his office window at Montana State, Phaedrus had looked at "The Madison Range and watched the storms come in" (p. 160) or had later "stared out into what had become a dark sky" (p. 163) until three o'clock in the morning. At the University of Chicago, Phaedrus sat at a round, cracked table and listened to "the ghost of Aristotle speaking down through the centuries—the desiccating lifeless voice of dualistic reason" while "the late-afternoon sun . . . hardly penetrated the window dirt . . ." (p. 326). The most brilliant image for Phaedrus is the Korean wall "shining radiantly, like a gate of heaven, across a misty harbor" (pp. 106–107), and even this is an image revealed by reflected sunlight or, perhaps, by the brilliance of Phaedrus' own nascent vision of Quality.

Pirsig allows the narrator to associate his changing emotional states with the absence or presence of the sun. This is obvious throughout the book. In addition, religious overtones sometimes creep into the narrator's words when he refers to the sun: "The rays of the sun create a cathedral effect through the pines" (p. 170). As he watches his wet socks dry on a rock, he says, "I stare at them meditatively as vapors from them rise up toward the sun"(p. 216). In fact, the narrator seems often to communicate better with the sun than with people, an irony that he does not recognize until late in the book. At the DeWeese party, several people are on the deck and the narrator sits "in the sunlight" and puts on his sunglasses and becomes "visually detached from everything but the sun and the sunlit slopes of the canyon" (p. 139). A little later, he is thinking about Phaedrus, a man "who was creatively on fire with a set of ideas no one ever heard of before" and is troubled because "DeWeese thinks that person is here now" (p. 141). Then he shifts from thought to description:

> For a brief moment, way up at the top of the ridge, the sun diffuses through the trees and a halation of the light comes down to us. The halo expands, capturing everything in a sudden flash, and suddenly it catches me too.
> "He saw too much," I say. . . .
> Now suddenly the sun is gone behind the mountains . . . [p. 141].

Thus the narrator, caught in the sun-created halo, blurts out to his confused friends his deepest fears about the madman who formerly resided in his body. Because Phaedrus "saw too much," the light went out for him just as the sun set for the narrator that day on DeWeese's deck. The episode is a clear example of Pirsig's artistic manipulation of imagery in an autobiographical book.

The visual imagery obviously changes and seems less vivid when the narrator explains Phaedrus' quest for Quality and his own attempts to bring metaphysical Quality down to earth, by "caring." If one cares enough about what he or she is doing, the narrator suggests, the duality of self and object is diminished.

"That's what caring is, a feeling of identification with what one's doing" (p. 267). Much of the imagery in these parts of the book revolves around Phaedrus' apparently gloomy life and obsessive search for Quality and the narrator's prolonged attempts to explain "stuckness" and "gumption traps," often by using his motorcycle as his image and example. Caught up in the abstractions of Phaedrus and in his own desire to teach us to avoid dualities by caring, the narrator cannot grasp the depth of his blindness regarding his son. And he cannot see that before he can have a genuine "caring" relationship with Chris, he must first come to terms with Phaedrus.

It is on this level, the emotional and personal, that visual imagery—especially of darkness and light—has its strongest impact on the reader. We are first introduced to the "ghost of Phaedrus" in a vividly dramatic manner. Late in the afternoon on their first day of the trip, three flashes of lightning break through the darkened sky to reveal a farmhouse, a windmill: ". . . oh, my God, he's *been* here! . . . throttle off . . . this is *his* road . . . a fence and trees . . ." (p. 26). We learn the name of Phaedrus that night when the narrator tells it to Chris, as they lie in the dark of their motel room (p. 33). At the end of the second day while they are in their sleeping bags near Lemmon, South Dakota, "a full moon comes up" and the narrator measures "hour after hour of semisleep" filled with "strange dreams . . . and odd fragments of memory" (p. 56). "And in the fog there appears an intimation of a figure. It disappears when I look directly, but then reappears in the corner of my vision when I turn my glance . . . It is Phaedrus. Evil spirit. Insane. From a world without life or death" (p. 57). Clearly he has neither a Quality nor a caring relationship with his previous personality which had been annihilated, we are told, by court-ordered electric shock treatments (p. 77). And with each hint of Phaedrus' reappearance, the narrator becomes more fearful of returning insanity. He tells us his eerie predicament by emphasizing vision: "I'm like a clairvoyant, a spirit medium receiving messages from another world. . . . I see things with my own eyes, and I see things with his eyes too. He once owned them. These EYES! That is the terror of it" (p. 77).

The relationship between the narrator and Phaedrus gradually becomes clearer to the reader as the journey continues and as Pirsig allows his narrator to reveal more about Phaedrus' life and thoughts—knowledge gained from dreams, from fragments of memory, from friends and family, from letters, and from volumes of notes left by Phaedrus.

It is through dream imagery that the narrator gets his strongest hints about the extent of his blindness regarding Phaedrus. After ten days on the trip, while camping with Chris in a mountainous area where Phaedrus had camped years before, the narrator tells about "a dream that has occurred often before." In the dream, he thinks he is in a "white-painted room looking at a glass door" (p. 203) that separates him from Chris and other family members. While they are again camping two nights later, the dream becomes more vivid and includes a "dark figure in a shadow" (p. 245) who keeps him separated from Chris. The next time the dream occurs, the dreamer attacks the "figure in the shadows" (p. 297) and sees its face—that of the narrator himself. Phaedrus has been doing the dreaming alone. Now, some of the narrator's blindness is dispelled. "*A mind divided against itself* . . . me . . . I'm the evil figure in the shadows" (p. 298), he says. With this insight, the narrator becomes even more fearful of reuniting with Phaedrus. All of his talk about eliminating dualities has no effect on his personal dilemma.

The fifteenth day of the trip is generally a cold, rainy one, and the "grey rainy skies" (p. 329) reflect the narrator's mood. But he doggedly finishes the story of Phaedrus' experiences at the University of Chicago and of his total insanity, the same state that he feels approaching again. He tells about Phaedrus' anger with the Greeks who had placed Reason over Quality and thus "had endowed our culture with the tendency . . . *to do what is 'reasonable' even when it isn't any good*" (pp. 323–324). Ironically, the narrator cannot see that he is following the same tendency in relation to Phaedrus. He is trying to be "reasonable" about his own painful emotional situation.

That night he and Chris almost reenact an experience they had had five years previously in Chicago, just before Phaedrus' insanity. At that time, Phaedrus and Chris were going to get some bunk beds and Phaedrus forgot where the beds were and how to get home. Six-year-old Chris guided him home (pp. 299–300). Now, just north of San Francisco, they search for a motel. They finally find one. "In the rain and the dark streets, even with directions, we almost miss it. They have turned the light out . . ." (p. 359). The imagery fits the despair of the narrator and of Chris, who tells his father that he (Phaedrus) used to be "fun" to be around. Chris even enjoyed the bunk bed episode. Thus, we now question the narrator's gloomy memories of Phaedrus, especially when Chris tells his current father, "You just sit and stare and you don't *do* anything!" (p. 361).

On the last day of the trip, visual imagery and internal perception both work together to reveal the integrative power of Quality and caring. But this integration does not take place until the worst crisis of the trip has passed. During the day, the narrator has an insight into his own hypocrisy, hypocrisy that most readers have probably sensed throughout the book: "Advice is given again and again to eliminate subject-object duality, when the biggest duality of all, the duality between me and him, remains unfaced. A mind divided against itself" (p. 363). This recognition is significant, but he is still unable or unwilling to allow the fusion of himself with Phaedrus to take place. He feels "pushed toward something and the objects in the corner of the eye and the objects in the center of the vision are all of equal intensity now, all together in one" . . . (p. 367). Phaedrus, who had earlier been seen in the "corner of [his] vision" (p. 57), has now taken his rightful position in the center—and the narrator makes the "reasonable" assumption that insanity is imminent. "Chris, you're looking at a father who was insane for a long time, and is close to it again" (p. 367).

Then he tells Chris that people are saying that Chris also has mental problems, and the boy lets out a strange cry and falls to the ground beside the foggy highway, "doubles up and kneels and rocks back and forth, head on the ground" (p. 368). A truck approaches through the fog, and the narrator fights his impulse to run and jump off the nearby cliff. At that moment, Phaedrus breaks through and speaks to Chris:

> *Everything is all right now, Chris.*
> That's not my voice.
> *I haven't forgotten you.*
> Chris's rocking stops.
> *How could I forget you* [p. 368].

Recognizing his "real" father's voice, Chris gradually responds and asks him about the "glass door" of the hospital. "A kind of slow electric shock passes through me," the narrator states (p. 369), as more of his blindness is removed when he realizes that

Phaedrus' dream had been based on reality. When Chris is assured that Phaedrus had wanted to see him, "the fog begins to lift . . . and I see the sun on his face makes his expression open in a way I've never seen it before" (p. 369). The sun, once almost belonging exclusively to the emotionally blind narrator, is now also a part of Chris's world. It now shines on an integrated father, a healing son, and a caring relationship.

The last chapter of the book confirms this observation, as the two are back on their motorcycle again. Thinking to himself, the narrator says, "That's what Phaedrus always said—*I* always said—years ago " (p. 370). He thus accepts his newly integrated personality. They take off their helmets and can now hear each other without yelling. Chris stands up on the foot pegs and looks over his father's head for the first time on the trip. "The sunlight makes strange and beautiful designs through the tree branches on the road" (p. 372). When Chris comments that he can see "everything" now, his father asks, "What do you see?" (p. 372)—rather than telling him what to see.

In his search for a "Quality" father, Chris has, ironically, been doing some of the best "seeing" on the trip, and the narrator had been too blind to understand. It now seems obvious that Pirsig planned the visual imagery of his work to complement the narrator's emotional blindness and eventual integration. Although *ZMM* is an autobiographical book, it was not written solely by "life." To paraphrase Bokonon in Vonnegut's *Cat's Cradle*, "Life never wrote a good book."[7] Life supplied Pirsig with his materials, but his own artistry gave visual form to the narrator's "feeling" that, he says, "is not just on the surface of things, but penetrates all the way through" (p. 373).

NOTES

[1] Robert M. Pirsig, *Zen and the Art of Motorcycle Maintenance* (New York: Bantam Books, 1979), p. 3. Subsequent references are to this edition and are included parenthetically.

[2] The narrator carefully blocks out the days of his journey, even telling us that they leave on a Monday (p. 9) in July (p. 4). And he tells where they spend almost every night. The only problem about discovering the exact number of days on the trip is his leaving out most of the activities of a day or parts of two days and simply saying, "For two days John and Sylvia and Chris and I loaf . . ." (p. 168) while they are at the DeWeeses. They seem to have left the Minneapolis area on Monday (Day

1), arrived at the DeWeeses on Saturday afternoon (Day 6), and loafed on Sunday (Day 7) before John and Sylvia left for Minnesota on Monday (Day 8) after which the narrator and Chris visit Montana State again. On Tuesday morning (Day 9), they begin backpacking in the mountains, spend one night there, and return to a Bozeman hotel on Wednesday night. On Thursday morning (Day 11), they see the DeWeeses before leaving for the West Coast. The book ends on a Tuesday afternoon (Day 16). By days and by chapters, *ZMM* is arranged this way: 1(1,2,3), 2(4,5),3(6,7),4(8,9,10),5(11,12),6(13,14),7 and 8(15),9(16,17,18),10(19, 20,21),11(22,23),12(24,25),13(26),14(27,28),15(29,30),16(31,32). Relating the events and the narrator's Chautauquas to days on the trip—rather than to chapters or parts of *ZMM*—can add another dimension to this book.

[3] In a note to me (January 4, 1983), Richard Rodino said that Pirsig's own abbreviated version is *ZMM*. Rodino chaired a special session on *ZMM* at the MLA meeting in New York, December 29, 1981. In a rare public appearance, Pirsig himself attended this special session, according to Rodino.

[4] Richard H. Rodino, "Irony and Earnestness in Robert Pirsig's *Zen and the Art of Motorcycle Maintenance*," *Critique*, Vol. 22 (August 1980), p. 22. This article offers a thoughtful analysis of some of the fictional complications of *ZMM*. Although Rodino says little about imagery, his analysis of the limited narrator with an "earnest" voice is a significant contribution to an understanding of *ZMM*.

[5] Even with the diversity of books we call "novels," one would have to stretch the guidelines significantly to call *ZMM* a novel. Pirsig's narrator obviously does not think of it as a novel; see p. 130 of *ZMM*.

[6] For some widely varying approaches to *ZMM*, see the following: G. Thomas Couser, "*ZMM* as Prophetic Autobiography," *Rendezvous*, Vol. 12 (Fall 1977), pp. 31–38; Scott Consigny, "Rhetoric and Madness: Robert Pirsig's Inquiry into Values," *Southern Speech Communication Journal*, Vol. 43 (Fall 1977), pp. 16–32; William C. Placher, "The Trinity and the Motorcycle," *Theology Today*, Vol. 34 (Oct. 1977), pp. 248–256; Nancy Corson Carter, "1970 Images of the Machine and the Garden: Kosinski, Crews, and Pirsig," *Soundings*, Vol. 61 (Spring 1978), pp. 105–122; Thomas J. Steele, "Zen and the Art . . .: The Identity of the Erlkönig," *Ariel*, Vol. 10 (Jan. 1979), pp. 83–93; Ronald J. Lee, "Pirsig's *ZMM*: The Fusion of Form and Content," *Western American Literature*, Vol. 14 (Fall 1979), pp. 221–226; Donald Benson, "*ZMM*: Technology Re-Valued," *Iowa Journal of Research*, Vol. 54 (Nov. 1979), pp. 267–273; Steven Weiland, "The Humanities and the Art of Motorcycle Maintenance," *Southern Humanities Review*, Vol. 14 (Fall 1980), pp. 301–309; Richard H. Rodino, "The Matrix of Journeys in *ZMM*," *Journal of Narrative Technique*, Vol. 11 (Winter 1981), pp. 53–63.

[7] Kurt Vonnegut, Jr., *Cat's Cradle* (New York: Dell Publishing Co., 1963), p. 161. Bokonon's actual words are, "God never wrote a good play in His life."

SECTION 9

BIBLIOGRAPHY OF WORKS ABOUT *ZEN AND THE ART OF MOTORCYCLE MAINTENANCE*

The earlier items of this bibliography are mostly book reviews that assumed that the reader had not yet read *Zen and the Art of Motorcycle Maintenance,* so the reviews mainly advised readers either to buy and read the book or not to. After a couple of years, after *ZMM* had become the subject of some ongoing discussion and critical publication, subsequent authors took for granted that their readers were familiar with Pirsig's book and pursued critical discourse on that assumption.

The present bibliography first lists reviews by year and journal, then some reviews that have been quoted more often along with all the critical articles by year and author.

REVIEWS
1974

America, Vol. 130 (May 25, 1974), p. 420.
Booklist, Vol. 70 (July 15, 1974), p. 1227.
Book World, (May 19, 1974), pp. 1–2.
Choice, Vol. 11 (July 1974), p. 774.
Commentary, Vol. 58 (October 1974), pp. 87–91.

Commonweal, Vol. 100 (August 23, 1974), pp. 461–462, and Vol. 101 (December 6, 1974), pp. 242–243.
Economic Survey, Vol. 253 (November 30, 1974), p. 9.
Kirkus Review, Vol. 42 (March 1, 1974), p. 285.
Library Journal, Vol. 99 (May 1, 1974), p. 1287, and (October 15, 1974), p. 2753.
London Magazine, Vol. 14, No. 5 (December 1974–January 1975), pp. 136–138.
New Leader, Vol. 57 (May 27, 1974), pp. 15–17.
New Republic, Vol. 171 (December 21, 1974), pp. 24–26.
New Statesman, Vol. 88 (November 15, 1974), p. 709.
Newsweek, Vol. 83, No. 17 (April 29, 1974), p. 95; Vol. 83, No. 22 (June 3, 1974), pp. 76–79; and Vol. 84, No. 27 (December 30, 1974), p. 63.
New York Times Book Review (December 1, 1974), p. 76.
Observer (October 27, 1974), p. 30.
Psychology Today, Vol. 8, No. 3 (August 1974), pp. 12–14.
Publishers Weekly, Vol. 205 (February 11, 1974), p. 59.
Spectator, Vol. 233 (December 14, 1974), p. 764.
Time, Vol. 103, No. 15 (April 15, 1974), p. 99, and Vol. 104, No. 27 (December 30, 1974), p. 57.
Village Voice, Vol. 19 (April 11, 1974), p. 25.
Wall Street Journal, Vol. 183 (June 13, 1974), p. 16.

1975

Books and Bookmen, Vol. 20 (September 1975), p. 43.
Book World, (July 13, 1975), p. 3.
Christian Century, Vol. 92 (April 30, 1975), p. 448.
Cycle World, (February 1975), pp. 30, 34.
Front, Vol. 18 (Summer 1975), pp. 119–120.
New York Times Book Review (March 30, 1975), p. 6.
Publishers Weekly, Vol. 207 (February 17, 1975), p. 82.

1976

Communication Quarterly, Vol. 24 (1976), pp. 49–51.
Observer (March 7, 1976), p. 26.

1977

New Society, Vol. 39 (February 17, 1977), pp. 346–347.

1978

National Forum, Vol. 58 (Spring 1978), p. 44.

1979

English Journal, Vol. 68 (March 1979), p. 95.

CRITICAL ARTICLES
1974

Adams, Robert M. "Good Trip." *New York Review of Books,* Vol. 11, No. 10 (June 13, 1974), pp. 22–23.

The reviewer suggests that *ZMM* always seems precariously close to disaster because of its picaresque character and its great diversity, but concludes that its strength is in its capacity to disturb the reader rather than ingratiate itself with him. The Chautauquas, the "inquiry into values" of the title, turn the narrator into an Ancient Mariner reciting the intellectual and spiritual autobiography of his quest for a definition or reason larger than can be built of reasonable materials. The ideas of the Chautauqua, in themselves fragile and precious, are hateful in terms of the plot because they ignore Chris, the narrator's only human tie. Adams notes the twin troubles—between the narrator and Phaedrus, and between the narrator and Chris. He ascribes the former to paranoia and self-pity and describes the Chicago University breakdown as melodramatic nearly to the point of comedy. He identifies Chris as the fundamental source of value and Phaedrus as the answer to the narrator's problems but seems baffled by the reason for this outcome.

Hoffman, Eva. "*ZMM.*" *Commentary,* Vol. 58 (1974), pp. 87–91.

The reviewer compares *ZMM* with Annie Dillard's *Pilgrim at Tinker Creek* in that, like Thoreau, the authors try to free their thinking from prejudice. Hoffman immensely prefers Dillard to Pirsig, thinking that *ZMM* tries too hard, solves pseudoproblems, oversimplifies, and loses judgment because of the narrator's isolation. It is a hostile reading.

Lehmann-Haupt, Christopher. "The Motorcycles of Your Mind," *New York Times* (April 16, 1974), p. 37.

The mixing of philosophical inquiry and autobiography makes *ZMM* a special book. For overt plot, there is the narrator's trip with the troubled son; for psychological interest, the cat-and-mouse game with Phaedrus; and for intellectual entertainment, the question of the status of Quality as a solution to the modern world's impasses with technology.

Lhamon, W. T., Jr. "A Fine Fiction." *New Republic*, Vol. 170 (June 29, 1974), pp. 24–26.

Pirsig searches, this reviewer says, for a vision or voice that is not partial but whole, not a compromise between opposites but a reconciliation that yokes both powers. The important dichotomies are mythos versus insanity, machine versus garden, and technology versus life. Lhamon prefers the end to all else, relishing Phaedrus' voice speaking through the narrator. He notes, on the one hand, the destructive rationality of Greek philosophy and the reaction to it that turns Phaedrus into Ahab and, on the other hand, the movement away from the feminine (land, woman) into the thought, thought, thought that turns the narrator into J. Alfred Prufrock.

Steiner, George. "Uneasy Rider." *New Yorker*, Vol. 50, No. 8 (April 15, 1974), pp. 147–150.

Steiner's seminal essay ascribes the book's shift from the very personal and confessional to the rigidly impersonal to its American Manichaeism. He explores the book's background of mythology, literature, and history of ideas. He discusses various views of Chris—as Saint Christopher, Hercules among the centaur-motorcyclists, and the *Kind* in Goethe's "Erlkönig."

Times Literary Supplement. "On the Road with Aristotle." London *Times Literary Supplement*, No. 3763 (April 19, 1974), pp. 405–406.

The anonymous reviewer (R.C. Zaehner) especially admires the way the book's title joins Phaedrus and the narrator, but he often confuses Pirsig with the narrator (a common failing) and even Phaedrus. The breakdown at Chicago University is "the mystic's usual grave"; the capital letters used just before that event are taken to be symptomatic.

Todd, Richard. "Praise God from Whom All Ball Bearings Flow." *Atlantic Monthly*, Vol. 234, No. 3 (September 1974), pp. 92–94.

Todd calls the book alternately inspired and banal, "both long-winded and laconic." He describes the Faustian Phaedrus at the University of Chicago misreading the classics of Greek philosophy, dropping into "heated personal quarrels that almost surely existed only in Phaedrus' mind but are reported as though they had occurred in fact," and finally crashing psychologically. Todd has a problem distinguishing author and narrator, whom he describes as moving through life gingerly and exercising a reverence toward machines that generates a "technological theology." Todd claims that the author-narrator lacks "a developed sense of the inevitable mutuality of experience."

1975

Basalla, George. "Man and Machine." *Science,* Vol. 187 (January 24, 1975), pp. 248–250.

Basalla says only in the twentieth century has there been any systematic study of the effects of technology (as old as mankind) or the effects of science (several centuries old). Such study shows the Western world is not unified and that we need to reconcile the subject-object and knowing-valuing dualities so we can move beyond the illusion that science and technology are value-free and give ourselves a chance at finding Quality. As it stands, *ZMM* applies to individuals rather than to assembly plants full of workers mass-producing items in a context where "quality control" means bare-minimum standards; but the book opens the way to a more satisfactory approach to the problems and to the possibility of redirecting technology to worthy social goals.

Schuldenfrei, Richard. Review of *ZMM. Harvard Educational Review,* Vol. 45 (1975), pp. 95–103.

Granted that *ZMM* is in a way novel and autobiography, Schuldenfrei studies it as "an inquiry into values," a philosophical exploration. Alternating from abstract principles to concrete examples, the book explores scientific rationality and its relation to the good. Though people generally favor the physical products of technology, they often dislike both the processes themselves and their by-products (pollutants both physical and emotional, aesthetic, and spiritual). This critic's summary traces the development of the idea of Quality from the naïve scientific method of Hume and Mill to today's thought (Thomas Kuhn, Richard Gregory, Ernst Gombrich, Max Wartofsky, E. A. Burtt). Schuldenfrei notes that many of the Chautauqua's principles are inapplicable in our complex mass society and, identifying author and narrator, accuses Pirsig of being a partisan of William James's subjectivist and individualist pragmatism.

1976

Coe, Richard. "Zen and the Art of Rhetoric." *Rhetorical Society Quarterly,* Vol. 6 (1976), pp. 66–67.

This critic uses *ZMM* as the central text for a course in contemporary rhetorical theory because it makes the right assumption—that perceiving, thinking, and communicating are closely related levels of a single process—and therefore asks the right questions, though it gives the wrong answers. The theme of Part I is perceptual relativity owing to diverse root metaphors (Kenneth Burke); the theme of Part II is technology and scientific method. Coe then discusses Quality, method, and content in Aristotle and other Greek questions. Coe accuses author, narrator, and book of philosophical idealism, but citing Gregory Bateson he admits that Western dualistic rationality is a form of paranoid schizophrenia.

Crusius, Tim. "In Praise of Pirsig's *ZMM*." *Western Journal of Speech Communication*, Vol. 40 (1976), pp. 168–177.

Crusius chooses to subordinate the discussion about Western dichotomies, which Pirsig places up front in the Chautauquas, to emphasize the technical and formal side of *ZMM* so that we can see the book's movement though all divisions to wholeness—as a modern Jungian instance of the archetypal quest. Thus *ZMM* is a discovery-event; the immediacy of the present-tense narrative plays off against the narrator's evoking and judging Phaedrus' ideas—often negatively. When we remember the divided nature of the narrative, we see that the book is neither essay nor novel. The narrator's reaction to his Phaedrus-dream leads to avoidance and obsession (fascination) rather than to confrontation and burial.

Parker, Richard B. "A Review of *ZMM* with Some Remarks on the Teaching of Law." *Rutgers Law Review*, Vol. 29 (1976), pp. 318–331.

Parker uses *ZMM* as a guide to a better way of teaching law—or anything else. The good teacher helps the student learn to *do* with confidence what the teacher does; the student does not become a disciple, permanently dependent. Parts I and II of the book ask what is best, leading to the question of Quality. Parker admires Pirsig's use of analogies (like the Bergsonian railroad train) to make abstractions concrete. Good teaching is not just imparting objective and abstract information, nor is it just presenting one's own actual experience; it is the sort of blend of the one and the other that *ZMM* is.

Perry, Joan Ellen. "Visions of Reality: Values and Perspectives in the Prose of Carlos Castaneda, Robert M. Pirsig, Ursula K. LeGuin, James Purdy, Cyrus Colter, and Sylvia Plath." Dissertation, University of Wisconsin, 1976; also in *Dissertation Abstracts International*, Vol. 37, No. 9 (1977), p. 5818A.

Whereas rigid human subjectivity rejects the unknown, a more flexible psyche can adopt values that thoroughly change its perspectives. If it recognizes that its own unconscious (by definition part of the unknown) is an ally rather than an enemy, this enlarged consciousness can become more optimistic about the personal and cultural future.

Primeau, Ronald. "Regeneration and Motorcycle Maintenance in *Paradise Lost*." In John Karl Franson, ed., *Milton Reconsidered* (Salzburg: Salzburg University Press, 1976), pp. 103–121.

ZMM serves Primeau as a jumping-off point for an article showing that "Milton's literary career rejected the dualism that pervades western thought."

Wagner, Tony. "A Second Look at Motorcycle Maintenance and Zen." *Humanist*, Vol. 36 (1976), pp. 45–46.

Asking why *ZMM* is so widely popular, Wagner notes that it has a clear, craftsmanly style; a deep and thought-provoking concern with technology (motorcycles) and important philosophical questions; and the suspense of a good thriller. Wagner suggests that the book lacks conscience because the narrator offers no explicit apology for his poor relationship with Chris, preferring instead pure thought in isolation from the world, without modesty or compassion.

1977

Brodsky, Stanley L. "Go Away—I'm Looking for the Truth: Research Utilization in Corrections." *Criminal Justice and Behavior*, Vol. 4 (1977), pp. 3–10.

Several factors lead to the successful application of theoretical research in any correctional institution; mainly, one should know in practice what "good" means and have some idea of what "better" would be. Brodsky's editorial encourages using Phaedrus' guidelines for creative organizational change. He imagines what Phaedrus would pronounce as his principles: Don't get stuck; ask answerable questions; entrust the power to reform only to good people; learn from successful people; select on the basis of Quality; feel free to fail; learn to live with some frustration; go for long-range values like peace of mind.

Consigny, Scott. "Rhetoric and Madness: Robert Pirsig's Inquiry into Values." *Southern Speech Communication Journal*, Vol. 43 (1977), pp. 16–32.

We are alienated owing to a crisis in Western rationality that we can neither flee nor finesse; this crisis invaded the life of Phaedrus/the narrator in the form of madness. By a new integration of art and technology exemplified in tuning the bike, the narrator constructs a working alternative to the old rationality, a sort of aesthetics to replace the traditional epistemology that commonly presupposed that the objective was real and that subjective states were somehow bogus. A working worldview based on caring leads to personal sanity and can lead to a truly human control of technology; a correlating rhetoric of that new sanity would identify the emotions as ways of engagement with the world, aids to knowing and choosing. Such a rhetoric would supplant the adversarial world of Socrates and Plato, for whom dialectic—the union-in-conflict of two persons struggling for truth—is the highest form of love. Consigny comments on a broad range of earlier criticism.

Couser, G. Thomas. "*ZMM* as Prophetic Biography." *Rendezvous*, Vol. 12 (1977), pp. 31–38.

Autobiography is a term that fits more uneasily and paradoxically with "Zen" than with either "art" or "motorcycle maintenance." *ZMM* is a very American book because it is prophetic autobiography. It creates an exemplary didactic pattern out of a mix of personal and cultural history. The motorcycle's hereness and nowness, contrasted with the "reality" of TV, appears in present tense; the motorcycle, which is both designer's idea and physical reality, serves to unify inner and outer journeys and ultimately, for Chris's sake, all the other dichotomies as well.

Goldstein, Jeffrey. "Spiritualization of Technology: A New Vision for the 1970's." *Drew Gateway*, Vol. 48, No. 2 (1977), pp. 26–31.

ZMM and the films *2001*, *Star Wars*, and *Close Encounters of the Third Kind* show a new understanding of technology in which it is a medium of the merciful aspect of the sacred absolute, not an evil, destructive, and antihuman force. Goldstein deals mainly with *Close Encounters*.

Placher, William C. "The Trinity and the Motorcycle." *Theology Today*, Vol. 34 (1977), pp. 248–256.

ZMM states that technology and value are split and can be joined again only if our culture accepts a new metaphysical basis, an expanded intellectuality that affirms the preconceptual. But Phaedrus' Quality *as idea* becomes a romantic night in which all cows are black, where all distinctions among particulars are illusory or at least relative, and thus seems to defeat the coprinciple of caring. Augustine placed the Trinity (as intelligibility and value) at the heart of his thought to solve a similar impasse in Neoplatonism. Pirsig's successful identification of today's need suggests that a fresh look at the Trinity will safeguard structured intelligibility and real value.

Pritscher, Conrad. "Some Comparisons Between Gestalt Educators and Pirsig's View of Pre-Socratic Philosophers." *Philosophical Studies in Education* (1977), pp. 81–86.

Positing responsibility and freedom generates the fundamental ideas of Gestalt theory. In that context, the pre-Socratic philosophers mentioned in *ZMM* are found to be at the root of Western assumptions that authentic knowledge requires a definable object—leaving problematic all preconceptual and preverbal Quality experiences, which are based on caring.

Stark, John. "*ZMM*." *Great Lakes Review*, Vol. 3 (1977), pp. 50–59.

The characteristically American power of *ZMM* stems from the narrator's eventual acceptance of his former self, Phaedrus. Phaedrus' derivation of Greek cultural history and therefore Western civilization renders this sequence: prehistoric Quality, archaic mythos (communal context), Sophistic rhetoric, Socratic-Platonic dialectic, Aristotelian formal logic. If we are to make sense of the narrator's acceptance of Phaedrus, from whom he is separated by what Stark infers are two bouts of mental illness, this acceptance must occur *within* the mythos. Stark refers to Leo Marx's critical study *The Machine in the Garden* and the writings of Emerson, Thoreau, Melville, and Twain, concluding that Phaedrus as literary symbol is a better answer to the problems posed than Quality as idea.

1978

Allis, Una. "*ZMM.*" *Critical Quarterly*, Vol. 20 (Autumn 1978), pp. 33–41.

Since literary realism assumes the tally of thought and language with the object, it is not congenial with the alienated and relativized contemporary world; but Pirsig uses realism in *ZMM* and succeeds. The book is both a romantic epic with an interior landscape and battleground (the overt plot in present tense and the intellectual autobiography—the narrative connected with the Chautauqua—mostly in past tense) and a philosophical search for the point of bifurcation, the Greek discovery of the self and the consequent separation of self from community. The experience of trip and Chautauqua together leads to a complete reversal of roles at the end of the novel: Anomaly becomes norm, the glass door becomes reality, insane becomes sane, and the objectified past personality becomes subjectivity. Allis concludes that Pirsig is no naïve realist (positivist), that instead he incorporates realism, redeems it for his tale, and earns his happy ending.

Carter, Nancy Corson. "1970 Images of the Machine in the Garden." *Soundings* (1978), pp. 105–122.

Carter subjects Crew's *Car*, Kosinski's *Being There*, and Pirsig's *ZMM* to analysis in terms of the intrusive machine in nature's virginal garden. Americans say they want to worship nature, but American history shows we worship machines. Since the machine is an instrument of a human being, a reconciliation is possible—luckily so, since it is necessary and urgent. Unlike *Car*'s bizarre iconoclasm or *Being There*'s ironic reunion, by traveling west to arrive at the East, *ZMM* reconciles Western rationality with Eastern religious intuition. Once the narrator has retrieved Phaedrus' enlightened "understanding from outside" of our disjunctive, technology-producing mythos, he has mastered it, can use it for personal reintegration, and can offer it for cultural use.

Del Col, Jeffrey Anthony. "Early Clues for the New Direction? The Technocratic Myth in Pynchon and Pirsig." Dissertation, University of West Virginia, 1978; also in *Dissertation Abstracts International*, Vol. 39, No. 7 (1979), p. 4239A.

The contemporary world's myth of technology perceives humanity and the rest of the world solely in empirical, pragmatic, positivist, and behavioral ways. It separates human knowledge from human interests. Today's literature needs to grapple with the technological myth and critique it morally. Del Col presents Pynchon as a deep pessimist and Pirsig as a naïve optimist. Like many other critics, Del Col does not discriminate among the three "I" voices of *ZMM*, author, narrator, and Phaedrus. He seems to dislike both the classical-Aristotelian narrator and the romantic-Platonic Phaedrus, accusing them ("Pirsig") of superficially identifying the technology problem and hence of failing to give any solution.

Krus, David J., and Patricia H. Krus. "Contributions to Psychohistory: III. Measuring Value Systems As Related to Societal Change." *Psychological Reports*, Vol. 43 (1978), pp. 3–9.

These researchers formulated a questionnaire out of *ZMM* sentences on value and tabulated it statistically along with Charles Reich's *The Greening of America* and various scales that index Apollonian (Consciousness I and II) and Dionysian (Consciousness III and *ZMM*) orientations to explore how values are presently changing.

Plank, Robert. "*ZMM*: The Voyage As a Quest for Self-Discovery." *Exploration*, Vol. 5 (1978), pp. 33–43.

The narrator thinks he is more different from Phaedrus than he is. His travel, modeled after Goethe's "Erlkönig," to recover his own lost past (Phaedrus) results finally in a euphoric self-unification; but this at-one-ment is unconvincing because his selective memory of the poem, in which the father himself must in some manner be ghost and potential killer both, throws doubt on the narrator's present sanity and on Phaedrus' Chicago University experience.

Sacks, M. "*ZMM*." *Psychoanalytic Review*, Vol. 65 (1978), pp. 351–352.

The technology that concerns the author includes not only motorcycles but also electroconvulsive therapy. The motorcycle is not only a narcissistic representation but also the beginning of a self-versus-object differentiation and thereby a transitional object for relating to others. Phaedrus' quest on behalf of his students ended with only the idea of an answer and psychotic catatonia; the narrator's full recovery requires him to retrace in memory the road to psychosis and thereby explore its meaning.

Staudenmaier, John M., S.J. "*ZMM*." *Technology and Culture*, Vol. 19 (1978), pp. 257–259.

This brief review article compares *ZMM* and John Jerome's *Truck*, preferring the former. *ZMM* takes the reader along on a triple journey—geographical, by motorcycle; familial, by psychological relationship; and intellectual, by autobiographical memory. The reviewer especially applauds the complete and subtle inquiry into the mental process of technological creation.

1979

Benson, Donald. "*ZMM:* Technology Re-Valued." *Iowa State Journal of Research*, Vol. 54 (1979), pp. 267–273.

Because they lead to alienation, Pirsig totally rejects the dualistic foundations of the scientific revolution, including especially mind-versus-body and values-versus-technology. Instead, mind and nature are expressions of a single prior reality, and technology, the historical interaction of man and nature, is a realm in which man discovers and expresses value.

Brabner, George. "A Link Between the Arts and the Sciences? B.F. Skinner's Concept of Contingencies of Reinforcement." *Psychological Record*, Vol. 29 (1979), pp. 57–64.

The behaviorist notion of reinforcement as applied to *ZMM* and Tom Robbins's *Another Roadside Attraction* suggests that most literature distorts human reality by separating being from doing and by using metaphors unscientifically.

Cawelti, John G. "Ringer to Sheehy to Pirsig: The 'Greening' of American Ideals of Success." *Journal of American Culture*, Vol. 2 (1979), pp. 147–161.

Charles Reich's notion that Consciousness I (self-made man) and II (organization man) have yielded to III (liberated man) may be premature. Cawelti studies Ringer's *Winning Through Intimidation*, Sheehy's *Passages*, and Pirsig's *ZMM* and concludes that personal success in overcoming crises with no transcendent help is still paramount in popular writing. *ZMM*'s exploration and quest for wholeness within—not transcendent escape from—a fragmented culture places the book in dialogue with *Walden*.

Lee, Ronald J. "Pirsig's *ZMM:* The Fusion of Form and Content." *Western American Literature*, Vol. 14 (1979), pp. 221–226.

Indefinable Quality must be embodied in the events of the plot as indefinable Zen is in archery or calligraphy. The novel asserts the inefficacy of mere philosophical discussion; one must *do*—live and experience—a holistic life, since to conceptualize the holistic is to foster the very subject-object dualism that prevents it.

Steele, Thomas J., S.J. "*ZMM:* The Identity of the Erlkönig." *Ariel*, Vol. 10 (1979), pp. 83–93.

The narrator (who must always be differentiated from the historical Pirsig even more than from Phaedrus) first correlates the persons in *ZMM* with the characters in Goethe's "Erlkönig," identifying himself as the father, Chris as the son, and Phaedrus as the lethal ghost. As the book proceeds, the narrator gradually perceives that he is the Alderking. By the end of the story, he has overcome the Phaedrus-narrator dichotomy, has again become Phaedrus without ceasing to be narrator, and sees that Chris—Christopher, Christ-bearer—"has been carrying me."

1980

Gilgen, Albert R., and Jae Hyung Cho. "Comparison of Performance on the East-West Questionnaire, Zen Scale, and Consciousness I, II, and III Scales." *Psychological Reports*, Vol. 47 (1980), pp. 583–588.

The authors got 140 college students to take five questionnaires: one designed to measure Eastern and Western views of reality and man-in-the-world, another derived from the Oriental themes of *ZMM*, and a third, fourth, and fifth derived from Reich's *The Greening of America* for testing Consciousness I (individualism), II (organization), and III (co-operative personal relationships). East-West, *ZMM*, and Con III scores correlated positively, but Con I and II scores did not correlate negatively as had been predicted.

Krus, David J., and Harold S. Blackman. "Contributions to Psychohistory: V. East-West Dimensions of Ideology Measured by Transtemporal Cognitive Matching." *Psychological Reports*, Vol. 47 (1980), pp. 947–955.

The recent romantic revival closely resembles the original romantic movement in its way of structuring reality, its styles of thought, and its preference for and support of certain social movements. The authors measured the similar cognitive structures of late-eighteenth and late-twentieth-century romanticism by using Goethe's *The Sorrows of Young Werther*, and Reich's *The Greening of America*, Pirsig's *ZMM*, Apollonian-Dionysian cognitive scales, and East-West value scales.

Rodino, Richard H. "Irony and Earnestness in Robert Pirsig's *ZMM*." *Critique: Studies in Modern Fiction*, Vol. 22 (1980), pp. 21–31.

Irony generated by the contrast between the Chautauqua and the action of *ZMM* provides the book's postmodern strength and richness but occasions much confusion in interpretation. The reader must distinguish among Pirsig, Phaedrus, and the narrator and not let the narrator's limited and partial perspective fool him into taking his voice as normative. All the dichotomies need to be dissolved, but especially that between

Phaedrus and the narrator, so that the reconstituted father can bridge the gap between Chris's mute or clumsily expressed love and understanding and the narrator's silent absorption in his thoughts, even when his thoughts concern his son.

Tokarski, Stanislaw. "Zen i psychidelika [Zen and Psychedelics]." *Przegląd Socjologiczny*, Vol. 32 (1980), pp. 243–269.

This Polish-language article is said to discuss the role of Zen in the United States counterculture, examining its history and functions and studying the central place of satori. The hippie subculture described a biochemical "satori" around 1960; Pirsig describes a similar enlightenment in *ZMM*.

Weiland, Steven. "The Humanities and the Art of Motorcycle Maintenance." *Southern Humanities Review*, Vol. 14 (1980), pp. 301–309.

The humanities are open to two apparently opposed defenses: They are value-centered and therefore personally relevant, or they are logical and scholarly. Any good novel, though, joins the two. Weiland summarizes some parts of *ZMM*; he appeals to A. R. Ammons's poem "He Held Radical Light" to elucidate the struggle that led to Phaedrus' breakdown; and he concludes that *ZMM* does not explain humanistic knowing, either scholarly or everyday, so much as it embodies it.

1981

Bernstein, Gene M. "*ZMM* as Quest Romance." Paper delivered at the Modern Language Association national convention, December 29, 1981.

As quest-romance—a narrative of an urgent journey, despite an obstacle, to an all-important goal—*ZMM* operates on four symbolic levels: the physical-geographical, the psychological (narrator-Phaedrus and father-son), the metaphysical-philosophical, and the spiritual-religious. Bernstein's article shows how links forged from level to level help the story move to a successful finish on all four levels simultaneously.

Binion, Rudolph. *Soundings: Psychohistorical and Psycholiterary* (New York: Psychohistory Press, 1981), pp. 116–121.

Pirsig's story moves west to get East, crossing a map of wholeness in order to reconcile reason and nonreason. On behalf of an entire culture yearning for unity, it attempts to find nature and human spirit fused in the indefinable Quality-event. *ZMM* is a more complex and satisfactory multilevel treatment of images of nature and technology than *Car* or *Being There*.

Chaney, Norman. "Pirsig's Piety for the Age of Aquarius." *Renascence*, Vol. 33 (1981), pp. 162–171.

Our anxiety about alienation from ourselves, from others, and from the world leads us to Zen. While admitting that analysis is inevitable, the book emphasizes the experiential aspects of Zen rather than the theoretical. Chaney objects to the book's final vagueness about Quality, the narrator's disdain for the value of persons, and the book's coolness to religion, suggesting that an impersonal and imminent Absolute will leave the self cut off from the world and multiplex in itself.

Oates, Mary I. "Vroom at the Bottom: *Zen* and the Art of English Composition." Paper delivered at the Modern Language Association national convention, December 29, 1981.

Oates found *ZMM* a "good read" and discovered that it conveyed good ideals and had good effects on her own work, but she found that she could not pass those benefits along to her students; she used *ZMM* as a reader for college remedial and conditional composition classes. Questions she found effective are included in Section 10 of this guidebook.

Raymond, Michael W. "Generic Schizophrenia in *ZMM*." *CEA Critic*, Vol. 43 (1981), pp. 18–25.

Confusion about certain parts of *ZMM* leads naturally to confusion about the whole. The book's apparent tangle of different threads is symptomatic of the split personality of contemporary culture. That sort of autobiography joins fiction and history so the reader can attain an "imaginative comprehension of another's historic identity"; thus the book features a persona who serves as narrator, lecturer, and protagonist; a diversity of styles; and a multitude of mythic allusions and references. In the end, however, the dichotomies converge.

Rodino, Richard H. "Introduction to Interpretation and Application of Robert M. Pirsig's *ZMM*." Address delivered at the Modern Language Association national convention, December 29, 1981.

Introducing the special MLA section on December 29, 1981, Rodino welcomed the participants and author Robert M. Pirsig, surveyed the academic fields that treated *ZMM*, and spoke of the developments of the papers by Oates, Sorrentino, Bump, and Bernstein.

———. "The Matrix of Journeys in *ZMM*." *Journal of Narrative Technique*," Vol. 11 (1981), pp. 53–63.

Only a sophisticated reading will reveal *ZMM*'s ironies and the complex unity of its four plots: the overt geographical journey, the pilgrimage to the theory of Quality, the quest for Phaedrus, and the progress toward a satisfactory father-son relationship. Naturally, change in one plot usually causes change in another, often the ironic opposite of what might be expected. The article explores some of the connections among the different levels of action.

Sebouhian, George. "From Abraham and Isaac to Bob Slocum and My Boy: Why Fathers Kill Their Sons." *Twentieth Century Literature*, Vol. 27 (1981), pp. 43–52.

This article treats *ZMM* in the context of numerous stories about fathers who kill or almost kill their sons, from Abraham and Isaac in Genesis, Chapter 22, through *Billy Budd* to Joseph Heller's *Something Happened*. Owing to Phaedrus' dream-emergence, the narrator's realization that "I'm not giving [Chris] strength. . . . I'm killing him" enables him to fade out and allow Phaedrus to take over a reintegrated single paternal personality.

Singer, Barnett. "Reflections on Robert Pirsig." *Durham University Journal*, Vol. 73 (1981), pp. 213–219.

Today's central question is, How can people in the modern age relate to technology morally? Singer posits that an obedient commitment within an almost pragmatic religion can lift one's life to a new level. He uses John Dewey, Theodore Roszak, Arthur Clarke, Allen Ginsberg, Tom Wolfe's Las Vegas, and giant chemical plants as vantage points to comment not so much on *ZMM* as on the American mind.

Sorrentino, Paul. "Using Pirsig's *ZMM* to Teach the Nature of Objectivity in Scientific and Technical Writing." Paper delivered at the Modern Language Association national convention, December 29, 1981.

Pirsig attacks implicit assumptions about literary, philosophical, and scientific knowledge and discourse by asserting that objectivity is an illusion. Galileo, Descartes, Locke, nineteenth-century empiricism, and twentieth-century logical positivism closed "objective" disciplines to feelings and values. Pirsig looks back to the Greeks for the start of the dissociation in human consciousness, but he moves forward to quote Heisenberg, "Method and object can no longer be separated." Therefore, science, like *ZMM*, is "An Inquiry into Values."

1982

Abbey, Edward. "Reviewing *ZMM*." In *Down the River* (New York: E. P. Dutton, 1982), pp. 199–202.

If imitation is the sincerest form of flattery, parody is the most enjoyable form of criticism. Abbey claims he subcontracted the writing of this review to Dave Harleyson, a member of the Southern Arizona Road Huns and a world-class virtuoso in using the bluest of bikers' language.

Bolin, Meb. "The Independent, Simultaneous Development of Instrumental Thought in Various Disciplines." *Journal of Economic Issues*, Vol. 17 (1983), pp. 345–352.

Clarence Ayres, Jacob Bronowski, and Pirsig, says Bolin, have independently formulated variants of instrumentalism, a Deweyite anticeremonialism that judges truth and goodness only in terms of pragmatic life-enhancing workability and that does not need to separate value from science (as does logical positivism).

Brugger, Winfried. "Max Weber und der American Way of Life." *Stimmen der Zeit*, Vol. 20 (1983), pp. 779–784.

A German reader, Brugger says, finds a second book hidden within *ZMM* that might be called "Max Weber and the American Way of Life" or "Max Weber as Motorcycle Builder and Buddhist Monk." For the narrator and Chris, the trip west is an escape from scientific America and its false promise of a meaningful life. Meaning originates not in theory but in our hearts, minds, and hands during our relationships with each other and with technologized nature. Max Weber (1864–1920), the great German sociologist of religion and theoretician of the social sciences, got psychically ill, then recovered, but ultimately lost out; Phaedrus officially dies—but not completely.

Bump, Jerome. "Creativity, Rationality, and Metaphor in Robert Pirsig's *ZMM*." *The South Atlantic Quarterly*, Vol. 82 (1983), pp. 370–380. (See Rodino, 1981a.)

Rational intelligence is not the same as Aristotelian logic. The creativity of genius is often characterized by both—and also by metaphors and odd rebellions against either-or thinking. The One and the approach to the One are better described by holistic analogies than by dead literal discourse, so Pirsig turns to such images as ghosts, horses, churches, mountains, and avalanches.

Cullis, Tara Elizabeth. "Literature of Rupture: Science and Literature in the Twentieth Century." Dissertation, University of Wisconsin, 1983; also in *Dissertation Abstracts International*, Vol. 44 (1983), p. 1782.

Literature is such an alien in our technological world that when it reflects science it does so more in its form than in its content. This formal representation shows rupture within characters, especially artist-heroes, and in society, especially by undermining structures of authority and meaning. Among the many authors and books Cullis studies, *ZMM* is rare in that it treats science as content and technologist as hero.

Shearon, Forrest B. "Visual Imagery and Internal Awareness in Pirsig's *ZMM*." *Kentucky Philological Association Bulletin: Best Papers* (1983), pp. 53–62.

The article offers a thorough treatment of seeing, both literally and as a symbol of emotional awareness. The unreliable narrator, who is not identical with Pirsig the author, does not see as well as he thinks he does. He sees the technological world pretty well, but he relates to it better than he does to people. Caring diminishes visuality and its distancing of object from subject.

1984

Gross, Beverly. "A Mind Divided Against Itself: Madness in *ZMM*." *Journal of Narrative Technique*, Vol. 14 (1984), pp. 201–213.

ZMM dramatizes the human need to synthesize potential greatness (Phaedrus) with normalcy (narrator). The narrator's Chautauquas, which cohere symbolically and nearly allegorically with the plot, are unsuccessful avoidance measures, for his attempts to bury Phaedrus lead luckily to resurrection and union with the narrator. The latter never gives in to "stuckness," but paradoxically it is only when he gives in to what he supposes is madness that he finds authenticity.

Hayles, N. Katherine. "Drawn to the Web: The Quality of Rhetoric in Pirsig's *ZMM*." In *The Cosmic Web* (Ithaca: Cornell University Press, 1984), pp. 63–84.

ZMM experiments with three rhetorics to express preverbal Quality. For Phaedrus, the most nearly suitable is the Sophists' rhetoric of Good, but his mystical ecstasy (or insanity; the reader has his choice) leaves only an offstage Phaedrus as the rhetorical equivalent of unspoken Quality. The narrator's more complex rhetoric strives not to baffle the rational mind but to find the Buddha within analytic, scientific, technological, linear thought; his verb tenses, however, separate experience into past Quality-event and present Chautauqua, which creates and reinforces duality. The author and reader, who are aware of more than Phaedrus and narrator are, should realize by a third sort of rhetoric that when the offstage Phaedrus comes onstage, this book on preverbal Quality must end.

Tiechert, Marilyn Chandler. "A Healing Art: Autobiography and the Poetics of Crisis." Dissertation, Princeton University, 1984; also in *Dissertation Abstracts International*, Vol. 45, No. 10 (1984), p. 3130A.

Autobiography can enable a writer to recover from personal crisis and restructure his self-image. His narrative perspective toward the past can aid health; moreover, his narrative form can help him to perceive and symbolize his past in a new way and achieve wholeness. In *ZMM* and six other works of the last sixty years, art and therapy merge in such a way that literature reacts on life.

1986

Burnham, Christopher C. "Heroes Obscured: *ZMM*." *South Dakota Review*, Vol. 24 (1986), pp. 151–160.

The historical Phaedrus was the first-century A.D. Greek freedman who retold Aesop's fables in Latin and introduced their chatty moralizing narrator. He offers Burnham occasion to retell the plot of *ZMM* and comment on it as a tale of transcendence, where Quality overcomes many divisions, especially triplets like the three voices of narrator, Phaedrus, and storyteller, which finally merge as the real father reasserts himself.

George, Roger Allen. "The Transcendental Traveler." Dissertation, University of Washington, 1986; also in *Dissertation Abstracts International*, Vol. 47, No. 12 (1986), p. 4390A.

The subjective autobiographical travel narrative is a distinctly American subgenre that tests spiritual ideals during a journey to personal conversion. From Parkman and Muir to Pirsig and Least Heat Moon, New England Transcendentalism has strongly influenced both form and content. Despite the associative looseness of the narrative and the seeming randomness of its events, the work is carefully crafted to get the reader to reexperience the journey and thereby share the conversion.

Rodino, Richard H. "Robert Pirsig." In Larry McCaffrey, ed., *Postmodern Fiction* (New York: Greenwood Press, 1986), pp. 483–486.

This is a brief treatment of the author's career and the book's origin, development, and success. Since the center of the book is the father-son relationship, the completion of all its threads is the father's ability finally to love and share.

1987

Smith, Richard. "Skills: The Middle Way." *Journal of the Philosophy of Education*, Vol. 21 (1987), pp. 197–201.

Contemporary talk about "skills" implies that their lack subtracts nothing intrinsic from the unskilled person; but a real craft-skill intrinsically enhances the successful craftsman, for by his work he relates himself properly to the world, avoiding both alienation from it and total identification with it.

Harpham, Geoffrey Galt. "Rhetoric and the Madness of Philosophy in Plato and Pirsig." *Contemporary Literature*, Vol. 29 (1988), pp. 64–81.

ZMM echoes the near identity of literature-rhetoric and philosophy in the near identity of narrator and Phaedrus. The narrator tells the story of the trip and he speaks the Chautauquas. But when the Chautauqua repeats Phaedrus' theorizing about Quality, Phaedrus' implied biography increasingly becomes the narrator's autobiography; that convergence requires another level of discourse that comprehends all the rest, and thus it requires a unification of narrator and Phaedrus. Harpham suggests how that occurs by interpreting Plato's *Phaedrus* to show that it represents speech in writing as duplicitously as does *ZMM*.

1990

Charlton, Bruce G. "The Quality of Pirsig Is Not Feigned: The Value of *ZMM*." *Durham University Journal* (forthcoming).

Pirsig wrote *ZMM* as a novel because he wished to do philosophy for practical, moral reasons. Real solutions to practical problems do not proceed from philosophizing in the highbrow academic tradition but come about by adopting a pragmatic precritical or postmetaphysical stance and then doing lay philosophy.

INTERVIEWS WITH AND ARTICLES BY AND ABOUT R. M. PIRSIG

The items below are arranged chronologically.

Pirsig, Robert M. "Quality in Freshman Composition." Paper delivered at the Rocky Mountain Modern Language Association regional convention, October 13, 1961.

Gent, George. Interview. *New York Times* (May 15, 1974), p. 36.

Kinsman, Clare D., ed. *Contemporary Authors*, Vols. 53–56 (1975), pp. 465–466.

Contemporary Literary Criticism, Vol. 4 (1975), pp. 403–405, and Vol. 6 (1976), pp. 420–422 (reprinted excerpts of reviews and articles).

Hefner, Christie. "Conversation with Robert M. Pirsig." *Oui*, Vol. 4, No. 11 (November 1975), pp. 67–68, 123–126.

Pirsig, Robert. "Cruising Blues and Their Cure." *Esquire*, Vol. 87, No. 12 (May 1977), pp. 65–68.

Who's Who in America, Vol. 39 (1976–1977), p. 2498; and subsequent editions.

Zuckerman, Ed. "Zen and the Art of Sailboat Maintenance." *Mother Jones,* Vol. 2, No. 4 (May 1977), pp. 56–61.

Haley, Charles William. "Dream Forms," original composition. University of Missouri, Kansas City, 1983; also in *Dissertation Abstracts International,* Vol. 44, No. 4 (1983), p. 905A. (Haley set to music various literary texts that represent nightmares, including one of Pirsig's "Erlkönig" passages from *ZMM.*)

Pirsig, Robert. "An Author and Father Looks Ahead at the Past." *New York Times Book Review* (March 4, 1984), pp. 7–8. (In slightly different form, it appears as Introduction or Afterword in Morrow/Quill and Bantam editions of *ZMM* since 1986.)

Commire, Anne, ed. *Something About the Author,* Vol. 39 (1985), pp. 169–173.

SECTION 10

TOPICS FOR FURTHER
RESEARCH

By providing these topics, we do not wish to suggest that *ZMM* is at home only in an academic setting. Any interested reader can find ideas here for further rumination on this rich book.

The first group of fourteen topics are perhaps more suitable for a first reading of the book on a high school or lower-division college level. They come from a paper by Mary I. Oates O'Reilly, "Vroom at the Bottom: *Zen* and the Art of English Composition," delivered at the Modern Language Association national convention in New York City, on December 29, 1981; we use them in a slightly revised form with her kind permission.

The first ten topics are designed to be *discussed* class after class, topic after topic, as the student reads and the class discusses the book a chapter or two per session.

PARTICULAR *ZMM* QUESTIONS

1. Read the "Author's Note" right after the title page. Does it suggest that the book is fact or fiction? What does "rhetorical" mean? Now read the epigraph on the next page. It is from Plato's dialogue called *The Phaedrus*. How would you answer the question it asks?

2. In three or four sentences, how does Pirsig use the term

The first fourteen questions are copyright © 1989 by Mary I. O'Reilly.

"Chautauqua"? Your dictionary will help, but the book itself helps more. (See *ZMM*, p. 7 and passim.)

3. Study Pirsig's distinction between "classical" and "romantic." Are you more classical or more romantic? Write a paragraph in which you identify yourself as one or the other, giving examples of your behavior. For instance, how does a classical person pack for a weekend at the shore or on the ski slopes? A romantic person? What is the classical approach to dental hygiene? The romantic? (Pp. 60–62, 102, and passim.)

4. Why did Phaedrus come to see his early failure as a lucky break? Can you think of any "failure" of your own that turned out to be a lucky break? A "failure" of anyone else's? (Pp. 99–103, 106, 109.)

5. What does "allegory" mean? Using a figure different from Pirsig's mountain, write an allegorical paragraph describing what it's like to get through freshman year of college. (P. 167; see also Index of this guidebook.)

6. What is the relationship between the dream from which a voice says to Chris, "I'll meet you at the top of the mountain," and the narrator's decision not to make the trip all the way to the summit? (Pp. 204, 219–220.)

7. What does "gumption" mean? How does it relate to "enthusiasm"? (Pp. 272–294.)

8. What allegory does Pirsig develop by relating Phaedrus to a wolf? What does the dog in the allegory stand for? Who are the sheep? Who is the shepherd? (Pp. 347–355; see also pp. 74–75, 143.)

9. What is the significance of the narrator's realization that throughout the bike trip Chris has been staring at his back? How does that relate to details in Chapter 1? (Pp. 3–17, 372.)

10. What answer does the last sentence suggest for the question in the epigraph? (P. 373.)

GENERAL ZMM QUESTIONS

—This book by Robert Pirsig is, among other things, a very good mystery story. As you read, think, and write answers to the foregoing questions, try also to work out answers to the following four questions:

11. Who is Phaedrus, and why is he called by that name?

12. What is the narrator's attitude toward Phaedrus? It is con-

sistent throughout the book, or does it change? If you come to some point where it changes, note the page number.

13. How is the narrator's son Chris involved in the mystery-story plot?

14. What happens at the end to the three central characters—Phaedrus, the narrator, Chris?

The second group of topics is perhaps more suitable for discussions or papers at the upper-division or graduate level. They are divided into four subject categories: the literary, the philosophical, the mystical (especially Oriental), and the scientific.

LITERARY

1. Pirsig's use of the motorcycle as example and/or as metaphor for technology in general; his use of motorcycle maintenance as example and/or as metaphor for Quality activity or its opposite.

2. Use the last section of this book, the Index, to identify sets of page numbers for some recurrent motif that interests you. Examine the recurrences in place—in the context of *ZMM*—checking to see if there are helpful notes in Section 11 of this book.

3. "Zen and the Art of Faulkner." In the second chapter of Faulkner's late novel *The Reivers*, Boon Hogganbeck and Mr. Buffaloe get hold of an automobile. What novelistic use does Faulkner make, in the context of the whole novel, of what *ZMM* would call "classical" and "romantic" approaches? Does Boon turn out to be a "romantic" character most if not all the time? Does he have a "classical" correlative?

4. "Toward a *Diagramme Raisonné* of the Chautauqua in *ZMM*." Is the subject-object, the romantic-classical, or the will-intellect dichotomy most basic? What occupies the middle ground in each case? How many middle grounds are there? Can you construct a rational and systematic diagram of the ideas in the Chautauqua?

5. Compare and contrast *ZMM* and Henry David Thoreau's *Walden* and/or *A Week on the Concord and Merrimack Rivers*. Use Leo Marx's seminal *The Machine in the Garden*.

6. Specify and apply the notion of Quality to some very limited range of literature: How can you discern "what is good, Phae-

drus, and what is not good"? Where is there a right balance of objective and subjective? of classical and romantic? What is good subjective, and what is good classical writing, and why?

PHILOSOPHICAL
Early

1. Study the notion of psyche in Heraclitus, Democritus, and Plato. Use Eric A. Havelock, *Preface to Plato* (Cambridge, Mass.: Belknap/Harvard University Press, 1963), Chapter 11, fn. 3.

2. "Thinking, Writing, and Speaking." Differentiate the Chautauqua as the narrator's thoughts and the Chautauqua as Robert M. Pirsig's literary product, and contrast both of them with the father's conversation with Chris at the end of the book. As background, look at Plato's/Socrates' comments on the alphabet in *Phaedrus;* Havelock, *Preface to Plato*, pp. 36–49; and Charles Rowan Beye, *Ancient Greek Literature and Society* (Ithaca, N.Y.: Cornell University Press, 1987 [reprint of 1975 edition]), pp. 242–243, on the sexual analogy of conversation.

3. Read some pertinent works of Eric Havelock, Bruno Snell, and/or Walter J. Ong and treat *ZMM* in the light of what these scholars say.

4. "Dialectic in Speaking, in Writing, and in Private Thought." See the note to *ZMM*, page 329, in Section 11, below.

5. The allegory of the line in *The Republic*, Book VI, suggests that there are four stages of Platonism; some students claim there are five stages of Buddhism. Do they mesh, and if so, how?

6. For the primitive, ultimate reality is to be found in the patterns set down at the beginning of time (see works of Mircea Eliade); for Plato, ultimate reality is to be found in the world of ideas (though for the Neoplatonist Saint Augustine of Hippo, those ideas are located in God's memory). Now what might Aristotle say? Or William of Occam? or Karl Marx? or yourself?

7. What is the difference between Plato's Good and Phaedrus' Quality (*ZMM*, p. 332)? Why did Phaedrus consider Plato to have originated all dichotomies?

8. Plato's Allegory of the Cave (*The Republic*, Book VII) is an analogy (like the analogy of the chariot and its two horses in Phaedrus) that expresses in a nonliteral manner the truth about metalogical reality.

9. Plato's *Ion* treats of prophecy, poetry, and madness. How does this dialogue shed some light on *ZMM*?

Late

1. "Existentialism and the Maintenance of One's Own Past"— *ZMM* in the light of Camus' *The Stranger*, Wright's *Native Son*, and/or Faulkner's *The Reivers*.

2. René Descartes is not mentioned in *ZMM*, but some would accuse him of perfecting the separation of subjective and objective in the West. T. S. Eliot claimed that what he called the "dissociation of sensibility" dated from the same period as the Cartesian separation of mind and matter.

3. Survey the subject-object problem as the problem of knowledge in Descartes, Hume, Kant, Hegel, Nietzsche, Heidegger . . . and Pirsig.

MYSTICAL-ORIENTAL

1. Enlightenment in Zen Buddhism has been said to require (1) purification from possessions and pride, (2) meditation, (3) the direction of a master, and (4) the koan. Does Phaedrus attain enlightenment?

2. Some religious groups believe in a God who is totally other—*totaliter aliter, ganz anders*—but the God of the mystic seems to be quite immanent. Is mysticism possible in relation to a merely and wholly transcendent God?

3. Read Rudolf Otto and/or R. C. Zaehner and/or other writers on mysticism, and apply what you learn to *ZMM*.

4. Thesis: Enlightenment concerns only the subliminal (subconscious, latent, alien) self; therefore the narrator's conscious self was wholly ignorant of the fact that Phaedrus had reached enlightenment.

5. Metaphor, analogy, Gospel parable, Zen koan: the nonlogical as gateway to enlightenment.

6. Insanity and enlightenment: How can they be told apart (with exemplification from *ZMM*)?

7. How can the eight (or in other sources ten) circles of Buddhism be shown to be relevant to *ZMM*?

8. Eastern (Hindu, Buddhist, and Taoist) and Western (Jewish, Christian, and Muslim) mysticisms.

9. Movement in *ZMM* and the Oxherding Pictures: the spiritual journey as symbol of progress, aimless motion as symbol of regress, barriers (mountains, glass door, helmets in *ZMM*) as either obstacles or opportunities, depending on how the pilgrim reacts.

SCIENCE

1. Physics has received a fair amount of comment from Taoist perspectives in recent years. Find, analyze, and criticize the positions of several such commentators.

2. "Scientific Model as Metaphor, Scientific Model as Catalyst of Scientific Discovery." Use, for instance, the Bohr model of the atom, the wave and particle models of light.

3. "The Beholding of Elegance." How can you manage to choose the good hypotheses and not have to test the infinite number of bad ones? What do Poincaré and Einstein say in their writings that might help answer that question? Perhaps you might want to look at Section 11, the note to p. 240; that might in turn lead you to Jacques Maritain's *Art and Scholasticism* and *Creative Intuition in Art and Poetry*.

S E C T I O N   I I

NOTES TO *ZEN AND THE ART OF MOTORCYCLE MAINTENANCE*

Directions: The more ordinary notes in this section, which resemble the usual explanatory footnotes or endnotes, may be related to *ZMM* by referring to the page numbers given (which correspond to those in any of the Bantam paperback editions printed since 1979).

All occurrences of any motif that recurs frequently in *ZMM*, however, are treated together in a single note. The location of each of these thirty-one MASTER MOTIF notes may be found most easily by using the next section of this book, the Index. Once found, the note will refer the reader both to all the pages in *ZMM* where versions of the MASTER MOTIF appear and also to any closely related MASTER MOTIFS.

p. vii—"Author's Note"—Mark Twain's note to *Huck Finn* reads: "Persons attempting to find a motive in this narrative will be prosecuted; persons attempting to find a moral in it will be banished; persons attempting to find a plot in it will be shot."

p. ix—"And what is good, Phaedrus?" (See *ZMM*, pp. 7, 164, 185; see especially p. 357).

PART I
CHAPTER 1

p. 3—The author uses the present tense for motorcycle trip, the past tense for narrative associated with the "Chautauqua"; but see the note to *ZMM*, p. 299, and Rodino (above, p. 349).

————"duck hunting sloughs . . . red-winged blackbirds," BIRD: The bird motif or symbol remains obscure for the present, but it occurs too often to be ignored (see *ZMM*, pp. 4, 169, 244, 361, 367, 368). Related MASTER MOTIFS are 4 LATERAL MOTION and 32 WIND. (The numbers before the motifs [4 and 32] refer to the [*ZMM*] page numbers preceding entries in this section.)

p. 4—"Secondary roads . . . Paved county roads." William Least Heat Moon's *Blue Highways* (Boston: Little, Brown, 1982) is reminiscent of this passage. See 4 LATERAL MOTION.

————"you bank into turns and don't get swung from side to side." LATERAL MOTION: This motif involves moving from left to right either positively (because at the same time going forward) or negatively (because not moving forward). Examples of positive lateral motion are: banking into turns or wind on a motorcycle (pp. 4, 17, 370, 372); secondary-road travel, which is higher-quality than arriving (pp. 4, 5, 43, 103, 136, 190); the partridge (pp. 169–170); seeing from the corner of the eye (pp. 57, 271, 308, 367); drifting laterally—at an angle—toward "lateral truth" (pp. 71, 103, 108, 150, 198, 301); and non-Euclidean geometry—where the straight line is not the shortest or best (p. 234). Examples of negative lateral motion are travel in an auto (pp. 4–5); the silt-choked stream of thought that floods the lowlands (p. 7); and Chris rocking back and forth on the ground (p. 368). Related MASTER MOTIFS are 3 BIRD, 18 SEEING, 31 INSANITY, 32 WIND, 85 QUESTION UNANSWERED, and 93 HYPOTHESIS.

p. 7—"Chautauqua." Sinclair Lewis describes the Chautauqua coming to Gopher Prairie in *Main Street*, Chapter 19, section VII. *We Called It Culture: The Story of Chautauqua* by Victoria and Robert Case (Garden City, N.Y.: Doubleday, 1948) opens with a scene in Bozeman. See also John Noffsinger, *Correspondence Schools, Lyceums, Chautauquas* (New York: Macmillan, 1926); Harry P. Harrison and Karl Detzer, *Culture Under Canvas* (New York: Hastings House, 1958); and Joseph Gould, *The Chautauqua Movement* (New York: SUNY Press, 1961).

ZMM is, among other things, both an entertaining narrative and a serious intellectual and moral autobiography. The Renaissance ideal for any literature, that it ought both to amuse and to improve, comes principally from Horace, *Ars Poetica*, line 333 and especially lines 343–344: "Omne tulit punctum qui miscuit utile dulci/Lectorem delectando pariterque monendo—A poet will succeed completely if he mixes the useful with the pleasant, delighting the reader as he admonishes him." Here is rooted *ZMM*'s moral aspect as "An Inquiry into Values" (its subtitle): What is best, what is good, what has Quality?

The narrator's solipsistic Chautauqua and the author's record of it in *ZMM* stand in contrast to the Socratic dialogue, of which Charles Beye says:

> In the *Phaedrus* Socrates says that he objects to the written word, preferring oral discourse. The context for this observation is a walk into the countryside in the company of the beautiful young Phaedrus, for whom he is developing his ideas. Phaedrus has brought along a written text of Lysias on love which Socrates answers viva voce. . . .
>
> It is not too much to say that Socrates' preference for the spoken word has a sexual element in it. The dialogue or delivered speech requires a partner, the hearer, just as sexual intercourse requires two people. In both instances the partners work energetically to create something greater than their separate selves. Speech, like sexual desire, works outside of the body; the two are splendid expressions of the transcendence of the flesh, an idea so important to Plato. The dialogue form, therefore, was most likely adopted by him not simply to mask certain inadequacies, but because of this very transcendence. [*Ancient Greek Literature and Society* (Ithaca, N.Y.: Cornell University Press, 1987). p. 242]

Geoffrey Galt Harpham (1988, pp. 77–78; in Bibliography) draws out other possible sexual innuendo. Aware of the problem with much nonnarrative writing, Pirsig has the narrator tell Gennie DeWeese that "essays always have to sound like God talking for eternity" (*ZMM*, p. 153).

———"What is best?" For the Confucian dimensions of this question that the narrator asks, see p. 87 above.

p. 8—"a funeral procession." BURIAL: This motif joins to burials proper (pp. 53, 58, 60, 219, 345) the numerous references to coffins, graves, or tombs (pp. 128, 135, 140, 153, 245) and to funeral processions (pp. 6, 8, 230, 293, 294). Related MASTER MOTIFS are 26 ELECTRICITY, 28 GHOST, 128 ARCHAE-OLOGY, and 245 ITALICS.

p. 9—"I'm not sure I have any solution either, just ideas." The contrast between practical action and mere theory is typical of the narrator, who views his previous self as a self-destructive dreamer.

p. 14—"To get away from technology out into the country." John and Sylvia's supposed escape from technology on a motor-cycle exemplifies the divided American mind about nature and art.

p. 15—"ugly strange shapes of metal" (pp. 86, 88, 144, 194).

p. 16—"The Buddha, the Godhead, resides." This passage has been commented on by many critics.

Buddhism is the ascetical Asian religion founded by Siddhartha Gautama in the sixth century B.C. to offer enlightenment, happiness, and salvation. For a thorough treatment of Buddhism in general, see pp. 62–84 above; for a thorough treatment of Zen Buddhism, see pp. 118–133 above.

CHAPTER 2

p. 17—"something peculiar about this road, apprehension" (pp. 21, 26–27, 58, 71, 128).

p. 18—"See? . . . See?" SEEING: This motif is the modern visualist analogue to enlightenment. It occurs on pp. 4, 5, 42, 70, 74, 141, 152, 171, 253, 363; see also pp. 118–120 of this book. Related MASTER MOTIFS are 4 LATERAL MOTION, 24 CARING, 26 ELECTRICITY, 31 INSANITY, 69 AWARE, and 85 QUESTION UNANSWERED.

p. 21—"this freeway." Interstate 29 north from Sioux Falls, South Dakota, to Fargo, North Dakota.

p. 24—"not in such a way as to care." CARING: This motif contrasts with the lack of personal involvement of a spectator viewing an object. Care would be a characteristic of what Martin Buber called the I-Thou encounter; it is the affective face of the Quality event. This motif further occurs on pp. 25, 33, 38, 146, 247, 253, 267. See also pp. 173 and 186–199 of this book. Related MASTER MOTIFS are 18 SEEING, 69 AWARE, 70 FIGURE IN THE SCENE, and 160 QUALITY.

CHAPTER 3

p. 26—"in the brilliance of the next flash . . . oh, my God, he's *been* here!" ELECTRICITY: This motif gathers together all sorts of electricity, whether natural (lighting, p. 26), man-made (electroconvulsive therapy, p. 77), or metaphorical (pp. 129, 340, 369). The "he" of the quotation "he's been here" is Phaedrus, the narrator's former personality, as we will learn in due time. This dramatic entrance-line symbolically associates Phaedrus with Frankenstein's monster. As electricity dispatched him, so "a sort of slow electric shock" will recall him into full being. Related MASTER MOTIFS are 8 BURIAL, 18 SEEING, 77 PERSONALITIES, and 245 ITALICS.

p. 27—" 'Intuition.' " The narrator's "intuition" is really a memory fragment from his prior personality's life.

p. 28—" 'any good ghost stories.' " GHOST: This motif takes many forms in *ZMM*. When the narrator first uses the term, it applies to Phaedrus, whom he wishes to bury properly so he will stay dead (p. 60; this also echoes Marc Antony's "I come to bury Caesar, not to praise him" in *Julius Caesar* [Act 2, scene 3, ll. 78–257]; Caesar's ghost appears in the play in Act 4, scene 3, l. 275). The "ghost" of Plato (or of any other thinker) is defined as something without physical matter or energy which nevertheless exerts power through its mental effects (p. 28; see also pp. 143, 224). Tom White Bear's Indian grandmother would probably think of "ghost" as the dangerous objective power that endures after a person's (or animal's) death, especially if sudden or violent; such a power exists and acts whether living persons are conscious of it or not. The ghost motif occurs extremely often (pp. 28–34, 55, 71, 72, 74, 75, 84, 88, 97, 127, 128, 143, 153, 157, 158, 200, 221, 224; see especially p. 363, where the narrator recognizes himself as rightfully the ghost). Related MASTER MOTIFS are 8 BURIAL, 75 WOLF, and 77 PERSONALITIES.

p. 29—"quants." This is a variation of "quanta," most often found in the singular in the phrase "light quant."

p. 30—"gravitation and the law of gravitation." As expressed in a mathematical formula, gravity did not exist before Newton. The narrator is obviously not claiming that things began to behave—fall or orbit—differently after Newton published *Principia* in 1687.

p. 31—"feigning twentieth-century lunacy." INSANITY: The

narrator feigns insanity in order not to draw attention to his different way of thinking—which will increasingly become the way his former personality, Phaedrus, thought. At one point, the narrator thinks, "The things I was saying about science and ghosts, and even that idea this afternoon about caring and technology—they are not my own. . . . They are stolen from him" (p. 33). Insanity and enlightenment can at times be difficult to differentiate—but not impossible (see R. C. Zaehner, *Mysticism Sacred and Profane* [London: Oxford University Press, 1961], Chapter 5, "Madness," pp. 84–105). The motif of insanity, understandably in view of the narrator's past, occurs quite frequently in the book (pp. 54, 57, 62, 71, 72, 77, 140, 151, 159, 160, 225, 311, 316, 318, 332, 334, 356–358, 367, 369–370). Related MASTER MOTIFS are 4 LATERAL MOTION, 18 SEEING, 54 FOLIE À DEUX, and 77 PERSONALITIES.

p. 32—"Except for the wind." WIND: This motif occurs on pp. 17, 50, 51, 55 (in the Goethe poem), 142, 143, 149, 152–154, 203. Related MASTER MOTIFS are 3 BIRD, 4 LATERAL MOTION, and 69 AWARE.

p. 33—" 'No one you know.' " This is a very ironic reply, as will become apparent at the very end of the book when the father says of Chris, "He's been carrying *me*!"

CHAPTER 4

p. 36—"*Chilton's Motorcycle Troubleshooting Guide.*" This was written by OCee (*sic*) Rich (Radnor, Pa.: Chilton Book Company, 1966).

p. 39—"its own unique personality." For analogues to a bike's "personality," see Gerard Manley Hopkins's "As Kingfishers Catch Fire," especially the line about bells, which were "baptized" and given proper names in traditional Catholicism. In one part of the *ZMM* manuscript that was cut, the man who sold the bike to the narrator bid it farewell with "Well good-bye, old motorcycle," like Billy Budd's "And good-by to you too, old Rights of Man" (see p. 227 above). In another cut part, a bike responds to care in a personified manner (p. 213). Martin Buber, in *I and Thou*, says that an item of fine art can be a "Thou."

p. 41—"CHICKENMAN!" Chickenman, a parody of Superman, was a Chicago disc jockey's creation during the mid-1960s.

Each two-and-a-half-minute episode began, "Bawk, bawk, bawk, baaawk—CHICKENMAN! He's everywhere, he's everywhere!" Under his assumed name, Clark Kent, Superman wore glasses, though he really had X-ray vision; Lois Lane was his girlfriend.

p. 43—"just moving down the empty road." This is a rather Zen approach to a journey (pp. 4–6, 103, 136).

CHAPTER 5

p. 46—" 'What's shim?' " The hero as *bricoleur* makes a shim out of a found object.

p. 47—"Baron Alfred Krupp" (1812–1887) not literally a baron, though he was known as the Cannon King and Alfred the Great (see William R. Manchester, *The Arms of Krupp* [Boston: Little, Brown, 1968]; see also p. 112 of this book).

p. 53—"Lone prairie." An echo of the old cowboy song "Oh Bury Me Not on the Lone Prairie." (see 8 BURIAL, and compare p. 358, "that lonesome valley."

p. 54—"the beginning symptoms of mental illness." FOLIE À DEUX: This motif is not quite rightly named, perhaps. Since the narrator's statement comes between a reference to his near breakdown (at bottom of p. 53) and an anticipation of Phaedrus' breakdown ("My cigarette is down to my fingers"—compare p. 358), the reader may think of something like *folie à deux*, the copying of the symptoms of mental illness by a person close to the real sufferer. The motif occurs on pp. 79, 121, 157 (Chris is frightened because the narrator is), 282–283, 360 (where Chris says, "I don't want to do anything" because the father does not do anything), and 364. The reader should note that the reference is to "the beginning *symptoms* of mental illness" and not to "the beginning of mental illness." A young boy like Chris, because of the strength of his identification with his father during his process of socialization, can display the symptoms without having the illness a parent or other role model suffers from. Related MASTER MOTIFS are 31 INSANITY and 77 PERSONALITIES.

————" 'What do the psychiatrists think?' " The narrator is perhaps unwilling to send Chris to a psychologist or psychiatrist because his subconscious self (Phaedrus) has an aversion to the technology of psychology at least equal to John Sutherland's aversion to the technology of motorcycle maintenance.

pp. 54–55—"*kin.*" This Johann W. von Goethe poem may be found in the article on *ZMM* by Thomas J. Steele on p. 283. The text changes a little from one edition of *ZMM* to the next: "*ein*" to "*der*" in line 2. In 1815, Franz Schubert (1797–1828) composed a stunning setting to the poem (D. 328d) which is best performed by Dietrich Fischer-Dieskau, baritone, Gerald Moore, piano, on a recording from Deutsche Grammophon.

Note that the ocean does not appear in the original poem but is introduced into the narrator's account of it from the symbol system of the book.

"Kin" and "king" are etymologically related words. For a suggestion that the father in Goethe's poem is in some way the Erl-king, see Plank (1978, pp. 37–38, in Bibliography, citing Steiner, pp. 250–254, above).

p. 56—"a great big sandpile." The image of the sandpile is important in the Chautauqua (pp. 69–70).

p. 57—"It is Phaedrus." The narrator here begins to identify the Erlkönig as symbolically equivalent to his former personality; for an interpretation of the plot thread that originates here, see the article by Steele, reprinted here on pp. 282–292.

CHAPTER 6

p. 57—"to explore Phaedrus' world." The narrator wants to bury his dead former self (p. 60) in order to prevent his resurrection; but the optimistic narrator fools himself, for the net effect will be to elicit Phaedrus' return. See 8 BURIAL.

p. 58—"things will probably get better" (pp. 154–155, 214, 373).

pp. 58–59—The mechanical trouble here will be mentioned again on p. 155 and solved in a passage that is reprinted here on pp. 211–219.

p. 59—" 'where to start.' " STARTING POINT: This motif echoes Eugen Herrigel's problem of the starting point in *Zen in the Art of Archery:* how to get beneath all the layers of being that are accessible by Western methods of reflection. The motif in *ZMM* may be found on pp. 97, 109, 150, 247–248, 353–354. A related MASTER MOTIF is 85 QUESTION UNANSWERED.

p. 60—"classical understanding and romantic understanding." CLASSICAL and ROMANTIC: In this pair of motifs, which almost always accompany and define each other, the classical mode seems to resemble what Greek philosophy would have called *episteme*, real if "square" knowledge, wheras the romantic mode resembles *doxa*, a "groovy" communal interpretation of the thing's immediate appearances. Examples occur on pp. 45, 47–49, 61, 62, 102, 108, 112, 149, 199, 200, 212, 240, 248, 260, 262, 264, 266, 366. A related MASTER MOTIF is 160 QUALITY.

p. 62—"a house divided against itself." The phrase recalls Matthew 12:25 and Abraham Lincoln's speech of June 16, 1858. See 77 PERSONALITIES.

————"self-stroking cycles." This is a typographical error; "stoking" is correct; the phrase recurs, correctly printed, on pp. 140 and 284.

p. 66—"there is a knife moving here." KNIFE: This motif is always purely metaphorical. Any literal knife that may appear in the story (as for instance on p. 182, the hunting knife used to slice some cheese) has no discernible status as motif.

As metaphor and motif, the mental knife of rational analysis carves the world up prior to sorting it into some hierarchical order. The knife motif (or split or division) occurs on pp. 62, 63–67, 69, 70, 196, 212, 215, 223, 225, 325, 326 (the crack in the table), 332.

Eugen Herrigel's *Zen in the Art of Archery* (New York: Random House, 1971) p. 70, offers the comparable motif of a bowstring that cuts right through the archer.

Related MASTER MOTIFS are 69 AWARE, 87 HIERARCHY, 92 LOGIC, and 108 CONTINUUM.

CHAPTER 7

p. 69—"All the time we are aware." AWARE: The motif of awareness is usually identified with the Quality moment (pp. 6, 199, 215, 228, 240, 255, 265, 358, 367). As such, it relates the figure-in-the-scene to the *whole* scene of which he is part, to the entire undifferentiated aesthetic continuum of F.S.C. Northrop's *The Meeting of East and West: An Inquiry Concerning World Understanding* (New York: Macmillan, 1946 [reprinted, 1960, 1966]). But a few times (pp. 221, 222, 261), "aware" names the postsensory knowing that occurs after the figure takes the handful of conscious sand and sorts or divides it with a knife. Related MASTER MOTIFS are 18 SEEING, 24 CARING, 32 WIND, 66

KNIFE, 70 FIGURE IN THE SCENE, and 108 CONTINUUM.
p. 70—"a figure in the middle of it, sorting sand." FIGURE
IN THE SCENE: This motif gathers together some apparently
disparate figures: the literal motorcyclist (pp. 4, 19), the Erlkönig
of the narrator's dream (pp. 57, 245, 297), and some human's
"caring-awareness" (p. 70). This last figure turns Northrop's "undifferentiated aesthetic continuum" (p. 108; the landscape) into
differentiated and analyzed mental discontinuities. See Crusius
(1976, pp. 170–171) and Weiland (1980, p. 305), in Bibliography.
Related MASTER MOTIFS are 24 CARING and 69 AWARE.

———"Mark Twain's experience." A passage from *Life on the
Mississippi*, Chapter IX, reads:

> Now when I had mastered the language of this water, and had
> come to know every trifling feature that bordered the great river as
> familiarly as I knew the letters of the alphabet, I had made a valuable
> acquisition. But I had lost something, too. I had lost something
> which could never be restored to me while I lived. All the grace, the
> beauty, the poetry, had gone out of the majestic river! . . .
> No, the romance and beauty were all gone from the river. All the
> value any feature of it had for me now was the amount of usefulness
> it could furnish toward compassing the safe piloting of a steamboat.

p. 75—"it was a timber wolf." WOLF: Through this powerful
motif, the narrator presents the solitary Phaedrus as a sort of Step-
penwolf; he introduces his mistaken etymology of the word "wolf"
as deriving from the Greek work *phaidros* (which actually means
"bright" or "shining"; and it can serve as an epithet for Apollo).
Oddly, *lukeios*, "Lycian," "wolfish," is equally the sun god's epithet; it turns up in the English noun "lyceum," the temple of
Apollo in Athens where Aristotle and his students walked and
talked (see p. 155).
The motif of wolves joins that of ghosts. Perhaps coinciden-
tally, Greek werewolves were supposed to have hung their clothes
on Zeus' sacred oak next to a stagnant pond when they wished to
metamorphose from human to lupine form (see Arthur B. Cook,
"Zeus, Jupiter, and the Oak," *The Classical Review*, Vol. 18
[1904], pp. 88–89; H. W. Parke, *The Oracles of Zeus* [Oxford:
Basil Blackwell, 1967], p. 21, citing Pliny, *Natural History*, Book
VIII, Ch. 34).
References to wolves appear on pp. 143, 347, 350, 353, 354. A
related MASTER MOTIF is 28 GHOST.

p. 77—" 'You have a new personality now.' . . .'You *are* a new personality.' " PERSONALITIES: This motif would have elicited some pointed remark from David Hume. It touches upon the dichotomy between Phaedrus and the narrator and thus permeates every page of the book, but it reaches out in many other directions as well. Some examples are pp. 29, 39 (a motorcycle's personality), 52, 55, 56, 62 (house divided), 122 (the spy movie), 141, 142, 201–204, 214, 220, 240, 269, 283, 298, 363, 370. Related MASTER MOTIFS are 26 ELECTRICITY, 28 GHOST, 31 INSANITY, 54 FOLIE À DEUX, and 245 ITALICS.

The shock therapy was technologically faultless but existentially inauthenticating (see article by Steele, pp. 282–292, and also Susan Squire, "Shock Therapy's Return to Respectability," *New York Times Magazine* (November 22, 1987), pp. 78–79, 85, 88–89).

PART II
CHAPTER 8

p. 83—"it's become a ritual." The ritual and iconic aspect of tuning the cycle elevates it metaphorically to a religious act; the art of motorcycle maintenance, a miniature instance of the art of rationality itself, is an example or ritual enactment of the myth—the sacred story—of modern technological man (pp. 84–85, 87, 97–100, 133, 285–286). See notes to *ZMM*, pp. 97–100 and 133 below, and see Bump (1983, p. 377; in Bibliography).

p. 85—"I just leave it as a hanging question." QUESTION UNANSWERED: This motif concerns inability to solve a problem (pp. 85, 100–103, 106, 113, 198, 214, 304) and hence getting stuck (pp. 249–258). It approaches the Zen koan (p. 256) or the *mu* state (pp. 288–290), and it can take the form of "just sitting" or "just looking" (pp. 280, 286; see also the omitted text on p. 217, above). The narrator's fundamental personal answer seems to arrive only on p. 370. Related MASTER MOTIFS are 4 LATERAL MOTION, 18 SEEING, and 59 STARTING POINT.

p. 86—"the shapes of the steel." That is, the ideas (pp. 15, 88, 144, 194). The motorcycle, as an artifact, is an expression of human ideas and hence primarily a mental phenomenon.

p. 87—"a hierarchy." HIERARCHY: The name of this motif was invented by Pseudo-Dionysius, a fifth- or sixth-century Christian Neoplatonist theologian, who viewed Trinity, angels, Church, and state as interconnected flow-charts of holiness-power.

A philosophical realist's analysis of the universe can readily posit a chain or ladder of being where each link or rung is a discrete species or essence; a nominalist's analysis, by contrast, will see the multitude of individuals as a sort of inclined plane, a calculus of infinitesimal variations that might lead to a theory of evolution. Either way, once the philosopher's mental knife cuts the universe apart, his mind organizes the resulting pieces as a set of higher and lower rungs of a ladder or steps of a stair or links of a chain.

Examples occur on pp. 188 (contrasted with concentric waves), 199, 238, 251. The related MASTER MOTIF is of course 66 KNIFE.

————"A *real* system." Projecting a worldview in a classical manner, the totality of objects in the world is "the system."

p. 88—"systematic thought itself, rationality itself." RATIO-NALITY: This motif recalls the end of Nathaniel Hawthorne's "Earth's Holocaust," when reformers have burned all the vain and evil things in the world but have not cleansed the human heart. In the second to last paragraph of the story, the devil comments, "Unless they hit upon some method of purifying that foul cavern, forth from it will re-issue all the shapes of wrong and misery—the same old shapes, or worse ones—which they have taken such a vast deal of trouble to consume to ashes. I have stood by, this live-long night, and laughed in my sleeve at the whole business. Oh, take my word for it, it will be the old world yet."

The motif occurs notably on pp. 71, 84, 97, 120, 129 ("Church of Reason"), 130–133, 150 (expand reason), 248, 263, 315, 323. See also p. 123 and Section 5, passim, of this book. Related MASTER MOTIFS are 28 GHOST, 92 LOGIC, and 93 HYPOTHESIS.

————"there's no steel in nature." Shakespeare has King Polixenes in *Winter's Tale* say this about the relationship of nature and art:

> Yet nature is made better by no mean
> But nature makes that mean. So, over that art
> Which you say adds to nature, is an art
> That nature makes. You see, sweet maid, we marry
> A gentler scion to the wildest stock,
> And make conceive a bark of baser kind
> By bud of nobler race. This is an art

Which does mend nature—change it rather—but
The art itself is nature.
[Act 4, scene 4, ll. 89–95]

But Perdida is not convinced any more than John Sutherland
would be.

p. 91—"the governor of Montana." Donald Grant Nutter
(1915–1962) (p. 130). Gallatin County lies in southwest Montana;
Bozeman is the county seat. Eleanor Roosevelt (1884–1962), wife
of President Franklin Delano Roosevelt, was controversial, but
only the most brittle personalities felt seriously threatened by a
seventy-five-year-old gentlewoman.

CHAPTER 9

p. 92—"Two kinds of logic." LOGIC: This motif treats any formal reasoning process. Logic is mentioned on pp. 31, 161, 205
(dilemma), 210 (*reductio ad absurdum*), and 236 (definition). Inductive logic typically proceeds from particulars to a generaliza-
tion; it projects a hypothesis and attains *probability* at best.
Deductive logic proceeds with *necessity* from premises to a conclusion and attains a certainty as great as that of its premises.
Related MASTER MOTIFS are 66 KNIFE, 88 RATIONAL-
ITY, and 93 HYPOTHESIS.

p. 93—"hypotheses as to the cause." HYPOTHESIS: This
motif deals with a part of scientific method, but since hypotheses
are formed by induction, they are capable of multiplying faster
than they can be tested. Further examples of this motif can be
found on pp. 98–100, 109, 147 (the many ways to assemble the
rotisserie), 237, and 251. Related MASTER MOTIFS are 4 LAT-
ERAL MOTION, 88 RATIONALITY, 92 LOGIC, 160 CRYS-
TALLIZATION, and 188 WAVE.

CHAPTER 10

p. 97—"In the temple of science." The five quotations (pp. 97–
100) from Albert Einstein (1879–1955) come from a charming
birthday address he composed for Max Planck (1858–1947). See
notes to ZMM, pp. 83–85 above, and p. 133 below; and see Bump
(pp. 316–328 in Section 8, "Critical Reception").

p. 100—"The number of rational hypotheses." This rueful principle about hypotheses multiplying is quoted in Arthur Bloch, *Murphy's Law and Other Reasons Why Things Go Wrong* (Los Angeles: Price-Stern-Sloan, 1977), p. 87. See 93 HYPOTHESIS.

p. 103—"expelled from the University." Later, Phaedrus' students who most resemble him will also flunk out (pp. 122–123, 344, 355).

CHAPTER 11

p. 106—"although he has hit the bull's-eye." In Eugen Herrigel's *Zen in the Art of Archery,* pp. 4–5, 62–63, arrow, archer, and target finally come to make a single entity.

————"a picture of a wall." WALL, KOREAN: This motif gathers together all the exemplary artifacts that demonstrate Quality in human productivity. Such items are mentioned on pp. 222, 261, 267, 288 (the ditch), 321 (the weld), and perhaps 358–359 (the bedroom wall in Chicago); see also pp. 126–127 above. A related MASTER MOTIF is 160 QUALITY, and as the WALL exemplifies Quality, the motif 254 TRAIN allegorizes it.

p. 107—"the twenty-six written characters." The Roman alphabet; the Orientals politely but firmly deny that language, especially in its chirographic or typographic forms, can encompass reality either totally or adequately.

p. 108—"undifferentiated aesthetic continuum." CONTINUUM: Regarding this motif, F.S.C. Northrop's *The Meeting of East and West* (New York: Macmillan, 1946), pp. 335–343, 352–357, and 366–371, presents the "undifferentiated aesthetic continuum" as the experiential event prior to "sorting out" into subject and object. It is both the landscape (p. 69) and the figure in the landscape (p. 70). That continuum can appear either benign (p. 4) or cruel and senseless (pp. 6, 126), but it is in itself the ultimate reality (pp. 117–18, 145, 228) from which all else flows. Related MASTER MOTIFS are 66 KNIFE, 69 AWARE, and 160 QUALITY.

p. 109—"science . . . a branch of philosophy." What we call science used to be called collectively "natural philosophy" (or "natural history"); it has long since made a clean getaway from philosophy. The philosophy of science, however, has developed as a branch of philosophy that studies the logic of scientific method,

3 7 7

the status of scientific concepts, and the degree of scientific certitude.

p. 112—"the romantic condemnation of rationality." This is a function of the success of that very rationality in freeing humanity from its toil and, by pure and applied science (technology), granting us noetic and practical control over the world we inhabit (pp. 62, 102, 112–113, 149). See especially Walter J. Ong, S.J., *Rhetoric, Romance, and Technology* (Ithaca, N.Y.: Cornell University Press, 1971), pp. 276–283.

pp. 114–120—Kant and Hume. Kant's aesthetic categories (time and space) are subjective differentiations of what Northrop calls "the undifferentiated aesthetic continuum" into discrete events, each of which is identified by its proper space-location and time-sequence. In this context, "continuity" (pp. 117, 118) would be difficult to assert if the narrator did not make reference to substance (p. 117). See also pp. 116, 142–143, and 163–166 of this book.

p. 115—" 'Nature' and 'Nature's laws.' " This phrase perhaps echoes Alexander Pope's epigram "Nature and Nature's laws were hid in night;/God said, 'Let Newton be,' and all was light."

p. 119—"a passive observer, a 'blank tablet' "—*tabula rasa* is a Lockean term for the mind as it is in itself, the "erased slate" on which the external world can write, by means of human sensations, the record of its presence. See pp. 163–166 above.

CHAPTER 12

p. 122—"a movie about a World War I spy." In *The Lancer Spy* (Twentieth Century-Fox, 1937) George Sanders played both Baron Kurt von Rohback and Lieutenant Michael Bruce, the latter of whom resembles the narrator at the DeWeeses' as the narrator pretends to be Phaedrus. Compare 77 PERSONALITIES.

p. 123—" '. . . are all *failing!* ' " The students most like the teacher flunk out as he did (p. 103), not from stupidity or lack of interest but from an excess of the opposite traits (pp. 344, 354, 355).

p. 124—"he knew what he liked." This comment is surely, on DeWeese's behalf, Pirsig's jesting rejoinder to the silly remark every artist hears: "I don't know anything about art, but I know what I like."

p. 125—"this strange perspective." The perspective from

which Bob DeWeese views the world is never described explicitly, but it probably is aesthetic-synthetic.

————"Benares [or Varanasi] Hindu University." This university was located in the ancient city on the Ganges between Delhi and Calcutta. The English theosophist Annie Besant (1847–1933) was instrumental in founding the Hindu University. The city is holy because in the Deer Park of Saranath on its outskirts Gautama Buddha preached his first sermon.

Hinduism is the ancient religious-cultural ensemble of India and Southeast Asia. For a thorough treatment, see pp. 52–62 above.

p. 126—"*Tat tvam asi.*" This doctrine affirms absolute monism: Thou art the thing itself, i.e., there is no subject differentiated from any object, for only the One is. Oriental theory of knowledge from India through China to Japan (*dhyana, chan, zen*) tends toward holism and monism; Western "major logic"(epistemology), by contrast, separates knower and known, dancer from dance. See pp. 4, 6.

————"the atomic bombs that had dropped on Hiroshima and Nagasaki." In early August 1945.

CHAPTER 13

p. 128—"the archeologist's feelings." ARCHAEOLOGY: This motif presents the memory of the narrator as he "digs up" his dead and buried former personality, Phaedrus. The narrator's conscious intention is to bury Phaedrus so he will stay dead, to lay his ghost forever. But ironically the effect of the excavation is to bring Phaedrus back, for he still exists in the subconscious—dead but able to rise, dormant but able to awaken, or hidden and secretly managing events as he sees fit. Other appearances of this motif are on pp. 135, 140, 144, 153, 169. See Bernstein (1981, p. 4; in Bibliography). Related MASTER MOTIFS are 8 BURIAL and 245 ITALICS.

p. 130—"A nationally known professor." Leslie Fiedler, a seminal thinker and a very well known critic of American literature, had taught in the Montana State University English department in Missoula during the early 1960s. Some of his more important books are *Love and Death in the American Novel, The Return of the Vanishing American,* and *An End to Innocence.*

————"The newly elected governor." A standard history of Montana says:

Montana's political pendulum swung even farther to the right in 1960 with the election of Donald Nutter to the governorship. An archconservative from Sidney, Nutter soundly defeated liberal Democrat Paul Cannon by running on a platform that called for a better business climate, reduced taxes, major cuts in government services and payroll, and, if necessary, a sales tax. Governor Nutter proved, as anticipated, to be an extreme rightist once in office, even refusing to proclaim United Nations Day in Montana. The 1961 Legislature, faced with a six million dollar deficit, followed Nutter's proposals and slashed expenditures for the custodial institutions, the university system, and other arms of government. With some measure of truth, many Montanans trace today's budget problems and erosion of state services back to the wholesale cuts of 1961.

Governor Nutter never had a chance to pursue his retrenchment program, for he died in a terrible January 1962 plane crash. Replacing him was Lieutenant Governor Tim Babcock, a wealthy trucker from Billings whose conservative leanings approached those of his predecessor. Babcock . . . would later find himself caught up in the fund-raising scandals of Watergate.

[Michael P. Malone and Richard B. Roeder, *Montana: A History of Two Centuries* (Seattle: University of Washington Press, 1976), pp. 298–299]

The extremist conservative John Birch Society, founded in 1958, "explained" nearly everything as the result of a Communist conspiracy.

Roland Renne was president of Montana State College from 1945 to 1964.

p. 133—" 'the church' and 'the location.' " The account describes Phaedrus' rational "knife" cutting the university into process and buildings. See 66 KNIFE and Bump (1983, p. 377; in Bibliography).

The text seems to suggest that the Jesuits resembled the Player Queen in *Hamlet:* "The lady doth protest too much."

———"Socrates' old goal of truth, in its ever-changing forms." Phaedrus would later suggest that for the human person goodness is a more important goal than truth, while Socrates would have said that "ever-changing" is the worst adjective to apply to truth, since for him truth is by its very nature eternal and immutable.

p. 135—"I feel like an archeologist." (pp. 128, 153, 169). See Bernstein (1981, p. 4; in Bibliography).

p. 136—"the main east-west highway . . . over a low pass." Interstate 90 goes west from Livingston over Bozeman Pass (elevation six thousand feet) into the Gallatin River headwaters of the Missouri.

CHAPTER 14

p. 137—"wave a leg back." Robert DeWeese recalls the wave with the leg as the narrator approached the house.

pp. 137–144—The host and hostess of the party (Robert and Gennie DeWeese) and their guests—the art instructor and his wife (who were in fact department chairman John Basher and his wife Pat, p. 138), Jack and Wylla Barsness (moving to Boise State University, p. 144), and the sculptor-sheepherder from northern Montana (Bill Stockton, actually a cattleman, p. 144)—are all, like John and Sylvia Sutherland, real and historical persons.

p. 141—" 'He saw too much.' " That is, for his own good; this unthinking inappropriate remark affirming Phaedrus' enlightenment is the sort of blunder the narrator implicitly agreed not to commit as a condition for leaving the mental hospital.

p. 142—"lonely here." The remark should probably be understood as having been made by Phaedrus, talking in the narrator's sleep, to Chris.

p. 143—"ghosts . . . wolves." Seeing that Chris is disappointed by his first, literally true reply, DeWeese adds the satisfying "But they could." His perceptiveness suggests the difference between DeWeese and the narrator's undemonstrative fatherly love. The historical Robert DeWeese disclaims having said this; it would seem to be the author's creation for the purpose of showing, by contrast, the narrator's restraint in responding to his son's needs, which were often expressed in a quite childish fashion. See 28 GHOST and 75 WOLF.

p. 143—"Peter Voulkos." Note the correct spelling. This very well known ceramicist studied under DeWeese at Montana State from 1946 to 1951; he has since studied, worked, and taught in California.

p. 145—"lack of smoothness and continuity" (pp. 4, 6, 108, 117–118).

p. 146—" 'Assembly of Japanese bicycle require great peace of mind.' " This refers both to doing and to being validated when done (pp. 99, 264).

p. 150—"expand the nature of rationality." Calculus is a

branch of math involving the idea of a limit and studying such matters as rates of change and areas and volumes created by compound curves; calculus, which was developed independently and simultaneously by Leibniz and Newton, is an expansion of human reasoning. See the concept *mu*, pp. 288–289, and the MASTER MOTIF 88 RATIONALITY.

p. 151—"The whole Renaissance." The characteristics and timing of that cultural period suggest that the narrator might have chosen "Mannerist" rather than "Renaissance."

The flat earth theory was held during this period only by the uneducated; from Greek times, learned persons knew that the earth was a sphere, and Eratosthenes of Cyrene (c. 276–c. 194 B.C.) had even calculated its circumference to within a few hundred miles.

The passage might echo Matthew Arnold's "Dover Beach" (1851): "The Sea of Faith/Was once, too, at the full . . ./But now I only hear/Its melancholy, long, withdrawing roar."

p. 152—"The ancient Greeks . . . listened to the wind and predicted the future." The priests of chthonic Zeus at the shrine of Dodona listened to the sound of the wind in the leaves of the sacred oak or beech trees or to the noise of bronze vessels hung from the branches. See H. W. Parke, *The Oracles of Zeus* (Oxford: Basil Blackwell, 1967), pp. 27–28; see also *The Iliad*, Book 16, ll. 233–227; *The Odyssey*, Book 14, ll. 327–328 or Book 19, ll. 296–297; 2 Samuel 5:24; Herodotus, *History*, Book 2, l. 55; Aeschylus, *Prometheus Bound*, ll. 830–835; Arthur B. Cook, "Zeus, Jupiter, and the Oak," *The Classical Review*, Vol. 17 (1903), pp. 178–179. Plato's *Phaedrus*, 275B, refers to the priests of Dodona. See 32 WIND.

p. 153—"their graves." See Bernstein (1981, p. 4; in Bibliography).

CHAPTER 15

p. 155—"peripatetic . . . academy." The *peripatos* was a covered walk around the Lyceum (a temple of Lycian Apollo, Apollo as wolf god) where Aristotle and his students strolled, and hence they came to be called Peripatetic philosophers; the Academy was a gymnasium where Plato taught.

p. 156—"most freshman-rhetoric courses." The Montana State College catalog for 1960–1962 describes English 101-102-103 as follows: "A writing course giving special attention to the elements of effective modern style, including organization of ideas into sentences, paragraphs, and longer units, and current usage in grammar and phrasing. Wide reading in contemporary prose, and constant emphasis on improvement in vocabulary and spelling."

————"had a certain syrup . . . didn't pour." This Gertrude Stein *mot* appears in her *Autobiography of Alice B. Toklas* (New York: Harcourt Brace, 1933), p. 269: "There was also Glenway Wescott but Glenway Wescott at no time interested Gertrude Stein. He has a certain syrup but it does not pour."

p. 157—"he turns and runs." Why should Chris be afraid when he and the narrator return to the classroom building where Phaedrus taught, since it would seem that he might hope to contact his "real" father there? One plausible if not very likely reason for his fear is that he senses the narrator's tension (pp. 26, 27, 57, 58, 71, 128) and fear, so he echoes his emotion (pp. 54, 121, 282–283). Another reason is that he senses the narrator's hatred of Phaedrus and his wish to bury him permanently and thus is frightened.

p. 158—"She has an aggressive face . . . not very pretty." This was actually a very friendly male custodian who (Pirsig says in a letter of May 3, 1987) "enjoyed my lectures which, being delivered in a loud voice, he got to hear regularly."

p. 160—"Feininger's 'Church of the Minorites.' " Minorites are Franciscans, priests of the Order of Friars Minor. This painting is at Minneapolis's Walker Art Center.

————"an avalanche of memory." This is part of the motif 183 MOUNTAIN.

————"Sarah." Sarah J. Vinke (A.B. 1914, Grinnell College; A.M. 1921 and Ph.D. 1923, Wisconsin University) was formerly chair of the English department at Montana State College; she indeed retired about 1961. Pirsig notes in his letter of May 3, 1987, that "Gennie DeWeese took courses from her and admired her very much. 'I am a mystic,' she once said to me at a faculty party when there wasn't much to talk about. 'You can't be a mystic,' I said. 'A mystic doesn't define himself as anything.' She thought about this and said, 'You're right. I am not a mystic.' She smiled a little, and that was the last she ever said on the subject."

————" 'I hope you are teaching Quality.' " QUALITY: Sarah, who starts this motif, is thinking in terms of the Greek noun *aretê*. According to a folk etymology, *aretê* was originally the name for Ares-ness, a human participation in the virtue of the god of war Ares (Mars). The references to Quality from p. 160 to the end of the book are too numerous to cite, but two earlier references may be found on pp. 7 ("best") and 153. Related MASTER MOTIFS are 24 CARING, 60 CLASSICAL and ROMANTIC, 106 WALL, 108 CONTINUUM, and 254 TRAIN.

————"the seed crystal." CRYSTALLIZATION: This motif recurs when the narrator describes something "jelling" in Phaedrus' mind. There will be three stages, which are sometimes referred to as waves (pp. 188, 239); the phrase "waves of crystallization" might seem to be a mixed metaphor unless the reader imagines not the lines of ocean waves all moving in one direction but instead (as on p. 188) concentric ripples moving out from a single source on the surface of a pond or (even better) moving rhythmically in all three spatial dimensions from a seed crystal (p. 160) in the center of a beaker of supersaturated liquid. See pp. 181, 188, 191–193, 196, 205 (the second, or metaphysical, wave), 221 (the third, or mystical, wave), and 239. On the relationship between the metaphysical stage and the mystical stage, see pp. 117–118 above. Related MASTER MOTIFS are 93 HYPOTHESIS and 188 WAVE.

p. 162—"good table manners and spoke and wrote grammatically." These are marks of a caste system, but Montana was still residually frontier and therefore egalitarian.

PART III
CHAPTER 16

p. 167—Gennie and Bob DeWeese recall Chris being less than enthusiastic about taking the hike, but it might be worth mentioning here that no part of the trip could have occurred if Chris had not agreed to go.

p. 169—"When I first discovered this debris." For the imagery, see 128 ARCHAEOLOGY; see also Bernstein (1981, p. 4; in Bibliography).

p. 170—"They rock back and forth." There are two different sorts of connections: to the motif 3 BIRD (red-winged blackbirds, ducks, teal) and 4 LATERAL MOTION (rocking from side to side or back and forth as a physical activity indicative of psychological paralysis).

p. 176—"school of hard knocks." This echoes the title of a frequently delivered and famous early Chautauqua lecture, "The University of Hard Knocks," by Ralph Parlette. See Harry P. Harrison and Karl Detzer, *Culture Under Canvas* (New York: Hastings House, 1958), pp. 11, 183–184, 267.

p. 178—"figure you are going to fail and then go ahead and do what you could . . . relax." The response seems to be an effective existential reaction to the academic equivalent of death: Face it squarely and be liberated to live (or learn) authentically (pp. 183, 189–190). As to be ready to die is to be ready to live, so to be ready to flunk is to be ready to learn something.

p. 180—"a Kafkaesque situation." Some students—often those Phaedrus thought most resembled himself—are reduced to a degree of absurdity reminiscent of the writings of Franz Kafka (1883–1924), especially *The Trial*, in which the hero, Joseph K., is punished but never told why. Thus the withholding of grades creates a situation with which some of Phaedrus' students cannot cope.

———"Reed College in Oregon." Burton R. Clark, *The Distinctive College: Antioch, Reed, and Swarthmore* (Chicago: Aldine Publishing, 1970), says that withholding grades aids Reed in "attracting intellectually adventuresome students while repelling the more routine types" (p. 130) but that in actual practice it makes the school "strongly punishment centered" (p. 131).

CHAPTER 17

p. 183—"each footstep isn't just a means to an end but a unique event in itself" (pp. 4–6, 42–43, 103, 136, 178, 189–190).

———"the sides of the mountain . . . sustain life." MOUNTAIN: This motif is both literal and symbolic. As life-sustaining, Zen is more proper to mountainsides and valleys than it is to mountaintops, but a top is always needed to define the sides. The motif occurs on pp. 74, 98, 103–105, 111, 114, 153, 160, 167, 168, 183, 204, 216, 217, 220, 228 (mental avalanche), and 246. A related MASTER MOTIF is 220 OCEAN. Death limits and thus defines life.

———"what they hear is unimportant." That is, what they hear in their mental reflection.

p. 188—"Cromwell's statement." As translated from French,

it reads: "One never rises so high as when one does not know where one is going" (letter to M. Bellièvre, in Cardinal de Metz's *Memoirs*). It must have gained something in translation.

————"like waves in all directions." WAVE: Note the uniting of the new motif of the wave with the crystallization motif introduced on p. 160. The wave image is sometimes used in Zen Buddhism to suggest the birth-and-death cycle of samsara. In *ZMM*, concentric waves contrast with hierarchies. Here the three waves of crystallization—not a mixed metaphor (see the note to p. 160, above)—lead to psychological death. The wave motif occurs also on pp. 193, 196, 205, 221, 239. Related MASTER MOTIFS are 93 HYPOTHESIS and 160 CRYSTALLIZATION.

p. 189—"holy Mount Kailas." Popularly known as Kangrinboqê Feng, this Tibetan mountain may be found at latitude 31° 05′N, longitude 81° 21′E. The very holiness of the mountain is the pilgrims' strength; because they submit to it, it becomes theirs. See p. 183, and Dom Denys Rutledge, *In Search of a Yogi* (New York: Farrar, Straus, 1963); Sorrel Wilby, "Nomads' Land: A Journey Through Tibet," *National Geographic*, Vol. 172, No. 6 (December 1987), pp. 766–773; and Jere Van Dyk, "Long Journey of the Brahmaputra," *National Geographic*, Vol. 174, No. 5 (November 1988), pp. 677–678.

CHAPTER 18

p. 190—"forcing Quality into its servitude." As Quality under the title of Good becomes Plato's number two Idea—after Truth—so Quality in the guise of Beauty becomes an even lower-ranking Idea.

p. 192—"Definitions are the *foundation* of reason." Reason can only determine the connections between assertions if the terms of the assertions have meanings that are fixed by definitions.

p. 193—" 'It isn't any fun' " (p. 360).

————"called itself *realism*" This kind of philosophy takes the position that the objects of human thought exist in themselves and continue to do so though no human is conscious of them. There are two types of realism: that of natures (opposed to nominalism and including Platonism, Aristotelianism, and medieval scholasticism), and that of things (opposed to idealism and including naïve and critical realism). See pp. 139–151 above.

p. 194—See p. 345 and Aldous Huxley's *Brave New World* (1932) and George Orwell's *1984* (1949), two famous dystopian novels.

————"quit smoking." Note the correction of typo.

p. 195—"Some artist friends . . . Negroes." Pp. 205–206 above, includes an omitted section of the original typescript on African-American and white families.

p. 201—"the paperback by Thoreau." *Walden* (p. 36). John Sutherland's antitechnological mentality might be reminiscent of the romantic Thoreau, who lived at the start of the American industrial-technological age, whereas the very contemporary narrator is trying to unite pro- and antitechnological currents.

CHAPTER 19

p. 203—"helps dispel a dream." For the narrator's memory of dream and interpretation, see the article by Steele on pp. 282–291 of this guidebook.

p. 204—" 'drunk or something.' " Again, Chris is reporting the Phaedrus voice speaking to him from the narrator's sleep (pp. 218, 368, 369). Chris might have said that his father sounded as if he were speaking in italics. See 245 ITALICS.

p. 205—In line 6, "the" is correct, not "and."

————"A *dilemma*, which is Greek." A lemma is a postulate or proposition (from *lambanein* "to take," "something taken"); a dilemma is a pair of propositions that fit together as a single major premise.

p. 208—"the historic roots of the word *quality*." Marcus Tullius Cicero (*Quaestiones Academicae*, Book 1, Ch. 7, sects. 25–26) formed the technical abstract noun *qualitas* from the adjective *qualis* in order to translate the Greek philosophical word *poiotês*, apologetically coined by Plato (*Theatetus* 182 A-B): "The passive [subject] perceives but does not become perception itself, as the active [object] acquires a quality [literally, 'becomes such and such'] but does not become the quality itself. Now perhaps 'quality' seems an extraordinary word, and you do not understand when it's used abstractly, so let me give some concrete examples."

p. 210—"*reductio ad absurdum*." *Reductio ad absurdum* is a simple form of dilemma (p. 205): a *single* premise, the results of which are per se impossible, de facto false, or highly undesirable.

The dilemma is made up of a proposition and its contradictory, one of which seems bound to be true (for the middle is excluded) and *both* of which have unacceptable implications. Both dilemma and *reductio ad absurdum* can begin 4 LATERAL MOTION toward higher truths.

————"the number zero." As a concept, zero seems to have arisen in the Hindu world as much as two millennia ago, certainly by the ninth century; the Arabs learned it and introduced it into Europe.

p. 211—"Berkeley . . . Bosanquet." Idealism holds that the objects of knowledge are within mind and therefore are ideas; nonmental entities, should any exist, are thus unknowable except by inference. The philosophers named are all idealists of different schools: Bishop George Berkeley (1685–1753), David Hume (1711–1776), Immanuel Kant (1724–1804), J. G. Fichte (1762–1814), F.W.G. Schelling (1775–1854), G.W.F. Hegel (1770–1831), F. H. Bradley (1846–1924); see the note to p. 267, below), Bernard Bosanquet (1848–1923). See Section 5's discussions of "metaphysical" and "epistemological" idealism, pp. 139–151, 175–176, and 182–185 above.

p. 214—"Quality *decreases* subjectivity. Quality takes you out of yourself, makes you aware of the world around you. Quality is *opposed* to subjectivity." In his seminal essay "Tradition and the Individual Talent" (1919), T. S. Eliot enunciated some similar thoughts:

> What happens is a continual surrender of himself as he is at the moment to something which is more valuable. The progress of an artist is a continual self-sacrifice, a continual extinction of personality. . . . Poetry is not a turning loose of emotion, but an escape from emotion; it is not the expression of personality, but an escape from personality. . . . The emotion of art is impersonal. And the poet cannot reach this impersonality without surrendering himself wholly to the work to be done.

p. 215—"Quality . . . is an *event*." From it the existence of the subject and object are deduced—the separate identification of subject and object is the differentiation and intellectualization that puts an end to Northrop's "undifferentiated aesthetic continuum." In Judeo-Christian terms, "mystery" refers to an historical event.

p. 216—" 'We made it.' " See p. 373 for an example and

Rodino (p. 309 above) for a study of Chris's "we" as contrasted with the narrator's "he" and three repetitions of "I."

CHAPTER 20

p. 217—"A sound of falling rock." An August 1959 earthquake just west of Yellowstone National Park and just southwest of Bozeman left about twenty persons dead and buried under millions of tons of rock and earth. In *ZMM*, it serves also as a symbol of the mental avalanche of 31 INSANITY; see also 183 MOUNTAIN.

————In the 13th to last line, "of" should be "to."

pp. 217–218—" 'drunk' " . . . " 'not drunk' " . . . " 'different.' " This is exactly like the dream material on p. 245. See 245 ITALICS.

p. 220—"far down. . . . To the ocean." OCEAN: The motif of the ocean, which appeared in the narrator's paraphrase of the Goethe poem though it does not appear in the poem itself (pp. 55–56), was also mentioned on pp. 17 and 110 and will recur increasingly from here to the end of the book (pp. 246, 265, 328, 331, 342, 360, 362–364, 366, 367). For the narrator's refusal to proceed to the top of the mountain as a refusal of authenticity, followed by his acquiescence in going to the ocean to integrate his two selves, see Hayles (1984, pp. 73–81; in Bibliography). A related MASTER MOTIF is 183 MOUNTAIN.

————"some Doppelgänger." This is an apparition of a living person in a place apart from the real person. See 77 PERSONALITIES.

————"Zen is the 'spirit of the valley.' " That is, of normal life (p. 183). See p. 112 above, where the phrase is identified as Taoist.

————"a great big heavy stone tablet." This refers to the Ten Commandments, as in Chapters 20, 31, and 34 of the Book of Exodus.

p. 222—"the tree . . . is always in the past." The great Jewish theologian Martin Buber comes to the same conclusion in *I and Thou* (New York: Charles Scribner's Sons, 1958), p. 22.

————"the *source* of all subjects and objects." This will be identified as Tao. The statement recurs on pp. 254–255 in the form of the image of the train of boxcars.

p. 224—"see ghosts . . . seeing the law of gravity." See 28 GHOST and 88 RATIONALITY.

p. 225—"to create the world in which we live." See pp. 280, 317; p. 226, the monism of oriental religious philosophy.

p. 226—"*Tao Te Ching* of Lao Tzu." This sixth-century-B.C. book is central to Taoism, which humbly seeks human harmony with the universe by balancing opposites. For a thorough treatment, see pp. 100–118 above.

p. 231—" 'value freedom' " (pp. 309, 323).

p. 232—"a much larger creek in the distance." This was Hyalite Creek, parallel to and northeast of Cottonwood Creek from which they had ascended. "The main downtown hotel" was the Baxter, at 105 West Main.

CHAPTER 22

p. 232—"Jules Henri Poincaré." Note that Phaedrus was not aware of Poincaré's thinking. See p. 169 above.

p. 233—"Robinson Crusoe's discovery of footprints." Daniel Defoe, *The Life and Adventures of Robinson Crusoe* (Baltimore: Penguin, 1965 [original ed. 1719–1720]), p. 162.

p. 234–235—Lobachevski, Bolyai, Riemann. All three of these nineteenth-century mathematicians were powerfully influenced by the works of Carl Friedrich Gauss (1777–1855). In 1823, Lobachevski drafted a scheme of non-Euclidean geometry by postulating more than one coplanar line parallel with another line through a single point; he presented his scheme in a lecture in 1826 and published his proposals in 1829–1830. In 1823, Bolyai independently created a geometry without Euclid's fifth postulate about parallel lines; when Gauss saw it in 1831, he recognized that it might demand a revision of Kant's aesthetic category of space.

p. 237—"the axioms of geometry . . . disguised definitions." Geometrical axioms and axioms in other areas, which serve as the basis of reason (p. 192), are quite often tautological definitions, not statements about things; and an axiom that is not a tautology can be altered in order to make it more helpful. Hence math and other bodies of knowledge should be thought of as convenient and advantageous rather than true in the traditional sense of the word.

————"Metric system . . . avoirdupois system." The metric system is a complete decimal system of measurements, whereas the avoirdupois system is the British and American "system" that measures weight in ounces, pounds, tons, etc.

————"*Which* hypotheses?" (pp. 93, 98–100).

p. 240—"the 'subliminal self.' " This aspect of the ego is capable of a preintellectual awareness without apparently being self-conscious. Elegance (*claritas* or *splendor formae*) was a property of beauty in Thomism.

CHAPTER 23

p. 245—"*There it is.*" ITALICS: This typographic motif serves as a sign of Phaedrus' voice independent of the narrator; see Harpham (1988; pp. 69–70; in Bibliography). Chris has already reported a different speaking voice (pp. 204, 218), and its return will be marked typographically on pp. 297 and 368–370. Related MASTER MOTIFS are 8 BURIAL, 26 ELECTRICITY, 77 PERSONALITIES, and 128 ARCHAEOLOGY.

p. 246—"*The mountain is gone. 'AT THE BOTTOM OF THE OCEAN!!'* " The Zen master Dogen Kigen (1200–1253) quoted Yueh-shan Wei-yen as stating that "being-time stands on the top-most peak and in the utmost depths of the sea" (pp. 183, 220).

CHAPTER 24

p. 254—"an image of a huge, long railroad train." TRAIN: Parker (1976; pp. 321–324; in Bibliography) comments on this motif. It will recur on pp. 272, 288, and 317. A related motif is 160 QUALITY. As each particularization of the KOREAN WALL motif (106) lists a concrete *example* of Quality, so the present train motif offers an *analogue* for Quality.

pp. 255–256—"Harry Truman . . . 'We'll just try them.' " The quote may be a recollection of Franklin D. Roosevelt's "It is common sense to take a method and try it. If it fails, admit it frankly and try another. But above all, try something" (speech delivered at Oglethorpe University, May 22, 1932).

CHAPTER 25

p. 260—"never separated art from manufacture." The Greeks distinguished between servile arts and liberal arts; the former, involving physical effort and performed only by slaves, would have included sculpture and painting. Too great expertise in anything would have seemed inappropriate to the free generalist. The Balinese are reputed to say, "We have no art; we simply try to do everything as well as we can."

p. 261—"the *tat tvam asi* truth of the Upanishads." This is the affirmation of the sacred Hindu writings that the individual (thou, *tvam*) is identically anything other (that, *tat*) including the Absolute; thus there can be no valid subject-object or mind-matter distinction.

p. 264—"The passions, the emotions." Stoic and Epicurean philosophers carried this Platonic tendency to its extreme. The affective life of emotions and will naturally seems valid to a voluntarist thinker such as Pirsig is and Phaedrus was.

p. 265—"three levels." The three categories of quietness seem to equal the three on p. 274: physical equals psychomotor, mental equals cognitive, and quietness of value or of desire equals affective quietness.

p. 266—"his mind is at rest . . . material is right." When the competent and caring craftsman's aesthetic conscience tells him the artifact is satisfactory, he is satisfied; see Jacques Maritain, *Creative Intuition in Art and Poetry* (New York: Meridian, 1955), pp. 34–39, 301–302. See the rotisserie and Japanese bicycle (pp. 145–146) and pp. 358–359, "his soul is at rest."

_____" 'just sitting.' " See pp. 152, 280, and 286. See also pp. 118–119 and 217 of this book, and 85 QUESTION UNANSWERED.

p. 267—"the end is the beginning." T. S. Eliot cites F. H. Bradley in the footnotes to *The Waste Land* on the separation of one self from another self. The other self becomes an object ("it") instead of remaining a transobjective subject ("I"), and the ego remains locked up in an exaggerated individualism that nearly becomes solipsism. See 77 PERSONALITIES.

On the other hand, in the Elizabethan theater, a railer was never permitted to be either the reformer of the chaotic world or even the spokesman for the cosmic vision. Thus Duke Senior in *As You Like It* says to melancholy Jaques that if the latter tried to reform society, he would commit

Most mischievous foul sin, in chiding sin:
For thou thyself hast been a libertine,
As sensual as the brutish sting itself;

And all th' embossèd sores and headed evils
That thou with license of free foot hast caught
Wouldst thou disgorge into the general world.
[Act 2, scene 7, ll. 64–69]

The reader should be wary of the narrator's prescriptions for reform and not accept them uncritically. The end of the book will show that he himself needs a major change for the better. Nor should the reader identify the narrator with the implied author or with the historical Robert M. Pirsig.

Also, "in the end is the beginning" recalls the last line of Eliot's *Four Quartets*, "East Coker": "In my end is my beginning."

p. 269—"the idea that one person's mind is accessible." The solipsism here is quite exaggerated (see also pp. 77, 292–293, 315, 323). The plot of *ZMM* (like the thrust of *The Waste Land*) denies the theory.

CHAPTER 26

pp. 270–271—"*The Rubáiyat of Omar Khayyám.*" In Edward Fitzgerald's translation, this very romantic poem must have been more Phaedrus' type of reading than the narrator's; it is loaded with Coleridgean exoticism.

p. 271—"Rajasthan." A region of northwestern India located on a high plateau surrounded by mountains.

————"Mogul." Also spelled Mughal. Babur (d. 1530), the first of the sixteenth- and seventeenth-century Muslim Mogul rulers of northwestern India, was descended on his mother's side from the Mongolian Genghis Khan (d. 1227) and on his father's from the conqueror Tamur (Tamerlane, d. 1405), a soldier of the Turkic people of central Asia who had been conquered by Genghis Khan.

————"*his* memory . . . mine." The convergence of memory in this section of the book will lead to a coalescence of their identities. See 77 PERSONALITIES.

p. 272—"*where leaves the Rose of Yesterday?*" The "Ubi sunt" theme suggested by the *Rubáiyat* stanza derives from the medieval and Renaissance past, going at least as far back as Chaucer's "Yea, fare-well al the snow of ferne-yere" (*Troilus and Cressyde*, Book 5, l. 1176) and the refrain "Où sont les neiges d'antan" (François Villon's "Ballade des Dames du Temps Jadis").

————"*enthousiasmos.*" That a god can take over a man's personality is one of the fears of Plato in *Ion* and other works.

p. 273–"*Audel's Automotive Guide.*" Frank Duncan Graham, *Audel's New Automobile Guide for Mechanics, Operators, and Servicemen* (New York: T. Audel, 1963); the Theo Audel Company has published many such guides.

p. 280—"just *stare* at the machine." See pp. 152, 266, 286, and p. 217 of this guidebook.

p. 283—"I'm forever on the other side of a glass door." This is another reference to the solipsistic illusion. But who's who? The reader must cautiously distinguish Phaedrus and the narrator, not falling into the latter's cognitive value-rigidity.

p. 285—"you've lost your 'beginner's mind.'" See p. 119 above.

p. 285—"a kind of ritual" (p. 83).

p. 288—"the Japanese *mu.*" See p. 150, the need to expand reason to include some new awareness that will break the logjam. Bernard Lonergan (1904–1984) talks in *Insight* (pp. 19–25) about what he calls "inverse insight" in a way that echoes the narrator's discussion of *mu.*

pp. 291–292—The three paragraphs on "mechanic's feel" are reprinted in Sylvan Barnett and Marcia Stubbs, *Practical Guide to Writing*, 4th ed. (Boston: Little, Brown, 1983), pp. 126–127. Dave Harleyson works the concept over in Abbey (1982, p. 201; in Bibliography): "Somebody should maybe tell that poor ———— about torque wrenches."

pp. 292–293—"live right too. . . . Make yourself perfect." See pp. 267, 269; Leviticus 11:44 and 19:2; Matthew 5:48; and 1 Peter 1:16.

p. 293—"The real cycle you're working on is a cycle called yourself." See pp. 20–30 above for some further light on this cyclic interpretation of human destiny.

PART IV
CHAPTER 27

p. 298—"*I hear Chris's voice through the door.*" Phaedrus' italicized voice has once again entered Chris's world, but now for the first time Chris's voice enters Phaedrus' world. The meeting of father and son is becoming more and more possible, especially because at this point the father, like the queen in "Rumple-stiltskin," names the real name of the ghost and thereby gains power over it: " 'It was my own face, Chris.' "

CHAPTER 28

p. 299—"It's a cold, snowless November day." The present tense for Chautauqua narrative (see the note to p. 3, above) suggests a convergence of Phaedrus' experience and narrator's memory; also and very especially, as memory becomes more recent, Chris remembers it as well. Therefore there is a convergence of the three subjectivities—the narrator's, Phaedrus', and Chris's (p. 77). See Allis (1978, p. 266 above) and Couser (1977, p. 38; in Bibliography).

p. 300—"Don't throw anything away." The admonition recalls what Boss Priest says to his grandson Lucius Priest in William Faulkner's *The Reivers* (New York: Random House, 1962), p. 302: " 'Nothing is ever forgotten. Nothing is ever lost. It's too valuable.' " It is good existential advice.

p. 302—"like a Delphic oracle." The oracle at Delphi was sacred to Apollo; it is a parallel to the wind-tree oracle of Zeus at Dodona (pp. 152–154).

p. 304—Chairman Richard P. McKeon (1900–1985) was the author of *The Philosophy of Spinoza* (1928) and editor of *Basic Works of Aristotle* (1941) and *Introduction to Aristotle* (1947, 1973). Note well: The reader should presume that Phaedrus' paranoid condition has twisted the facts into an unreliable account. Todd (1974, p. 94; in Bibliography) is justifiably suspicious that much of the remainder of the Chautauqua narrative did not really happen the way Phaedrus experienced it, and on p. 311 the narrator warns the reader to be suspicious: "He admitted the claim was grandiose. . . . Just outrageous." Indeed, it sounds like an academic version of James Thurber's "The Catbird Seat." See also p. 305.

Further, the narrator's version of Phaedrus' version of the Chicago years is doubly dubious.

p. 305—"Procrustean bed." Greek legend tells of a villainous brigand and kidnapper who stretched small people to fit a large bed and lopped tall people to fit a short bed. Procrustes would not have said that man is the measure of all things.

p. 309—"Robert Maynard Hutchins . . . Mortimer Adler . . . Scott Buchanan . . . the present chairman [Richard McKeon]." *Time* once referred to these philosophers as "peeping Thomists."

p. 312—"cut a Gordian knot of dualistic thought." A Gordian knot is an insoluble problem of some sort. Alexander the Great could not undo a knot tied by Gordius, the father of Midas, that bound a yoke to his wagon-tongue, so he drew his sword and cut it. See Arrian's *Anabasis of Alexander*, Book II, Ch. 3.

p. 315—"the 'mythos over logos' argument." Mythos, or myth, is the sacred narrative, a group's telling of a story that it continually creates and re-creates in order to create and re-create itself as a society. Logos (reason) is the rational thinking that began to characterize Greek thought during the classical period, starting about 500 B.C. (see p. 88). As a body of common knowledge, mythos serves as the context for all social speech; it might be thought of as a sort of specification and localization of the Jungian collective unconscious. In time, logos becomes the new mythos, the mutually accepted story that guarantees anyone's ability to communicate with anyone else (p. 336). For the opposite presumption, see pp. 267, 269, 292–293, 323.

p. 316—"only one kind of person . . . rejects the mythos." Compare Miles Bjornstam in Sinclair Lewis's *Main Street*, Ch. 7, sect. I. See Frederick D. Wilhelmsen, "The Philosopher and the Myth," *The Modern Schoolman*, Vol. 32 (1954), pp. 39–55, and R. C. Zaehner's *Mysticism Sacred and Profane* (New York: Oxford University Press, 1961), pp. 84–105. Emily Dickinson's poem 435 begins, "Much Madness is divinest Sense—/To a discerning Eye—/Much Sense—the starkest Madness—"

p. 317—"Men are invented by religion." Anthropologist Clifford Geertz grants that culture (of which religion is a part) creates man, but man creates all of human culture including religion. It may be—a believer would say so—that mankind does not create its religion out of nothing, that instead a deity offers some self-revelation. See Geertz, "The Impact of the Concept of Culture on the Concept of Man," pp. 93–118 in John R. Platt, ed., *New Views of the Nature of Man* (Chicago: University of Chicago Press, 1965).

———"the mythos grows this way." Logos becomes the new mythos, so that the "sacred" story we now tell ourselves, as members of the Greco-Roman-European-American mainstream, is that human linear reason is absolute. We could characterize this mythos of ours as insane. For instance, the cacique of Taos Indian Pueblo told Carl Jung that whites were all mad because " 'they say they think with their heads.' 'Why of course. What do you think with?' I asked him in surprise. 'We think here,' he said, indicating his heart" (*Memories, Dreams, Reflections* [New York: Pantheon, 1963], p. 248).

CHAPTER 29

p. 319—In line 11, "grease" is the correct word.

pp. 319–320—"village-smithy . . . spreading chestnut tree." These are a couple of memorable phrases from the opening of Henry Wadsworth Longfellow's moralistic and sentimental poem "The Village Blacksmith."

pp. 320–322—"Lonely." See p. 8; the trip has returned to the primary, urban, individualistic, alienated America which it left (pp. 4–5).

p. 324—"whose organization appears extremely poor." Perhaps Aristotle has seemed disorganized since Pierre Ramee (Petrus Ramus, 1515–1583) developed the method of information presentation that presently strikes us as reasonable.

————"*Rhetoric is an art.*" Aristotle's *Rhetoric*, Book 1, Ch. 1, sect. 1. For Plato, art (*techne*) is the middle ground between experience and real knowledge; since rhetoric is more organized than raw experience and less organized than science, it qualifies as art.

p. 325—"They are anger . . . shame." This material occurs in *Rhetoric*, Book 1, Ch. 1, sect. 12, Ch. 2, sects. 3, 15; and Book 2, Ch. 1, sect. 1 to Ch. 11, sect. 16. Anger and shame recur on p. 327; "fear" recurs on pp. 328, 352. Note that the list presents "contempt" both as a subdivision of "slight" and in parallel with "slight."

p. 326—"this enormous table had a huge crack that ran right across it near the middle." Critic N. Katherine Hayles (1984, p. 66, in Bibliography) notes that the crack symbolizes "the cultural schism being re-enacted there." See 66 KNIFE.

p. 327—" 'Forensic, deliberative and epideictic.' " This material may be found in Aristotle, *Rhetoric*, Book 1, Ch. 3, sect. 3 and Ch. 9, sects. 28–40.

————"His shame becomes Phaedrus' anger." The professor's tyranny builds among the students a sort of community to which

Phaedrus belongs, though the rest of the students do not realize that he does.

pp. 328–329—"Practical Science . . . Theoretical Science." For the Greeks with their slaveholding mentality, practical or applied science—arts, crafts, and what we would call technology—because of its likeness to manual ("servile") work, took second place to theoretical or pure science. However, it should be noted that Aristotle viewed ethics, which he took seriously, as a practical science. See pp. 187–194 above.

p. 329—"the subject of 'dialectic.' " The word originally meant dialogue and implied a conversation undertaken to achieve truth; later, it came to mean logical argumentation, disputation, and cross-examination; and finally it has come to mean individualistic internalized logical thinking. For Socrates and Plato dialectic is the sole method of achieving truth; by contrast, for Aristotle it is a counterpart of rhetoric, though it has only a residual character of dialogue. See the note above to p. 7, "Chautauqua," above.

At the end of the classical period, Martianus Capella's *Marriage of Philology and Mercury* proposed as the trivium (the three initial branches of study) grammar, rhetoric, and dialectic; Walter J. Ong, S. J., *Ramus, Method, and the Decay of Dialogue* (Cambridge: Harvard University Press, 1958), p. 138.

p. 331—"I think it was Coleridge." It was, as critics George Steiner and Rodino point out, Goethe who said it first, in *Zur Farbenlehre* (*Theory of Color*) in 1810. But Coleridge, who had read Goethe's book, restated the idea more pointedly, more circumstantially, more memorably, and more often (see *The Statesman's Manual* [1816], *Table Talk* [July 2, 1830], and *Philosophical Lectures* [unpublished until 1949]; see also I. A. Richards, *Coleridge on Imagination* [New York: Harcourt, Brace, 1935], pp. 164–186).

p. 332—"His Quality and Plato's Good." One difference is that Plato's Good is intrinsically the object of knowledge, the leading Idea, whereas Phaedrus' Quality is primarily the object of the will and desire, or perhaps more accurately it is prior to the will-intellect division and no object at all; a second difference is that Plato's Good does not change whereas Quality changes (p. 338 and especially pp. 342–343). See pp. 170–171 of this book.

———"rhetoric is 'the Bad.' " See Eric Havelock, *Preface to Plato* (Cambridge: Belknap/Harvard University Press, 1963);

Bruno Snell, *The Discovery of Mind* (Oxford: Oxford University Press, 1953).

————"*Gorgias.*" Plato named this early dialogue for the Sophist Gorgias (c. 483–376 B.C.), who wrote a philosophical treatise proving that nothing exists. Appropriately, it is lost. He may have been the first theoretician of epideictic oratory.

The dialogue first treats the nature and worth of rhetoric, then makes a plea for morality (and against expediency) as the chief rule of private and communal life, then denounces political oratory and propaganda, and finally evokes the destiny of the just soul.

p. 336—"that which destroys the old mythos becomes the new mythos." In common understanding, myth is a false imaginative creation of degraded art, and dialectic, working on abstractions, ought to be put in its place. Socrates was called an atheist for his pains. See p. 315.

p. 337—"these dichotomies." The word means "cutting in two"; Greek rationality divided the world into mind-body, subject-object, form-matter, and accidents-substance. See 66 KNIFE.

pp. 337–338—" 'Man is the measure of all things.' . . . the Sophists." The saying goes back to the Sophist Protagoras (c. 480–410 B.C.). Owing to their perception of Quality, human beings are participants in the creation of all that is.

Contradicting the pre-Socratic philosophers, the Sophists denied the existence of any unifying objective principle (water, air, fire, etc.). Therefore, there being no eternal extrinsic basis of absolute knowledge, man had to be the measure of all things. For a Taoist perspective, see pp. 115, and 116 above.

p. 338—"subjective idealists . . . objective idealists and materialists." The word "idealist" shifts its meaning from century to century and from context to context. See pp. 175–176 and 182–183 of this book.

pp. 339–340—H.D.F. Kitto's *The Greeks.* Kitto treats the archaic Greek's duty to himself in terms of honor and glory, which are altogether relative to the members of his in-group.

p. 339—In line 8, "predecadent" is the correct word.

p. 340—"the Sanskrit word *dharma.*" In Hinduism, this word names the holistic cosmic order that implies all natural laws and especially all personal moral obligations.

p. 341—" 'You never gain something but that you lose something.' " See Ralph Waldo Emerson, "Compensation" (1841): "For anything you gain, you lose something else."

p. 344—"their Aristotelian A's." For the motif of students passing and failing, see pp. 124, 355.

p. 345—"Aristotelian ethics." These two paragraphs sound a bit like Aldous Huxley's World Controller Mustapha Mond dismissing all past culture in *Brave New World* (New York: Bantam, 1968), pp. 22–23. See p. 194.

CHAPTER 30

p. 346—"November wore on. The leaves . . ." This is reminiscent of Shakespeare's Sonnet 73: "That time of year thou mayst in me behold/When yellow leaves . . ."

————"Its title was *Phaedrus*." The title character of the dialogue is a young orator and a student of the orator Lysias. *Lukos* means "wolf"; the Greek word *phaidros* means "bright" or "shining" and serves as an epithet of Apollo the sun god, who has symbolic ties to Christ as the light of world and the principle of order of world.

Phaedrus, son of Pythocles of the Attic rural district of Myrrhinus, about fourteen miles southeast of Athens, was also a disciple of the Sophist Hippias of Elis and a younger contemporary of Plato and (according to Diogenes Laertius, Book 3, Chs. 25–31) an object of his passion. Phaedrus seems to have preferred the rather euphuistic southern Italian rhetorical style. In *The Symposium*, he pronounces the opening speech in praise of Eros the god of love (178A–180B), which concludes: "Thus say I: Love, among all the gods, is the eldest, the most honorable, and the most powerful in eliciting virtue [*aretê*] and happiness in human beings, be they alive or dead." See Bump (1983, pp. 374–375; in Bibliography).

p. 348—"none other than the Chairman." Richard McKeon. See the note to p. 309, above.

————In line 23, "this status" should be "his status."

p. 349—"the soul, self-moving, the source of all things." The Soul, as the Absolute, is the Atman, Tao, etc.

p. 350—" '*Phaedrus* in Greek does mean wolf.' " As above in the note to p. 346, *Phaedrus* does not mean "wolf."

p. 351—"Phaedrus . . . knows he will sign another kind of death warrant." Phaedrus will kill his own authenticity if out of cowardice he backs off from asking the question; as with Socrates, there would be the possibility of having " 'forfeited his own soul.' " See 8 BURIAL.

————"just an analogy." The chariot and the horses are not univocal literal statement; there cannot be such for the One, which "can only be described allegorically" (p. 349).

p. 353—"Aristotle's opinion is." The proposition that dialectic gives rise to the forms would have been much more than an opinion to Aristotle; for the backing-up problem, see pp. 59, 97, 247, 353–354. The history-of-ideas sequence as Phaedrus gives it is: (1) Quality, (2) myths and poetry, (3) rhetoric, (4) dialectic, and (5) forms.

p. 354—"The Church of Reason." Rationality is a defense against the weakness of the human mind. The narrator has suggested that the Jesuits (p. 134) were so strident because of the Church's weakness during the sixteenth-century period of Reformation.

p. 357—"What is good, Phaedrus." This is the book's epigraph; see 160 QUALITY.

p. 358—"his desires too." Phaedrus attains a sort of value quietness in which loathsomeness, shame, pain, and all other bad and good things mean nothing.

————"cross that lonesome valley." The song of this name began as a black spiritual and has developed a multitude of variants, some of which have themes of death and resurrection; some performances of the song may well sound western.

————"out of the mythos." Phaedrus never betrayed Quality; his unitive vision leaves him perfectly at rest, a "dream of himself . . . with himself in it." See, on the other hand, pp. 141 and 363, where the narrator comes to a recognition of himself for what he has been, someone who survives and thrives by pleasing others. The real Phaedrus stands in contrast to the ghostly narrator on p. 363; the narrator is an existential *anti*hero, an inauthentic man who has acquiesced and cooperated in destroying some of his very own being. See p. 316, and the chapter "Madness" in R. C. Zaehner's *Mysticism Sacred and Profane* referred to in the note to p. 316, above.

p. 360—" 'I don't want to do *any*thing.' "—This is not a typographical error but an example of the motif 54 FOLIE À DEUX: because the narrator doesn't *do* anything, Chris doesn't *want* to do anything.

4 0 1

CHAPTER 31

p. 362—" 'Let's go back.' " Critic Bernstein suggests (1981, p. 6; in Bibliography) that by saying this Chris is (not consciously) asking for an impossible return to the past, to when the narrator and Phaedrus had not yet been separated.

p. 364—"a mystery that can never be fathomed." Nature, whether external or internal (human) or in unitary conjunction, is a mystery. See the last dozen lines of Emily Dickinson's great little poem 1400: "What mystery pervades a well"; and see p. 142 above.

p. 367—"the objects . . . are all of equal intensity." Hayles (1984, p. 82; in Bibliography) comments:

> The completion of the [book's] design has been accomplished by moving what had been peripheral into center consciousness, but at the cost of losing the periphery that had been the text's greatest strength. As Phaedrus joins with [the narrator], and as they speak again with one voice, there is nothing left unsaid, no aspect or part of Quality that has not been drawn into the realm of discourse. Hence the synthesis that allows formal closure also sabotages the text's rhetorical strategy of making the hidden Phaedrus the rhetorical analogue of the unspeakable Quality.

———"and yet so aware." See 69 AWARE. In this event may be seen the narrator's symbolic killing of Chris or at least a temptation to kill him.

p. 368—"I'm killing him." The narrator recognizes that since, because of his alienation from himself, he fails to give Chris strength in a nourishing parental manner, he is his own son's enemy.

———Note the italicized Phaedrus voice; see 245 ITALICS.

CHAPTER 32

p. 370—Note the father's four repetitions of the "I knew it"; the father (i.e., the narrator plus Phaedrus) treasures the affirmation Chris has given him.

———"The cycle swings into each curve effortlessly." See 4 LATERAL MOTION. The description here perhaps echoes T. S. Eliot's *The Waste Land*, lines 419–423.

———"what Phaedrus always said—*I* always said." The father's ability to appropriate his Phaedrus self without at the same time killing off his narrator self enables him to fulfill his command to himself: "Be one person again." See 77 PERSONALITIES.

p. 371—"leaving this helmet off." With the removal of the helmets, ready dialogue between father and son can resume.

p. 372—" 'Can I have a motorcycle when I get old enough?' " The father's supportive and strengthening paternal relationship to his son contrasts to the cool distance that had characterized the narrator's attitude.

p. 373—"You can sort of tell these things." Placher (1977, p. 252; in Bibliography) notes that this final sentence of the book is thoroughly romantic, and he suggests that it is so because the classical narrator has relinquished primacy in the new reintegrated personality to the romantic Phaedrus.

S E C T I O N 1 2

ANALYTIC INDEX

An asterisk indicates a MASTER MOTIF; the single *ZMM* page number appended to such a motif directs the reader to a note in the previous section of this book where there is a thorough treatment of the motif, including a complete list of page numbers indicating where the motif appears in *ZMM*, and references to other closely related motifs.

The page numbers refer to Pirsig's ZMM, Bantam edition, 1979+. They are your key to items in Section 11 of this guidebook.

The page numbers refer to Pirsig's ZMM, Bantam edition, 1979+. They are your key to items in Section 11 of this guidebook.

myth, mythos—267, 269, 292–293, 315, 323, 336, 358; see also ritual

narrator's inadequacy as father—29–31, 52, 121, 202–203, 217, 229, 244–245, 290, 362–363, 367–368

Northrop, F.S.C.—108

Nutter, Donald G.—91, 130

observer—see FIGURE IN THE SCENE 70 *

OCEAN—220 *

Orwell, George—194

Parmenides—336–337, 343

pattern—169, 188

PERSONALITIES—77 *

Poincaré, Jules Henri—232, 252–253, 258

Procrustean bed—305

Pythagoreans—336

QUALITY—160 *

QUESTION UNANSWERED—85 *

quietness—145

RATIONALITY—88 *

realism, philosophical—193

reason—see RATIONALITY 88 *

rhetoric—324

Riemann, Georg Friedrich—234

ritual—83, 85, 285; see also myth

rocking back and forth—see LATERAL MOTION 4 *

ROMANTIC—60 *

Rubáiyat of Omar Khayyám—270

sand—see CONTINUUM 108 *

sand, figure sorting—see FIGURE IN THE SCENE 70 *

Sarah (teacher of classics and English)—160–162, 302

Schelling, F.W.J. von—211

sea—see OCEAN 220 *

secondary road—see LATERAL MOTION 4 *

SEEING (enlightenment)—18 *

shapes of metal—15, 86, 88, 144, 194

shock—see electricity 26 *

side-to-side movement—see LATERAL MOTION 4 *

solipsism—55–56, 267, 269, 292–293, 315, 323

sorting—see FIGURE IN THE SCENE 70 *

split personality—see PERSONALITIES 77 *

STARTING POINT—59 *

Stein, Gertrude—156

stuck, stuckness—249–252, 256–258; see also QUESTION UNANSWERED 85 *

system—87

Taoism—226

tension—26–27, 58, 71, 128, 219–220

Thales—336

theories—see HYPOTHESES 93 *

Thoreau, Henry David—36, 201–202

tomb—see BURIAL 8 *

TRAIN—254 *

travel (rather than arrive)—see LATERAL MOTION 4 *

Truman, Harry—255

Twain, Mark—vii, 70

unsolved problem, unanswered question—see QUESTION UNANSWERED 85 *

Upanishads—261

"Village Blacksmith," Longfellow—319–320

Voulkos, Peter—143

WALL, KOREAN—106 *

WAVE—188 *

WIND—32 *

WOLF—75 *

Zen Buddhism—16

Zeno—337

zero—210

The page numbers refer to Pirsig's ZMM, Bantam edition, 1979+. They are your key to items in Section 11 of this guidebook.